# GRIZZLY BEAR SCIENCE

## AND THE ART OF A WILDERNESS LIFE

*Forty Years of Research in the Flathead Valley*

BRUCE McLELLAN

RMB

First Edition, reprinted 2024

For information on purchasing bulk quantities of this book, or to obtain media excerpts or invite the author to speak at an event, please visit rmbooks.com and select the "Contact" tab.

RMB | Rocky Mountain Books Ltd.
rmbooks.com
@rmbooks
facebook.com/rmbooks

Cataloguing data available from Library and Archives Canada
ISBN 9781771605656 (hardcover)
ISBN 9781771605663 (electronic)

All photographs are by Bruce McLellan unless otherwise noted.

Design: Lara Minja, Lime Design
Cover photo credit: Lubos Chlubny/Shutterstock

Printed and bound in Canada

We would like to also take this opportunity to acknowledge the traditional territories upon which we live and work. In Calgary, Alberta, we acknowledge the Niitsítapi (Blackfoot) and the people of the Treaty 7 region in Southern Alberta, which includes the Siksika, the Piikuni, the Kainai, the Tsuut'ina, and the Stoney Nakoda First Nations, including Chiniki, Bearpaw, and Wesley First Nations. The City of Calgary is also home to Métis Nation of Alberta, Region III. In Victoria, British Columbia, we acknowledge the traditional territories of the Lkwungen (Esquimalt and Songhees), Malahat, Pacheedaht, Scia'new, T'Sou-ke, and W̱SÁNEĆ (Pauquachin, Tsartlip, Tsawout, Tseycum) peoples.

The Flathead Valley, where most of the research for this book was based, is within the traditional territory of the Ktunaxa People.



We acknowledge the financial support of the Government of Canada through the Canada Book Fund and the Canada Council for the Arts, and of the province of British Columbia through the British Columbia Arts Council and the Book Publishing Tax Credit.

Canada | Canada Council for the Arts | Conseil des arts du Canada | British Columbia | British Columbia Arts Council

# GRIZZLY BEAR SCIENCE

*Written for our grandchildren, Tia, Elise, Emma and Soren*

# Contents

## ACKNOWLEDGEMENTS

Being able to spend a lifetime studying grizzly bears, most often in the remote and wild country of British Columbia, has been, for me, the most amazing life imaginable. But on top of this blessed opportunity, I have been able to share my experiences with really good people. Many are in this book, and I hope, by the time you're finished, you will understand how much I owe them for enriching my life; really wonderful people dedicate themselves to wildlife research. In alphabetical order, I thank Clayton Apps, Dan Carney, John Flaa, Randy Heggs, Dave Horning, Fred Hovey, Clayton Lamb, Dave Mair, Rick Mace, Rob McCann, Garth Mowat, Robin Munro, Steve Nadeau, Bill Noble, Joe Perry, Tom Radandt, Dave Reiner, Steve Rochetta, Volker Scherm, Irene Teske, Tim Thier, Clay Wilson and John Woods. Thanks so much, my friends.

I thank Bill Noble and David Shackleton, for reviewing and editing some early drafts, and copy editor Peter Enman of Rocky Mountain Books.

But there is more to wildlife research than being in the mountains following bears. Research takes thought, planning and scientific discussion, as well as funding. I thoroughly enjoyed the seemingly endless discussions that all of us field workers had on wildlife and wildlife research. I also sincerely thank Fred Bunnell, Chuck Jonkel, Chris Servheen, Dave Shackleton, Tony Sinclair, Kari Stuart-Smith and in particular Ray Demarchi for their scientific insights and dedicated support. As well, Steve Herrero for suggesting, several times, that I write a book on our life in the Flathead.

Most authors thank, as they should, their family – spouse, children and parents. Only by finishing this book will you will understand how much Celine, Michelle and Charlie contributed to the bear research. The project was as much theirs as mine. How, in a sentence or two, can I thank people enough for their support, day after day, year after year, for a lifetime? How many evenings did we, as a family, spend watching grizzly bears in the mountains? Yep, there were a few mosquitoes, but it was better than watching TV.

Over the decades, the Flathead bear study was funded by many private and public sources in both Canada and the US. These include the BC Ministry of Forests, BC Forest Investment Account, Forest Renewal BC, BC Ministry of Environment, BC Habitat Conservation Trust Foundation, US Fish and Wildlife Service, Shell Canada Ltd., University of British Columbia, Canadian Wildlife Federation, National Fish and Wildlife Foundation (US), Boone and Crockett Club, National Rifle Association (US), World Wildlife Fund (Canada), Canadian Wildlife Service University Research Support Fund, East Kootenay Operators (seven BC forestry companies), Plum Creek Timber Company, Crowsnest Resources Ltd., Sage Creek Coal Ltd., Guide Outfitters Association of BC, and Safari Club International (BC chapter).

# PROLOGUE

Like many people, I suspect, I can't remember far enough back into my childhood to a time when I was not fascinated by living creatures and in particular wild animals. I have a vague and very distant memory of finding a small dead trout that had washed ashore on a sandbar where I had been playing in the sand. The fish was so firm yet flexible and glistened so beautifully in the sunshine. I also recall how devastated I was when it slipped from my hands and fell down among large boulders and was gone forever. Even my mother couldn't recover it, and back then I thought my mother could do anything. My grandparents became aware of my fascination with animals and bought me several books on animal life. Once they bought me a Classics Illustrated comic book, *Frank Buck's Bring 'Em Back Alive*, which, I recall, was mostly hand-drawn pictures. I would go through it, cover to cover, perhaps once or twice a week, and imagined myself catching huge snakes and orangutans.

As I grew through adolescence, my fascination expanded to include wild country, as well as wild animals. My father had built the first rope-tows on a local ski hill in the 1940s and although they had since been replaced by chairlifts, my parents still owned an old cabin near the top of the mountain. The cabin was perched above a steep gorge on the very edge of a large, mostly roadless wilderness, some of which was the watershed for the city of Vancouver, British Columbia. Because that area was where the drinking water came from, nobody was supposed to enter the wilderness. My parents kept having more kids until they never had time to use the cabin, but soon I did. Beginning in our early teens, my buddies and I often stayed in the cabin, and it became a base from where we explored our private, out-of-bounds wilderness. During summer, we hiked all over the forests and alpine. In winter we went on skis. Because we would be leaving tell-tale tracks in the snow, we usually stayed out of the fully protected watershed that was officially out of bounds to everyone. Of course, when the snow was new and deep, we couldn't resist a run into some distant valley. Who really knows why, perhaps it was the feeling of independence and freedom from the human-dominated world, but we all felt great exploring the wilderness that we had all to ourselves. When I grew older, I wanted to feel the pure freedom from social constraints by spending a lot more time in wilderness.

Half a century later, I was following Celine as we headed south towards our cabin along the east bank of the Flathead River. We were on a trail that animals and no doubt Indigenous People had used for millennia. We had often maintained the trail by cutting trees that had fallen across, most often individually but also after major windstorms and even a huge "one-in-200-year" flood. The trail went across a terrace of tall grass and wildflower meadows interspersed with a few old, gnarly Douglas fir trees just above the river. The water in the river below moved smooth but fast; it was cold and clean enough to drink. Not a road or logging scar could be seen from the trail. Celine moved quickly, particularly for a senior citizen and old-age pensioner. Although we were more than 40 years older than when we first walked this trail, she seemed even more agile. Perhaps decades of following generations of radio-collared grizzly bears over this portion of the Rocky Mountains, where there are very few trails, had fine-tuned her ability to move efficiently over rough terrain. This story is not as much on what Celine and I did over those 40-plus years, but more about what we learned about grizzly bears.

Much of what we learned has been published in about 40 research articles in various scientific journals. But, because the format and writing style of science journals is so strict and boring, I doubt anyone other than research scientists and a few wildlife managers have ever read these papers. Yet it seems that many people, from wilderness travellers to condo-dwelling urbanites, are interested in grizzly bears and grizzly bear conservation. There is just something about grizzly bears that often has a deep and lasting effect on people. I don't remember the first deer, elk or moose I saw, but even though it was in 1958 and I was 4 years old, I can still clearly recall the first grizzly bear I saw. We were living in a log house in Banff National Park. My mother woke us early one morning to see a small grizzly on the far bank of the Pipestone River. It just stood there for a short while, moving its head back and forth. It then it turned and walked back into the forest.

I don't know anyone, except other scientists, who read science journal papers. Most people are largely unaware of what scientists know about grizzly bears and even how we learn about them. Often journalists become the interpreter between scientists and the public. Some journalists do an excellent job, but many have limited understanding of the science, are often sensationalists, and sometimes seem biased and only report what fits their own beliefs and values or will sell more copy.

I'm a research scientist, not a populist writer, but after decades of doing wildlife research, I thought it was worth my time to summarize some of what we have learned in a format that I hope more people will read and understand. To do this, I have mixed chapters on grizzly bear ecology with chapters about Celine and I living and raising our family in a small log cabin along the Flathead River. In these chapters I've sometimes combined events to save space and improve flow. I have included stories of bears and families of bears and a few of my many encounters with grizzly bears, as well as a few descriptions of bear capture and tracking these animals in an effort to keep readers engaged. Some sections are somewhat technical and may not be easy reading, but I encourage readers to be patient and not ignore the science. By reading those sections, you may learn about bears, wildlife science and even something about ecological science in general. Chapters are really stand-alone accounts and do not have to be read sequentially.

You will notice that I have included the latitude and longitude of where many events happened. If you like, you can type these into the search box in the top left corner of *Google Earth* and you will be zoomed in to the spot where the event happened. I wish I could be zoomed in time as well. We had an amazing life following about 170 different radio-collared grizzlies in the Flathead over the past 42 years. I hope you allow me to share some of these experiences with you.

# MAP OF FLATHEAD STUDY AREA

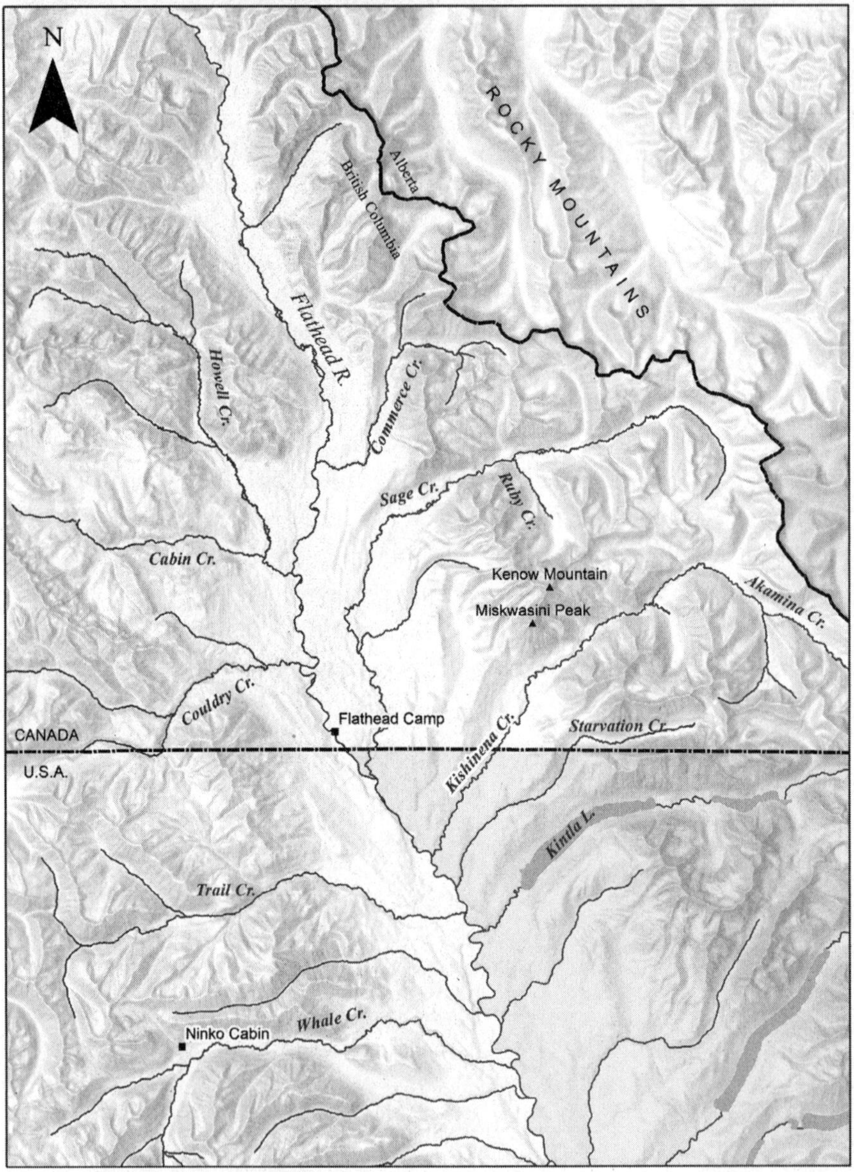

N
ROCKY MOUNTAINS
Alberta
British Columbia
Flathead R.
Howell Cr.
Commerce Cr.
Sage Cr.
Ruby Cr.
Cabin Cr.
Kenow Mountain
Miskwasini Peak
Akamina Cr.
Couldry Cr.
Flathead Camp
Kishinena Cr.
Starvation Cr.
CANADA
U.S.A.
Kintla L.
Trail Cr.
Whale Cr.
Ninko Cabin

# MAP OF REGION AROUND THE FLATHEAD

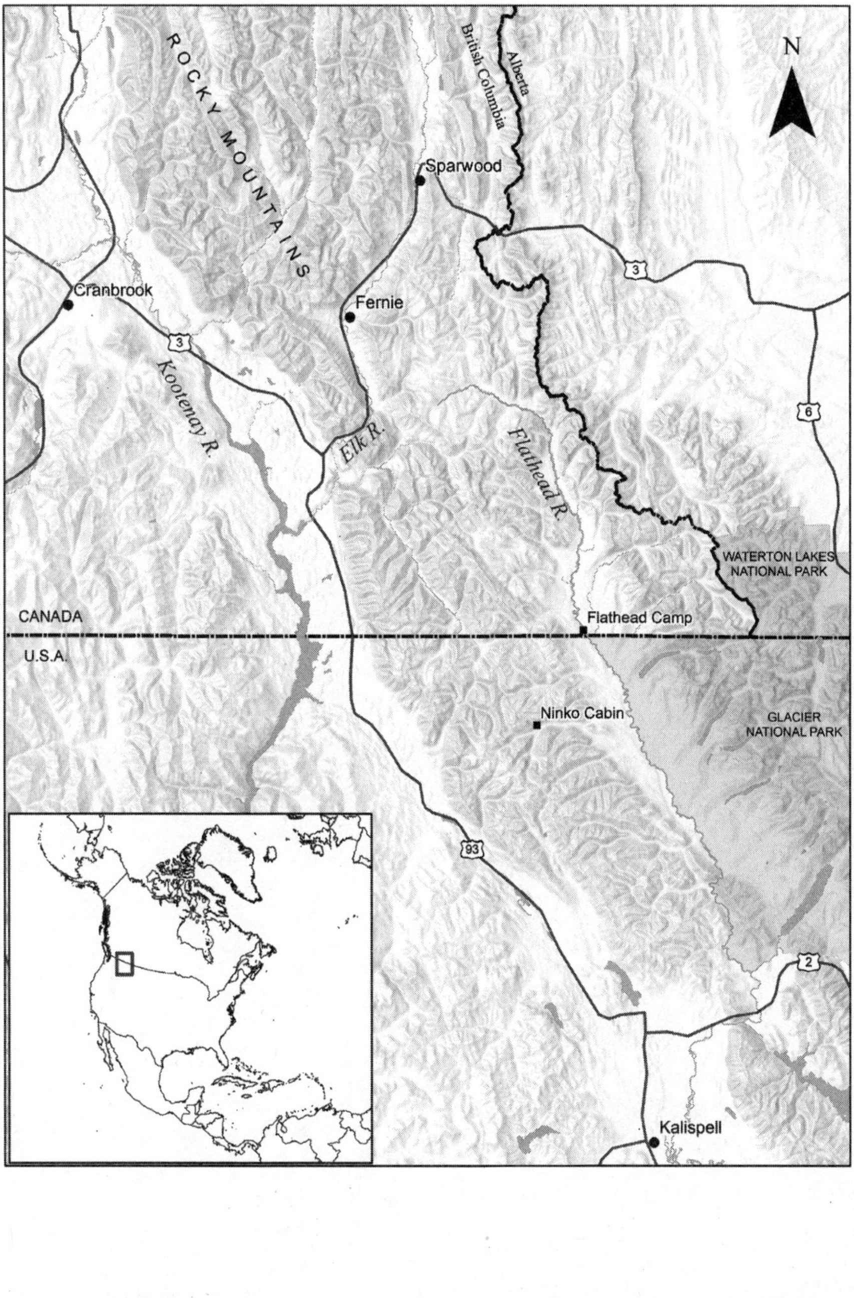

CHAPTER 1

# OPENING THE PORTAL TO UNDERSTANDING

The road wasn't really a road but a rough track left by jeeps and 4x4 pickups that had wound their way through the spruce forest growing near the bank of the Flathead River. Smooth, round gouges from where truck differentials had scraped the mud showed that the wheel ruts were about as deep as they could get without high-centring vehicles. It had frozen hard overnight. The ruts, full of rainwater, were now covered with over an inch (2 cm) of ice. Joe Perry, a 25-year-old cowboy, was at the wheel. Joe was a solid and pretty well rectangular-looking Montanan with a dirty old ball cap covering his rapidly thinning hair. He almost always had a lip full of Copenhagen chew and used a three-fingered pinch for restocking his lower lip.

Joe was trying to keep the Dodge Power Wagon out of the deep ruts by balancing on the rut edge and just next to the trees – something we all try to do but rarely succeed at. Sure enough, the truck slid off the edge and crashed through the ice and into the ruts. Joe gunned the engine to keep up the momentum as we continued smashing ice while we powered ahead. Of course he cursed. Joe often cursed. I find most cowboys frequently curse.

We left the spruce forest and continued a couple of hundred yards (200 m) through a dryer, grassy meadow scattered with small pine trees and a few aspen that had lost all their leaves. It was, after all, early November 1978. The sun was finally coming up over the high, snow-plastered peaks of Glacier National Park in the distance, but it was still darned cold. We stopped the truck at the end of the rutted track and casually got out. Joe slid four three-inch magnum slugs into the pump-action, short-barrel, 12-gauge shotgun, and we wandered along the now beaten path to check the foot snare, just as we had done every morning for the past couple of weeks.

Simultaneously we stopped. The site (49.0374 -114.5078) wasn't the same. It had totally changed. From behind a mound of freshly piled dirt, boulders and cubby-trap logs, I noticed, backlit in the sunlight, large puffs of condensing steam rising at about one-second intervals. Something very large was breathing deeply and rapidly. A dark brown, silvery-tipped hump appeared, and then, seemingly out of nowhere, a bear many times larger than the black bears Joe and I had caught in the previous weeks exploded into view. That bear didn't try to climb a tree or flee, as the black bears had, but instantly was coming right at us with a deep, guttural bellow.

"Grizzly!" Joe flicked the safety off the shotgun.

The bear hit the end of the snare cable, flipped over, and then almost as quickly was back in the big hole it had dug. Joe blew the air out of his lungs, took in a fresh breath, and cursed.

"Back to the truck," and then he really started talking non-stop. "That's a real bear, man, a real big real bear. How's he caught? Did you see the snare?" Joe was focused – his endless jokes were over. We got into the truck, slammed the doors and felt much safer behind a shield of steel.

"I don't know how he's caught. I wasn't really looking at such details," I finally got a chance to answer, "but he must be caught well because he's still there."

In the past month I'd heard stories, all second-hand, that bears could be caught by just a toe or two and slip free in a full charge. I'd been taught that our first job was to see how the snare was attached to the bear's foot. If the snare wasn't in the perfect spot on the bear's wrist, then I presumed it would affect how we proceeded.

Joe dug out his hunting rifle, a tool he trusted more than me and the shotgun. We grabbed our binoculars, then, bent over low so we couldn't be seen, slinked our way back towards a small mound and got behind some shrubs to try to see into the pit the bear had dug. We could see brown fur, small ears spaced far apart, but that was all.

"Try to see how the snare is on his foot," Joe directed again.

"I can just see his back." But, looking a little further beyond the hole and the top of the bear's head, I asked, "Joe, buddy, what's the other end of the snare attached to?"

Usually, the cable is wrapped around a strong, live tree, but there was no tree, just a torn-up field with mounds of dirt, boulders and cubby logs.

"Holy shit – back to the truck!"

Once again, we felt a lot safer inside the pickup while we discussed the anchor end of the snare. It had been on a tree, but there wasn't a tree left standing; the area looked like it had been clearcut and excavated. But the bear was clearly still anchored to something. We also knew it was a big, very pissed-off bear, undoubtedly an adult male grizzly.

The drug we used at the time was safe over a wide range of doses, so we decided to load a big dart with a big dose and knock him right out so we could get this over with. Why did my first grizzly have to be so big and so mad? Why did he have to clearcut the anchor tree and dig a pit so deep that we couldn't even see him? Joe had been on a few grizzly bear captures, but he certainly wasn't a seasoned expert. We got out the drug kit and prepared a big "harpoon" of a dart. I was wishing we were already finished with him.

"You sure you're a real hunter and can handle that shotgun?" Joe asked, once again.

"Don't worry, Joe, I'll get off at least two shots before he eats you."

"Any idiot can get off two shots, but they have to hit the bear right in the chest, no fancy head shots."

"They will, don't worry about me. Besides, I know I'm way faster out of the blocks than you." I used the tired old joke – you don't have to outrun the bear, just outrun your partner.

We snuck back to our little hill behind the shrubs but were too far away to shoot. I had the 12-gauge and Joe had the dart gun. We approached, side by side, with a level of focus that I'd never before experienced. All my senses were on overdrive and my entire body seemed to be humming on high alert. The bear started making low guttural groans, so deep they seemed soft. Then he came straight at us. The shotgun was up, safety off, pointed right below his head at the left side of his chest. He flipped at the end of the cable. Joe shot and the dart hit the bear somewhere on his broad back. We backed off towards the truck and climbed inside – time, 11:40.

As you can imagine, when you're pumped with adrenaline, sitting and waiting for the drug to take effect is a painfully slow business. There is not much to do but watch your watch as time ticks away. A couple of minutes later we returned to the little hill with our plan to quietly watch as the bear became immobile and to ensure he conked out in a safe position and not with his face bent back under him in the corner of his hole where he could suffocate. But he was in the hole, so we couldn't see more than his shoulder. At 11:50 we thought he should be going out so we advanced to check.

No noise this time, but out of the hole he came, head down, straight at us. Maybe he was a little less coordinated than before, but maybe not. This time he picked up a solid, five inch (13 cm) diameter log in his mouth and shook it. The log snapped in half and he dropped it and returned to his hole.

"Whooo, looks like he's going to need a tad more," says Joe.

"You don't say, Doc." We loaded another half dose and repeated step one – there was no procedure manual; I was a complete novice and Joe was certainly no veteran. We were simply winging it.

Once again we approached and once again the bear rushed straight at us and Joe fired a second dart into the bear's rump this time – time, 12:35. Again we returned quickly to the truck and waited. After a few more minutes, we went back to the little hill, and then to the bear to check his status. Again the bear lifted his head, bellowed deeply, then came out of his hole and took two quick, short, stiff-legged prances towards us, pulling soil backward at each step. "Damn," is all Joe said as we hustled back to the truck.

The bear was big and had a lot of fat stored for winter hibernation. "He's so fat the drug isn't getting through to the bloodstream" was the theory we agreed on. So we loaded a third dart with another half dose, and approached. This time the bear lifted his head, growled his deep growl, but stayed in his hole. From where we had shot the previous times, we could only see the top of his head and the long guard hairs on the top of his hump. We waited, hoping he would come out again. He stayed in his hole. We waited, he stayed – a standoff.

"We can't wait forever, Joe. Won't the drug from the first dart be wearing off? We won't know if he's going down or waking up?" I guessed out loud.

We slowly approached closer – still no shot. We moved closer to where we certainly didn't want him to come charging out, as we were within 20 feet (6 m) of his hole and the snare was almost 10 feet (3 m) long and he was a big bear and could stretch. We just wanted to get to where we could put a dart in the top of his big hump. Joe stretched up on his tiptoes, aimed at the hump and fired. The bear came out of the hole at us instantly, but we had leapt back to safety just as the dart had hit him. The big bear stumbled at the end of the snare, right where we had stood half a second before. We backed off to the truck, hoping this would end and he would go out.

Ten minutes later we returned to check the bear. He lifted his head but put it back down. He was positioned well so we went back to the truck and waited some more. In another ten minutes we went back. Again he lifted his head. He was definitely very groggy. Joe cut a small tree and cleaned off the branches to make a pole about ten feet (3 m) long. With electrician's tape he attached to the end of the pole a previously whittled, home-crafted syringe plunger. On this he put the rubber plunger and the outer, plastic cylinder of a regular, medical syringe. We loaded it up and approached again. The bear lifted his head and just stared at us. With the little syringe on the end of the ten-foot (3 m) pole, Joe poked the bear in his upper arm where there would be little fat and kept pushing until all the drug was injected. The bear didn't flinch, but still we moved away.

Ten minutes later we returned – clapped hands, yelled and tossed sticks on his back. The bear didn't move. Finally, he was out. Joe removed all the darts and checked each one to ensure that the internal charges had gone off and the drug had actually been injected into the bear. All had worked properly. After such powerful charging rushes ending with the big bear flipping over, I wanted to get the snare off and check his foot, but I had to move his arm from under his chest. His forearm was the size of my thigh but so hard it was like grabbing a log. Being covered with coarse, short black hair, it was difficult to grip.

"Joe, want to help me a bit so I can get the snare off?" We rolled him a little and pulled a lot until I could get the snare off. His paw was a little swollen and rubbed where the cable had been, but there were no cuts and it surprisingly seemed fine. There is a good reason why we use heavy leather when making boots to be worn in rugged mountains. His feet were amply tough to spend a lifetime wandering barefoot over the Rocky Mountains.

We then checked the anchor tree. Originally it had been a ten inch (25 cm) diameter lodgepole pine, but the bear had chewed it right off about a foot (30 cm) above the ground. Large chunks of splintered wood lay about that he had torn out of the tree by simply biting and pulling. Fortunately, the snare was still wrapped around the base of the tree. A good lesson about anchoring snares on smaller trees – don't do it, but if you must, use a spike to keep the snare right at the bottom of the tree.

In 1978, Joe and I were both in our mid-20s and, combined, would have weighed about 400 pounds (181 kg), but we sure struggled to get the bear out of the hole. We had to get the front half of his body partway out and then roll him over while pushing his rear end up and out. But, after a lot of pushing and pulling, mixed with arm-waving bouts of planning our next moves, we succeeded and finally had him out and in place to work on him. We cleared a level spot and positioned him chest down, then put ointment in his eyes in case his blinking reflex was disturbed, and then covered his eyes with a blindfold to keep out any dust that we might stir up. After a quick check of his vital signs and airway, we started measuring many parts of his body and feet. Even taking basic measurements was not easy on a big animal. We had to dig a trench under him to poke a tape measure through just to measure his chest circumference. For an accurate age, we removed a tiny premolar tooth that poked about an eighth of an inch (3 mm) above the gum line, right behind the canine tooth that rose about an inch and a half (38 mm) above the gum. This very small tooth is *vestigial*, or a structure that has no apparent function but appears to be residual from a distant ancestor. We put in small ear tags so he could be more easily identified if his collar came off, and even tattooed his lip so he had a permanent marker. We extracted blood from the femoral vein in his crotch, because other biologists were interested in blood chemistry. Unfortunately, we didn't weigh him. Weighing big bears is not easy, and Dr. Jonkel, who directed the program from the University of Montana in the US, told us that a "hog tape" that measured the chest circumference in pounds was surprisingly accurate. That was a mistake. I found out later that while the hog tape was pretty close, it wasn't exact. According to the hog tape, this bear weighed 642 pounds (291 kg).

Finally, we started to put on the radio collar. It was the first collar I had helped put on a bear, and it was much trickier than putting a collar on the elk or deer that I had collared before. The bear's neck was 36 inches (91 cm) in circumference, and his head was about the same size around. But, unlike an elk, a bear has dexterous paws and he would no doubt try to pull it off just like a person would. So the collar had to be fairly snug. While we were fitting the collar, the bear jerked his head up, just a little. He was beginning to recover. We certainly didn't want to put more drug into him, so we began to rush. While Joe tightened the bolts after our final collar adjustment, the bear was lifting his head and moving it back and forth, even though I had him by the ears trying to keep him still. We cleaned up and tossed all the tools into our kit. Before we left, I gave him a quick pat on his head. "Good luck, old buddy. I'll see you in the mountains." We were certainly pumped as we drove away. "Let's call him Rushes," Joe suggested. "After all, the big fellow gave me more rushes with every one of his rushes."

**WE HEADED OFF TO CHECK** the rest of our snares before heading back to camp. The temperature was dropping noticeably and a light snow was starting to fall as we got back to the small cabin along the Flathead River.

Joe told me that, after catching a grizzly, it was a tradition to have a few beers in celebration. This was expected, as Joe liked his beer as much, if not even more than I did. Perhaps Joe just made up the beer drinking tradition, and that was fine with me. We knocked them back and had finished the few we had before we began cooking dinner.

Joe was feeling the beers and was on an entertaining bear-trapper's rant. "Now you know I'm not full of crap when I made you take out that snare that you set with old Chuck. Could you imagine catching that bear in a place like that? We wouldn't have even seen him until he was about to bite a big chunk out of your ass. You gotta be able to see the site from a good, safe distance."

He went on and on.

"Big bears scare me, but not nearly as much as very small bears. I once caught a grizzly cub. Just a tiny 30-pound bear, but that really freaked me out. Just to hear that baby bear bawling away makes my last four hairs stand on end. When I hear it, I know it might not be long before momma bear sinks her teeth right into my nice, sweet, soft ass." He was rambling while I began to cook.

"Where the hell does Celine keep her wine? She must have a stash somewhere. We could polish off a bottle before she gets back and she won't even know," Joe went on.

"I think she has a bottle or two back there behind the cups," I replied. "But she'll certainly know if we finish one off. She knows exactly how many damn potatoes we have left, maybe every carrot. But go ahead and crack one. We'll need some for the gourmet dinner I'm working on anyway."

It's a two-hour drive each way from our cabin along the Flathead River (49.0094 -114.4834) to Fernie, the nearest town in Canada. Celine, my travelling partner, had gone on a supply run in the morning. Now Celine can spend an amazing amount of time buying groceries. She always checks for the lowest sugar content, fewest ingredients with unpronounceable names, and the best price of everything, but it had now been snowing hard for several hours and it was well after dark. There was nobody, except one rarely used forestry cabin, along the entire gravel logging road to town, and she had to drive many miles through a high, steep mountain pass in our old two-wheel-drive Volkswagen van. And our van, like all old VW vans that I know of, had its share of mechanical issues.

The wind was often strong in the mountain pass and the snow blew into deep drifts. She could pull the van into a snowbank for the night, as we always slept in the van when Joe was in the cabin, but I knew she wouldn't unless she was really stuck. After all the beers and Celine's wine, neither Joe nor I was in great shape for driving, particularly in the snowstorm, but

I was starting to worry and was thinking of heading out into the night with the Power Wagon to look for her.

Then, through the total darkness, I saw the flickering of distant headlights reflecting off whitened, snow-covered trees. The old van, snow-caked over the entire front except two small spots where the wipers struggled, pulled up through the big frozen puddles. Celine, whose English was still pretty limited at that time, came out of the storm, stomping the snow off, and into the warm cabin. She again stomped some remaining snow off her boots.

"Dat was a very long trip, I 'ate to go to town."

"Hey, we had quite a day too," I said, but she wanted to tell her story first as she thought it was so funny (for ease of reading, I will no longer give Celine an accent, but decades have passed and she still has one).

"It was so dark and bad for seeing with so much snow coming at me in the headlights and so many new logging roads all over the place and covered with snow that I got completely lost. I don't know where I was at all. Lucky for me, I see a pickup coming so I get out, wave my hands and stop them. They were forestry guys who know all the roads so I ask them the way to the Game Warden cabin on Lower Sage Road. They think it's crazy to find me lost and driving the old van way out here in the dark with all the snow falling. They asked me where I lived. They think it's very funny when I tell them that I live in the Game Warden cabin on Lower Sage Road."

**THE NEXT MORNING** was clear and cold but perfectly calm. The storm had passed, leaving the outside world white and quiet. Joe was anxious to call it a year and head back to Missoula, so we set off early to remove the few remaining snares. We stopped on the terrace above the wide Flathead flood plain just above where we had caught Rushes. I took out the bear tracking receiver and antenna. There was no signal at all; the big guy had gone. We drove down to the trap site. There were no tracks, just smooth white snow. Nobody would have guessed what had happened there the day before. We could only guess at the direction Rushes had gone.

About eight miles (13 km) further north (49.1055 -114.4949), the main Flathead road gets close to the terrace above the river. We stopped and again tried listening for Rushes' radio signal. This time, I heard the beeps. Swinging the directional antenna left and right told me the general direction of the bear.

We both knew it was very unlikely that there would be a bear caught in our remaining snares with so much new snow, so I asked, "Hey Joe, give me an hour. Why don't you pull the snares and I'll go see if I can cross his tracks."

"Be careful, man, he'll have a worse hangover than me, and I know that he'd just love to sink his big choppers right into your ass."

I felt great and took off, walking fast through the soft, knee-deep snow, down an old seismic trail that wound its way towards the river. I stopped at the terrace edge above the broad cottonwood flood plain and switched on the receiver. The signal was now much louder and the directionality was clear. The bear was to the southwest.

I left the seismic trail, boot-skied down a steep bank to the flood plain and went southward, flipping on the receiver every few hundred yards just to make sure the bear had not turned towards me. Who knows, maybe he did have a nasty hangover and didn't really know or care where he was heading. I was excited and travelled fast through the snow-covered meadows. He seemed now to be a little northwest towards the river, so I headed southwest where I thought I would cross his tracks. Soon I was rewarded. There were his big, pigeon-toed tracks shuffling through the new snow. Almost like magic, the radio collar was my portal into a new world of learning about bears. I followed him step by step until a strong radio signal suggested I was getting close. To avoid a confrontation, perhaps it would have been wiser to have followed his tracks backwards away from where he now was. I had a lot to learn about using telemetry, but I found out that if I put in the effort, I could find a known individual grizzly bear whenever I wanted to. Clearly, radio tracking is a very powerful tool for learning about bears as they make their living wandering over rugged mountains and thick forests.

CHAPTER 2

# PEERING THROUGH THE PORTAL ON BEAR NO. 1

There are a few places on Earth, such as along some salmon spawning streams, where grizzly bears can be safely and reliably watched. In these areas bears can easily be studied by observation. But even in these rare areas, simple observational studies only work when the bears are there catching fish. The rest of the time, which is most of the time, little or nothing will be known about what is going on in their life.

In other areas, a highly skilled tracker can sometimes follow bear sign and try to interpret what the bear had been up to, but nobody can keep up with a grizzly bear, day and night, day after day, so information is fragmented at best. Observations and tracking provide some insights and, based on these, people have generated hundreds of ideas and theories about bears and bear behaviour. It seems that almost everyone who has seen a bear has theories of what, where and even why bears do what they do. And more observations often support previous theories because the person will be looking in the same types of locations and seeing the same types of bear sign and activities, and so, in their mind, they reconfirm their theories or mental models. Once a bear wears a radio collar, however, a whole new world of relatively unbiased information becomes available. Instead of going where the observer or tracker decides to look for bears or bear sign, now the observer goes to where bears really spend their time. Once the bear locations are known, then someone interested in observational or tracking-based data can go to a sample of a bear's locations and watch the bear or find bear sign of what the animals were recently up to. In addition, the person will know the bear's age, sex and reproductive status (if it's a female). They will also know where the bear was the day before, the previous week or year and maybe where the bear's mother and grandmother are that day. With this kind of information, the real world of bear behaviour and ecology becomes focused on what bears are really doing, not what the observer thinks bears should be doing and where they should be. And we soon learn that each bear is an individual with unique behaviours and ways of using the landscape they live in. Learning a great deal about a few bears will only provide a limited understanding of a population. Detailed information about many individuals is really needed.

Being able to accurately locate a known individual certainly enhanced my efficiency for gaining observational, or what has sometimes been called more traditional, knowledge. This type of knowledge is how we most often learn about grizzly bears and is usually the basis of generating hypotheses on bear behaviour and population processes. Using spatial or temporal ecological differences that occur naturally, or better yet, human-caused experiments, these hypotheses can be tested and these tests can even be replicated in different study areas with different conditions.

**WHEN I BEGAN MY GRIZZLY BEAR WORK IN 1978,** Ray Demarchi was the British Columbia (BC) government's regional wildlife biologist based in Cranbrook, and, if I had a boss, he was it. Ray was tall and thin with wavy, almost black hair and, perhaps because he was only one generation from Italy, extremely animated and loved to put on an act. Celine and I went back to town for supplies about two weeks after collaring Rushes and stopped by the Fish and Wildlife office to check for mail (now called snail mail) and phone messages (written on pink slips of paper).

"Goddamn it, man, a month of bear work you look more like a grizzzzed bar than my old friend Adams." Ray went on with his performance, "but you've got even more damn whiskers than Adams had. Well, Bruce my boy," he went on, "for you, I've got some really great news, until reality sets in. Then, my friend, maybe it's just pretty good news."

I wanted to tell Ray about catching Rushes, but when he was performing it was hard to squeak a word in. "Well, old Crows Nest Industries has been given millions and millions worth of trees from the good citizens of our generous province, but in the big scheme of things, that's nothing, as the government also gave us 15,000 buckaroos to study the impacts of their damn logging on grizzly bears and we can start spending it on December first. The minister, being such a wonderful guy, has already announced what a great job his government is doing investing in grizzly bear conservation and how they really care about wildlife in the Flathead, oh, such great news." On Ray rambled. "But, of course, all the funding must be spent by

March 31 or it all goes back into general revenue, and very likely go, in one goddamn way or another, to offset road building costs for Crows Nest, so the fat-cat shareholders, living in goddamn glass towers in big cities can make even more money while gutting the province's forests."

It was obvious where this rant was going. The bears would be under many feet of snow hibernating until after the end of March, so we couldn't do any bear work, and then the promised money would simply disappear. Ray sensed my disappointment.

"Well, amigo, welcome to the world of government crap. Learn to accept and adapt, or you'll go crazy and burn out in frustration. Government is guaranteed to take young, keen people and break their spirit until they are useless old farts counting the days to retirement. Just look at me for Christ's sake! Don't worry, my boy, we'll use the money as best we can."

Ray then put both hands over his heart, tilted his head to the side and closed his eyes, and then in a higher-pitched voice, "Don't worry, I'll let you two love birds nest away in the Flathead all winter." He then laughed, "But the romance living out there in that little shack when it's 50 below in winter and with a billion mosquitoes in summer will wear off pretty damn fast."

Ray then told me of the proposed Sage Creek Coal open pit coal mine in the heart of the Flathead Valley and that he would like me to document and map where the deer, elk, moose and mountain goats spend their winter. "It would be great, just for once, for us to have some real information to base land-use discussions on rather than the crap the industry consultants fabricate after a day riding around in a helicopter." So Celine and I wintered in the Flathead, and I even got paid to do so; life was wonderful.

**FROM HIS RADIO COLLAR,** we knew that for the rest of November 1978 Rushes remained in the wide Flathead Valley bottom, and usually near the river. By going to his locations the day after he had moved on, we knew he spent much of his waking hours digging the long taproot of yellow sweet vetch, or *Hedysarum sulphurescens* as the botanists call it. We later learned that this plant grows in a variety of habitats, from valley bottom to some places high in the alpine. Sweet vetch was often abundant along the gravelly flood plain, where it was sometimes mixed with low-growing mats of yellow-flowered dryas and purple-flowered asters, but it grew more often along the forest edge. Compared to most other areas where vetch grew, it seemed relatively easy for bears to dig it up along the river because the soil was gravelly and loose and there were fewer roots of other plants entangling the taproot of the vetch.

By the second week of December, the snow was getting deep and, at about −20°F (−29°C), it was bitterly cold. Rushes settled into one spot right on the bank of the Flathead River for over a week. Through my binoculars I watched him, belly deep in snow, but I could only guess what kept him there. The day after he moved on, we checked the site and found that he had likely scavenged a dead bull elk. What little remained of the carcass was frozen solid and Rushes had been gnawing away on it. When he left the frozen remains of the elk, he ploughed his way through deep, light snow into the mountains to the west of where we had caught him. The radio collar told us the general area of his winter den, but because the days were so short and the snow so unconsolidated and unstable, we thought it wise to wait until March to ski into the mountains and find his den. Besides, I was now being paid to find out where the moose, elk, deer and mountain goats were spending the winter, not follow bears.

By mid-March, days were noticeably longer. It was still well below freezing on clear mornings, but by afternoon the sun was now strong enough to feel warm after a long, cold winter. Spring was approaching and soon some bears would emerge from their dens. It was time to find my first grizzly den. Just as the sun rose over the distant peaks in Glacier National Park, Celine and I crossed the frozen river on an old and very heavy twin-track Ski-Doo. From the main Flathead Valley we snowmobiled on a logging road into a side drainage and to the bottom of a narrow valley leading back into the higher mountains. With the antenna held on its side and getting the gain on the tracking receiver just right, we could hear a very weak signal from Rushes' collar. We put synthetic "seal skins" on our long and thin wooden touring skis and began working our way through the lodgepole pine in the valley. The snow had a drip-crust, where melting snow in the tree canopy had dripped on the snow below and then frozen hard overnight, making edging with light skis difficult at times. In a couple of hours we had crossed through the pine forest and, zigzagging back and forth, climbed about 1,500 feet (450 m) and up through the spruce forest and into the more open, subalpine fir-dominated elevations. There the snow was deep, firm and more even. The surface ice from yesterday's afternoon melting had softened and we could move quickly with our light skis. We soon broke out of the trees and into open alpine below some almost vertical rock faces. I had been ski touring since the 1960s, when I was a teenager, but the feeling of leaving the forest and entering the high mountains on a clear, bluebird day where there is just snow, sky and sun still made my insides explode with joy. Celine was now very light on her skis and it was obvious that she felt the high-mountain magic too.

Following the radio signal, we worked our way up between the rock and onto a high, open ridge. The beeping sound from the receiver grew strong and clear as we crossed over into a small alpine bowl. Even with the gain and volume of the receiver turned down, the signal had that chirping sound that meant the collar was very close, and the direction of the strongest signal changed rapidly as we moved along one side of the bowl.

"He must be right over there on the far side of the bowl," I said after scanning once more with the receiver. Celine was scanning the area through the binoculars. "I don't see anything. No tracks, no marks and no bears. I think he's still sleeping." The area was mostly treeless and it was easy to visualize where the den must be (49.036 -114.632). I flagged a few small trees that poked through the snow and jotted directions in my notebook.

"I guess that's good enough for now," I said. "Time to make a few turns."

"OK, but I will go slowly 'cause these skis are pretty bad and my skiing is pretty rusty. Is that the good word, rusty?"

"Yes, but it also has other meanings," I answered.

Off went the seal skins from our skis, and we pointed our tips back down our up-track, gained speed, and then off the track into the open snowfield; the snow had softened nicely. A fun run of wide-open turns with skinny skis, at least until the trees got thick. We were starting to learn some important things about Rushes' life.

**WE REPEATED OUR SKI TRIP** into the mountains on the first of April, but Rushes was still in the same place under the snow. On the morning of April 5, however, something had changed. I tried the tracking equipment right from the cabin just as I had most mornings. Previously I couldn't hear anything from there, but on April 5 I heard very faint beeping. Rushes must have emerged from his den.

We packed our gear, fuelled and loaded the snowmobile. The ice was now off the river so we had to motor an extra 20 miles (32 km) each way to cross a bridge. That route would add a lot of time as the twin-track Ski-Doo was far from fast. Once across the river, we followed our old snowmobile track up the side drainage towards the den. I stopped on an open curve of the road that had a wide view of the valley and mountains. Celine stood and stretched after the hour and a half long, bumpy ride from our camp. I pulled the antenna and receiver out of my pack and twisted the four ends of the antenna together. I turned on the receiver and the signal chirped in; he was right below us. Before I'd had a chance to say anything, Celine, who knew what such a strong signal meant, was already back on the machine. Would Rushes be grumpy after such a long sleep, or maybe just hungry? Luckily, the engine started right away and up the road we roared with the antenna and receiver bouncing on the seat, held there with my knees. In about 50 yards (46 m) we crossed big, fresh grizzly tracks coming down the road. Rushes had been heading our way on our old snowmobile track, where the snow was firmer and he would sink less. I kept the equipment bouncing on the seat for a while before stopping to put it away. We had scared him off the road just as he had scared us; humans and grizzly bears – two of the world's scariest species scaring the hell out of each other.

For the third time, we skied up to his den. We went quickly, back and forth, up through the forest and into the high, open mountains because we knew Rushes was far away down in the valley. We skied right to the alpine basin where we knew he had spent the winter. In the basin there were both big muddy grizzly tracks and clean tracks wandering all over. The den was easy to find, as the muddy tracks radiated from it. It was a hole, just under 2½ feet (0.76 m) in diameter, disappearing into the snow. I took off my skis, took a flashlight out of my pack and shone it down the hole. It didn't do any good as it was not a very bright light and my eyes were used to the very bright whiteness of snow and sun. So I slid in, feet first. It wasn't straight down through the snow, but it was at a steep angle. I thought if Rushes climbed out, I should be able to climb out too; after all, at about 600 pounds (272 kg), he was three times my size. Yet the passage down was amazingly tight. My head was below the surface of the snow when my feet hit the firm ground, or the top of the real entrance to the den. I looked up and all I saw was Celine looking down at me.

"I hope they don't den with friends," Celine said with a bit of a grin. "If I had to den in a hole all winter, I think I'd do it with you. Why wouldn't Rushes want to cuddle a friend to keep cozy and warm?" My first exploration of a small, tight hole in the ground where a grizzly bear had just spent months was exciting enough without her suggesting that maybe his lazy buddy was still down there, just sleeping in a little bit.

I then dropped below the snow and into the real den that Rushes had dug into the soil and rocks of the mountainside. Now I was lucky to have my flashlight, as it was too dark to see much without it, and it was strong enough in such darkness when my eyes adjusted. I called up to Celine, "Nobody's sleeping in my bed."

The actual den had been dug back into the mountain only about six feet (1.8 m) at the deepest corner. It had a short entrance and then a small room just under five feet (1.5 m) across. I didn't realize at the time that this was a shallow den and not one I would have wanted to spend even one wintry night in. It was so shallow that the snow would have drifted in and all over his backside, at least until the snowpack completely covered him. It was the worst of his three dens that I found – Rushes did a rushed job. Because he had stayed in the valley until late December, there would have been several feet of snow up here high in the mountains, and that would have made finding a good spot, and then digging, more difficult. But once I got in the den what was most striking was how wet it was. Recent afternoons had been sunny and warm and the bottom of the den was soggy. Was all the water from the snow that he must have dug away when scraping out his exit hole?

Over the next decades I crawled into dozens of black bear dens during March when they were still there hibernating (we immobilize them first), and I know that dens are usually amazingly dry; dusty dry like a dirt road at the peak of fire season in August. Not surprising, since keeping dry to maintain body heat is very important. The bed where Rushes had spent the past three months was just dirt and rocks. Again, I didn't know at the time, but bears often make large beds in their dens with vegetation, sometimes enormous amounts of vegetation. I have been in dens with about one, or even two, 50-pound (23 kg) bales' worth, if it had been hay, but it was usually beargrass or subalpine fir boughs that had been packed in. Although trees were not abundant, Rushes could have broken conifer branches and brought them in, but he hadn't. I used the toes of my boots and fingers to claw my way back up and out of the hole. I was covered in mud and, just like Rushes, I left muddy footprints away from the den hole, then a muddy snow angel when I rolled around in the snow to clear some of the muck off my ski gear.

Once out of his den, Rushes did break branches. From his tracks, it looked like the first thing he did after coming out was to test his trusty bite. He chewed a small, four inch diameter (10 cm) fir tree to bits and then he did the same to another. He made one bed of fir boughs on the snow and then headed right down the mountain. We skied out along his path, and partway down the mountain I found and bagged his first poop of 1979. It looked like dirt and hair.

Just to make sure Rushes wasn't on our path on our way home, I stopped the snowmobile when we got near to where he had been in the morning and took out my tracking gear to listen for his collar. He sounded to be about a mile (1.6 km) from the road we were on. I stopped where we had met him on our way up the valley. Sure enough, his tracks in the snow showed that he left running, slid down a little slope and had likely been on a small bench about 30 yards (27 m) below us when we had stopped earlier in the day. No doubt such events often happen to people, but when there isn't snow to make clear tracks and tell the story, they are blissfully unaware that there's a big grizzly bear just off the trail beside them – fully aware and just listening and watching.

**OVER THE NEXT TWO WEEKS,** when there were still patches of snow in the Flathead Valley bottom, Rushes stayed at low elevations and wandered from just below the US border, past our cabin to about 15 miles (24 km) north of the border. By following his tracks in the snow, I noticed that he often moved from one thick clump of trees to the next, perhaps because there was less snow in the thickets so he wouldn't sink in as often. He was feeding mostly on sweet vetch roots along the gravelly riverbanks and terraces just as he had the previous November. He also grazed on emerging green grasses that were only found along the banks of small streams. Rushes visited the remains of the same bull elk carcass he had been feeding on the previous December, but it was now mostly just hide and bones. He tore the plywood door off a small Forest Service shed and scattered garbage bags about. Fortunately, a bear getting into garbage is very rare in the Flathead because no people lived on the BC side of the border, but a few lived in Montana south of the border.

On April 28, 1979, from clear tracks left in a snow patch, I noticed that Rushes was travelling with a smaller bear whose front track was only five inches (12.7 cm) across compared to the 6¾ (17.1 cm) across Rushes' track. Although it was early in the year, I presumed he had found a mate. But I now know this might not necessarily be true. I've since found some adult males travel with younger males for short periods of time in the spring, even during the mating season, which for Flathead grizzly and black bears is usually mid-May to mid-July.

On May 12, Rushes left the Flathead Valley. I watched him through my binoculars, chest deep in snow, slowly ploughing his way up an avalanche track. He would struggle uphill for about a minute and then stop to rest before continuing. In an hour he had reached the ridge crest, just above where he had left his den a month and a half before. He then headed west.

I was once again setting snares to catch and collar more bears, so I couldn't follow him daily anymore, but once a week I would climb into an airplane and find Rushes, as well as all the other collared bears. When I located him from the plane ten days later, he was ten miles (16.1 km) to the west, and a week later he was in an avalanche chute another 12 miles (19.3 km) to the northwest. He gradually moved southward 30 miles (48.3 km) and into the US.

IN THE LATE FALL, almost a year after we first captured him, I followed Rushes, step by step in a dusting of snow, as he crossed the entire Flathead Valley. As I often did, I had tracked him down using the telemetry gear when he was in a basin in the west side of the valley. There are very few human-built trails in the Flathead so, as usual, I'd follow game trails when I could but usually just bushwhacked through the forest and brush up into the mountains. Once I was near the basin where I thought Rushes was, the radio signal from his collar was bouncing in all directions among the vertical limestone cliffs. I knew he was close to me, but I was unsure of where. I found myself working my way along a narrow ledge on a cliff face when, unexpectedly, there he was, maybe 30 or 40 yards (27 to 37 m) away. He didn't see or smell me, but he was working hard, rapidly digging sweet vetch roots with his long claws. His silver-tipped fur shimmered in the sunlight as he flexed his incredibly powerful shoulders while pulling rocks and dirt out of the ground – shoulders that had evolved for digging and then been exercised, hour after hour, by tearing away at the hard ground. Being a big bear and a serious root digger, Rushes had immense power in his shoulders and arms.

It had been a poor year for berries, and he dug and ate roots steadily as if he was still trying to add a little more fat for winter hibernation and next spring's mating season, when, with luck, he would be too busy with the females to eat much. He was big and intimidating when I was that close. I had handled him before and understood his ridiculously immense power compared to mine. Yet I felt relatively safe even at such a close distance perched along the cliff face. He was likely more frightened of me than I was of him, plus I thought my hands must be better than his paws for climbing. He never did detect me that day, so, after an exciting time so close to the big guy, I backed off the way I'd come. I've always been impressed that he, and all other grizzlies, stay in the mountains, sun, rain or snow, day after day, year after year, while I return to the warmth and comfort of our cabin. It's so nice to be a human.

A few days later, after a light snow fell in the valley, I followed his big, pigeon-toed tracks as he left the mountains (49.035 -114.608) and walked down a logging road heading east. I had a trap (49.642 -114.559) about ten yards (9 m) from the road, baited with ripened butcher cuttings (fat and unusable meat). When he got near the trap, he veered the opposite way and crossed a wide logging landing. As I followed his tracks I thought, "What a cagey old bear, no wonder he has avoided hunters for all these years." Maybe he had picked up my scent from my daily trap checks, or perhaps he spotted the way I built my traps and remembered what that led to. But then I learned that no, it was nothing so thoughtful. At the far side of the landing, behind a pile of logs, he put his nose right into the snow and must have had a good sniff. Then I remembered that a few days before, a visitor from the city had asked where was the nearest toilet. I answered, "Behind any tree you like but not near the trap." He had headed across that same landing to do something he had never done before.

Rushes headed straight down the road for a few miles and then through the forest to the Flathead River. He waded the river, wandered through more forest, roads and clearcuts before he waded Sage Creek and continued going east. About ten miles (16.1 km) from where he began this trip, he walked right to a dead mule deer buck (49.091 -114.409) that had likely been fatally wounded by a hunter. Could he have detected the dead deer from ten miles away? I don't know, but he did walk almost straight to the deer from the mountains on one side of the Flathead Valley to the edge of the mountains on the other side. I've never since tracked another bear on such a long and direct path to a dead deer.

Three days later Rushes was back on the west side of the valley and was caught in the same foot snare that he'd avoided earlier by preferring to sniff the frozen turd. He was still big, aggressive and noisy but, likely reflecting the very poor huckleberry crop in 1979, his girth was only 49 inches (124 cm) where a year before it had been 59 inches (150 cm), and his neck circumference was now 31 inches (79 cm) where it had been 36 (91 cm). We did weigh him this time and he was only 465 pounds (211 kg). It was too bad we'd only used Dr. Jonkel's hog tape the first time we caught him. Almost exactly a year before he had taped out at 642 pounds (291 kg). He was obviously a lot lighter now, but I really didn't know how much lighter.

He was still pretty fat, but could he be 177 pounds (80 kg) lighter than the year before? Likely near that.

Because of their long daily movements and huge home ranges, it's difficult to follow adult males in sufficient detail to get a good understanding of their day-to-day lives. But I learned more from Rushes than from most other male bears I've followed over the decades. I tracked him from 1978 to his death on May 11, 1981, when I located his collar in the hand of a hunter an hour or two after Rushes had died. He had been shot from a road (49.041 -114.540) either by an American who had crossed the border illegally because the border was not open until June 1, or by his hunting partner, a Canadian who had the permit. The big bear was on the far side of a creek that ran parallel to the road. The hunters spotted him and leapt from the truck. Rushes was running straight away. The bullet hit him from behind, one inch (2.5 cm) from his anus. The .338 magnum went up through his organs and the bear died about 200 yards (183 m) from where he was hit. Joe, the Canadian with the tag, told me that the bear knew him because as he died, the bear repetitively cried out, "Jooooe." Both hunters had a good laugh at their joke.

I left the hunters and went up along the creek to where his naked carcass lay. Even without his hide, head and paws, he was a big, solid animal. He had been the first grizzly I'd captured and radio-collared, and I'd learned a lot about how this big bear lived over the previous two and a half years. But, as I stood looking at his lifeless shape, I wondered how much I really knew. Who was his mother? Where was he born? Did he have any litter mates when he was a cub? Did he still encounter them? Did he know them? Was he the father of any cubs?

I sat beside him and put my hand on his lifeless body and could feel the surface gradually losing heat. I wondered what he had seen in his life. I knew he had an incredible knowledge of space and how to efficiently find many important features in his range that provided him with food, shelter and mates. I also knew he had an extraordinary knowledge of plants, dozens if not hundreds of species that he knew he could eat, and even of how to find roots and tubers early in the spring before the plant had broken out through the surface of the soil. I wondered what he thought about. He had outsmarted many of my traps, so I knew that he did learn, think and remember. His brain had evolved to work well for important bear thoughts. For some things, I knew his brain was much better than mine. For others, I like to think most things, mine was much better than his. After all, a lot of time and energy goes into developing and maintaining a human brain. But I'll never know what he thought about or even what his thought processes were like.

"I'm sorry, old buddy," I whispered. "Life isn't really fair, is it?" Then my damn eyes started to lose focus and water and I was becoming overcome with emotion. Although I was alone with the cooling carcass and the clear creek that was unchanged, flowing slowly past, I felt a bit silly getting emotional over a dead bear. As a young researcher I thought I should really do something like dissect him, but I certainly wasn't in the mood for that. So I met my complex, dual personality of being an objective and inquisitive scientist yet having strong human emotions partway. I took out my knife and cut a roast from his rump. I had never eaten grizzly meat and thought I should at least give it a try so I would continue to learn something from Rushes.

I had to cook it myself because Celine was emotionally sickened with the events of the day and thought I was as mentally unstable as the hunters and a deranged cannibal for wanting to try old Rushes on the barbeque. I tried, even struggled as I have often had to do, to be as objective as possible and separate my human, highly emotional self from my totally objective recorder and interpreter of data. He tasted okay, but the way I cooked him, he was as tough as my boot. I should have used a pressure pot for a few hours with a lot of garlic and black pepper – and then maybe just eaten the pot.

The nine-foot (3 m) grizzly bear rug ended up with the American in the US. This amazing animal became just another stack of statistics. I recorded the event into a computer database with the death as certain, legal resident hunter kill of a collared bear, shot from a road with a known latitude/longitude. I doubt that the Canadian really shot the bear, as he owned a pub with a mountain theme and would have loved to have had the bear rug on the wall so he could tell guests stories of how he had hunted down the great bear.

THIS WAS THE BRIEF STORY of a few selected observations out of many possibilities, of just one collared bear, but he was my first. Over the next 40-plus years, we captured over 200 different grizzly bears in the Flathead study area, and hundreds more elsewhere, and put radio collars on most of them. Although he was the first bear I tracked and watched, I would follow the lives of many others in much more detail than old Rushes. Two females, Maggie and Mammie, I followed from their birth to their deaths, when they were both over 27 years of age. I first saw Aggie, another female, as a tiny cub only a few days after she emerged from the den where she and her two sisters were born. I was still tracking her when she was shot and killed 32 years later.

Although an observer learns an enormous amount about bears from a collection of many thousands of diverse observations, that is not really science. After all, if someone else had had exactly the same experience, they would be unlikely to have exactly the same understanding or develop the same beliefs about bears as I did. Science is more than just describing what one thinks they have learned from observations, even from thousands of unbiased observations of collared bears.

CHAPTER 3

# THE CANADIAN FLATHEAD

The Flathead is a region that is mostly in the state of Montana. The name comes from the Indigenous Peoples that lived there who were part of the great Salish Confederacy. Although now called Flatheads, these people did not have flat heads. But a few centuries ago, it was the custom of some people living towards the Pacific Coast to gradually pressure the skulls of some infants so they developed flattened or even wedge-shaped heads. So, with ample confusion from translating both spoken and sign language among early French- and English-speaking fur traders and the many Indigenous languages, people living in this region ended up being called Flatheads even though their heads were not.

Some Flatheads lived near Flathead Lake (47.919 -114.100), which is one of the largest natural lakes in the western US. This lake is filled by the Flathead River, which has three major tributaries. Unfortunately, early French fur traders, who created imaginative place names such as Pend d'Oreille, Gros Ventre and Grand Teton across the American West, never got around to naming these rivers, so they ended up being called the North, Middle and South Forks of the Flathead.

The source of the South Fork is high in the mountains of the Bob Marshall Wilderness in western Montana. From there it flows wild and free for about 40 miles (64 km) before being backed up behind the Hungry Horse Dam, which floods 30 miles (48 km) of valley bottom. The Middle Fork also starts in "the Bob" and flows through a relatively narrow valley to where it meets US Highway No. 2 and the Burlington Northern/Santa Fe Railway along the south edge of Glacier National Park. From there the highway, railway and river run side by side through the tight valley. The North Fork is the largest of the three. It is about 60 miles (96 km) longer than the other tributaries and has about as much water flow as the other two combined. The headwaters of the North Fork are in the Rocky Mountains of British Columbia, Canada, where it is simply called "the Flathead." From there it flows through a wide, spacious valley with no permanent human habitation for about 45 miles (72 km). It then crosses the international border and enters the US (49.000 -114.4744). Once in the US, its legal status changes from just an ordinary Canadian river to a Wild and Scenic River, and it forms the western boundary of Glacier National Park.

In Canada, mountain passes must be crossed to enter the valley. From Montana, however, the Canadian Flathead is just across an important line – the 49th parallel or the US–Canada border. Although this line really exists only in the minds and maps of people, it's important enough that a wide swath of forest has been cut down along its length for hundreds of miles. This oddity of geography has had interesting ramifications. Historically, it was difficult for Canadians to live in the Flathead because it was a long, rugged trip through mountain passes to get in or out of the valley. Americans couldn't live there because it wasn't in the US. A few trappers and hunters have cabins that they use seasonally and some have even lived there for a few years, but there is no private land with permanent residents in this broad valley bounded by ranges of the Rocky Mountains towering above the quiet forests below.

Although remote, the valley hasn't always been silent. For centuries, people travelled from permanent settlements located further west, crossed the Flathead and then the Continental Divide to get out of the mountains and onto the Great Plains. There, great herds of bison once migrated freely across the vast expanse of tall and short grass prairies unaware of the 49th parallel. Two of these prehistoric trails over the divide are now grown over, but the ground, compacted by centuries of foot traffic weighted down with dried bison meat, can still be seen by those who are looking closely. Other trails have been modified with early versions of the bulldozer. Bulldozer trails are obvious and will remain obvious for a very long time. The bulldozer operators, however, were not thinking of bison. When they weren't thinking of pushing dirt and rocks around, they may have thought of the oil under the ground because that was why they were there.

The early people in search of bison knew of the slimy, smelly liquid oozing from the ground along the Continental Divide near Akamina Pass (49.021 -114.057) and used it for waterproofing and medicine. In the 1880s, the "smelly water" springs were found by the European newcomers on both sides of the pass, and in 1901, drilling for oil began just east of Akamina Pass in what is now Canada's Waterton Lakes National Park (Monahan 2000). In 1902, a well briefly pumped 300 barrels a day (Dormaar and Watt 2007).

That was a huge amount for the time and sufficient to attract many "wild-cat" drillers. The oil rush, with drilling and seismic exploration, has come and gone several times over the past century. The smell of oil naturally seeps from the earth in several places, but very little has been pumped.

Along with oil there is coal in the Flathead. In places it can be picked out of a road-cut and tossed into the wood stove for more intense heat to take the chill off a clear, deep-cold Flathead night. There is more coal further down in the earth – a lot more. Enough for large multinational companies to propose several developments, but so far the coal remains untouched. And of course there are the forests. Early in the 20th century, most of the valley was full of western larch and Douglas fir forests with trees that were often several hundred years old and many of them more than four feet (1.2 m) in diameter. Back then there had been few and scattered major forest fires since the mid-17th century (Barrett, Arno and Key 1991). I was told by the few old-timers that were still alive in the 1970s that "you could ride your horse anywhere through open larch forests." In the 1920s and again in the 1930s, a series of hot and dry summers resulted in the "Dustbowl" across most of the prairies, and enormous forest fires in the Flathead. Most of the old stands burned, leaving a sea of tall, blackened snags. Over the years the snags would turn a light grey, standing like ghosts from an earlier time. But ecosystems are anything but static, and under these snags, lodgepole pine, a species of conifer that responds quickly after fire, soon began to grow.

The mountains and valleys of the Flathead had another, less tangible value than coal and lumber. Tall, up-thrusted Rocky Mountain peaks rising above wide forested valleys and its untamed nature still unsettled by people just begged to be left alone. Some early visionaries appreciated the wild beauty of this landscape, and in 1895, a small Kootenay Lakes Forest Park, Canada's fourth Dominion Park, was established along Waterton Lake in Alberta (MacDonald 1992). In 1910, the Americans set aside a much larger area called Glacier National Park that spread from the prairies to the North Fork of the Flathead and right up to the Canadian border. The Canadian park shifted boundaries many times, but by 1932 the two national parks were joined as the Waterton-Glacier International Peace Park. In the north-western corner of this international park, there is a large, wedge-shaped piece of landscape that is obviously missing, and it includes the Akamina, Kishinena and Starvation creek tributaries of the Canadian Flathead. As early as 1917, there was a plan to add this last piece to the puzzle and make a park in the corner of the Canadian Flathead (Wood 2000). In 1931, the BC

Forest Service excluded the "Kishinena Park" from their measurements of available forest for logging because the area was to become a park (Andrews 1930). Although this area was coloured green and was named as a special place on many maps, decades came and went, but nothing happened to convert talk to action and give the area an official designation.

**IN THE MID-1970S,** a small insect brought great changes to the Flathead. The vast lodgepole pine forests that filled the valley following the huge wildfires of the 1920s and 1930s were now 40 to 70 years old – the age when they are often attacked by the mountain pine beetle. These little black bugs bored through the bark of the trees and then ate their way upward in the cambium layer where the nutrients flow up and down the tree. Along their upward path, female beetles laid their eggs, and the hatched larvae ate the cambium horizontally around the tree. When a tree was attacked by enough beetles, so many larvae ate the cambium that nutrients couldn't flow and the tree died. In the Flathead Valley, the needles of thousands, if not millions of trees turned red, then grey, and then the trees died (Young 1988). What was to be done with all the dead and dying trees?

In a meeting room in Cranbrook, BC, a forester who worked for the logging company, Crows Nest Industries, was on a rant: "It's the cancer of the forest. We have to cut it out right now before it spreads and destroys forests everywhere and there are no living forests left."

Then the habitat biologist explained, as much for the media present as for the forester who certainly wasn't going to change his mind, "Oh, come on, let's calm down and not get so excited. This is a natural process that has come and gone many, many times. It's not the end of the world and it's not even all bad. It's just nature's way and may even benefit the ecosystem over the long run. For example, numbers of rare three-toed woodpeckers are finally starting to increase with all the insects under the bark."

"Come on, man, the forests are being wiped out and you're worried about some three-peckered wood toads?"

It was 1977, and then the forest industry had all the power in Victoria, the provincial capital, because the BC economy was dominated by logging revenue – and the industry people knew it.

The decision to log the dead and dying pine in the Flathead was simple and there was little opposition. But then the loggers turned their eyes to the forests in the Kishinena drainage just below Miskwasini (49.0608 -114.3369) and Kenow (49.07742 -114.3243) peaks, and then up Akamina Creek (49.0419

-114.1077) right to the boundaries of both Waterton and Glacier national parks. Logging right to the boundaries of the International Peace Park finally woke up the anti-logging activists in both Canada and the US. There were letters to politicians and local newspapers and town meetings in Canada and the US, and the threat was highlighted in Canada's national *Maclean's* magazine and was the cover photo in *Life* magazine. The decision had been made, and it included the drainages that, decades before, had been slated to join the International Peace Park. Using a common strategy to appease those against development, the bureaucrats from Victoria had their playbook ready.

"There is really no need for concern. We will make this a special study area and ensure this will be a textbook case of how a valley can be logged sustainably and have no environmental impact."

I doubt anyone really bought the snake oil that day, but it likely made the bureaucrats think they had pulled the wool over the eyes of some backward country folk, a few hippies and a handful of "anti-progress" types.

CHAPTER 4

# GRIZZLY BEARS AND PEOPLE TO 1978

Over the eons of time there have been many species of bears living around the world. Most evolved and then disappeared over time. Currently there are only eight species of bears. The giant panda, sun bear, sloth bear and Asiatic black bear, or moon bear, are only found in Asia. The Andean bear is found only in South America, and the American black bear is confined to North America, including parts of northern Mexico. The polar bear ranges across the Arctic, so is found along the edges of North America and Asia, as well as Greenland and Svalbard, a small archipelago north of Scandinavia governed by Norway. By far the most widely distributed species of bear is the brown bear, which is called the grizzly bear in non-coastal areas of North America.

In Eurasia, there are small populations of brown bears in Spain, France and Italy, and some individuals occasionally move to other countries that share the Alps. Larger populations of brown bears remain in Eastern Europe and their numbers have been rapidly increasing in Scandinavia (McLellan et al. 2017). Much larger populations remain across Russia and brown bears are also found on the northernmost Japanese Island of Hokkaido and even on some of the small Kuril Islands that are scattered towards Kamchatka. In the mountains and deserts of western and central Asia, brown bears remain usually in small and often isolated populations (McLellan et al. 2017).

WHEN ALEXANDER MACKENZIE and his team of mostly French-Canadian voyageurs crossed North America in 1793, grizzly bears were found across the prairies to Manitoba and North Dakota. They were likely most common along river flood plains where there was a variety and abundance of bear foods. The prairie bears were also linked, at least seasonally, to the millions of bison that roamed the grasslands. Grizzlies were found on the open tundra of northern Canada, including east of Hudson Bay in northern Quebec and perhaps out to the Atlantic Ocean in Labrador (Loring and Spiess 2007). Grizzly bears had spread southward through western mountain ranges and into northern Mexico. However, they were rare in the western boreal forests and absent from both the eastern boreal and the rich, mixed broad-leaved forests that covered most of the eastern half of North America. It is likely that the two other large omnivores, black bears and humans, kept grizzlies out of the eastern deciduous and mixed woodlands through competition over important foods (exploitive competition), and perhaps displacement and even direct killing (interference competition) (Mattson, Herrero and Merrill 2005).

Bears in general, but particularly grizzly bears, had an enormous yet complex significance for all Indigenous Peoples who shared their range. Far beyond a simple respect for a large and aggressive carnivore, many Indigenous Peoples had a deeper, spiritual connection with these great bears. This deeper relationship was likely rooted in bears and people having diverse yet virtually identical diets and somewhat similar body structure. Unlike other large mammals in North America, bears have five toes and are plantigrade – they walk on their entire foot as we do, although we walk on two and they walk on all fours. Also, like people, they have separate radius and ulna bones that enable a rotating forearm that provides some dexterity. Bears are flat-chested and frighteningly resemble a large, very strong but short-legged man when skinned. Understandably, a variety of legends were built around the bear's amazing ability to hibernate.

Although it was not always peaceful, there was a respectful coexistence between grizzly bears and Indigenous Peoples in western North America for millennia. Any form of stability between the two species disappeared when Europeans arrived. The first Europeans to encounter grizzly bears were likely either members of the Narváez expedition, who crossed the continent near the present Mexico–US border in 1532, or the group led by Francisco Vásquez de Coronado, who explored northern Mexico and southwestern US between 1540 and 1542. In 1666, Claude Jean Allouez, a French missionary, appears to be the first European to describe rumours he had heard of bears of frightful size, all red, and with prodigiously long claws and that they sometimes ate people; he thought they were likely lions (Shoalts 2017). In 1691, Henry Kelsey described the grizzly on the Canadian prairies as "a great sort of bear which is bigger than any white bear and is neither white nor black but silver hair'd like our English Rabbit" (Bentley 1990).

Samuel Hearne is thought to be the first to describe the bear as "grizzled" when he explored northwestern Canada from 1769 to 1772 (Hearne 1911).

About a decade after Alexander Mackenzie crossed Canada, Meriwether Lewis, William Clark and the Corps of Discovery made their own cross-continental journey. They were also accompanied by several French-Canadian voyageurs, as well as by the somewhat less savoury interpreter, Toussaint Charbonneau, and one of his wives, Sacagawea. The goal of this epic journey across the United States was to explore the territories that had just been purchased from France. On this trip, they didn't record any grizzly bears along the Missouri River in areas where the Indigenous Peoples cultivated corn (twice, they likely saw tracks), but as they travelled westward, they encountered their first grizzlies in western North Dakota. These exploring naturalists described the grizzly bear in great detail and compared it to the better-known black bear. Lewis noted in his journal that "it is a much more furious and formidable animal, and will frequently pursue the hunter when wounded.... It is astonishing to see the wounds they will bear before they can be put to death" (Lewis and Clark 2003). It is estimated that at least 43 bears were killed by this expedition, foreshadowing what was to become the fate of the grizzly bear in the lower 48 states and across the Canadian prairies (Burroughs 1961).

THE ACTUAL DISTRIBUTION of grizzly bears before 1800 was not well documented. In the lower 48 states of the US, it was generally thought that they were found across an area of about 1.7 million square miles from the Pacific Ocean throughout the West to a great arc across the prairies. Dave Mattson and Troy Merrill combined early writings, their own ecological knowledge of bears, and statistical analyses of a variety of factors important to bears to refine the occupied area to under one million square miles (2.6 million $km^2$) (Mattson and Merrill 2002). Their analyses largely excluded the deserts where grizzly bears were unlikely to have been found due to a lack of sufficient grizzly bear foods. They also failed to find evidence of grizzly bears over the coastal plains of Washington and Oregon. They suggested that salmon were so abundant there that Indigenous People dominated the productive salmon spawning streams and excluded grizzly bears. No such refinement of the grizzly bear range has been done in Canada, but because there are no major deserts or a coastal plain, their distribution was more or less west of a line through southern Manitoba and central Saskatchewan to northern Alberta plus the Barrens to the north. Such detail of their historic range is no longer really important; the Canadian prairies are now largely farmland and, except for the westernmost fringe, the grizzlies are gone.

In the lower 48 states, the number and distribution of grizzlies plummeted at an amazing rate. Bears were shot, poisoned and trapped, and the land was settled, overgrazed and logged. In less than a century of carnivore cleansing, grizzly bears south of the 49th parallel were all but extinct, surviving only in and around Glacier and Yellowstone national parks, plus three other very small populations crossing in from Canada. The number of grizzly bears in the Glacier National Park area was likely at a minimum in around 1910 when the park was established. With ongoing predator control inside the park until 1931, and adjacent to the park until the mid-1950s or 1960s, bear numbers remained low (Keating 1986). In Yellowstone, bears were a great tourist attraction and were deliberately fed at several garbage dumps. As a result they were offered greater protection than other carnivores such as wolves, which were extirpated, and cougars, which came close to extinction in that park.

In 1959, twin brothers John and Frank Craighead began a research project on the grizzlies of Yellowstone. They learned how to capture bears, use drugs to immobilize them, and apply identifying ear tags, as well as inventing and using radio collars. They were also able to systematically and reliably observe large numbers of bears at several garbage dumps, enabling them to accumulate by far the most complete data set on grizzly bear population characteristics up to that time (Craighead, Sumner and Mitchell 1995). Their work was well known to the public. Not only did Yellowstone resonate with the American public, but their research was also highlighted in *National Geographic* magazine and TV documentary specials. But major changes to park policy, the grizzly bears and the Craighead research program all began from events that happened a few hundred miles to the north in Glacier National Park, and these had ramifications that rippled across the US and Canada.

From 1872, when Yellowstone became the world's first national park, to 1967, three people had been killed by grizzly bears in all national parks in North America (Herrero 1970). Of these, two deaths were in Yellowstone and included a tourist in 1907 when he (I'm guessing, due to the stupidity of the action, that it was a man) chased a grizzly cub up a tree and was poking it with his umbrella and the mother bear roughed him up a little excessively (Cole 1972). Similarly, in 1916 a fellow tried to chase a large grizzly from a wagon containing food. That was the last dumb decision he made (Cole

1972). But by a weird coincidence, on the night of August 12/13, 1967, two 19-year-old women were killed by grizzly bears in separate incidents and distant locations of Glacier National Park (Olsen 1969). These seemingly independent events shocked the US and Canadian parks services and other wildlife managers, and stimulated the US Parks Service to fast-track a long-term plan to stop allowing bears access to human foods, including garbage, in national parks.

For decades, bears in Yellowstone had regarded garbage dumps as a rich and almost traditional food source, somewhat like salmon returning to spawn are to coastal grizzlies (Craighead, Sumner and Mitchell 1995). The Craigheads suggested a gradual reduction in garbage availability as a weaning-off period, but their advice was ignored and the dumps were closed quickly (Craighead 1979). The "cold turkey" approach left bears that had grown dependent on the garbage without the know-how to find sufficient natural foods, particularly since they were spending their time looking for the garbage that was no longer there. These bears had also grown far too large feeding at the dump to survive on natural foods. And of course, after decades of people dumping garbage out for them, the bears had relatively little fear of humans. As predicted, bears came into campgrounds and many had to be killed by park employees (Craighead 1979). Parks officials, however, thought there was a large segment of the grizzly population that did not use the dumps and that these bears would be unaffected by the dump closures (Cole 1972; Craighead 1979). Based on the proportion of the bears seen in the dumps that were ear-tagged research animals compared to the proportion of the bears that had been killed over the years outside of the park that were ear-tagged research bears, the Craigheads estimated that by far most bears in the entire Yellowstone ecosystem used the dumps (Craighead, Varney and Craighead Jr. 1974). Combining their estimated population size with measured vital rates (age-specific mortality and reproduction), the Craigheads argued that the population was going to crash and could get dangerously close to extinction (Craighead, Varney and Craighead Jr. 1974). As it involved Yellowstone and also grizzly bears, the situation became highly politicized. A National Academy of Sciences committee was established to review the data, and many opinions were posted (Cowan et al. 1974). In 1973, the US Congress passed the Endangered Species Act, and in 1975 the grizzly bear was listed as a Threatened Species.

Concern over the status of grizzly bears was not limited to the US. By 1976, research projects using radio telemetry had been initiated in Kluane

National Park in Yukon Territory (Pearson 1975), Jasper (Russell et al. 1979) and Banff (Hamer and Herrero 1983) national parks in Alberta, as well as in very remote portions of northern Yukon (Nagy et al. 1983, *Ecological studies*) and Tuktoyaktuk Peninsula of the Northwest Territories (Nagy et al. 1983, *A study of grizzly bears*). With the few remaining grizzly bears in the entire continental US being largely restricted to two national parks, and all the grizzly bear research work in Canada being done in either national parks or very remote arctic areas, it became almost common knowledge that grizzly bears were a "wilderness demanding" species and that viable populations required huge areas of pristine habitat (Hamer 1974; Craighead 1976; Herrero 1976). The conflict between the increasing rate of resource development and the needs of species such as the grizzly bear was obvious, and managers responsible for grizzly bear conservation were understandably concerned.

In the late 1970s, the greatest storm brewing over grizzly bear conservation was in the Flathead Valley. The Flathead was not only adjacent to the Waterton-Glacier International Peace Park, but it contained the missing piece of the park reserve. Even more than Yellowstone, the Peace Park was recognized as the best place left for grizzlies in the continental US. The Flathead also formed the critical link between the large "green blob" on the map of protected areas in the US (Glacier National Park, Bob Marshall, Scapegoat, Great Bear wilderness areas) and the large "green blob" on Canadian maps showing the Banff, Yoho, Kootenay and Jasper national parks, plus many provincial parks in both BC and Alberta. The Flathead was also going to be heavily roaded, logged and developed for oil and gas, and maybe mined for coal and gold. In the late 1970s, there was serious concern over grizzly bears in this valley.

CHAPTER 5

# WHY STUDY GRIZZLY BEARS?

Over the years I have sometimes been asked why I chose grizzly bears, of all animals, to study. This question sometimes gave me an inclination that they thought I must be a little odd, or even a macho egotist, to pick such a species for study. After all, for at least six reasons, they are among the worst subjects for pure ecological research. First, grizzlies, and particularly those that live in the interior of the continent with no salmon spawning streams, are rare animals. Unless the study is a major, high-budget project with packs of technicians, biologists and graduate students, their scarcity makes it challenging to obtain sufficient sample sizes to make meaningful inferences about their behaviour and ecology. The naturally low density of these animals also makes the spatial scale of a manipulative experiment, the backbone of science, a daunting task. Experiments over hundreds if not thousands of square miles come with social, economic and political complexity that most field biologists spend their lives avoiding. A second problem is that grizzly bears mature slowly, and when they finally do, they only have cubs every three or four years. As a result, it takes a long time to learn about mechanisms that influence animals that reproduce so slowly and live so long – fruit flies and rodents provide quicker results.

A third difficulty is that, unlike many other species, grizzlies rarely have natural markings that can be used to identify individuals. Again, bears living in the interior of the continent travel and mix with other bears over such huge areas that they really cannot be individually identified by sight with any degree of certainty.

A fourth challenge is that most grizzlies live a solitary life. Except moms with cubs and relatively brief encounters of adults during the mating season, bears are almost always alone. This is not to say they are not social, but their interactions with each other are more through chemical scents detected by their sense of smell, so interactions among individuals cannot be simply observed as they can for species that live in groups.

Fifth and maybe most obvious, they are very powerful and can be explosively aggressive, particularly when a mother with cubs, or any adult bear feeding on a high-quality food source, is surprised at close range. And for me, their power and potential aggression were not simply distant legends and stories. A fellow UBC student and a co-worker of mine, Barb Chapman, was killed by a mother grizzly in 1976 when we both worked in British Columbia's Glacier National Park. Finally, grizzly bears often live in dense forest where they are rarely seen, and this was certainly the case in the Flathead.

**I DIDN'T CHOOSE TO WORK ON GRIZZLY BEARS.** I had never thought about working on grizzly bears until I fell into the job. As we all know, many major life-changing events happen by chance. In 1977, Ray Demarchi wanted someone to complete an elk study towards the Continental Divide in the Rocky Mountains, and through connections with my university professors, I met Ray for an informal interview at the University of British Columbia in Vancouver.

While licking the sticky cinnamon bun sugar off his fingers in the "Barn" café at UBC, Ray had finished the social pleasantries and started to ask a few questions in his expressive and animated way.

"This work is many long, damn cold miles from town. It's, well, way back in the mountains, and in the middle of winter, it will be minus 30 with a stiff wind blowing for days and days and nobody else will be around for weeks. Have you spent much time in really remote wilderness?"

Ray was cleverly trying to assess if I would end up being a benefit to him or, perhaps more probable, a huge pain in the ass or even a serious liability.

"Well, I'm only 24, so not as much as people like you likely have." I buttered him up as he finished his cinnamon bun.

"But I have done many long-weekend to maybe ten-day trips into remote areas. And two years ago I paddled a canoe with only one other guy, Harvey, for about 700 miles. But it wasn't simply a downstream float. We went from the Yukon River drainage upstream for 75 miles, and that took about three weeks of mostly lining the canoe. We then crossed the Continental Divide and went downstream on the Peel River system to the Mackenzie Delta, and then out to the Arctic Ocean. We didn't see another person and really no sign of anyone for over two months."

"Two months without restocking, or did you have food caches or air drops?" Ray asked.

"No, this was a low-budget trip by a couple of poor students. We certainly couldn't afford air drops. We packed everything we needed with us."

Ray seemed really interested and it became more of a dialogue than an interview. "What the hell did you eat for two months?"

"We took 80 pounds of flour, 25 pounds of beans, 25 pounds of rice, and some spices, sauces and jams that made the basics taste better, and once the flood waters went down, we caught a lot of fish in some places."

Ray was a government biologist, so I avoided telling him that we shot ducks and geese and maybe a larger animal too.

"No veggies?" he asked. "Let me see your teeth, did any fall out from scurvy?" Ray laughed at his joke.

"I don't know how much vitamin C is in it, but we drank Labrador tea once in a while, also a tea we made of spruce needles that we liked better. No scurvy, but we didn't eat any fresh fruit or veggies the whole time."

Ray joked a few times as he must have been feeling good about my answer, so before he could get onto another topic I added, "And last year my girlfriend and I, with two other friends, drove a '64 VW van that we bought for $300 in Scotland across Europe and then across the middle of the Sahara Desert to Nigeria. The Sahara is really one very huge wilderness, about the size of the entire US."

"You drove a crappy old hippie van to Nigeria? How the hell did that go?" Ray laughed.

"Well, it certainly would have been more relaxing in a new four-wheel-drive Range Rover. We must have had the old Volks stuck in the sand a thousand times, and we had to rebuild the engine, do some transmission work, and one of the reduction gears gave us a lot of grief."

Ray still seemed interested. "Now I know what an engine is, and I think I know about a transmission, but what the hell is a reduction gear?"

"In the old vans, there's a gear in the rear wheels that is linked to the transaxle." I sensed that Ray didn't know much about mechanics so I could use my newly learned terms and maybe impress him – let him know that I wouldn't be an endless pain in his butt. So I went on.

"One reduction gear came apart in southern Algeria, near the Niger border when we were a couple of hundred miles of sand from anywhere. I put it all back together fine, but I had to remove an old, rusty filler plug to get the gear oil in because, without oil, it would have seized up in no time. I first tried a vice grip but there wasn't enough lip on the plug sticking out. I then tried to unthread it by tapping it with a cold chisel. The chisel just ended up cutting it away, one bit at a time, until it was flush with the gear housing. I needed, I think it was a 9/16-inch Allen key, which is about three times bigger than I've ever seen. We were really in the middle of nowhere, sand pretty well forever, and we hadn't seen another vehicle for a couple of days. But just as I announced to the others that we were screwed, we spotted a dust cloud away on the horizon. The dust cloud grew, and in about half an hour, a 4x4 van with 'Clarke Equipment' written on the side drove up. The driver got out and I asked him if he had a 14 mm Allen key. Sure, he said, after all he was a real mechanic driving a truck full of tools and his job was to keep the bulldozers and other big machines running that countries like the US and France gave to some African countries. He popped that plug out in a few seconds and gave us some gear oil, as we only had engine oil left after the tranny work. He then told us that we could have used some non-critical 14 mm bolt for an Allen key and strip a nut on the end if we had to. He had a cup of tea and then took off towards Tamanrasset in central Algeria. It was all sort of magical, like a desert mirage that happened to be true."

"Magical? No kidding. What's the probability of that happening? What would you have done without the magic?"

I could sense Ray might think we were just stupid, so I answered, "We would have figured it out, and if not, someone else would have come along with the know-how. Most people who spend time in the Sahara are good at fixing things; some fix trucks, others fix camels. But, if we really couldn't figure it out, then we would have had to leave the van and hitch a ride with some desert truck. The van was so rusted that it would have been sandblasted to just an engine block in no time. It wouldn't have been much of a financial loss, as we each had only 75 bucks invested in it. But I think we would have figured it out – likely a Eureka moment in a dream. I've never had to leave a machine, but always got them going one way or another." I was happy with my answer. It was true, and I'm sure it left Ray thinking that I was some sort of mechanic, which of course I wasn't.

Ray got the interview back on track. "So we don't have enough funding to hire a helper, so you will have to work alone out there in the mountains."

Here was my chance to sew up this interview. "My girlfriend will come along and help out."

"Is this the same girl that crossed the Sahara with you?"

"Yep, the same one. She has been my travelling partner for a few years now. Besides Africa, we hitchhiked all over western North America down to central Mexico together a few years ago. She may not look it, but she's a really tough person – just not very big. I don't mean tough for a week and then back to central heating and a long, hot shower, but deep-down tough. Maybe it's her French-Canadian, *coureur de bois*–type genes, but I think she's tougher than I am, unless it gets really hot. She hated Lagos as it was steamy hot and total chaos. And she needed more shade than I did in the northern Mexican desert in July when it got around 115 degrees in the shade. She's a farm girl who worked, lying belly down on a wagon to pick cucumbers, when she was 6 years old. She's tough."

I was sure that having Celine come along really pleased Ray. After all, there would be a safety issue with having a 24-year-old spending weeks alone in the winter many miles from pavement. One way or another, the interview went well because I was hired by the BC Fish and Wildlife Branch and a group of seven local logging companies to investigate conflicts over the management of elk winter range in the Rockies. A few days later, Celine and I drove my 1968 VW Beetle to Cranbrook to start my first wildlife research project. I had never heard of the Flathead Valley and the conflict brewing there at that time. I had never thought about working on grizzly bears – but I was very excited to get paid to work on elk.

MY JOB WAS TO FIGURE OUT how elk used an area that had been heavily logged. Dead and dying lodgepole pine trees, killed by the mountain pine beetle, were to be salvage logged about 100 miles (161 km) north of the Flathead. In particular, Ray wanted to know how elk responded to the large clearcuts when it became extremely cold and the snow got really deep. The general belief at the time was that elk needed "thermal cover," and that on very cold days they would stay deep in the forest where conditions were thought to be less harsh. It was also thought that elk would avoid areas that had been logged by clearcutting, or at least remain very close to the edge of the clearcuts. If the cuts were large, a lot of the land base would not be used by the animals and therefore would be of no value to them.

Celine and I were lucky that winter. Around New Year's the weather turned very cold and then, a few days later, a big storm moved in from across the mountains and it snowed and snowed. Although it challenged our comfort, extreme cold and deep snow were great for learning about animals in nasty conditions. We'd been given a very old, dilapidated travel trailer to live in that winter, and it had been dumped off in the middle of a big clearcut in the mountains. The old trailer could suck the cold right out of the night. Although it wasn't really a big trailer, we put in two wood stoves beside each other. One stove would be burning hot and stoked full of wood before we went to bed, but it would burn out hours before morning. The second stove would not be lit in the evening, but before we went to bed, we set it with paper, kindling and larger wood, ready to ignite. On cold mornings, I would just have to put my arm out from under the warm blankets, strike a match and poke it into the second wood stove and then get back under the deep stack of covers. In half an hour it was warm, at least at head height, but a cup of steaming coffee put on the floor would soon freeze over.

On the coldest night in December 1977, the temperature dropped to minus 42 Fahrenheit (–41°C) inside the trailer; even our bottle of Canadian Club whisky started to freeze. As we lay under the deep covers with our toques on, we could hear elk squeaking to each other through the bitterly cold, still air. In the morning they were still in the middle of the clearcut, hundreds of metres from the forest, pushing the shallow snow aside with their hooves to expose and eat the dried grass buried below. The first of Ray's hypotheses tested and falsified. Elk did not need to seek forests when it was extremely cold. That was easy – we didn't even need to get out of bed. Hypotheses about life in the cold developed by an almost hairless species that evolved in the heat of Africa were bound to be a little off. We found snow depth and hardness had a major effect on elk movements.

After catching, radio-collaring and tracking elk in winter, I next moved to working on mountain goats. I was supposed to capture and move about a dozen from an area where they were abundant to an area where they had been all shot off decades before. Although these animals are usually found above treeline on very steep, rugged cliffs, this job was surprisingly easy. In the spring, many, if not most, mountain goats in some areas wander down from the high mountains along well-trampled trails to the valley, where they eat mud at mineral licks. So, with some steel pipe, heavy commercial fish netting that I picked up for free at the docks in Vancouver, and rat traps for triggers, I made a box trap with a drop door on each end. When set, it was like a net-covered, pipe-framed tunnel. Then, with some boards and plywood, I made a mountain goat carrying box with sliding drop doors on each end. At one end of the carrying box, I also put some heavy, one-inch (2.5 cm) wire mesh, so when the doors were off, the goat could see daylight right through the box.

I put the tunnel trap on a goat trail and piled brush and poles to make the trap difficult for the goats to avoid. A goat coming along the trail would enter the tunnel trap and hit a fishing line crossing in the middle of the trap.

Snap, snap, both rat traps would go off. A wire attached to each trap pulled hooks holding up the net-covered drop doors, which then would simultaneously drop in front of and behind the goat.

When I arrived in the morning and a goat was caught, I quietly put the carrying box with both doors off at the end of the trap. I then pulled open the drop door of the trap and quietly walked around to the far end of the trap. As soon as I was on the far side of the animal, the goat would jump right into the carrying box and hit the wire mesh. I would quickly slide the doors of the box down and the goat was now ready to be carried to a pickup and then driven 150 miles (241 km) to its new home.

In late August 1978, I was writing up my mountain goat report when Ray came to me, with his arms waving all over, and told me of the many issues facing grizzly bears in BC. He went on about loggers and miners, and then hunters and anti-hunters. Finally he asked me if I wanted to work on grizzlies in the Flathead. At that time I wanted to go to graduate school to do an M.Sc. so I asked if that was a possibility. Ray told me that the work would be done cooperatively with Dr. Chuck Jonkel, who was a professor in charge of the Border Grizzly Project at the University of Montana, so there was already a direct link to a university.

**ON SEPTEMBER 10, 1978,** Celine and I first drove to the Flathead. On yellow note paper Jonkel had scribbled a very rough map of how to get from the US border near Eureka, Montana, over the Whitefish Mountains to Ninko Cabin (48.8597 -114.5994), on the US side of the Flathead Valley. He told us that we would find some field biologists staying in the cabin who were working on his grizzly bear research project. From them, we were to learn how to capture, immobilize, radio collar and track grizzlies.

It was a clear, early autumn day when we wound our way on old single-track logging roads towards the Flathead Valley. The VW Beetle was stuffed with camping gear and food. The aspen leaves had their first tinge of yellow, the larch were still green, but the shrubs high in the mountain basins above us were turning deep, purplish red. To me at the time, they were just pretty reddish plants covering the high, open basins. I didn't know what they were, and certainly not how significant these huckleberry bushes would become to my understanding of grizzly bear ecology.

It was late afternoon when we arrived at Ninko Cabin. A couple of pickup trucks, one with the University of Montana, and the other a Power Wagon with Montana Fish, Wildlife and Parks decals, were parked at the end of the road. From there a foot bridge crossed a small creek. We parked the Beetle, got out and stretched in the afternoon sun. We were a little shy as we had never met the American grizzly bear researchers and weren't sure that they even knew that we were to join them; after all, with hundreds of things going on, Jonkel, like all busy professors, seemed a little scattered at times. Then, in the shifting air, not strong enough to be called wind, an extremely foul smell of rotting flesh drifted our way. I then noticed the continuous buzz of thousands of flies around the pickup trucks. I didn't know for sure what the smell was at the time or how I would live with its putrescent aroma for decades to come.

We crossed the bridge and then passed the outhouse on the way up the trail to the cabin. There was a sign on the door of the outhouse that read "Dr. Jonkel's Office." Scribbled below was "Joe Perry in the basement." We passed a big wall tent and then, further up the trail, approached the cabin. The cabin had been built years before from logs cut from the nearby forest. The door had dozens of spikes pounded through from the inside so the outside resembled a bed of nails – ready for some guru to meditate on. The unwelcoming design was intended to keep the once-famous "Geifer Creek Grizzly" from pushing the door down. Three fellows about our age were inside. They had just cracked into a case of the cheapest American beer money could buy.

"Hi, I'm Rick. Chuck said you'd show up here sometime."

"Howdy, I'm Dan, Dan Carney. You guys look like you could use a beer."

I readily accepted while Celine declined, telling them that she was not a big beer drinker. As expected, the BS thickened, and as a few more beers went down, I really liked these guys – teasing each other, lots of laughs, storytelling and beer drinking – perfect for a bunch of mountain men, well, maybe mountain boys in our 20s. At the time, of course, none of us knew the future, but Rick Mace would study grizzly bears for the next 35 years and write some excellent science papers on their ecology and management. Trappin' Dan Carney would spend decades working for the Blackfoot Indian Tribe in Montana and would become one of the most competent on-site grizzly managers on the continent.

But that afternoon we were drinking beer and swapping stories and almost all of these were about wildlife. Most were about grizzly bears they had captured, tagged, measured, radio-collared and tracked. It was clear that they were extremely impressed with the great bears, and with traps set, they also seemed perpetually nervous. Over the past two summers they had caught dozens of black bears but very few grizzlies. So far this entire year, they had only caught one small female grizzly that was too young to have had cubs. I learned from the stories that she had a radio collar on and lived in Red Meadow Creek, but was not often tracked. From these stories, it was clear that it might take a long time to get first-hand experience catching and radio-collaring even one grizzly bear.

While the boys and I were drinking beer, Celine took out a real wine glass from our cooking box and poured herself a few ounces as she began preparing dinner. She chopped and cut food under one of the small windows where there was enough light to see. But the light continued to fade in the dark-walled cabin, until finally one of the bear trappers put down his beer and began to pump an old white-gas lantern. It hissed, burst into a tall orange flame until toggled down, then flamed up again until it finally hissed away and the room became light. The others took this as their cue and began rummaging around the cupboards looking through boxes for some food. Dan opened a can of pork and beans and warmed it in the can, over a low flame on one of the burners of the propane stove that Celine had left unused. Rick, we found out, had the habit of making a huge pot of oatmeal porridge in the morning so he could refry the leftovers into a soggy pancake for dinner. The third bear trapper, Davie Gillespie, had a three-pound coffee tin of granola that his wife had made. He ate handfuls right out of the tin. He seemed to do this for every meal, every day, for weeks. Meanwhile, Celine was well on her way to finishing a wonderful plate of coq au vin – chicken with small onions, ham, carrots and mushrooms in a herb and wine sauce. Under the light and steady hiss of the gas lantern, we all sat down to dine at the long table made of planks. Half-burned, half-cooked beans, soggy oatmeal pancake topped with cheap, fake maple syrup, a fistful of granola, and coq au vin.

Over the previous couple of years together, Celine had changed and was slowly dragging me unknowingly along. It was clear that she had moved beyond being content spending weeks with a bunch of boys drinking beer, telling hunting stories and eating Kraft dinners sometimes spiced up with a wiener or two. I hadn't yet completely grown past that stage of life, but the end was approaching. We both enjoyed their company immensely, but in private Celine made it clear that we should be heading to Canada, even if we failed to catch even one grizzly in the US. I too was anxious to move north across the border. Certainly not to get away from my new friends, but I was keen to start my own program.

We stayed in the wall tent and worked out of Ninko Cabin in the US for a month. We didn't catch a single grizzly bear. We didn't even see one. I did, however, learn to set a foot snare to catch bears by the paw, and a few ways to help direct a bear to put its foot in the right spot to be caught. With about a dozen foot snares set, we did catch a lot of American black bears, so the traps were at least working. These animals were smaller and much more common than grizzlies, at least where we were trapping in 1978. When we approached a captured black bear to immobilize it for releasing, the bear would almost always make an effort to flee. Usually it would climb the tree that it was attached to as far as the snare cable would let it. Between the "fight or flight" reaction, black bears rarely had much fight in them.

In late September, Dr. Jonkel came to the field for a weekend. With Jonkel driving, Celine and I crossed the border to the Canadian side of the Flathead for the first time. It was pretty obvious that Chuck, as all the students called him, came to the field mostly to get away from his office and the headaches of running a large bear project. He clearly felt good in the bush just slowly poking around enjoying nature, as he was an amazing observer. We drove around stopping here and there to look for bear sign and to build potential trap sites. Where Chuck thought we should build a trap site, the three of us would pile about 10 foot-long logs on top of each other in a V shape, or what is called a cubby. At the back corner of the cubby was where bait would eventually be placed when we actually began trapping. Also at the back of the cubby was a sturdy anchor tree. When the trap was set, this anchor tree held one end of the quarter-inch diameter steel cable, and the noose at the other end is what held the bear's foot if successfully captured. The trick was getting the bear to step inside that noose. The logs of the cubby made the bear approach the bait from a very limited direction, at least bears that were not yet wise to traps. Although some bears suffered abrasions, and I have no doubt that some had sore feet for a few days, there were no dislocated shoulders or elbows and extremely few serious injuries when I used these foot snares in the Flathead – bears are very tough.

Chuck stopped again to get out and poke about. I took out my binoculars and scanned open slopes on Commerce Mountain (49.1584 -114.4215), where forest fires had burned the trees decades before and avalanches helped keep areas open. There was a bear, and then another. Across the mountainside we could see ten different black and grizzly bears. A large grizzly was in the centre of one of the avalanche chutes with its head down, busily feeding.

Two smaller grizzlies were also busy feeding close together on a sparsely forested ridge, perhaps a few hundred yards away from the larger bear. Another grizzly was further along, but also high up on the mostly treeless mountainside. The rest were black bears. Most were lower on the mountain than the grizzlies, but one was just as high up and feeding in just as open an area as the grizzlies.

We sat on the road in the warm September afternoon sun with our binoculars and watched the bears for perhaps an hour. Their gradual movements suggested an ursid solar system, with the large grizzly being the slowly moving, fur-covered sun and the other bears slowly rotated around him. The berries, combined with the other bears, were the forces maintaining the planetary-like orbits. Some of the smaller bears moved like moons around mid-sized grizzlies. We saw no interactions at all, but by their movements, I was sure that all bears on the mountain were aware of each other. In my enthusiasm, I thought that next September I should get a little travel trailer and stay right there all berry season and plot out this bear solar system. That would be fun, but what would it really tell us or what question could I test? Now, if I were to also map the locations with reference to the forest and also the abundance of food, then I might test trade-offs that bears were making between security and food abundance.

I could tell that Chuck was more interested in just enjoying a wonderful autumn day 200 miles (322 km) from his office, sitting watching bears, than he was talking research with yet another potential graduate student. But I wanted to somehow get onto the topic of grizzly bear research and how I wanted to fit in.

"We've been working out of Ninko for a month and didn't see a grizzly. Sure great to see four at once right in front of us. I wonder if it would be possible to use forest cover maps and air photos to map in detail the mountainside and then record bear locations from right along the road to test which factors influence where the different bears feed?" I waited for a reply. Through his binoculars, Chuck was now looking at the mountaintop, way above the bears.

"Is that a repeater of some sort up on the mountaintop?" was all he said.

"Yep, I think it's a Forest Service repeater," I replied.

He didn't seem too eager to discuss the bears on the mountainside, but then he said, "You know, foresters in Montana and in BC, and even in Oregon and Washington, are really interested in tree girdling by bears. It's a damn big issue for them, particularly in 30- to 40-year-old plantations. The darn bears don't pull the bark off young trees to eat the cambium, which would probably help thin the stand, but they wait until the trees are three-quarters grown before pulling the bark off to eat the cambium, and that usually kills the trees. They want to know how big a problem it is and if there is anything we can do about it. There seems to be some funding for such a study in BC, and some American companies are interested too."

Aha, that's why Chuck was so interested in bear tree girdling. Foresters might be more apt to fund grizzly bear research if they could tell their bosses that the money was directed at a forestry issue like bears killing trees. I got along well with the BC forestry companies that had funded my elk study, and they had told me that they wanted to continue working with Ray and me on the grizzly bear study. It sounded like Chuck was trying to redirect the BC forest industry funding into his Border Grizzly Project, and with it, leverage similar funding from US companies where tree girdling was a much bigger issue. I was worried that some if not most of the money would be spent on the variety of other topics Jonkel's students were working on; he had at least four bear studies under his direction, as well as trying out his idea of using red-hot pepper in a spray for defending hikers from attacking bears. But I wasn't really keen on this tiny aspect of bear behaviour, and I didn't want to be a pawn in the big, multifaceted Border Grizzly Project. Fortunately, I knew that Ray, whom Chuck liked and respected, was also not interested in tree girdling by bears.

"That would be interesting, Chuck," I sort of lied, "but Ray really wants me to look at the bear population. You know, how many bears there are, how fast they reproduce, how they die, and how hunting and particularly logging affect the population. I'm really supposed to be looking at the effects of the salvage logging on the bears, not the effect of bears on the trees."

I went on: "It would be sort of an experiment, with the logging being the treatment, and I could measure the bears' responses and what happens to the population."

To this somewhat ridiculously ambitious statement from a potential M.Sc. student, Jonkel just replied, "I'm not sure you want to start getting into life tables and all that." He paused for a few seconds. "How long do you plan on being here?" He laughed. That question and his laugh shut me up and pulled me back into reality, but it didn't stop me from thinking about what I felt really should be studied.

**ON OCTOBER 20, 1978,** a few weeks after the bears had left the mountainside, Celine and I finally moved to the Flathead cabin in British Columbia. The cabin had been built in 1947 by two game wardens, Max Ewert and Gordon Hascal. It was 16 feet (5 m) long and ten feet (3 m) wide and made of logs, so the actual usable inside space was just under 135 square feet (12.5 $m^2$). Moss had been stuffed between the logs for chinking, and on the inside of the cabin, thin poles had been nailed to cover the moss, while on the outside, white mortar covered the moss. Much of the mortar had cracked and fallen out, but over the years others had added steel wool to the chinking in hopes that mice would have a more difficult time getting through matted metal. There was a six by ten foot (1.8 × 3 m) addition made of planks on the front. The cabin had been built about half a mile (0.8 km) north of the US border and about 20 feet (6 m) from the east bank of the Flathead River. Although it was just about at the lowest spot in the Canadian Flathead, the cabin was at an elevation of 3,900 feet (1188 m).

For the first few weeks, Celine and I slept in our old VW van, while Joe Perry stayed in the cabin. The three of us set snares in the log cubbies we had built with Dr. Jonkel, but Joe wasn't impressed with a couple of them. With tobacco drooling from his lips, he said, "Old Chuck's going crazy, man. Can you imagine catching a cub here? Mumma griz would have your ass sure as shit." So we built new trap sites by piling logs in a V-shape cubby, and began to learn more about the Canadian Flathead.

By Halloween, it was getting cold and winter was clearly arriving. A light snow had fallen during the first few days of November and the ground was frozen hard. We were beginning to discuss how long we should keep trapping, even though we hadn't caught a single grizzly bear on either side of the border. Having no bears caught was not a good position to be in when it came to keeping a project funded. In the US, Jimmy Carter was struggling with mid-term turmoil, even though the Iranian hostage crisis was a year in the future. We decided that when Joe went to vote in mid-term elections, we would pull the snares and call it a year. Then we caught our first grizzly – Rushes.

**JOE THEN HEADED HOME** and Celine and I moved from the van to the cabin. As the nights got longer and the mid-winter deep freeze set in, we spent less time working outside and more time reading under the hiss of a gas lantern. Celine read Tolstoy's *War and Peace*, followed right after by *Anna Karenina*, "to help with my English," she said. I continued to read papers and books on bears, animal behaviour and ecological theory.

In the late 1970s, perhaps stimulated by Edward Wilson's *Sociobiology* and *The Selfish Gene* by Richard Dawkins, the field of behavioural ecology was rapidly emerging. For someone working on bears, this field of study goes beyond describing what bears do but asks, *Why do bears do what they do?* This question is not only academic but clearly important for grizzly bear conservation and management. The little I had read of optimal and risk-sensitive foraging, for example, suggested that human-bear conflicts occur when bears are making risk-sensitive foraging decisions when attracted to foods that people grow, discard as garbage or hang in hunting camps. These foods are of very high quality, but to get them is risky. It's a gamble that many bears make, particularly when they are not quite as fat as they need to be to survive hibernation or to reproduce.

I also happened to find a new ecology textbook written by UBC professor Charlie Krebs in the Cranbrook Fish and Wildlife office, and brought it down to the Flathead cabin. According to Krebs, ecology is *the scientific study of the interactions that determine the distribution and abundance of organisms*. To a research neophyte like me, this definition cleared a pathway through the huge and distracting clutter of topics that abound in wildlife science journals. I realized that my goal should not only be to know how many bears are there but to answer: *What are the interactions that determine how many grizzly bears there are?* or more simply: *Why aren't there more bears?* Answering these questions is the basis of population ecology and, when applied to small and declining populations, becomes the foundation of conservation biology.

The general understanding in the 1970s was that grizzly bears were a *wilderness demanding species* and did not do well when they overlapped with any form of human activities. My job was to determine the effect of the salvage logging program on grizzly bears, and if possible, how these developments could be done so as to minimize impacts. That winter I spent a lot of time on skis in the forest, mapping where the elk, moose, deer and mountain goats were, but I was often thinking of grizzly bears and science. I began to turn my questions into hypotheses, and my basic one was simple: *if the logging and all the associated human activities were bad for grizzly bears, as conservation theory and general knowledge suggested, then the population should decline while and after the valley was logged.* Although it might take a few years, this hypothesis could be put to the test and, of course, all scientific hypotheses must be testable. After all, deriving a hypothesis from observations or existing theory that can be tested with empirical data is what science is all about.

But, of course, nothing with grizzly bears is that simple. I had talked about grizzlies with a great variety of people and had been told by old-timers, as well as by some not-so-old-timers, of numerous bears that had been shot in the past. Some stories, such as those told to me by Andy Russell, author of *Grizzly Country*, whose guiding territory was once in the Flathead, were from decades ago, but others were more recent and certainly within the lifespan of the bears living in the Flathead. These stories suggested that the Flathead population could have been greatly reduced in the past. But now shooting a grizzly might not be the "knee jerk" reflex that it had been a decade before, given the stricter hunting regulations Ray had applied in this part of BC and the generally increasing concern over grizzly bear conservation since the US listed these bears as Threatened under the Endangered Species Act. So, as in many fields of science, I had to include the *initial conditions*. To do this, I added a caveat to my hypothesis: *or the population is at a low density compared to other populations in the nearby Rocky Mountains*. After all, if there were very few bears left in the Flathead, as many people including Andy Russell had suggested, then the logging might not be enough on its own to cause the population to decline even more. This addition to my hypothesis, which would make me estimate the number of bears as well as the trend of the population, would make Ray happy.

But if I were to test the hypothesis that logging the valley would cause the grizzly bear population to decline, it would not have been very useful or even insightful. I really wanted to know which factors caused the population to change. To get a greater understanding of the interactions or mechanisms behind any population response, I would have to dig much deeper into the ecology of the bears while the valley was being logged. I would have to do a lot of basic, natural history type observational work, plus test more focused hypotheses within the overall logging experiment. Did the population change because of reduced reproduction or because mortality of one or more age classes of bears increased? Or maybe the bears were bothered so much with all the activity that they just packed up and moved to the adjacent Glacier or Waterton Lakes national parks? Was the reproduction low because the bear's habitat was destroyed by logging, as was commonly suggested, or because the bears were displaced from important habitats from all the activity so could no longer use the landscape efficiently? Or even more subtly, maybe the bears would be forced to become nocturnal and thus less efficient at foraging. Clearly, there were many possible interactions that could result in a population change. I wanted to look at as many of these that I could while the valley was roaded and the forests cut down. As I skied through the cold, quiet forests in the winter of 1978/79 and thought of these questions, I knew it might take a long time and a lot of work, but I didn't know that it would take up most of my life.

CHAPTER 6

# GRIZZLY GRUB

There are a few basic requirements that mammals need to sustain life. Understanding these necessities and what animals do to obtain them, as well as their ability to store them for leaner times, is fundamental to understanding why individuals do what they do and why there are not more of them. Oxygen, in the form of $O_2$, is one crucial need, but unless you're a high-elevation mountain climber or a free diver far under the surface of the ocean, you are unlikely ever to think about getting enough oxygen – it seems to be everywhere. Every few seconds of your entire life, you breathe in and then exhale. It's so abundant that mammals have not evolved mechanisms to conserve or store it, but without air, most die in minutes; all die in hours. Fresh water is also needed and is less ubiquitous than oxygen. Mammals don't need a drink every few seconds, but most, including ourselves, can only go a few days without it. In deserts, of course, fresh water is at a premium and animals that evolved in such arid areas can go much longer without a drink.

Then there is a huge variety of nutrients that are collectively called food. Major nutrients include proteins, fats and carbohydrates. These macronutrients can be converted within the body into a chemical form that can be used as energy needed to sustain life. However, only amino acids, which are linked together to form proteins, can be used as the main components of most body tissues. Usable forms of these macronutrients are relatively rare in all environments, and animals spend much if not most of their life seeking them. Furthermore, these nutrients are usually highly seasonal in abundance, and their availability can vary greatly among years. Most mammals live a life of feast or famine.

To deal with major changes in the abundance of macronutrients as well as the many micronutrients, such as vitamins and minerals, animals have evolved ways of conserving and storing them to buffer periods of scarcity. For these nutrients, their bodies are like a series of rechargeable batteries that can be slowly drained but will need recharging or the individual will die. While people have survived for almost two months without eating any food, bears are masters of storing energy and going months without eating. For them, obesity is not a health problem but a survival necessity. Knowing what bears eat during the year, what levels of digestible protein and energy are in the foods that they eat, and what foods enable them to recharge their bodies is so fundamental to understanding much of their ecology and behaviour that I have spent considerable effort investigating various aspects of their diet.

There are some foods that bears clearly crave. All bear trappers know that bears can't resist a nice chunk of moose meat or, better yet, a semi-rancid slab of fat or bacon grease. While tying nice chunks of pork on the trigger at the back end of an eight-foot-long, aluminum barrel trap, then another smaller chunk halfway into the trap, and a third at the entrance where the bear will certainly eat it in culinary bliss, Trappin' Dan Carney would say, "There ain't a self-respecting bear alive that can resist a smoked Tennessee apple glazed ham." And almost always they couldn't and we'd catch them. Once in a while, however, a big, clever bear would pick up the 350-pound trap, turn it on end, and shake out the bait. We learned to tie the trap to a sturdy tree, and then these bears would sometimes just dig a big pit in frustration.

But foraging decisions bears make are not always simple or obvious. Chuck Jonkel once told me, "There's not much point in trying to catch bears once berries are ripe. They seem to like berries as much as bait." And even when I was a kid, my grandmother, who had a dozen old fruit trees in her farmyard, as well as a sockeye salmon spawning stream about 50 yards (50 m) away, would say, "Why can't the bears eat fish like they are supposed to and leave my fruit trees alone?" The black bears in her yard seemed to like plums best, then pears and then apples. They didn't seem to go for the salmon very much, even though the big red fish would be easy to catch when they were busy spawning and then dying in the foot-deep (30 cm) stream.

**BEING OMNIVORES WITH A HIGHLY VARIED DIET,** yet needing to become obese every year, bears have a complex nutritional ecology. Fortunately, Dr. Charlie Robbins, a professor at Washington State University (WSU), began focusing on bear nutrition in the 1980s. Since then, he and his students have done many feeding experiments on captive bears, as well as some work on wild animals. A major finding from decades of work was published by Joy

Erlenbach (Erlenbach et al. 2014). She found that when large, adult captive bears were offered a variety of foods including salmon, apples and pork fat, they selected a mix that ended up with only 17 per cent of the energy coming from protein, and with this optimal diet, their weight gain was the highest. Pound for pound, fat contains over twice as much energy as carbohydrates, and bears preferred foods high in fat over foods high in carbs. However, if the protein content of the diet was above 17 per cent, or higher than optimal, then both fats and carbs were equally efficient at reducing the proportion of protein to approach the optimal target. This result helped explain why bears in parts of Alaska spent 70 per cent of their time in the mountains eating high-carb fruits when the streams were full of spawning salmon that are too high in protein for an ideal diet (Robbins et al. 2007). It also explains why bears eating spawning salmon often select the fat-filled brain, roe and skin and discard the meat (Gendle, Quinn and Willson 2001).

Laura Felicetti also did interesting experiments on the captive bears at WSU. She fed young, 100 to 200 (45 to 90 kg) pound grizzly bears diets with a variety of protein levels (Felicetti, Robbins and Shipley 2003). When on a very low-protein, fruit-based diet, the young and growing bears needed to eat more than twice as much digestible energy to gain the same amount of weight as they did when eating food with a more ideal amount of protein. But when eating the low-protein, fruit-based diet, all their weight gained was fat. These young bears, which should have been rapidly growing in stature and muscle mass, actually lost lean (mostly muscle) tissue while gaining fat when on the fruit-based diet. The inefficiency of the fruit-based diet was partially because the energy content, pound per pound, of the fat they were depositing was much higher than the energy content of the lean tissues they deposited when eating a diet with a more optimal amount of protein. Most interesting to me, the total amount of fat they put on was up to three times greater when the bears were on the low-protein, fruit-based diet than on the more optimal protein diet. On the fruit-based diet, the bears just ate a lot more food than they did when eating an ideal diet. Perhaps the young bears were striving to ingest a sufficient absolute amount of protein for their metabolic needs without depleting muscle tissue, and in doing so, ate far more food and therefore put on the blubber. Laura's results suggested that, like all animals, bears can buffer times of food scarcity by storing fat when times are good, but also that their lean mass is not static. Muscle tissue can also go up or down depending on their diet. Although it's likely not as efficient as ingesting the ideal protein target every day, body protein can also be charged and drained like a battery to buffer periods of protein scarcity.

Large-mammal ecologists generally agree that, ultimately, food supply usually regulates population size (Boutin 1990; Sinclair 1989). To begin to understand why there are not more grizzly bears, it was most important for me to know how the bears obtained sufficient energy and protein for body growth, and to pack away enough nutrients for months of hibernation. First, I had to know what the bears ate and the amount of digestible protein and energy that were in these foods. I also needed to know how the nutrient content of the foods changed over the seasons.

## 6.1 WHAT GOES IN MUST COME OUT

From time to time, grizzly bears eat just about everything from earthworms to willow bark, so making a never-ending list of bear foods becomes pretty well useless – to say all is to say nothing. What we really need to know is how much of each food they eat, but this is complex for an omnivore with such a varied diet. In the 1970s and 1980s, there were three ways to document the relative amounts of each food bears ate within a season, but all have potential for biases. First was to simply watch and see what wild bears were eating. This seems like a pleasant way to document their diet, but in reality this method is so problematic that it is rarely if ever used. In particular, grizzly bears often forage in thick enough vegetative cover that they will detect even the quietest observer. Then, if the observer is lucky, as they usually are, the grizzly will run off. If the observer is not so lucky, the bear will clearly communicate that they don't want to be watched. The unfortunate bear watcher will have had a powerful lesson and will likely try to study bear foraging using a different method next time.

There is, of course, one well-known exception, because where you can reliably and safely see what bears eat, tourists can safely and comfortably watch bears as well. Countless hours of film and millions of photographs have been taken at salmon spawning streams where bears, sometimes shoulder to shoulder, catch and eat fish. Likely because of the close contact among fish-eating bears and the abundance of food, these individuals have developed a culture with social graces that allow consistent and predictable viewing by people, and this has led to a safe and rapidly growing industry. But over most of their distribution, grizzly bears don't feed on salmon, nor have they developed these social graces that enable safe, close contact among bears, and among bears and people. And of course, at salmon spawning streams bears eat salmon – there is not really much to learn about their diet there except what parts of the salmon bears eat and which bears get the most. But put a radio collar on these fish-eating bears and in some areas you will find that even when salmon are spawning, bears spend most of their time away from streams eating other things (Robbins et al. 2007).

Although watching a bear feed from a distance is straightforward and requires little skill besides identifying foods from a distance and knowing something about sampling methodology, the second method requires skilled detective work. Bears leave sign when feeding, as well as where they wander. A skilled tracker, with or without the help of a well-trained dog, can see where the bear went and what it fed on. The fresher the sign, the easier it is to detect what the bear was up to. As with any detective work, being at the scene early is critical if one is to get the story correct, because some sign, such as digging for roots or ants, remains clear for many days while others, such as grazing on grass, disappear quickly. Again, this is where radio collars are all but essential to avoid major biases. With a collared bear, the site where the animal was located can be visited as soon as the bear wanders off, leaving very fresh sign from a known individual.

Dogs can help track bears, particularly if visual sign is difficult to follow. I used Mr. Buzz in the 1980s mostly to track detailed movements of radio-collared black bears for a graduate student because these bears spent a lot of time in closed canopy forests where I found following their sign to be challenging. Buzz was a German shepherd with a keen nose but had been culled from the police force because they thought he was a wimp. He was never frightened of black bears, but when I first got him when he was one year of age, he was so frightened of grizzly bears that he would not even look at a trapped grizzly. He would stare in the opposite direction and shake in fear. But, after he was enticed to many drugged grizzlies with dog biscuits buried in their fur, he gradually started to love grizzly bears. After a couple of years he was no longer a wimp. If he got off his harness, he would go nose to nose with a grizzly five times his size. He was a very intense animal who just never, ever stopped wanting to follow bears. Working with Mr. Buzz was more than a full-time job.

The third method was, until the 1990s, the standard way to assess bears' diets and one that my father seemed to enjoy. Dad was an engineer who designed ski lifts, suspension bridges and industrial tramways. His workplace was spotlessly clean. He loved to announce to his buddies that

I would meticulously pick through bear turds to definitively answer the age-old question, "Do bears shit in the woods?" How many times did I hear "Now, do you only go by what you see or do you also take a deep sniff, and then have a little taste to be sure?" To make him happy, I always went along with his joke. "Certainly, I first examine the bouquet, but one really needs to gently waft in the subtle scents and swirl the shit to detect the notes of huckleberry and overtones of sweet vetch root." It was mostly funny to me because he knew that I didn't do this, but he loved the story anyway. What I did was to collect and air dry the bear scats we collected and then send them to Bill Callaghan, the master of bear poop, who lived near Missoula, Montana. Bill had hundreds of small sample jars, each with a few seeds from all the plants that a bear would ever eat, as well as sample hairs of all the mammals and lots of leaf structure diagrams. Bill loved his work and was always so excited to find out what was in the scats. As everyone knew, Bill knew his shit.

To use scats to determine the diet, the first job, of course, is to collect scats. Now, collecting scats may seem pretty straightforward, but collecting an unbiased sample of anything is never straightforward. In an effort to reduce bias, I focused my collection at sites used by the radio-collared bears to make sure I was not collecting scats from places where I went but from places the bears went. Even in areas used by the radio-collared bears I limited the number of scats collected to a maximum of three because in some areas, particularly where a mother with cubs settled for a while, there were dozens of scats. I ended up collecting 1,190 grizzly bear plus 395 black bear scats and sent them to Bill Callaghan for analysis (McLellan and Hovey 1995).

**BUT OF COURSE,** all foods are not digested at the same rate (Pritchard and Robbins 1990). What goes in the bear's mouth isn't necessarily what comes out the other end. A highly digestible food such as fish, particularly if bones are avoided, is pretty much fully digested, and nothing comes out but slime. In contrast, fibrous plant roots come out looking much the same as they did going in. Fortunately, back at the WSU bear lab, Dave Hewitt quantified correction factors (grams ingested to get one millilitre of residue in the poop) for bear scats (Hewitt and Robbins 1996). With these numbers, we could estimate what actually went in the bear's mouth from what came out, and was, indeed, left in the woods. He simply fed the captive bears known mixed diets of various bear foods to compare with what the bears pooped out.

Bears eat a lot, so Dave needed large volumes of natural bear foods, some of which were not easy for him to find. I made him a deal. I would collect the glacier lily bulbs, cow parsnip stalks and buffalo berries if he would do nutrient analyses on all of my grizzly bear food samples. Every two weeks, I collected samples of most major bear foods from vegetation plots located where bears had fed. Having Dave do the analysis made sure it was done properly and consistently at the Robbins bear lab at WSU. The agreement I had with Dave meant I had to harvest a large volume of these bear foods, and by doing this I learned a lot, particularly about digging bulbs and roots efficiently. The number and distribution of plants, slope of the ground, and in particular soil texture and substrate, made huge differences in how fast I could dig roots. Doing what bears do is a good way to learn the minute-by-minute challenges they face.

Hewitt's results on correction factors were helpful for correcting scat analysis for ingested plants such as grasses, leafy forbs, berries, nuts and roots. Similarly, when bears ate small mammals, such as voles and ground squirrels, they swallowed the little animals whole, so the amount of hair and bone passing through was consistent. Determining correction factors for large mammals such as deer, elk or moose, however, remained a problem. The proportion of these animals that passed through the bear depended on the amount of their hide and hair the bear ate. The correction factor varied 18-fold when the consumption of hair and hide ranged from 5 to 100 per cent, assuming all the meat was eaten (Hewitt and Robbins 1996). However, it was worse. Bears are both predators and scavengers, so sometimes they are lucky and kill a deer and eat the meat, but often they take a kill from another carnivore, or simply find the remains of an old carcass with little or no meat left. If Dave had also fed the captive bears a deer hide with just a little fat on the inside, like one that a hunter would discard, then the correction factor would be less than most plants (less ingested to get 1 ml of residue) and would vary by much more than 18-fold. So we really needed a better way to estimate the amount of meat from large mammals in bear diets.

## 6.2 CLEAN CHEMISTRY

Fortunately, a fourth way to investigate the diet of grizzly bears was developed that was more high-tech and much easier than picking through hundreds of bear scats. This method is based on different ratios of stable isotope in animal tissue.

At the molecular level, bears' bodies, like those of all animals, are in continuous flux with the ecosystems they live in. The measurement of stable isotope ratios in a bear's body tissues indicates where the actual atoms that currently make up its body originated. Many elements have two or more stable isotopes, but because Carbon (C) and Nitrogen (N) are major building blocks of the body, these are primarily used. Importantly, not all C and N atoms are the same. For example, all N atoms have seven protons, or positively charged particles, in the nucleus and most also have seven non-charged neutrons (N-14). Some N atoms, however, have seven protons and eight neutrons (N-15). They generally act the same as N-14 atoms, but because they have an extra neutron, N-15 are slightly heavier. Now, when a mix of billions of N-14 and N-15 atoms pass through an organism every day, not all are incorporated into the body at the same rate. As with a prospector with a gold pan swishing around sand from a creek, the heavier stuff generally sinks to the bottom and the lighter particles go over the edge of the pan. Similarly, the heavy isotopes have stronger chemical bonds and are a little more apt to be retained longer by the organism, while the lighter ones are more likely to pass out in the urine. Although the ratios of heavy to light isotopes vary among species of plants, heavy isotopes are relatively rare in plants because they are at the bottom of the food chain.

Herbivores, such as deer and moose that eat plants, have higher levels of the heavy isotopes than their food does, because their bodies retain the heavier isotopes longer. Pure carnivores eating other animals have even higher proportions of heavy isotopes, because their food already has enriched levels. So the higher up the food chain a species is, the more enriched its isotopic signature. Bears that eat salmon have body tissues made of highly enriched N atoms because marine food chains are longer and more complex than terrestrial food chains. To date, isotope ratios cannot tell much about what species of leafy greens, roots or berries a bear has eaten. However, these ratios can us give an idea of what proportion of their diet that was assimilated into their tissues came from plants and what proportion was from meat.

Isotope ratios are especially useful because determining what proportion of a bear's diet came from meat is the main problem with Dave Hewitt's scat correction factors. Stable isotope analysis has also been a great tool because many samples can be inexpensively analyzed in a lab, a variety of tissues including hair can be used so samples can be easily obtained, and the measurements are from an individual whose sex and age we often know. With this information, we can compare diets among age groups and sexes.

Isotopes in hair reflect what the bears ate while the hair was growing. All healthy Flathead bears shed their thick underfur in June and July. Although the long guard hair on their hindquarters often thins out, and seemingly more so on males than females, they usually retain their long guard hairs throughout the year, at least on their front shoulders. Unlike the thick underfur, some of these longer guard hairs likely grow and are replaced across their active year, so isotope measurements from the shoulder guard hairs likely reflect an annual diet but are probably biased more towards August to October, particularly with males. I observed this pattern of moulting underfur, and sometimes guard hairs on the back half of the body, in many populations where I have caught grizzly bears every month of the year. Some coastal bears that eat salmon seem to moult differently. Unlike bears from the interior, many coastal, salmon-eating bears must shed their guard hairs as well as their underfur because they often have very short, usually simple brown coats early in the summer. The long guard hairs and underfur don't grow back until later in the summer. We now know that cutting hairs into sections and analyzing these separately may provide information on seasonal diets (Jones et al. 2006; Rogers et al. 2020).

In the Flathead, I collected hair samples from 18 female and nine male grizzly bears that I captured between 2003 and 2010 (McLellan 2011). The isotopes of ten females indicated that, on average, they had eaten very little meat while their guard hairs were growing. Although they no doubt ate some meat or at least some ants, most were essentially vegan. The hairs of only four females were derived from a diet that was likely over 10 per cent meat or insects, and the highest was a female whose hairs indicated a diet of 25 per cent meat. There was certainly more meat in the diet of the males than of the females. All nine males had hair that came from a diet with detectable amounts of meat; five had more than 20 per cent and the highest was 38 per cent. Also, adult males had more meat in their diet than did younger, subadult males.

Subsequently, we have collected many more hair samples from rub trees and hair traps. A friend I work with, Garth Mowat, sent samples from 29 females and 27 males from the Flathead to the lab. On average, these females had about 8 per cent meat in their diets, although five individuals likely had a diet of between 20 and 40 per cent meat. Hair samples from the males suggested that, on average, their diet was composed of 25 per cent meat, with three having a diet of over 50 per cent meat. Garth also analyzed samples of over 100 male and 100 female grizzly bears living in the Bull and Elk river drainages, immediately north of the Flathead. I found these results interesting because the plant bear foods in these areas are similar to those in the Flathead, but there are far more deer, elk, mountain goats and bighorn sheep (i.e., ungulates) living in those areas than in the Flathead. A simple statistical analysis of these isotopes found a clear difference in the amount of meat in the diets of males and females, but once sex was accounted for, there was no difference between the amount of meat in the diet of Flathead bears and those living in the Bull and Elk river drainages where large herbivores were more abundant. Female bears did not eat a lot of meat in either area.

In addition to the hair samples that indicate what bears had eaten when the hairs were growing, I had bone collagen samples analyzed that reveal the diet over many years. A couple of these bears I knew well; one I knew very well.

**BLANCHE WAS AN OLD FEMALE** grizzly that I named after Blanche McDougal. Blanche and her husband Joe were the only human residents of the Canadian Flathead between the 1940s and 1979 when Joe died. Blanche the bear lived in a 125 square mile (324 $km^2$) home range right in the middle of my study area. I saw her with three cubs early in 1979 and several times over the summer, but I didn't catch and collar her until autumn of that year. When she wasn't hibernating, I followed her pretty well every day from 1979 until her death in the autumn of 1986. In addition to her three cubs in 1979, she had three more in 1982, and another three in 1985. All nine cubs lived to at least 1½ years of age, and one that we called Melony lived to be 30, while her litter mate Aggie lived to be 32 years old. Blanche was not only one of the most productive females that I monitored in the Flathead or elsewhere, but an excellent mother whose cubs all survived at least through their first year. The bones of this productive female, over the years that she had nine cubs, had no detectable levels of meat at all. But, by tracking her day after day in detail, I know she almost always focused her feeding on a variety of plants, but she did eat meat too. I know she fed on the remains of at least two moose, three deer and an elk that she scavenged, as well as a lot of ants.

I had a bone sample of only one male, a bear we called Mitch, the son of Elspeth, another productive female that had 17 cubs over her life. We followed Mitch from his birth to his death five years later. Like several of Elspeth's cubs, Mitch was a character. Mostly he was the worst bait hound I've ever dealt with. He loved bait and learned where many of our trap sites were, so we spent considerable effort avoiding catching him when we knew, from his radio collar, that he was nearby. Even with this effort to avoid catching him, he ended up being caught eight times in 1988 alone. Luckily, he was caught in the aluminum barrel trap four times, so we just let him go without giving him any drugs. He seemed to love the barrel trap. There he was safe from bigger bears, sheltered from rain or snow, and had a pile of bait to eat. On two occasions, he was over 20 miles (32 km) away from the barrel trap when we set it. The next day, there he would be, curled up sound asleep with a belly full of fat.

When Mitch was 5 years old, we located him in the breeding season with young Melony. Although he had eaten his share of bait in his short life, Mitch was young and only weighed 245 pounds (111 kg). Then one morning I found that another male we called Wilt was with Melony and Mitch's collar had changed pulse rate, indicating that the collar was off or that Mitch was dead. Now, as you may guess, if you know anything about basketball, Wilt was tall. When snared to a tree, he stood up on his hind legs, bit into and then pulled at the tree. Out came a chunk of wood the size of a two-by-four and about three feet (1 m) long. We later measured the height of his bite and it was nine and a half feet (2.9 m) above the ground. I'm sure he would have stood over ten feet (3 m) tall if he stood up straight. Anyway, nature is anything but kind, and Mitch was dead. His skull was crushed by jaws that could rip a two-by-four out of a living tree. Not surprisingly, Mitch's bone collagen suggested that half was assimilated from meat. Only three of the 36 other males that Garth and I sampled in the Flathead had more meat in their diets than did little Mitch the bait hound.

## 6.3 THE ANNUAL DIET

To get a fairly clear picture of what foods the grizzly bears ate in the Flathead drainage at various times of the year, I combined several types of information. Most was combined from the isotope results with the analysis of over a thousand bear scats while incorporating Hewitt's correction factors. But I intertwined this information with hundreds of observations of grizzlies feeding, as well as the evidence they left after they wandered away.

### *6.3.1 April and May*

In the first decade of our study, when I was a graduate student, Celine and I were anxious to get away from the big city of Vancouver where my university was located. In late March or early April, we snowmobiled, usually

30 to 50 miles (48 to 80 km) from where the loggers had stopped ploughing the road that year, to the Flathead cabin. From the snow machine we would locate radio-collared bears and then ski along their tracks in the snow to learn what they were up to, and if lucky, find a scat. We followed bears, sometimes for several miles, and often didn't find a single poop and little or no feeding sign. They didn't seem to find much to eat early in the spring when snow covered most of the valley. But once in a while, after miles of skiing, there would be our reward melted into the snow. At that time of year I could usually tell without Bill's microscope that a scat contained almost 100 per cent elk or sometimes moose hair, but I would dry it and send it to Callaghan anyway. The scats that were mainly hair were likely from when the bear found little more than an old hide and some bones to gnaw on. When the bear ate mostly meat, scats were gross, greasy globs of grey goo that smelled significantly worse than a berry scat. Picking through meat scats is when Bill really earned his money.

In early April 1980, I was snowmobiling up a major side drainage when I crossed the fresh track of an uncollared grizzly with feet so big that it had to be an adult male (49.261 -114.638). It was only my second year of study and I hadn't been to many bear dens, so I thought I could follow his tracks backward and maybe find his den. I put climbing skins on my skis and set off uphill through the stunted spruce and fir forest, working my way back into a side drainage. There, the bear had crossed a couple of fairly threatening avalanche paths, but further up he had crested the ridge. From the ridge, he had come from a remote, unroaded valley. I pulled off the skins from my skis, and down I went, following his tracks into the distant forest. After about a mile (1.6 km), I had descended to the valley bottom where it was too low in elevation and too flat for a den (49.288 -114.626), but I was rewarded for my effort in the form of a scat on the snow. It was the good old grey goo, suggesting he had eaten a lot of meat and little hair.

It was now late in the afternoon. As I was alone in a remote valley as the temperature was starting to drop and the light beginning to fade, my imagination was wandering. There wasn't a lot of hair in this poop. Maybe the bear had been forced from his kill by an even bigger and meaner grizzly. I already knew that I might be evening skiing on my way out, and that it was going to be a long, cold snowmobile ride back to the cabin. So, not wanting to contest a kill from a bigger bear, I turned back and followed my route back up the mountain and then down to the snowmobile. When the results came back from Bill, it was 100 per cent black bear. The grizzly must have dug an unfortunate blackie out of its den and eaten it, because black bears are all still hibernating that early in the year.

I didn't collect a lot of scats in the first half of April. Only a few bears, and almost all of these would be males, were out of their dens and they didn't find much to eat as they strolled across a landscape still mostly blanketed with remaining winter snow. There was a little grass in one of these early season scats, and some that I collected in April consisted of sweet vetch roots, but the rest were the remains of elk. Often there was elk hair but little, if any, greasy goo, suggesting that little meat was available and feeding was often scavenging on old carcasses. Adult males emerge from their dens a couple of weeks earlier than other bears, likely because they are the only ones that can compete for the few elk, moose or mountain goats that either died or were all but dead after a long winter.

In most years, the great changes of spring were beginning by mid-April. The sun's arc across the sky was gradually getting higher. Days were getting longer and warmer, and the snow disappeared from the valley bottoms and from south- and west-facing slopes. The receding snowpack stimulated changes in the large mammal community. Mountain goats, clinging to windswept cliffs, remain in the Flathead all winter. Similarly, moose, with their long legs that keep them mobile in deep snow, also remained. Although some elk and mule deer spend the winter in the Flathead, most migrate out of the valley to dryer areas, generally at lower elevations where there is much less snow. All whitetail deer move elsewhere. Near the end of April and early May, the elk, mule deer and whitetail deer returned to the Flathead.

By mid-April, all adult male grizzlies were out of their dens, and by the end of April, most of the females were also out and foraging. During the second half of April some scats that I knew to be from males were still largely composed of elk and moose remains, but most were now full of sweet vetch roots. The long taproot on this two-foot (61 cm) tall, often multi-stemmed perennial, is usually tender in the early spring and again in the fall. It tastes a bit like parsnip but with a touch of almond. A similar species, *Hedysarum alpinum*, is known to have been an important food for Indigenous Peoples in Alaska, and no doubt *H. sulphurescens*, the sweet vetch most common in the Flathead, was also important to people further south. Early in the spring, sweet vetch is about 8 per cent digestible protein and, at 1.7 kcal/g, fairly high in digestible energy. Vetch grows well in open areas and is dug by bears along the river flood plain, and also on high-elevation mountain ridges. Bears also dig this root in clearcut logged areas, particularly if the logged area has been machine scarified, which acts like a farmer's plough, turning up and softening the soil. As with all roots, bears prefer to dig them in soft soil, and particularly where the taproots are not entangled with the roots of other, more fibrous trees and shrubs that make digging difficult. Scats known to be from female grizzlies in late April and early May were dominated by sweet vetch roots, but a few had a small proportion of elk hair from when they had scavenged remains left by others. Grass and horsetails were found in a very few scats before May.

By the latter half of May, the valley and the mountains were green with new plant growth. With such rapidly changing conditions, more feeding options opened up for bears. Foods eaten reflected changes in the abundance, nutrient content and distribution of foods, with each bear making decisions on where to focus their foraging effort. Although the number of large mammals in the valley greatly increased through May as most of the elk and deer returned, the bears' diet went from being dominated by sweet vetch roots and large mammals in April and early May to one almost exclusively of green vegetation by late May. In particular, bears fed on horsetails, grasses and some leafy plants or forbs. Early in the growing season, these green plants have 20 to 25 per cent digestible protein, so are even a little above the protein target for maximum body growth, and they are abundant. At around 1.3 kcal/g, however, these plants are fairly low in digestible energy.

### *6.3.2 June and July*

The digestible protein content of horsetails and grasses rapidly declined from over 20 per cent in early June to about 12 per cent at the end of the month, and continued to decline through July. The level of digestible energy also declined and so did their use by bears. Although some feeding on these plants continued, bears became more selective and appeared to pick areas and even individual plants that were greener and likely still had higher nutritional quality. But increased selectivity reduces ingestion rates, and horsetails and grasses were not commonly eaten by the end of June. While the consumption of horsetails and grasses declined, bear use of forbs, such as clover, creamy pea vine, but in particular cow parsnip increased. Although the quality of these foods was also in decline as spring progressed, they declined less rapidly than grass and horsetails did, and didn't drop below the optimal protein target until the beginning of July.

Cow parsnip (*Heracleum maximum*) is a very large herb. It has a one inch (2.5 cm) diameter stalk and is sometimes six feet (2 m) tall. At about two kcal/g of digestible energy and about 20 per cent digestible protein, it's not only a high-quality plant but one that bears can bulk feed on. Some sites had so much sign of grizzly bear feeding, trampling and snoozing in bear beds that we called them Heracleum Hotels.

Cow parsnip was a major food of Indigenous Peoples and is sometimes called Indian celery or rhubarb. At bear feeding sites, I sometimes peeled the strong-tasting outer layer from the stalks with a jackknife and ate the inner stem. When the plants are prime, they taste pretty darn good, but I like the inner stem of edible thistle even better. Although it takes some work to peel away the outer layer of thistles with its tiny thorns, there is no domesticated vegetable I've ever eaten that is so tender and tasty. I'm not sure if pea vine was a significant food for Indigenous People, but the flowers and new leaves are tasty and, of course, have the flavour of fresh raw peas. Unlike cow parsnip or thistles, pea vine doesn't need any preparation and can be picked and eaten while walking through open habitats. I have gobbled down a lot of pea vine as I wandered through the Flathead following bears. Although many species in the pea family have nasty alkaloids, I had no bad (or good!) effects from eating pea vine.

Some Flathead bears, particularly females, spend all of May, June and July in the wide Flathead Valley, rarely going into the mountains at that time of year. Other females lived in the mountains and rarely, if ever, went into the valley, whereas males often moved across all areas. Bears living in the mountains often dug glacier lily bulbs in June and July. These bulbs, however, did not often show up in the scats. Not only are they highly digestible with a correction factor four times higher than sweet vetch roots, but also scats containing glacier lily bulbs were not often found, I think mostly because of the way bears dig them. When bears forage on sweet vetch roots, digs are usually single holes spaced out, and scats are found at digs or where the bear moved between places they dug. For glacier lilies, bears often "rototill" entire hillsides; sometimes half an acre will be tilled. I've often searched excavated areas where it was obvious that bears spent considerable time digging and eating glacier lily bulbs, without finding a single scat. I think most scats got buried by all the digging.

Glacier lily bulbs are usually a little over an inch (2.5 cm) long, are tender and taste somewhat like a Jerusalem artichoke. They are high in carbs with

2.4 kcal/g of digestible energy, but have only 5 per cent digestible protein. As with sweet vetch and other roots grizzlies eat, bears usually dig glacier lily bulbs where digging is easy. Preferred sites are sometimes under a canopy of slide alder where soil is usually loose and deep. Other times they are dug where the soil is shallow over bedrock so the bulb lies close to the surface and the soil can be simply peeled back off the rock. Maybe most often they are dug in areas were the soil remains soft because bears dig there year after year. In such places, soil nitrogen increases due to the digging, and competition with other plants decreases, so the plants the bears miss grow well. Seed production of the surviving plants is higher than average, and since seed dispersal is limited to about three feet (1 m), these tilled sites regenerate with even more glacier lilies growing in the soft, tilled soil (Tardiff and Stanford 1998). Some of these sites are rototilled by grizzly bears year after year.

Although the isotope analysis suggested that female bears ate little meat or insects when their guard hairs were growing, I know that some ate newborn (neonates) deer, moose and elk near the end of May through the first half of June. These neonates are nursing so, from an isotope standpoint, they are feeding off their mothers and have enriched N-15 compared to adults. A bear feeding on already enriched animals should certainly have N-15-enriched guard hairs unless these hairs are not growing in early June. Mother deer, both whitetail and mule deer, usually let their fawns hide in the brush for the first few weeks of their life until they can outrun most predators. I have often bumped into fawns lying still in the forest shortly after they were born. Several times I've seen them curled up, motionless in the middle of a logging road, unaware that they were very obvious and were unlikely to live long lying there. After about a month of age, they sometimes explode from their hideout when I'm very close, and in grizzly country, this sends my heart rate skyrocketing. Undoubtedly, some if not most bears eat a newborn fawn or two in June when they are not so fast. In one area of Alaska, where plant food is relatively poor but moose and caribou are abundant, each bear monitored using video cameras on their collars ate an average of over 30 newborns during spring (Brockman et al. 2017).

Only a few June and July scats contained ground squirrel remains, but I've watched grizzlies dig for them on several occasions. Once, I was sitting alone, high in the mountains watching an uncollared bear about 100 yards (91 m) below me when it stopped sniffing ground squirrel burrows and started to dig into one. The bear worked hard for several minutes, grunting away and tossing dirt all over. Then a whole family of these one-pound

(0.45 kg) rodents took off running at once. The bear was an amazing display of athleticism. In almost a blur, it smacked one with its right paw, pivoted, hit another with the left, pounced to squash a third, spun and whacked another. It took only a couple of seconds but the bear had leapt, turned and contorted and killed most if not all of them. Then the bear ate them slowly, one by one.

People have suggested that a bear must lose net energy when digging for ground squirrels, but I think they can do well at times. Besides, by mid-July, the digestible protein content of even cow parsnip is down to about 12 per cent, well below the ideal level, so animal tissue really helps bears get back on their protein track. On the Tuktoyaktuk Peninsula in northern Canada, John Nagy found an adult female grizzly gained 1.8 kg per day eating mainly ground squirrels. From mid-May to mid-September, this female put on 220 pounds (100 kg), effectively doubling her spring weight by eating these rodents that had shallow burrows constrained by permafrost (Nagy et al. 1983, *A study of grizzly bears*).

From mid-May through July, bears fed primarily on green vegetation and in particular grasses, horsetails and cow parsnip, as well as on many other herbs. In the Flathead, these plants are abundant, and although bears had been eating them for over two months, they remained plentiful. The time when bears started focusing on these plants, in late May until their use declines in mid-July, coincides with the mating period of both grizzly and black bears. Mating is distracting and takes time. For bears, it's best done when foods are abundant, even if they are of relatively low quality. But in mid-July fruit starts to ripen. Then serious feeding begins and the mating season ends. It's now time for bears to grossly overeat and become obese as they prepare for the upcoming winter.

There are some saskatoon berries, or as the botanists say, *Amelanchier alnifolia*, in the Flathead, but these fruits are not a major food for Flathead bears, although they are in other places where I've studied grizzly bears. The first major fruit to ripen in the Flathead is buffalo berry, sometimes called soapberry, soopolallie, hooshum and even *Shepherdia canadensis*. Buffalo berry plants grow across much of the lower elevations in the Flathead but only produce an abundance of fruit in a few of the more open areas. In the same areas along gravelly river flood plains where bears dig sweet vetch, buffalo berry grows well and often produces enough fruit to be worthwhile for bears to stop and feed. They also produce fruit in areas that have been burned by wildfire in the past, but where conifer regeneration has been slow, including some high-elevation ridges. These shrubs also produce berries in some clearcuts, at least until the regenerating trees shade them. Although they taste like soap, or maybe worse, they are high in digestible energy, with 3.8 kcal/g. My Brix meter, a hand-held gadget with a digital readout that measures the sugar content of juice, usually finds between 18 and 25 grams of fructose per 100 ml of buffalo berry juice. For a worthy comparison, the higher number is about the same as ripe Cabernet Sauvignon grapes, and CabSauv is one of the sweeter grapes. At 6.3 per cent, buffalo berry also has a respectable amount of digestible protein, particularly for a fruit. But being a wild fruit, buffalo berry is unpredictable and does not produce a good crop every year. In years and places where it is abundant, bears start to not only gain weight but put on fat gorging on these berries.

Of course buffalo berry (hooshum) was a major food of Indigenous People. Although I find it tastes quite bad, it was whipped with a little water to make sxusem, or sometimes called Indian ice cream. This is a frothy food that tastes a little better than the fresh fruit, but an acquired taste is required for real enjoyment. Hooshum is also made into a juice drink that I find tastes bad enough that it must be healthy. I find a nice ale, as long as it's not over hopped, tastes much better on a hot day.

### *6.3.3 August and September*

In productive fruit years, buffalo berry continues to be a major food of Flathead grizzly bears into August. But a couple of weeks after buffalo berries first ripen, huckleberries in the mountains turn a dark blue if not almost black. Huckleberries, or *Vaccinium membranaceum*, have very little digestible protein and are lower in digestible energy (3.1 kcal/g vs. 3.8 kcal/g) than buffalo berry. Huckleberries are also not as clumped on each shrub as are buffalo berries, so ingestion rates of huckleberries are likely lower. Although not all bears prefer huckleberry to buffalo berry when both are ripe and abundant, most do. Overall, black huckleberry has been the major energy food for bears in the Flathead.

In the Flathead, huckleberry plants are common and found throughout the mountain forests, but in most areas they have very few if any berries. In general, these shrubs only produce enough berries for bears to feed on in open areas with few or no trees. In some other areas of the province where I have worked, productive areas for huckleberries included clearcuts, but in the Flathead, there is sufficient fruit on these shrubs only in areas that had been burned by wildfire decades before. Huckleberry fields are discrete areas and usually have little else for a bear to eat except some ants in the dead logs that remained years after the forest fires. Early in the huckleberry season, bears will move among berry fields, likely checking fruit productivity in several patches. But then some bears settle into one berry field for a week or two and don't seem to leave it. Others stay for several days but wander off for a few hours or even a day before returning.

When watching grizzlies in huckleberry fields, I sampled their activity by writing down what they were doing at the exact moment each minute started, during a total of 78 hours of observation of 42 bears. They were busy eating huckleberries 83 per cent of the time and 14 per cent of the time they were walking. Very unlike deer or elk, which have lots of predators to worry about, the grizzlies appeared vigilant (looking or sniffing) only 2 per cent of the time. During these sessions sampling behaviour in the old burns, I didn't see bears eat anything but huckleberries. Because huckleberries have little protein, a bear feeding only on these fruits will be on a diet far below their ideal level of protein. Although I didn't see bears tearing up logs for insects during sampling sessions, I have watched them eating ants in berry fields on many other occasions, and their scats suggest they ate more ants during the berry season than other times of year. By doing so, they would get a bit more protein in their diet.

THIS IS NOT TO SAY THAT BEARS don't do anything but eat and sleep when in huckleberry fields. Once in a while, other things happen in a bear's life, even when they are seriously trying to gobble down thousands of berries every day. For example, I was once sitting on a ridge (49.07618 -114.3558) watching Melissa with her three yearlings, Cindy, Sally and Bill (49.07918 -114.35743), late one August. With a stadium-like view from above, I saw a coyote sneaking up towards the bears. The little canid was getting close, I'd say about 20 yards (18 m) away from the nearest bear, but the bears were too busy eating to notice. It seemed the coyote didn't like being ignored so started to yap. Instantly, the bears were right after it, full steam ahead down the gully, but the coyote was so fast it left the bears behind in a second or two. This seemed to be so much fun that the bears all started rolling around, wrestling with each other. Even old Melissa got into the fun and joined the pile tussling with her yearlings. The coyote came back. It snuck right up again and began to yap. The bears forgot the fight with each other and were after the coyote again – full bore. But the coyote was gone in a flash. Then the wrestling started again. Four bears rolling around all in a big grizzly pile.

The coyote came back for a final yap, and again the bears were after it but of course didn't get close to catching it. Eventually the bears all went back to eating berries. Being a scientist, I couldn't simply assume the obvious – coyote and bears were all just having fun. Maybe the coyote had its pups nearby and was trying to lure the bears away from them. The old "broken wing" trick that I've seen grouse and other birds do a hundred times. I've even seen mother black bears try to lure me away from the tree their cubs were in using a similar diversionary tactic. But by late August I think coyote pups could easily outrun a bunch of fat grizzlies. Although some scientists may still avoid saying that non-human animals are having fun when playing and offer many reasons how play improves social and physical skills, which it likely does, it sure looks like they also are having a refreshing break from eating berries all day long. Just as with people, physical play is most often done by young animals, but I've watched adult elk, deer, mountain lions, wolves and bears playing. This was the only time I've seen different, undomesticated species playing the same game together.

And, for a second example, can acting tougher than you really are, just because your mother is there to protect you, be classified as fun? I was watching Elspeth and her three yearlings feeding on huckleberries on the side of Commerce Mountain (49.17613 -114.43382). They were acting like they most often act at that time of year and were focused busily feeding. Then another grizzly came into my view, also feeding on fruit, maybe 200 yards (183 m) from the family. I didn't have that bear radio-collared so I didn't recognize it for sure, but it was gangly and about the same size as Elspeth, so I guessed a 4- or 5-year-old male. The bears slowly got closer. Then, instead of continuing to feed while moving apart to maintain a respectable social distance, one of the yearlings took off running towards the lone bear. The other yearlings followed about ten yards (9 m) behind. Elspeth, who was 19 years old at the time, followed up a few yards behind her pack of little grizzly terrorists. The poor lone bear took off running, with the pack following in hot pursuit. After maybe 100 yards (91 m), Elspeth lost interest or tired, and stopped running, but just jogged slowly along. One by one, the yearlings lost interest too and fell behind, but the one keener kept going. The lone bear went into a gully, out of my view and I never saw it again. The keener followed into the gully and out of view. I was wondering, is that little dude going to get his ass whipped in there? The lone bear was at least twice as big, but the little guy came back half an hour later and joined his family eating huckleberries.

**LIKE MOST WILD FRUITS,** huckleberry varies in productivity year by year. Berries were likely abundant in 1978 when we first came to the Flathead and Celine, Dr. Jonkel and I watched the ten bears feeding on huckleberries on one broad west-facing side of Commerce Peak. The following summer was hot and dry, and there were almost no huckleberries, so collared bears spent little time in huckleberry areas. Jonkel once told me, "Everything in nature varies, but I think huckleberry production varies more than most." After hiking through all the huckleberry fields that the collared bears went to, I recorded production as not very good in 1979. I would refine this estimate to be a poor year, or a rating of two out of five. Lucky for the bears, the following six years were all fours and fives, or very good berry years. I continued to record huckleberry abundance every August for decades.

How late into autumn that bears would eat huckleberries varied among years. When there were few berries, some bears kept eating grasses and cow parsnip late into August. In these years, they also ate a greater variety of other, less popular fruits such as grouse berries, high-bush cranberries and cascara, before switching to typical late-fall foods early. In years when huckleberries were abundant and there were no serious frosts, I've watched grizzlies eating huckleberries in mid-October. I once watched Blanche with her three cubs, up to their fat bellies in snow, eating huckleberries in the latter half of October.

In average huckleberry production years, most bears continue to eat this fruit through September, but starting near the middle of the month, they gradually expand their diet to include more typical late-fall foods. In particular, bears would start eating the roots of sweet vetch again. The digestible energy and protein levels of this root were high in the early spring but declined from then through the summer when shoots, leaves and flowers were growing and using the energy that had been stored in the roots. But by mid-September the plant was becoming dormant again and nutrients had gone back into the roots, making them more profitable for bears to dig.

In addition to fruits and roots, large mammals start to show up more often in the bears' diet in the autumn. On September 10, the hunting season began and people came into the valley, set up their camps and went out into the bush in an effort to kill a deer, elk or moose. Although hunting regulations have become increasingly restrictive over the years for most of these animals, and the number killed has declined, hunters killed an average of 160 deer, elk, moose and mountain goats each year in the Flathead. During the 1980s, when both males and females were often hunted, twice this number of animals were sometimes killed. At every kill site, the hunters remove the entrails of the animal and leave these gut piles for scavengers. Ravens, eagles, turkey vultures and magpies are fast and numerous, and it seems they get much if not most of the remains, but bears get their share too. Because the Flathead is too far from town for hunters to go home at night, almost all stay and camp, and so many hunters skin the animals they shoot and discard the hides in the bush. Bears often chew away on these hides because they often have a lot of fat still attached. And of course, not all animals that are shot are found by hunters. Some die hours or days later. Unlike gut piles, birds have a more difficult time getting through the hide, so bears, wolves and wolverines seem to get most of these animals that are not found by hunters.

### *6.3.4 October and November*

During October, bears really eat almost everything. Huckleberries sometimes remained important, but as bears moved out of the high-elevation berry fields, other fruits such as high-bush cranberry, bear berry and cascara were also eaten. Some bears fed on clover that was often seeded as a cover crop along roadsides and in logging landings and sometimes became lush after fall rains. But through October, the amount of sweet vetch roots and large mammals continued to increase, to where they dominated the diet by the end of the month.

A common story among hunters in the Flathead and elsewhere is that rifle shots are the dinner bell for grizzly bears, and they have learned to associate the loud noise that echoes across the valley with a tasty gut pile. It is likely that some bears have made this connection, so I tried firing a couple of shots at some of my trap sites. Unfortunately for my trapping success, I didn't catch any more bears at these sites than others. But even if bears didn't come running whenever an elk or moose was shot, some hunters do provide grizzly bears with a lot of meat in the fall. For example, there wasn't even a hunting season for female moose in 1983, but someone shot a mother and her calf and just left them lying in a clearcut about 60 yards (55 m) from a rarely used road. I found them there (49.043 -114.393; clearcut has since grown into a forest) still untouched by scavengers, late in the day on October 18. The next morning, a 500-pound (227 kg) male we called Old Pete had dragged them almost 100 yards (91 m) to the forest just above the Flathead River. Six days later Pete had wandered off and not much of the two moose was left when I checked the site the following day.

Maybe Pete didn't eat all of the perhaps 1,000 pounds (454 kg) of moose meat in the six days himself. Other bears or even some wolves or a wolverine or two may have had their share. More than once I have found that when a radio-collared bear moved away from a kill site, it didn't mean that all the meat was gone. While checking kill sites the day after a collared bear had left, I've sometimes heard the deep, guttural growl that makes my hair stand right up. On one occasion I remember very clearly, a massive mound of brown fur rose out of the thick shrubs maybe 15 feet (5 m) from me. I was out of there in a flash, and presume the bear just settled back on the dead elk; I didn't stop to see. Although I'm not certain if Pete ate the entire moose, I know he ate a lot of meat. His diet was way over the optimal protein target for at least a week, but because he had been eating mostly huckleberries that are very low in protein for about a month and a half before this, the moose meat may have bulked up his muscle mass, which had likely been depleted. For an animal like a bear that must maximize fat deposition on foods that vary enormously in their composition, protein targets are unlikely to be strict daily targets, but likely can be optimized across longer time periods. Perhaps there are energetic costs to not having a perfect diet every day, but wild grizzly bears live in wild country and have to make do with what is available.

Grizzly bear diets in November are similar to those in April. There is snow on the ground and bears can be easily followed, step by step. Males are looking for the last bits of food, but females are starting to find their den sites for winter and are no longer focusing on feeding. Sweet vetch roots are still dug and some bears gobble up dry, tasteless bear berries. Large mammals show up in the scats, but I don't think much meat is eaten. In November, only deer are open for hunting and the Flathead is a long way from town to hunt deer. There are few hunters in November to produce new gut piles, and bears are usually limited to gnawing away on old frozen carcasses and discarded hides from October when hunters were more active. By late October and through November, bears are winding down for winter.

**THERE WAS A FOOT (30 CM) OF SNOW** at the cabin on November 10, 1982, and much more higher in the mountains. Elspeth had been high up in a remote basin in the Kishinena drainage for a week (49.090 -114.299) but had not yet denned. Through my spotting scope, I could see she had been ploughing through the snow and I wondered what she was doing up there. We didn't have a snow machine or even skis with us in November so I had to hike in. There were a lot of deadfall trees on the way into that basin from the Kishinena side, and deadfalls under a couple of feet of snow make travel very unpleasant. So I hiked in from Ruby Creek to the north, along the old logging road Celine and I had hiked up two years before (a few days before Michelle was born). From the back of the drainage it was only a 2,500-foot (760 m) climb to the ridge top; the back end of Ruby Creek was steep but had far fewer blow-downs. Ploughing my way uphill through the thigh-deep snow was slow, but I steadily worked my way up the steep, frozen terrain towards the ridge. Travelling alone in even light, autumn snow can become tiring because the footing is poor enough to make every step a challenge, plus there is nobody else to take their turn breaking trail. I was getting tired and hungry, so near treeline I trampled down the snow, broke some dead, dry spruce branches and started a fire. I leaned back against a subalpine fir snag, roasted an elk sausage and made tea from melted snow in a billy can. It was about –10°F, so the fire felt good. After my midday rest, I continued climbing up, getting above treeline, and finally over the ridge top and into the Kishinena drainage just above Elspeth.

I was only a few hundred yards above Elspeth and I could see many old tracks in the snow. I took out my binoculars and hunkered down out of the wind. There she was, just standing in the snow. What was she doing? She didn't move. She just stood like a statue. An hour went by and she hadn't moved at all. I had worked up a sweat climbing through the snow, and even though I was crouched down behind a big boulder, there was enough cold breeze to have an effect. I watched her for another 20 minutes or so, but she didn't move at all. Her body was preparing for hibernation. Her body temperature would have already dropped a couple of degrees and her heart rate had been slowly declining over the previous week (Evans et al. 2016). Was she sound asleep standing up? It certainly looked that way, but it's a different kind of sleep than we are used to. Some medical researchers would say she was beginning her magic act (Stenvinkel, Jani and Johnson 2013).

I was becoming very cold and it would be a long hike out in the snow, so I thought, good enough. She isn't doing anything and certainly isn't eating. "Nothing" seems to be the November diet of most females. A few days later, Elspeth went into her den for the winter.

At 230 pounds (105 kg) in the spring, Elspeth was an average-sized female for the Flathead. Both huckleberries and buffalo berries had been productive in 1982, so she was fairly fat – she sure looked to be in good shape. Elspeth had mated with a bear we called George in June and the fertilized eggs had developed into blastocysts, or clusters of 100 to 300 cells, but then their growth stopped. If and when they would implant into her womb depended on her condition. Bears with less than about 20 per cent body fat reabsorb the blastocysts and do not produce cubs that year (Robbins et al. 2012). Really fat bears (>35 per cent body fat) not only produce cubs but give birth a couple of weeks earlier than thinner bears (20 to 25 per cent body fat) (Robbins et al. 2012) and generally, but not always, produce larger litters. Fat bears can likely produce milk for a longer period of time before emerging from the den in spring, and consequently their cubs would be larger and more robust. I have seen many big, strong cubs early in the spring, but I have also seen some very feeble ones.

I would estimate that around December 1, or about three weeks after I was sitting in the snow watching Elspeth near her den, and after a five-month delay, her corpus luteum reactivated and the blastocysts implanted into her womb and two cubs started to grow. Her body temperature did not continue to drop from her active-season temperature of about 100°F (38°C) down to 90°F (32°C) as it would have in other bears. When the blastocysts implanted, and gestation began, her temperature would rise back up to almost normal – a temperature needed for proper development of embryos. A couple of months later, when there was eight feet (2.5 m) of snow above her, she didn't really wake up when giving birth to two approximately one-pound (454 g) cubs – about 0.4 per cent of the mother's weight. Their eyes and ears were unable to open and they were covered with thin, blond "peach fuzz" for hair (Tumanov 1998). These brand-new bears with sharp little claws crawled through their mother's fur to latch on to one of her six teats – most likely one of the four on her chest area as they are the most popular. Elspeth licked her babies clean and ate the afterbirth. Her body temperature then gradually dropped to near 90°F (32°C) like that of other hibernating bears. The cubs would nurse, making a surprisingly loud chuckling sound (more on hibernation in the next chapter). That sound is not only produced by small cubs while still in the den, but I have heard it from yearlings and even 2½-year-olds, who were almost as large as their mother, when still nursing.

## 6.4 BODY COMPOSITION DYNAMICS

To know the relative volume of the different plants and animals that bears eat during each one- or two-week period over the year is fundamental to understanding bear behaviour and ecology. Knowing how the digestible energy and protein of these foods also change over the year adds greater insight. But also of importance is how the total amount of food eaten changes over time. After following bears day after day, I have no doubt they ate far more food when bulk feeding on cow parsnip in late June than they did digging sweet vetch roots and chewing on the remains of a dead elk in April when snow still covered most of the Flathead Valley. And do they consume more pounds of cow parsnip per day in June or huckleberries in August?

Unfortunately, I couldn't measure actual intake rates of various foods with wild bears. For some species, scientists have used tame, hand-raised animals in wild conditions to estimate food ingestion rates, but having a grizzly bear on a leash in the mountains was not going to happen. Besides, wild bears are likely much more efficient foragers than a pet bear raised on dog chow would have been. If I knew daily ingestion rates over the seasons, then I could use equations derived by the WSU students to calculate the total digestible energy and protein provided by the different foods and even how much of each food contributed to the body growth, maintenance and fat storage needed for winter hibernation. So instead of building up my understanding of the energetics of grizzly bears from nutritional quality and ingestion rates, I used the actual daily changes in the bears' body weight and composition (fat and lean) over the seasons. To measure changes in body weight is straightforward, but to estimate changes in body composition I once again relied on the students at WSU.

In 1989, Celine, the kids and I drove to Pullman, Washington, and visited Sean Farley, a Ph.D. student, to learn first-hand how to estimate the body composition, or the amount of fat and non-fat, of captured bears. Although there are more precise ways of estimating body fat content, the bioimpedance meter that Sean was using was small and portable, and quick and easy to operate. The meter measures the resistance to the flow of electrical current through the body. Lean tissue, which is over 70 per cent water, is a good conductor of electricity, while fatty tissue, which is low in water, is a poor conductor, so the measurements provide an estimate of relative proportions of fat and lean in the bear's body. Sean had figured out the body measurements needed to make the meter work on bears (Farley and Robbins 1994).

From then on, I measured the body weight and estimated composition of all bears I caught. Although comparing averages for each age and sex class, for both black and grizzly bears, by season provides information on trends, measuring changes in the same individuals over time has a lot less "noise" or uncontrolled variability. Whenever I could, I had deactivated traps to avoid catching individuals when I didn't need to change their radio collar, but now I didn't mind catching specific bears more than once. Ideally, I had to catch the same bear at least a few weeks apart and within a distinct foraging season. To help with this task, I had been given two prototype recapture collars – radio collars that had two small syringes on the back. When I pressed the right combination of buttons on a remote communicating device, one of the small needles would slide out into the bear's neck muscle and inject the immobilizing drug. These collars also had a motion-sensitive tip-switch, a small ball of mercury in a glass tube that would tip back and forth making electrical contact. Usually I used the steady "beep once a second" mode to track bears, but I could remotely turn this switch on if I wanted to hear the irregular pattern of beeps when the bear was moving, or a steady beeping pattern if it was resting. Bears were usually awake and moving when I pushed the code for inject, and then the irregular beeping would get much more irregular and I guessed that the bear was wondering what kind of a monster mosquito just jabbed it in the neck. This rapid and erratic beeping would continue for a few minutes after injection, but then the beeps became slow and steady when the drug had taken effect and the bear was anesthetized.

The syringes on these collars were small and could only contain enough drug to immobilize a bear under 200 pounds (91 kg). We only used these collars on six black bears and one little grizzly bear, Mammie, when she was young. All of these small bears gained between 0.1 (45 g) and 0.8 pounds (363 g) per day from early June to mid-July when green vegetation dominated their diets. At that time of year, all of their gain was in lean tissue; they continued to use up some fat they had stored over winter from the previous summer and fall (Figure 1 from McLellan 2011). I also caught three young grizzlies in conventional traps in the spring. Each was caught twice, three or more weeks apart. They gained between 0.5 and 1.0 pound (0.23 to 0.45 kg) a day while two adult female grizzly bears, Rose and Melissa, remained almost the same weight.

The trends in weight gain by the wild bears I measured during spring closely fit the pattern of the small captive bears measured by Karyn Rode when the bears were fed herbaceous vegetation at WSU (Rode and Robbins 2000; Rode, Robbins, and Shipley 2001). Rose and Melissa, the adult female grizzly bears, did not gain as much weight as captive bears of similar size. Based on Karyn's equations, the wild bears would have ingested between 2700 and 8000 kcal per day during this season. The lowest energy ingested

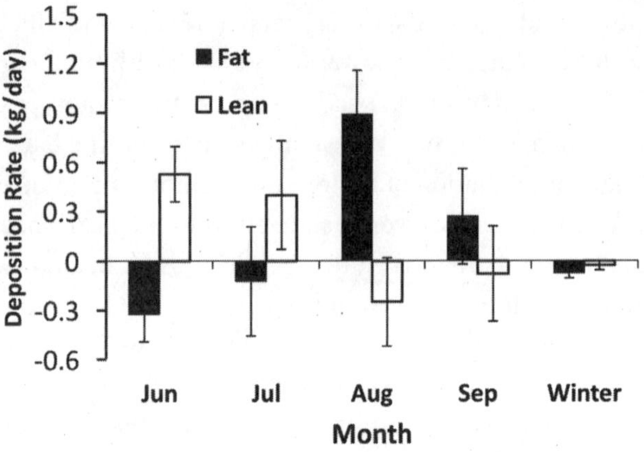


**Figure 1:** We all know that bears put on fat needed for hibernation, but the amount of lean mass also changes, at least in areas where they consume a low-protein but high-energy fruit-based diet for a portion of the year. This figure shows the amount of fat and lean (kg per day) that black bears in the Flathead Valley gained or lost per day.

was by a 90-pound (41 kg), 3-year-old female black bear, and the highest was, not surprisingly, by Mitch, the 4-year-old male grizzly that was a serious bait hound. Next to Mitch, Melissa's 4-year-old daughter Sally consumed about 7000 kcal per day. Melissa, at 315 pounds (143 kg) in June, was the largest female I ever caught in the Flathead. But during the spring that I caught her twice, she had been busy courting and mating first with George and then with Old Pete, and maybe some other males – there are good reasons for females to be promiscuous (that I will discuss later in section 16.3 on infanticide). She only ingested an average of 5100 kcal per day that spring.

**FOR GRIZZLY BEARS,** it is likely that internal physiological changes begin sometime in August. The expression of hundreds of genes in adipose (i.e., fat) cells are either cranked up or turned down, most likely activated by photoperiod, which is the amount of daylight. These types of genes have been called differentially expressed genes (Jansen et al. 2019). At this time of year the biochemical changes within the bears enhance their ability to deposit fat, a condition called hyperphagia, which of course means hyper-eating. Hyperphagia in bears, like hyperphagia in people, leads to obesity. Unlike in people, however, obesity or massive fat deposition is what bears need each year as they prepare for the real magic – hibernation (Stenvinkel, Jani and Johnson 2013).

In the berry season, I monitored two adult female black bears, Eva and Candice, and a 3-year-old female, Sophie, in detail because they had knock-down collars. The adults weighed 99 and 116 pounds (45 and 53 kg) when I first caught them in mid-July just before berries were ripe, and Sophie weighed 114 pounds (52 kg). To put their weight changes into a more personal context, Candice and Sophie were a few pounds heavier and Eva a little lighter than Celine is. Eva gained 1.6 pounds (0.73 kg) and Candice gained 1.9 pounds (0.86 kg) per day in the berry season. Sophie only gained one pound (0.45 kg) per day over a 49-day period between measurements. On this low-protein, fruit-based diet, all were losing lean tissue, so both adult bears put on more than two pounds (0.91 kg) of fat a day while Sophie put on 1.1 pounds (0.5 kg) of fat per day. In three weeks on berries, the adult female black bears gained 54 and 61 pounds (24.5 and 27.7 kg). Imagine a 107-pound (49 kg) person like Celine gaining 60 pounds (27 kg) in three weeks – I doubt she could even walk! While looking at the scale they hung from, I was really impressed at the weight gained by these wild bears that were only eating natural foods and were not eating out of a feed trough like the WSU captive bears – they had to work hard to get their food.

It was reassuring to know that the internal chemistry of these three black bears, as they fed on low-protein but high-energy berries, was the same as in the young captive grizzly bears that Laura Felicetti measured at the WSU bear lab. The 1-year-old captive grizzly bears Laura worked with, that should have been rapidly growing in body structure at that age, also put on fat but lost lean tissue when on a high-energy but low-protein fruit diet (Felicetti, Robbins and Shipley 2003).

Candice and Eva were not exceptions at putting on fat, but maybe the adult female black bear called Lucy was. I caught Lucy before I had the bioimpedance meter, so I couldn't measure her body fat. She weighed 125 pounds (57 kg) at the end of June before the berries were ripe. I caught her again in early October when she had finished eating berries for the year, and she had more than doubled in size to weigh 255 pounds (116 kg). If I'd had the bioimpedance meter, I would have likely found that Lucy, like the other females, would have lost some lean so would have gained even more than 130 pounds (59 kg) of fat. She was so fat she looked like a bloated tick with stubby little legs sticking out of a round body. Now, if any of you are about 125 pounds (57 kg) in size, just imagine what it would be like to gain an extra 130 pounds (59 kg) of fat in a month or two to pack around. Would you even be able to stand up?

Although Lucy was much fatter, Eva, Candice and even Sophie had packed away far more fat for bears their size than had any of the captive WSU bears when eating an endless supply of fruit, or even the pelleted mix with optimal protein content. The two adult females had gained as much weight for their size as hungry captive bears did feeding on an endless supply of chinook salmon and road-killed deer provided to them (Hilderbrand et al. 1999). Only captive adult grizzly bears that were hungry after a restricted diet, and then were given a continuously restocked smorgasbord of salmon, apples and pork fat, gained more weight for their size than had Eva and Candice. Some of these big captive bears ate so much fat in the first day of the experiment that they vomited. The 630-pound (286 kg) captive males consumed up to 58,000 kcals and gained up to 9 pounds (4.1 kg) a day (Erlenbach et al. 2014). If chubby Lucy had gained all her weight in the berry season, then her gains would have been the same for her size as the weight gains of the big captive bears on the dream diet of salmon, apples and pure fat. Chubby Lucy's weight gains would have been much further off the WSU charts for bears eating only fruit. I'm not certain how the small wild bears can gain so much weight on a fruit diet. Yes, wild huckleberries growing in open areas have an average Brix of 18 grams of sugar per 100 ml, which is higher than an average of 11 I've measured for fresh-pressed apple juice or 13 for commercial blueberries like those fed to the WSU captive bears instead of real, wild huckleberries. These bears were also eating some buffalo berries that have about 22 per cent more energy per pound than huckleberries and, because they grow more in clumps, can likely be ingested at a higher rate.

How many huckleberries or buffalo berries do bears eat to get so fat? In my huckleberry abundance plots that I measure annually, I have picked 4.5 pounds (2 kg) in an hour. After that hour my back was sore from bending over and I was pretty bored, but if a bear could keep up this rate for 14 hours, then it would eat 63 pounds (27 kg) of berries, or 13,300 kcals of digestible energy. If they ate 63 pounds of buffalo berries, they would ingest 19,600 kcals of digestible energy. The equations that WSU student Christy Welch (Welch et al. 1997) derived suggested that Eva and Candice would have eaten 58 and 70 pounds (26 to 32 kg) of huckleberries but only 49 and 59 pounds (22 to 27 kg), respectively, of buffalo berries per day to gain the weight they did. Lucy would have needed to eat an average of 81 pounds (37 kg) of huckleberries or 68 pounds (31 kg) of buffalo berries per day if she gained all her weight over the length of an average berry season.

The energetic relationships developed by Karyn Rode for a bear eating a 4 per cent crude protein, fruit diet (Rode and Robbins 2000) suggested that Eva, Candice and Sophie would have consumed between 10,500 and 14,900 kcal per day. Mitch, a young male grizzly that we caught twice in the berry season, would have ingested 21,500 kcal of digestible energy if he was only eating fruit. Myles, another young male grizzly bear, who gained 85 pounds (39 kg) in 49 days between captures, would have eaten 19,000 kcal, or almost 100 pounds (45 kg) of huckleberries or 70 pounds (32 kg) of buffalo berries per day. For comparison, the Mayo Clinic online calculator suggests that a six foot (183 cm) tall, 185 pound (84 kg), elderly yet active male, like I think I am, should consume 2450 kcal a day, while competitors in the gruelling, 22-day-long Tour de France bicycle race ingest, on average, 5900 kcal a day (Saris et al. 1989), or about the same as an NFL lineman.

I usually avoided catching grizzlies twice within a foraging season, so only ended up measuring Mitch and Myles. The average adult female grizzly bear, however, weighed 214 pounds (97 kg) before the berry season and 284 pounds (129 kg) after, so they likely gained in the neighbourhood of 70 pounds (32 kg) of fat (Figure 2). Karyn's equations suggest that, on average across a 51-day-long berry season, these females would have consumed 16,300 kcal per day. Adult males weighed an average of 354 pounds (161 kg) before berries were ripe but 424 pounds (192 kg) after, so they also would likely have put on about 70 pounds (32 kg) of fat and would have consumed 21,400 kcal per day. Overall, the grizzlies ingested about three times as much digestible energy in the summer berry season as they did in the spring when green vegetation dominated the diet.

Flathead grizzlies are a little smaller than grizzlies in other areas where protein is more abundant. In Yellowstone, for example, the average weight of adult females in the autumn is 297 pounds (135 kg), or about 5 per cent heavier than Flathead females. Similarly, Yellowstone adult males in autumn averaged 457 pounds (207 kg), or 8 per cent heavier than Flathead males (Schwartz et al. 2014). If Flathead bears were put in the WSU bear lab when they were cubs and fed a well-balanced, 17 per cent protein commercial chow, they would have grown to be almost twice their size. But at that size, they could not live in the Flathead because big bears can't eat enough

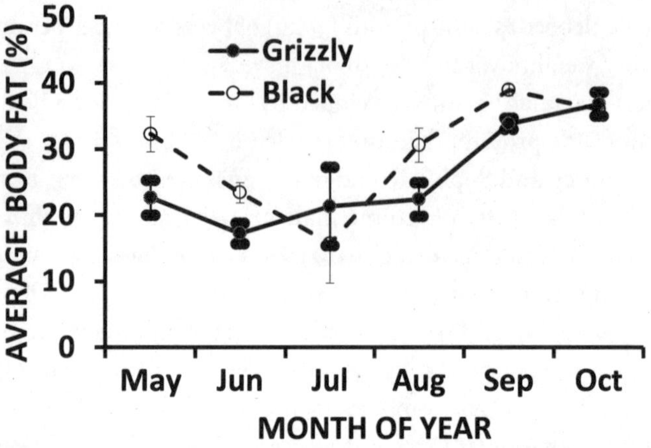


**Figure 2:** In the spring, when bears emerge from their dens, most have over 20 per cent body fat. The level of body fat usually declines for about two months but then rapidly increases when berries become ripe. Some bears get very fat, with some black bears being more than 50 per cent fat when they enter their dens in the late fall.

berries or other Flathead foods to maintain such a large body and still get fat enough for winter, whereas smaller bears can – after all, a small bear can likely eat berries almost as fast as a very large bear.

I HAD MEASURED THE CHANGES in Eva and Candice's weight and body fat over each season when the bears were active. Because the last measurements were in mid-October, just before they denned for the winter, I wanted to complete the job by doing a final measurement just before they woke in the spring. I had been working on caribou that winter in the deep-snow country in the northern Selkirk Mountains with Parks Canada warden John Flaa. It was easy to convince him to come to the Flathead. Not only does John love sitting around a glowing-hot wood stove in a remote camp, but as a national park warden, he is a well-trained, modern mountain man. It was easy to snowmobile into camp because each of us had a fairly new snow machine, very different from the ones Celine, the kids and I used years before.

Unlike many black bears that often den in the valley (one even denned downstairs in a rarely used outhouse!), Eva had denned in the mountains (49.2093 -114.5669), 2,000 feet (610 m) above where we could snowmobile. With the tracking gear, we could faintly hear her collar from the main

Flathead road where we parked the snow machines. There we put climbing skins on our skis and headed through the dense lodgepole pine forest. I liked touring with John because he never rushed. He was also six foot seven inches (2 m) tall, so when he was breaking trail, he either avoided or bumped into all branches that sometimes dumped snow down my neck; it all went down his neck instead. Slowly and steadily we worked our way through the pine and into the more open-spaced spruce forest. We were sinking less than a foot (30 cm) in the snow, but we still took turns breaking trail as we angled up towards the spot where the telemetry gear told us the bear was hibernating. After a few long switchbacks, we were getting close and so I began fine tuning the location. We didn't know if skiing over her would start waking Eva from hibernation, but the snow was deep, so we had to dig in exactly the right spot. If we missed her by a few feet, it would mean a lot more digging and a better chance she would wake up. We spent a few minutes of close, directional work to put an X on the snow where we thought would be right above her.

John began digging into the mountainside. I was below, clearing the snow he was removing out of the way so he didn't have to lift the shovel, full and heavy with snow, more than needed. Soon he started to complain. "I thought you said we would be just sitting around the fire, drinking whisky and telling stories."

"I've heard all your stories – most twice. We gotta make some new stories," I replied.

"Oh, I see, that's what we are doing. Digging a damn bear out of a hole in the mountain just to get a new story." Yep, in a way, Flaa was right.

We switched jobs a few times and in about 20 minutes I noticed he was "one Flaa down," which means the hole in the snow was six foot seven inches (2 m) deep. At one and a half Flaas deep, he hit rock.

I got in the hole with just my receiver and coaxial cable, and used it like a stethoscope searching for the strongest beep. I dug away more snow along the rock and a small hole opened up. John handed me a good Parks Canada headlamp and I looked in. Although we had been digging for over half an hour, Eva was deep asleep. I listened for cubs noisily humming away as they nursed but didn't hear anything. She had been in this hole under the boulder for five months. Eva hadn't eaten, drunk, urinated or defecated even once in this entire time, and would likely go on sleeping for another month or even more. To see her curled up under a Flaa and a half of snow is the closest thing to magic I've seen. Small animals like ground squirrels and hedgehogs drop their body temperature to almost freezing to hibernate, but they warm and even wake up every couple of weeks. Bears are the only large mammal that hibernates, and due to their size, they do it differently from the little guys.

For hibernation, thousands of genes, primarily in Eva's adipose but also her liver and muscle cells, would have had their expression enhanced or reduced, resulting in a host of physiological changes (Jansen et al. 2019). Eva's body temperature would have dropped from about 100°F (38°C) down to where it would cycle between 86°F (30°C) and 97°F (36°C) every two to seven days (Tøien, Blake and Barnes 2015). Her metabolic rate would have declined by at least 40 per cent, oxygen consumption down by at least 50 per cent, and her heart rate dropped from between 50 and 70 beats per minute to between 10 to 20 beats per minute (Evans et al. 2016; Stenvinkel, Jani and Johnson 2013; Tøien et al. 2011). But the real magic happens at the physiological and even biochemical level, and this is where she is saved from losing muscle tone, losing bone mass or being poisoned by all kinds of by-products from her ongoing metabolism. Unlike us, bears can recycle these poisons, even getting water as a by-product of burning fat (Stenvinkel, Jani and Johnson 2013; Nelson et al. 1983). There is certainly enough magic going on that medical researchers are writing dozens of journal papers on these processes in bears, hoping results will help people suffering from obesity, heart and vascular disease, diabetes, osteoporosis, kidney disease and even healing wounds (Stenvinkel, Jani and Johnson 2013). For me, and likely even more for six foot seven (2 m) John Flaa, a real benefit would be for space travel. I'm only a little over six feet tall (1.83 m) and yet a 12-hour flight in a jet is painful and I love it when I can sleep most of the way. Imagine getting onto a rocket and nodding off right away, only to be woken by, "We have started our descent into Mars, please make sure your seat backs and tray tables are in their full upright position.... It's been wonderful having you on board for the past six months."

I climbed out of the hole, took a vial of drug out of my pocket where it had been staying warm, and filled a little syringe on a shortened ski pole. I got back into the hole, scraped away a little more snow, and jabbed Eva in her rump. In five minutes, John and I blindfolded her and dragged her out of the hole. Eva had weighed 159.3 (72.3 kg) pounds in mid-October (45 per cent was fat), but now in mid-March she had lost 29.5 pounds (13.4 kg), and if the bioimpedance meter was exact, she had lost 27.9 pounds (12.7 kg) of fat and only 1.6 pounds (0.7 kg) of lean tissue. But Eva was not thin. She still had 43 pounds (19.5 kg) of fat on her, enough to keep her going for the rest of the winter and through the spring breeding season. She had had only 12 pounds (5.4 kg) of fat on her the previous July before berries had become ripe. If Eva had not been so fat, she would likely have had to use more lean tissue for her energy needs over the winter, but really chubby bears like Eva get almost all their energy needs from their fat stores (Hilderbrand et al. 2000).

After all the measurements, we pushed Eva back in her hole and made sure she was comfortable. We covered the entrance with blocks of snow, packed away our equipment, pulled the skins off our skis and headed down the mountain. It was pretty darn good skiing heading down until we hit some very fresh but hardened avalanche debris. A slide had come down, maybe 100 feet (30 m) across. It had gone right over the tracks we had left when climbing up the mountain an hour or so before. John and I had dug dead caribou out of smaller slides in the Selkirk Mountains on more than one occasion. The one that had just crossed our tracks was on the gentlest, most unthreatening terrain I had ever seen. That evening John and I enjoyed our whisky around a hot fire, warming our bones and drying our equipment. We had achieved all our goals for the day, including a new bear story. However, we talked about snow stability in the Rocky Mountains compared to other mountain ranges more than we did about bears.

We measured Candice the following day using the same find, dig, immobilize, measure and then ski home method. She had weighed 174 pounds (79 kg; also, 45 per cent was fat) in mid-October but was now down to 130 pounds (59 kg). Candice had not only lost 26 pounds (11.8 kg) of fat but also 18 pounds (8.2 kg) of lean, much of which would have gone into her rapidly growing, six-pound (2.7 kg) cub. Chubby Lucy, the female black bear that had gained 130 pounds (59 kg) over the summer, lost 43 pounds (19.5 kg) between October, just before she denned, to when we went into her den in mid-March, but she was still very fat. Surprisingly, she didn't produce any cubs that year. Losing fat but maintaining almost all of their lean body mass in non-lactating bears is due to several changes in the biochemical pathways of proteins used in metabolic processes (Nelson et al. 1983; Farley and Robbins 1995).

Lactating females lose both fat and lean tissue over winter, in part because protein is needed to grow the blastocysts into fetuses once they attach to the uterine wall. However, the production of mother's milk after cubs are born is when protein demand accelerates (Farley and Robbins

1995). Bears weigh only about a pound (450 g – black bears even less), and are extremely premature or "altricial," when born in mid-winter while the mother is hibernating. It is thought that they are born so uniquely small for a large animal (except marsupials, with an external pouch, have even smaller babies) because mammalian fetuses are unable to use fatty acids released from the mother's fat for energy. Instead they rely on energy in the form of glucose. In a hibernating animal that does not eat, the glucose comes from the breakdown of the mother's body protein, and that process produces enough ketone bodies to be toxic to the mother. It has been suggested that cubs are born when they are tiny to stop transplacental nourishment. Once born, they crawl up and latch onto a teat, and now can use the fatty acids coming from the mother's stored fat and into her milk – the start of an interesting evolutionary workaround to a serious constraint (Ramsay and Dunbrack 1986). To nurture altricial babies or "neonates," the transition from colostrum to main-phased milk production is gradual in bears, taking about a month. This transition of mother's milk goes through critical changes in composition that ensure proper development of various organs, including the central nervous system; a form of "external gestation" somewhat similar to that of marsupials (Zhang et al. 2016). Once main-phased milk is produced, it's certainly not skim or even 3 to 5 per cent fat like human breast milk, but at 20 to 30 per cent fat (Farley and Robbins 1995; Oftedal et al. 1993), it's more like whipping cream.

CHAPTER 7

# FERNIE FREE PRESS REPORTS

## *Flathead Baby Arrives*

In the autumn of 1978, the only grizzly bear we caught and radio-collared was Rushes. Having just one bear was enough to keep the government and industry funders sufficiently interested for me to continue for my first complete field season in 1979. That year we caught 12 grizzlies and 80 black bears, and by autumn, nine grizzlies wore radio collars. In the 1970s, that was a lot of grizzly bears to be tracking. There were other grizzly bear studies going on at the time, but most were monitoring less than half that number of bears.

With some level of security that the study would continue for another year or two, as well as our finances, I had enrolled as an M.Sc. student at UBC in Vancouver and Dr. David Shackleton was my supervisor. Both Dave and Ray Demarchi seemed pleased with the way the study was progressing and were my main supporters. Ray certainly told everyone from industry foresters to government bureaucrats that it was the greatest study of all time and they should get out their chequebooks. All signals suggested that the work was going to continue, maybe for another year or two.

In late September 1979, Celine and I hiked into a distant valley to track and watch a collared bear near the Continental Divide separating the Flathead Valley from Alberta. It had been a wonderful, sunny, bug-free day. We not only watched the grizzly bear for an hour or so but also a small band of mountain goats working their way across the cliffs. It was dusk when we drove down the old, mostly grown-in logging road. We passed a couple of hunters and I could see that they had shot a black bear that likely had been eating clover on the roadside. I usually avoided talking to hunters because I hear the same old stories and am asked the same old questions, but with a dead bear, we had to check it out. It was a young, fairly small male black bear and they told me, "We only wanted his overcoat, but he wouldn't give it to us, so we had to shoot him." That's a pretty standard joke among some bear hunters.

I had eaten black bear sausage before and it was excellent. I had been told that the fat, when rendered down, was the best lard in the world; they had said, "A French chef would simply drool over having bear lard to make his fancy patisseries." Now, why someone would shoot an animal and not eat it is beyond my understanding, but there was a skinned-out bear carcass lying right beside the road. The dirty work had been done. Now it was just 100 pounds (45 kg) of meat and a lot of pure white fat lying there.

"If you guys don't want the meat, can we have it?"

"You're not going to eat a damn bear? The bear's dead so he ain't going to eat you now, but if you eat him, his worms will eat you from the inside out."

Nice thought. "Don't worry, we'll cook him well."

I took out a knife and my hunting saw and in five minutes his guts were gone and they helped me toss the carcass into the back of our truck.

"What are you going to do with the bear?" Celine asked.

"We'll cut the fat off and render it down. Then we'll take all the meat to that old German butcher in Kimberley that makes such good sausage and see what he can do with it. It's going to be just fabulous. Don't worry, fabulous."

"Okay, because I don't want to make sausage."

We drove for a while and I was thinking about what an unbelievable day we'd just had, and about bear sausage, when, out of the blue Celine said, "You know, this living in the cabin along the river and hiking every day in the mountain is good. It's amazing, wonderful. I really like the cabin and the river. And you get paid to do it. It's the best job in the world. But this bear stuff is really your thing, not mine. It is your life and your career. I'm just a tagalong. Maybe I should be doing something too, but there's really nothing for me to do here living in the forest. We are so far from everything. Maybe it's a good time for us to have a baby?"

It was clearly the most important question anyone had ever asked me in my entire life. But it was not a question that required rational thought. We had no assets except for a canoe and two old Volkswagens that only worked because I crawled around with grease up to my elbows every few weeks. Although I was now getting paid, we still had very little money, and I was just starting an M.Sc. and wouldn't be finished for three more years. But none of these details crossed my mind, as they seemed irrelevant. I had full confidence in both of our abilities to do whatever we wanted as far as work was concerned. Besides, I had a dead bear in the back of the truck and was feeling great after a magical day in the mountains. It was a totally emotional no-brainer. "Sure, good idea."

That winter I did my required course work at UBC in Vancouver. We rented an illegal room in an otherwise unfinished basement for $120/month. There was a toilet and shower at the far end of the basement and a two-burner hot plate to cook on in the one room. We had one tiny window. It seemed to rain every day from December to March – typical "wet-coast" weather!

I would get up early, cook my breakfast and leave for my morning classes. Celine, being pregnant, would sleep in. Neither of us was getting paid anymore, so we didn't have much money. Luckily, I had a lot of bear sausage that was strongly spiced with a pile of garlic mixed in. I ate greasy sausage and eggs most mornings. Wow, were they great. I knew very little about pregnancy – well, I'll be more honest, I didn't know anything about pregnancy. It wasn't until years later when telling someone about how wonderful the bear sausage was that Celine let me in on the truth. She also woke when I got up and felt fine. But as soon as I started frying the sausage, the smell often made her stomach turn. I never knew. She never told me. She had morning sickness for months because of the darned bear sausages.

As soon as my classwork was done in early April, we left Vancouver and headed back to the Flathead. We borrowed the old Fish and Wildlife snowmobile, loaded the skimmer (toboggan) with food and jerry cans of gas, and snowmobiled about 50 miles (80 km) to the cabin. From there, we would find the bears' dens and then, when they woke, follow them.

Spring was coming, and by May the snow was gone in the valley. On May 19, 1980, it was daylight when I woke and wandered outside to drain my bladder and then go to the river to get water for coffee so I could thus refill my bladder.

It seems that most people think running tap water is a sign of civilization, and many friends had suggested clever ways of getting running water into the cabin. The general idea was to put a holding tank or cistern on a platform way up between some trees and fill it using a 12-volt pump running off the truck battery. Such a system was obvious and would have been simple to build, but then neither Celine nor I thought that having running water would make life more civilized. We thought the opposite. How many people in the world, particularly living within 50 degrees latitude of the equator, have the luxury of having not just a creek, but a river flowing 20 feet (6 m) from their doorstep, with water originating in high mountain basins and still clean enough to drink? I would usually walk, often barefoot, down the bank and over the rounded river rocks to the river edge. I liked the feel of cold rocks on my feet. I enjoyed looking at the river close up. Every day I could see how the water cleared, the algae grew, the insects that had metamorphosed and left their old exoskeletons on the rocks, and how the water level changed. There would often be a family of mergansers, or maybe a spotted sandpiper, or dipper going about their business along the river. Fetching water was not an inconvenience but a luxury to be enjoyed. Fetching clean water from a clean river is so much better than turning on a tap.

But the morning of May 19 was eerie. The air was thick with smoke that wasn't smoke. The ground was covered with ash but it wasn't fire ash. The sun was just a dull, deep orange ball. I couldn't even see the mountains. I got water and went back to the cabin and told Celine that there was something weird going on. She got up to check things out. A few days later we met a forester on the road and he told us that the Mount St. Helens volcano had blown, and how ash had spread across the western US and into southern Canada.

AS CELINE'S DUE DATE APPROACHED, we realized more and more that we knew nothing of childbirth other than what we'd learned from old westerns on TV; get warm water, towels and a clean string to tie the umbilical cord. But we often discussed the inevitable. We were only one and a half hours from town if we were in a work truck and not the old VW van. If there were any complications, then labour would be hours and we would have lots of time to get to town. If the baby came out really fast, well, it was out. What could be wrong with that? But I couldn't leave Celine at the cabin alone, so she had to come with me as I followed the bears.

The doctor had told Celine that the due date was August 1. But on that day, the baby was still happily inside. I was listening to strong beeps from Elspeth's collar coming out of Ruby Creek, a mountainous side drainage of the much larger Sage Creek. There are three small side creeks flowing into Ruby Creek and the signal was strong so I thought the bear was likely in the closest side draw.

"I think she'll be in Ruby One, but I can't really tell from here. What do you think? Want to walk a little up Ruby? It's only a mile or so to Ruby One." Celine was sitting uncomfortably in the pickup truck, trying to get her stretched belly into a preferred location. It was sunny and hot and Celine knew that I would not be content to hear the beeps but not find the bear, and she was always keen, even when very pregnant, to get out of the truck and walk.

To go up Ruby Creek means crossing Sage Creek (49.138 -114.352). Most of the bridge was long gone, but one old, barkless log was left. It was a thick log that had been a bridge stringer and still had old cables wrapped across it in places and it was over ten feet (3 m) above the creek. Sage Creek had receded since late June, but it was still flowing fast over some large boulders and deep pools. We parked and packed the equipment, and I headed quickly to the log, which I had crossed many times before. Celine was more hesitant than usual.

"I can't see my feet with my big belly," she said. "I don't like crossing logs when I can't see my feet."

"I'll hold on to your belt and follow close," she suggested. "Tell me when we come to the cables."

I walked slowly but at a steady speed. We came to the first cable and I tried to tell her, but with the roar of the water, I didn't know if she heard me. I could feel her slow down as she felt her way over the cables. We were over some big rocks now, but there was no way to turn back. We were committed. We slowed for another few cables and then the crossing went fine, maybe better than when she had crossed alone. We climbed up onto the old, overgrown road bed and started hiking up the valley.

Once we hiked up the first steep incline on the road, I knew from the signal that Elspeth was not in Ruby One. She was further back up the valley. Celine also knew that we had further to walk. After an hour we were getting close to Ruby Two, which was Elspeth's favourite of the three draws, but she wasn't there either. The signal was strong but coming from the back end of Ruby Creek. After three miles (4.8 km) and climbing up to almost 1,000 feet (300 m) in elevation, we came to the last old logging landing. Celine sat on a log in the shade of a young tree. After a few seconds she straightened quickly, bent almost backward, and cried out.

"Ohh, cramps, I've got cramps!"

"What do you mean cramps, are they contractions?" I didn't know much about childbirth, but I had heard of contractions and that sounded sort of like cramps to me.

We were over three miles from the truck, and if birthing was beginning we probably would not make it out. I didn't think we would even try to cross that log. Contractions halfway across might put us both in Sage Creek.

"If it's happening and it's a girl, I guess we'll call her Ruby." Celine ignored my joke, and seemed to be coming out of her cramps or contractions, or whatever they were.

We decided that Celine should stay in the shade and I'd go ahead and find the bear. Although there are no trails, I knew my route up Ruby Three well. A short bushwhack took me to the creek, and on the other side were meadows with little brush leading to a large talus field below a tall, 3,000-foot (914 m) cliff. I worked my way quickly as I didn't want to leave Celine too long. Cramps or contractions – I thought the time for action might be near. I crossed some open spruce forest and into an avalanche chute that was also good for fast travel. I had the receiver working, and due to the strength of the beeps, had a good feeling of where Elspeth was. I soon was at a good vantage spot so took out my binoculars and started looking for her (49.092 -114.326). It didn't take long to see her and her two yearlings. Usually I'd watch them for a while, but not today. Yes, I know where they are. I can get an X and Y from the map, and I know all three are still alive and they are digging glacier lily bulbs. So I'm out of here.

When I got back to the landing, there was no baby, Celine wasn't having contractions, and the cramps were gone. She looked very comfortable lying back against the log in the shade. If it wasn't for the few mosquitoes, it would have been near perfect. It was mostly downhill all the way out and we were in no rush. Celine and I had tallied another bear location before the baby was born.

**THE LAST TIME WE'D BEEN IN TOWN** to get supplies, Ray, being the father of two sons, had given us some sound advice on birthing.

"Just drive faster over those Flathead potholes and that will shake the baby out."

Maybe he was right. We were running out of supplies again so needed a trip to town. I didn't drive any faster than usual, but all the shaking may have had an effect. We were in town when things started to happen. Our perfect baby was born in the Cranbrook hospital. I suggested we call her Ruby anyway, but Celine wanted a name that worked in both French and English. So we called her Michelle.

A few days later, we had our supplies and our baby, and headed back to the cabin. We were driving down a long straight stretch in the Flathead road, about eight miles (12.9 km) from the cabin, when who do we see? Elspeth and her yearlings, Trouble and More Trouble, right there eating buffalo berries. I carefully took the baby out of her little car seat and held her up just as the bears ran off. Although I don't think a new baby can really focus, and certainly can't register anything, Michelle should have seen her first grizzlies when less than a week old. She would really see and even touch one before she was two months old.

THE SECOND HALF OF AUGUST to the end of September is the most wonderful time in the Flathead. The mosquitoes are all but gone, the days are warm but usually not hot, and the river is no longer icy cold. Even better, I don't trap bears at that time of year. Not so much because bears like berries more than bait as Chuck suggested, but because most bears are high in the huckleberry fields, too far from access roads and trap sites. Meanwhile, Celine had to recuperate and figure out the fine art of motherhood. She and Michelle usually stayed at the cabin and spent time on the beach beside the river. Sometimes they would join me if I was going to a bear site where the bear had fed on buffalo berries in the valley, but most often I was going into the huckleberry fields, which were too far a hike for them. A 135 square foot (12.5 $m^2$) cabin was a good size for a family of three in the late summer, when we lived outside most of the time and the mosquitoes had all but gone for the year. If the cabin got a little messy, it could be cleaned up in ten minutes and then it was time to hit our private beach.

By mid-September, I had put out a few traps because some bears were active in the valley again. We caught an old female we called Granny and her yearling daughter, Garnet. They were named after two women who lived just south of the border in Montana. But Michelle was not involved with bear captures until mid-October when we caught Rushes again. Although I was working with Trappin' Dan Carney, Rushes, being a big bear, took both Dan and me to move, measure and collar him. Celine took notes. Michelle lay bundled up against a tree. She was now old enough to focus, I think. So we let her sit next to the big bear and touch his fur. Maybe one day she would grow up to be a smelly old bear trapper like Dan and me.

CHAPTER 8

# IT'S THE HABITAT, STUPID

By now, everybody must know that we are living during an extinction crisis and species are disappearing faster than during any previous epoch. Most people must also know that habitat loss is the leading cause of this crisis. Decades ago I was told that *habitat is the animal*, and without habitat, the animals are gone. It's so obvious that habitat is overwhelmingly important for managing and conserving wildlife that habitat protection biologists dominated the BC Fish and Wildlife Branch in the 1970s. Yet in the 1978 edition of Charlie Krebs's ecology textbook that I read during my first winter in the Flathead, he stated, "Habitat selection is one of the most poorly understood ecological processes." Over 30 years and seven editions later, Dr. Krebs's textbook repeats the exact same sentence. The apparent lack of progress in our understanding of habitat selection is not due to a lack of attention. There have been thousands of valuable habitat studies published on many species over these decades, but there is still continued debate over analytical methods, and even definitions as basic as "what is habitat?" The lack of progress on developing a theoretical understanding of habitat selection is likely because habitat is a complex combination of food (and water), shelter, security and sometimes other features, that all vary across spatial scales. And, of course, the importance of each of these factors and scales varies among individuals and species, and often between years and almost always by season for the same species. The whole idea of habitat selection and the importance of various habitats is very complex.

At broad spatial scales, the entire Flathead Valley in BC is grizzly bear habitat – as is by far most of the province and the entire northwestern corner of North America. But people on the land, such as loggers, road builders, miners and recreationists, do not operate at this scale. So, because of the obvious importance of habitat management to animal conservation, I have tried to view habitat from a practical, applied viewpoint. When I began my bear study in the late 1970s, I wanted to learn about habitat in such a way and at spatial scales so I could explain my understanding to land managers to help them do a better job of grizzly bear conservation across the province by primarily protecting, but if possible enhancing or even creating, valued habitat conditions. To do this, I wanted to understand the fundamental mechanisms of the entire process as best as I could. Although it was not my actual research interest, I first needed some understanding of why the landscape was not homogeneous, but was extremely varied, creating vastly different conditions or habitats. From there, I wanted to understand the mechanisms that influenced where bears spent their time, and how different habitats affected bears' vital rates such as reproduction and survival.

Perhaps in mountains more than prairies, variation in the landscape is obvious to anyone who has observed the forests, fields and rivers as they travel, perhaps in a vehicle, crossing the countryside. Understanding why conditions vary, what aspects of this variation are important to grizzly bear populations, and how to explain it to habitat managers were my goals. Although I was interested in the various statistical methods used to determine selection, I did not want to spend much time investigating their mathematical virtues and elegance. And frankly, I think some of the fundamentals and assumptions of these analyses are flawed.

## 8.1 FORCES OF NATURE AND MOUNTAIN HABITATS

In the mountains of British Columbia, some well-known forces of nature strongly influence variation across the landscape. Some basic and very ancient, Aristotelian elements such as earth, air, fire and water seemed like good places for me to start. At least these forces are understood and can be communicated to land managers. In the mountains, earth becomes a combination of surficial substrate such as soils or rocks, but also of elevation, aspect and slope. In considering these factors, earth alone will account for much of the variation in the vegetative communities, from pine forests in the relatively mild valley bottoms to spruce and fir forests higher on the mountainsides where conditions are cooler. Higher up in the mountains, where the growing season is short, are more open subalpine forests of fir and whitebark pine. Higher yet are treeless, alpine meadows, and finally the rocky tops of mountains where only lichens grow. Add water, both in liquid or solid form, and there are more major effects. Ice age glaciers ground the U-shaped valleys to where low-gradient, slowly flowing streams are now often flanked by stands of mature cottonwood and spruce trees with roots reaching the water table. Sometimes these generally wet forests have a blanket of horsetails under the forest canopy. In other portions of these riparian habitats are treeless areas where the soil is deep and rich – the result of once being a pond held behind a beaver dam that gradually silted in. In these areas, lush grasses and forbs, such as cow parsnip and angelica, grow in abundance.

Water modifies large portions of the steep mountains as well. During cold, clear winter nights in the higher elevations, long, complex forms of hoarfrost slowly cover the snow surface. Wind on high mountain ridges deposits a deep snowpack over this fragile and unstable layer of hoarfrost. With warming weather and more snowfall, the weak layer fails and many hundreds of tons of snow flow down the mountain at high speed. If there were any trees in its path, there won't be when the avalanche stops and has piled the snow deep and hard in the run-out zone. After centuries of such action, a deep layer of soil may develop where the avalanche debris is deposited. Summer rain brings additional moisture down the channelled track, to the already wet soils near the huge pile of snow that slowly melts. With trees gone and moist, deep soil, alder and mountain ash shrubs are common. Centuries of the shed leaves of these shrubs form rich, deep soil where glacier lilies grow that are easily dug by bears. Also, lush slopes of cow parsnip, angelica and grasses grow in the more open areas in avalanche chutes.

Finally, we have fire. In wet, temperate ecosystems, some forests become ancient. In these forests, individual trees grow to be hundreds, if not a thousand years old. Eventually they die and begin to decompose when still a standing snag. Over time, snags fall to the ground, where decomposition slowly continues. Because stand-replacing events such as forest fires are uncommon in wet ecosystems, the undisturbed forest may be much older than the oldest trees. Most of the Rocky Mountains, however, are relatively dry and some forests have low-intensity, mostly brush fires every few years, but severe, stand-replacing fires burn these forests to the ground periodically. When fire removes the trees, the shrubs and herbs often respond to the released, post-fire nutrients and full sunlight not only with vigorous growth but by producing far more fruit. In the past century, people have replaced fire as the major agent of tree removal. Now we humans have become very effective at putting out fires before they get too large, but at the same time, have become even more effective at cutting down all the mature trees and replanting the clearcuts with seedlings. Areas burned by wildfire or logged and roaded are not static, but change as the new forest grows.

Pine forests, spruce forests, rock, riparian areas, avalanche chutes, post-fire burns, clearcuts and roads are all examples of the varied habitats across the Flathead landscape, with usually clear differences due to mechanisms that formed or maintain them. These habitat categories have, on average, vastly different amounts of seasonal bear foods and security for animals. Using these mechanistic habitat types to understand habitat selection and the value of different habitats to populations is important not only for conservation but for our understanding nature. After all, the variation in the landscape was caused by forces of nature, at least until people took their turn.

A walk, or sometimes a crawl, through the dense shrubs across an avalanche chute, for example, will show that the habitat types themselves are far from homogeneous. Although there is usually much less variation within a habitat type such as avalanche chutes, than across an entire valley, not all portions of avalanche chutes, or any other habitat types, are the same. To better understand habitat selection by grizzly bears and the importance of various habitats to them, it is essential that work also be done at finer spatial scales. Learning about grizzly bear habitat selection really requires spending a lot of time in the mountains following and watching an unbiased sample of bears, and when doing so, recording ecological features at their feeding and bedding sites.

## 8.2 ACTIVITY BUDGETS AND HABITAT SELECTION

In wide expanses of generally flat, plateau terrain, such as in central British Columbia, some grizzly bears hibernate in dens dug at low elevations, but in the Flathead, and all other mountainous areas where I have studied them, grizzly bears spend the winter in dens located high in the mountains. Of about 200 grizzly bear dens I have found in the Flathead, the lowest in elevation was 700 vertical feet (213 m) above the valley bottom. This low-elevation den, however, was a surprising exception. Almost all dens were within a few hundred vertical feet (100 m) of treeline or above the trees in the alpine.

Some bears, particularly females with their smaller ranges, lived in the mountains year round and never came down into the Flathead Valley. Other females moved down into the wide valley early in the spring before vegetation fully greened up. I accumulated enough radio locations on 31 females that lived all year in the mountains and 39 that moved into the wide valley to measure their selection of various habitats. I also collected data on

11 males that remained in the mountains while I tracked them, as well as on 55 males that moved into the valley, and often far beyond the Flathead.

Many of the radio collars had an electrical switch consisting of a ball of mercury that could move back and forth inside a tube. This switch altered the pulse rate of the collar when the animal was resting and when it was moving. In the Flathead, we originally recorded these activity patterns on chart-recorders. As technology advanced, more modern collars stored a record of the number of times the mercury switch moved back and forth over every five-minute period throughout the 24-hour cycle. The activity data could then be downloaded from the collar memory.

From when the first bears left their dens in April until the valley was starting to green up, usually in mid-May, the amount of daylight between morning and evening twilight increased from just over 14 to 16.5 hours per day. This early spring season, when snow still covered the mountains and much of the valley, was when bears fed mostly on sweet vetch roots and large mammals they killed or scavenged. Data from the activity collars indicated that bears were still lethargic, being active just under 11 hours a day. Even more than other seasons, the chance of bears being active during the night, or between 11 p.m. and 6 a.m., was less than 10 per cent. Not only did they sleep most of the night, they usually had a midday nap sometime between noon and 3 p.m. The chance of them being active was greatest between 7 a.m. and 11 a.m. and then again between 5 p.m. and 10 p.m., but even then, there was a 30 per cent chance they would be sleeping. Many females remained in or very near their dens throughout April, but those that had moved away from their dens in the early spring were active for about one hour more each day than were males.

It's not surprising that during the short season from when bears emerged from their dens to when the vegetation greened up, that they didn't show strong selection for any specific habitats – most areas were still covered with snow. Of the bears that remained in the mountains, 28 per cent of their locations were in closed canopy forests, 20 per cent were in open, rocky terrain, 12 per cent in avalanche chutes, and the remainder in all the other habitats. Bears that moved down to the wide Flathead Valley were found most often in closed canopy forests (35 per cent), followed by riparian habitat (26 per cent).

The proportion of radio locations in various habitats is an estimate of how the bears used the habitats, but does this equal their selection of the habitats? Selection depends not only on what bears use but also on what is available to them. Not being bears, we will never really know how they judge how available different habitats are. Most biologists have used the proportion of an individual's home range that is covered by each habitat as a measure of their availability. In this way, if an animal meandered around haphazardly, then its use of habitats would equal the area they covered and none would be selected for more than others; a random wandering animal shows no selection. This makes some sense. For example, bears in the mountains spent 28 per cent of their time in closed canopy forests, but this habitat covers 33 per cent of the study area, but they spent 12 per cent of their time in avalanche chutes and that habitat covers only 3.5 per cent of the Flathead. The relative rarity of avalanche chutes and the relatively high level of use suggests bears are selecting for them. There have been many ways proposed to crunch these numbers, and avalanche chutes always come out being selected more than closed canopy forests; some methods suggest four times as much. But still, bears were in forest more than twice as often as they were in avalanche chutes.

I have never been totally sold on the idea that the area covered was a realistic measure of a habitat's availability to bears (McLellan 1986). Perhaps this is because I'm a person and know my living room is three times larger than my kitchen, but I don't find it three times more available. Similarly, the huge building supply store in the mall is much larger than the wine store, yet I select the wine store much more often, and it has nothing to do with the number of square feet each store covers. When it comes to habitats, I'm pretty sure bears know their home ranges as well if not better than I know my home range.

Keeping avalanche chutes and forest as an example, I have found by watching and tracking bears in detail that sometimes they select to be in an avalanche chute to feed on grasses that emerge early where the snow has slid away. But when it's time for a nap, they often leave the chute and go into the forest and scrape out a bed on the uphill side of a big tree. There it's more level and they won't slide down the mountain as they might have if they fell asleep on the steep chute. A little later in the year, some females with new cubs choose to climb way up into the rocks and select a nice level spot to nurse and rest, presumably to avoid confrontation with other bears. Like the rooms in my house are to me, the different habitats in these areas seem equally available to the bears and they actively choose where to be for what they want to do at the time.

But then the bears leave the area with the avalanche chute and forest to go elsewhere. While on the move, they may be in more abundant habitats just because they cover more of the valley and just happen to be on their route. Do bears actively select some habitats for specific activities such as feeding, bedding or avoiding other bears, but passively select others just because they lie between selected habitats? When it comes to habitat selection, I like to present both bear use and area covered by the habitats. But to get my work published in science journals, I also used compositional analysis, which is a robust method that incorporates availability as the area covered by each habitat and uses each bear as the sample (McLellan and Hovey 2001a). This analysis provides the probability that apparent selection did not happen just by chance. Clearly, to understand habitat selection, we need to do finer-scale investigations of what the animals do in various habitats and how these habitats influence changes in body weight and even the composition of the bears' bodies and, ultimately, survival and reproduction.

**IN THE FLATHEAD VALLEY,** green-up usually begins in mid-May. Days continue to get longer until the summer solstice on June 21, when there is about 17.6 hours of daylight, after which days become shorter. During this season, when bears fed primarily on grasses, horsetails and forbs such as cow parsnip and pea vine, they were active an average of 13.3 hours a day, or almost two and a half hours more than before the vegetation had greened up (Figure 3). Bears still mostly, but not always, slept during the hours of darkness between 11 p.m. and 6 a.m., and then were usually awake until noon when most rested sometime before 4 p.m. Again, adult females were active about an hour a day more than adult males. Adults of both sexes were almost two hours less active than younger, two- to five-year-old, or what we call subadult bears.

During the season when green vegetation dominated their diets, bears that remained in the mountains more than doubled their use of avalanche chutes (26 per cent of the time) and decreased the time spent in closed canopy forest (21 per cent of the time). Bears that moved into the valley spent 43 per cent of the time in riparian habitat, although only 4.5 per cent of the area is covered with this habitat. Again, they were in closed canopy forest 21 per cent of the time. Riparian was the most highly selected habitat in the spring, followed by avalanche chutes, closed canopy forests and open canopy forests. There was, of course, considerable variation among individuals.

In most, but not all years, buffalo berries began to ripen and turn from orange to deep red in mid-July. Huckleberries ripened to a dark blue a couple of weeks later. Some bears that had spent the spring in the wide Flathead Valley remained in the valley but shifted their use from riparian to also include more open forests and clearcuts where buffalo berries were abundant. Once huckleberries ripened, most bears, at least during the first couple of decades that I followed them, moved into the mountains to treeless or sparsely forested areas that had been burned decades before in very intense wildfires, because that is where huckleberries were now by far most plentiful. The bears that were already in the mountains also shifted into these more open, old burned-off areas with huckleberry bushes. From early August to near the end of September, 34 per cent of the bear locations were in these burns, which covered 13 per cent of the Flathead, while 20 per cent were in closed canopy forests that covered 33 per cent of the area. Some bears continued to use riparian and avalanche chutes as they had in the spring, while others continued to use open forests and cutting units where buffalo berries were abundant. In the third decade of the Flathead study, a dramatic decline in huckleberry production led to a decline in the use of burned areas and an increased use of open forests and cutting units.

During the berry season, bears rapidly ingest these high-energy fruits and put on fat needed for winter hibernation. Although the hours of daylight are less than in spring, and continue to decline over the season, bears are active almost an hour and a half more each day than they are before berries ripen. Even adult males, who remain the least active group, are up and going for over 13 hours a day, while adult females are active about 15 hours per day. Even more than feeding on spring vegetative foods, feeding in the daylight for small berries is likely essential for maximum ingestion rates. When berries are ripe, bears are mostly sleeping from 11 p.m. to 5 a.m. From 7 a.m. to noon and again from 4 p.m. to 9 p.m. the probability that a bear will be active is over 80 per cent, with most bears taking a short midday nap.

**THIS PATTERN OF BEING MOST ACTIVE DURING THE DAY** in open habitats in August means that the bears have to deal with hot weather. Several times I've sat on a high mountain ridge watching bears on an open, southwest-facing hillside eating huckleberries when the temperature in the shade was about 80°F (27°C). In the direct sunlight, it's much hotter and more uncomfortable for me sitting in a T-shirt. The bears, now covered with a growing layer of fat under their fur coat, stayed out in the sun eating berries for several hours, but once in a while, I watched some make a dash down to the

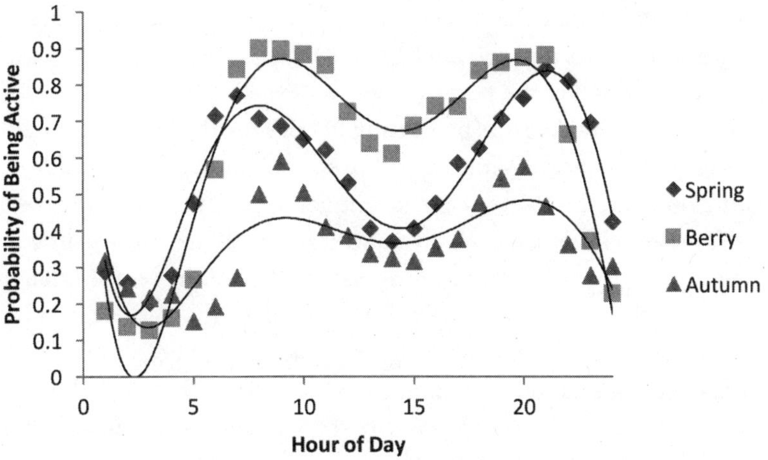


**Figure 3:** The probability of a grizzly bear being active during each hourly period. Spring, represented by the diamond-shaped points, is when bears feed primarily on grasses, forbs and roots. The berry season, indicated by the squares, is when they feed primarily on huckleberry and buffalo berry. Autumn, represented by the triangles, is the time of year they feed mostly on roots and mammals but a variety of fruits as well. Over each season, females were active about one hour more each day than males.

bottom of the draw and lie in a cool pool of water. Years later, with the fancy modern collars that recorded the number of head tips every five seconds, my daughter Michelle and I monitored grizzly bear activity near Lillooet, BC, which is one of the hottest places in Canada. There, female bears remained actively feeding on Saskatoon berries and chokecherries during the day in open, south-facing habitats even when it got to 100°F (38°C) in the shade (McLellan and McLellan 2015). When bears are feeding on other foods, hot weather may have some effect on the habitats they use (Pigeon et al. 2016), but berries are critical, and they will continue feeding on them during daylight hours even when it's darn hot.

BEARS BEGAN TO USE A GREATER VARIETY of habitats after buffalo berry and huckleberry productivity declined near the end of September. In the late autumn, bears were located in closed canopy forests 35 per cent of the time, but some remained in the open and in open forested burns (17 per cent), riparian (9 per cent) and cutting units (5 per cent). Bears were often in rocky habitat (9 per cent), sometimes in preparation for denning. The compositional analysis showed riparian to be most highly selected in the fall, but forest and open forest were also frequently selected. This analysis also suggested that when they were not at their denning areas, males and females, and adults and subadults, had similar habitat selection patterns during each season of the year.

Once the bears had finished eating berries for the year, their activity levels declined rapidly. While they were active almost 15 hours a day when feeding on fruit, they were active just under nine hours a day after berries were finished. Not only were they much less active, they were a little more active at night than they had been any other time of the year. Although in the autumn they were still active more during daylight hours than at night, the increase in their nocturnal behaviour might have been in response to all the deer, elk and moose hunters driving the road network during the day. Most, but not all, grizzly bears are more nocturnal when near human camps or habitations. In much of Europe, where brown bears were persecuted for millennia, bears tend to be more nocturnal, and particularly in regions with more people (Kaczensky et al. 2006; Ordiz et al. 2014).

**BESIDES DOING RESEARCH ON BEARS,** I worked with caribou in winter months. The caribou I worked on lived in areas with such deep snow that they walked on top of a 10 to 15 foot (3 to 4.5 m) snowpack and used that upward lift to reach lichen growing in the forest canopy. While following the lives of these animals, I realized how important the spatial configuration of habitats across the landscape was in the habitat selection process. These caribou strongly selected to be in very old forests early in the winter; however, small, isolated patches of old forest were almost never used because they were too far away from the "motherlode" of good habitat.

To deal with spatial scale and configuration during the early years of digital spatial data and Geographic Information Systems (GIS), I began working with Clayton Apps, who is a master of complex GIS-based analyses (Apps et al. 2001).. For caribou, and then using bear data, Clayton put a few dozen factors that we thought might influence habitat selection into a multi-spatial scale and multivariate statistical pressure cooker to see what factors and their interactions came out best (Apps, McLellan and Servheen 2013). For grizzly bears he included road densities, human access models and various images remotely sensed from satellites related to plant growth, as well as forest cover data. For this analysis he used data from 120 GPS and VHF collared bears that I had captured in the Flathead, plus 24 bears with GPS collars that Clayton and I captured in the lower Elk Valley, about 30 miles (48 km) to the north of the Flathead. Unlike the Flathead, the lower

Elk Valley has several towns, rural sprawl, a highway, railway, a ski hill and five open pit coal mines. Not surprisingly, factors that reduce human use such as steep, rugged terrain far from human population centres came out important at broad spatial scales for bears. At all spatial scales, habitat selection was most positively influenced by herbaceous and shrub-dominated landscapes, although shrubby habitats were, not surprisingly, most important during the berry season. At finer scales, a remotely sensed green vegetative index was also a strong predictor of selection, because it is correlated with rich herbaceous plant growth. Clayton's analyses also found that bears selected areas further from roads than close to roads at all spatial scales.

## 8.3 WHERE TO EAT AND SLEEP WITHIN HABITATS

Understanding the proportion of time bears spend in the various habitats each season, particularly when linked with the foods they eat and their corresponding change in body weight and fat deposition, should help managers make useful decisions on what habitats are especially important to the bears, and thus which ones to protect or even create. Using a complex multivariate, multi-scale analysis to predict where bears are most likely to be found, as Clayton did, may also prove useful, although difficult to extrapolate to areas with different combinations of remote-sensed conditions. However, I found that being on the ground and investigating detailed characteristics of the sites where bears actually foraged and where they slept within these selected habitats was by far the most revealing. After all, it's at this fine scale that bears make immediate decisions on where to stop and eat, and where to curl up for a snooze. It is also at this finer spatial scale where foraging theory is on display. Although wild grizzly bears are among the worst subjects for investigating foraging theory, I found it interesting at least to think about the theory when following grizzlies at fine-scale detail.

**FORAGING THEORY IS LARGELY ABOUT** the likely unconscious decisions or trade-offs animals make in order to ingest the most digestible energy, or any limiting nutrient, over a period of time without excessive risk. An early but interesting and even legendary experiment into foraging theory was done in the 1950s by Buzz Holling, who was once another UBC professor (Holling 1959). He bought a few boxes of two inch (5 cm) diameter sandpaper disks, some thumbtacks and a sheet of tack board. He cut the tack board so it was three feet by three feet (1 by 1 m) and laid it on a desk. He tacked five disks, to represent food items or prey, at random locations on the board. He put a blindfold on a friend, who was now the predator or forager. The blindfolded friend tapped her finger up and down while moving around the board until she found a disk. When she found it, she had to pull it off, and placed it on a pile. She did this for a minute and didn't find too many disks; after all, there were only five on the entire board. Then Buzz put ten disks on the board and they repeated the trial. Then he put 20 disks and then 30 and so on, until there were 256 disks tacked to the board. What was interesting is that the blindfolded tapper found and removed about twice as many disks when there were ten as when there were five but not quite twice as many when there were 20 as when there were 10. She removed nowhere near twice as many when there were 200 compared to 100. When disks were abundant she found almost the same number as when they were very abundant.

By watching the experiment, Buzz determined that there were two major components of foraging – at least "foraging" for sandpaper disks. One was searching for food which, in this experiment, was done by tapping. The second was handling the food, which in this experiment was removing the disk and putting it on the pile. From these factors, he derived a mathematical equation (most scientists love equations!) that predicted the number of disks removed from how fast the person tapped, the number of disks on the board (disk density), the time it takes to remove a disk and the total amount of time of the experiment. In animal foraging terms, how fast the person tapped is the searching rate that could be measured in miles per hour for a large predator like a wolf, or feet per second for an animal eating plants. The number of disks on the board represents the number of prey or food items in a defined area (prey density). Handling time for an animal may be the total amount of time it takes to chase, kill, eat and digest a large prey item, or simply to bite off, chew and swallow, and sometimes digest a plant food item. What is most important is that the relationship between food abundance and ingestion rate was not linear – doubling the amount of food in the area does not mean doubling the ingestion rate. At low food abundance, consumption rate is very low, but as the amount of food increases, consumption rapidly increases. Eventually, however, continued increase in abundance of food does not mean a steady increase in consumption. When food is highly abundant, the animal is spending less and less time searching, and most of their time handling food, and there is a limit to how much food can be handled. The graph of ingestion rate against

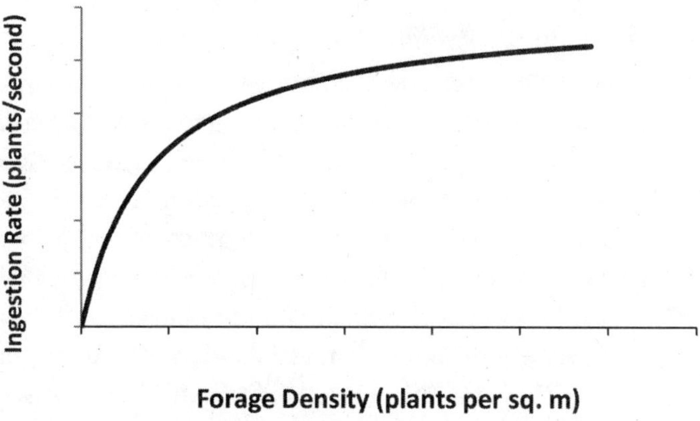


**Figure 4:** Holling's disk equation suggests that an animal's food ingestion rate is low when food is scarce because most foraging time is spent searching (moving and finding) for food. As the amount of food in the environment increases, the amount ingested increases because less time is spent searching and more time is spend handling (eating and digesting) food. As the amount of food in the environment becomes even more abundant, very little time is spent searching and almost all the time is spent handling, and thus a further increase in food availability does not lead to higher ingestion rates. The curve asymptotes when there is so much food that the animal spends no time searching and all the time handling food, so becomes fully satiated. The curved relationship between food abundance and ingestion rates is called a *Type Two functional response.*

food abundance is a curve – steep at first but then plateauing or reaching an asymptote where there is so much food available that the animal is never searching but just eating and digesting (Figure 4). The equation, which is famous in the world of ecologists, is known as Holling's Disk Equation, after the sandpaper disks. In ecology, the relationship between food abundance and ingestion rate is called the *functional response.* The curved relationship predicted by the disk equation is called a *Type Two functional response.* I don't want to leave you asking, "Well, what is a Type One?" – that is a continued linear relationship where food intake continues to increase proportionally with increased food abundance until a limit where the animal just can't eat any more – think of a filter-feeder or a spider on its web. Theoretical ecologists have developed others, but the curving slope of Type Two is by far the most common. The functional response is not limited to food abundance and ingestion rates but also habitat selection where increasing the amount of a habitat may not increase use because the animal can become satiated on what the habitat provides.

### *8.3.1 Springtime in the Rockies*

Grizzly bears in the Flathead showed strong selection for riparian habitats in the spring. It has been shown that major spring foods such as cow parsnip, horsetails and lush grasses are much more abundant in these wet areas than in the adjacent forests or clearcuts. There was no point in spending time doing plant plots to make this obvious comparison to show why bears select riparian. I wanted to know: *What were the characteristics of sites bears used within riparian, compared to all the sites in riparian that they could have used?* In other words, I wanted to understand what made the sites the bears used special. Knowing this would help target habitat protection to important portions of riparian areas, and also allow an estimate of how much bear food is needed to make it worthwhile for a bear to stop and feed. Understanding the relationship between grizzly bear selection and food abundance could be useful to habitat managers over large regions, or the entire province, even if the foods or habitats were not exactly the same as in the Flathead.

To document the characteristics of feeding and bedding sites within riparian habitat, I usually used radio telemetry locations of bears that I recorded from an airplane. When circling a hundred feet (30 m) above the ground and staring out of the window listening to the beeping signal get stronger and stronger and then weaker, as I switched between the left and right antenna, I could tell almost exactly where the bear was even if I didn't see it. I could also get accurate locations of a collared bear in riparian habitat by hiking to the edge of the terrace that overlooked most rivers and streams in the Flathead. Although I usually didn't see the bear in the very thick vegetation below, I could get accurate locations using a directional antenna and moving along the terrace because I was so close to the animal.

The next day, after checking the radio collar to make sure the bear had moved away, I visited the site. If I had to bushwhack through the forest for a mile (1.6 km) or so, I would go quickly and once in a while shout out to let any bears know I was there. When I dropped down from the terrace and into the thick riparian vegetation, I would yell out every couple of minutes, because many other grizzly bears spent their time in this densely vegetated habitat and I didn't want to surprise them at close range. I would work my way, often crossing streams back and forth on log jams, to where I thought the bear had been. I would almost always find the fresh trail of flattened grass, horsetails or forbs where the bear had walked and fed, sometimes with a fresh pile or two of bear poop along the route.

Unlike drier forested communities, riparian habitat is very complex and highly variable. The different plant species and their abundance varied greatly over short distances (often a few metres). As I followed the bear's trail, the variation in vegetation highlighted my first problem. Where do I locate the vegetation plot for a feeding site? If I centred the plot at one point, I would get very different data than if I centred it even 20 or 30 feet (6 to 9 m) further. So, to avoid biasing the plot centre location, I decided to centre my 18.5 foot radius plot (100 $m^2$) where I found a day-old scat plus evidence of feeding. I was assuming that when foraging, a bear would take a poop wherever it happened to be, so it was a random marker within the feeding site. Bears certainly appear to poop wherever they happen to be. A place where they slept was where I found a bed-site with either grizzly hair in it or a fresh grizzly dropping nearby. So, now I had my plot centre. My second problem was correcting for plants the bear ate or trampled at the feeding sites. In riparian, this problem was not as great as in other habitats because what remained was obvious, and what the site looked like before the bear had arrived could be estimated. Although I often didn't find a scat and so didn't do a plot, I did find 165 scats with evidence of feeding plus 65 beds in riparian areas, and here I recorded the data for bear use.

At this much finer spatial scale, was bear use of a site the same as selection for the site? I really doubt bears know and remember the distribution of all plants or patches of plants within their home ranges, and they certainly can't know which areas other bears have exploited a few days before, thereby reducing the amount of food. So at this scale, bears are likely not omniscient. I would have to know what was available to them within the riparian area if I was to estimate selection. To estimate what was available to bears within riparian habitats, I first mapped this habitat over the entire study area using air photos and detailed forest cover maps. Next, within the mapped riparian, I delineated 60 random points and at these I recorded the same data as I did in foraging and bedding sites. Data collected at these randomly located points told me the variation in vegetative characteristics that the bears had to choose from when they were in riparian areas.

Along the main Flathead River and some of the larger side drainages, I took our canoe and most often a fly fishing rod and went for a paddle. I did most of this work before GPS technology was available, so I used a printed map with previously measured compass directions and distances from recognizable features to the random points. Recording data at random points along small creeks that I couldn't paddle wasn't as much fun, but bushwhacking to a point along a creek is also a fine way to spend a day in the Rocky Mountains, because going where there are no trails is easy compared to other areas I've followed bears, such as the Selkirk Mountains near Revelstoke, or the Coast Mountains near Whistler, where the vegetation is relatively impenetrable and a large, nasty and aptly named plant, "Devil's Club," abounds.

Not surprisingly, the major difference I found between foraging sites and random sites was that foraging sites had far more of their favourite riparian area food, cow parsnip. Most random sites had no cow parsnip, and 90 per cent had less than 5 per cent coverage of this bear food. Compare this to all riparian feeding sites, of which 60 per cent had more than 5 per cent coverage, and 94 per cent of the sites where they fed on cow parsnip had greater than 5 per cent coverage.

When the coverage of cow parsnip at bear feeding sites was divided by the coverage at random to estimate selection, the relationship followed Buzz Holling's disk equation (Figure 5). Use was very low for sites with under 5 per cent cow parsnip coverage but increased rapidly to the 26 to 50 per cent cover category, and then remained at this level in the 51 to 75 per cent category. It appears that a bear can ingest cow parsnip as quickly when at about 30 per cent coverage as it can at greater coverages, This is the satiation threshold where they spend most of their time biting, chewing and swallowing, and little time moving between plants.

In riparian habitat, the canopy cover of conifer trees, mostly spruce and lodgepole pine, was also very different between random locations and feeding sites. Although 24 per cent of the random plots were in gravel bars or willow flats and under 5 per cent conifer canopy, 60 per cent of the feeding sites were in open areas with less than 5 per cent conifer canopy coverage, but these were not gravel bars.

When it comes to sleeping in riparian habitats, some bears would curl up and have a snooze right where they were feeding, but by far most bedding sites within riparian were in very different areas than they used for feeding. Almost half were under a conifer canopy of over 50 per cent and a quarter were under a canopy of over 75 per cent. Beds with no canopy cover were almost always in areas with high coverage of alder, willow or dogwood shrubs. These heavily vegetated areas are the kinds of places I could

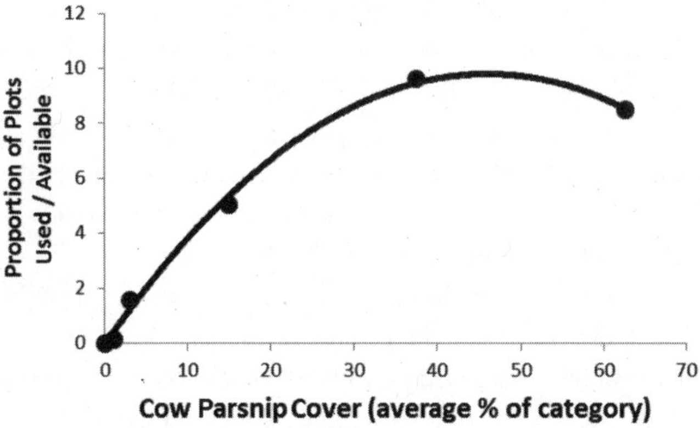


**Figure 5:** Where do grizzly bears stop to feed on their favourite food during late June and July? By comparing locations where bears fed on cow parsnip (used sites) to random locations (available sites) within riparian habitats, this figure shows very low selection of sites with little or none of this food. As the amount of cow parsnip increases, so does the selection for feeding in these sites. Once the coverage of this plant is about 30 per cent, however, further increases in abundance did not increase selection. As Holling's disk equation suggests, at 30 per cent coverage, the bear is no longer *searching* (spending time moving between plants) but spending all its time *handling* (eating) food. An increase in the abundance of cow parsnip beyond about 30 per cent coverage does not lead to greater ingestion rates, so bears do not show greater selection for sites with a greater abundance of this food.

bump into sleeping grizzlies if I wasn't making enough noise to alert them. I bumped into several anyway, because some grizzlies sleep deeply and are not easy to wake. Once I woke a sleeping grizzly when I was about three feet (1 m) away. Luckily for me, he was small and had little self-confidence. He shook his head, did a double take, and took off like a shot. So did I.

I collected similar springtime foraging information for grizzly bears using avalanche chutes, but recorded feeding at only 46 sites where I found a scat at a radio location, and again at 52 random plots. Comparisons between used and random sites in avalanche chutes were not as clear as they had been in riparian areas for cow parsnip or even grass coverage. Although it was sometimes difficult to reconstruct glacier lily abundance after a bear had rototilled a hillside, the coverage of this plant was greater at feeding sites than at random sites. Unlike cow parsnip, glacier lilies are small plants, and all combined, they rarely covered much of the plot. Three-quarters of the random sites had no glacier lilies, while most feeding sites had some, with 30 per cent of the feeding sites having over 5 per cent coverage, which is high for such a small plant.

The Flathead gets more snow than many if not most places in the Rockies, but it is not in the snowbelt so it doesn't really develop huge, rich, avalanche chutes like some other areas. To learn more about grizzly bear use of avalanche chutes, I worked with a UBC graduate student, Roger Ramcharita. We investigated grizzly bear use of avalanche chutes near Rogers Pass, BC, about 200 miles (320 km) north of the Flathead. Here, snowfall is extreme and avalanche chutes abound. National Park biologist John Woods and Park Warden John Flaa and I radio-collared 60 grizzly bears there between 1994 and 1999. Most bears were in avalanche chutes at least 60 per cent of the time in spring – far more than Flathead bears. Roger went to 49 sites where bears were located in avalanche chutes. He found sign of feeding at 41 of these and compared them to 45 random sites. Roger also found that when in avalanche chutes, bears selected to forage in relatively uncommon areas that had more than 25 per cent coverage of cow parsnip and glacier lily.

**HOLLING'S DISK EQUATION** predicts that with increasing food availability, ingestion rate increases but gradually reaches a maximum, after which increasing food abundance does not increase ingestion rates. This is the very basics of foraging theory. Most bear foods, however, are not evenly distributed even within selected habitats. Whether it's cow parsnip or glacier lilies, these plants grow in patches. Ingestion rate depends on the density or amount of food per area in a patch, so what happens when the amount of food declines because the animal eats it? As the animal depletes the food in a patch, it eventually faces the law of diminishing returns because ingestion rates decline the longer the animal stays and feeds in the patch.

Legend has it, at least among some UBC ecology students, that on a paper napkin at the UBC faculty club, Eric Charnov derived the equation (remember, scientists love equations) that predicts when a forager should leave a patch and move to find another, known as his Marginal Value Theorem (Charnov 1976). Not surprisingly, an animal should leave a patch when its ingestion rate drops to the average rate it has experienced while foraging over the broader habitat unit. The depletion rate of the patches of food and the travel time between patches are the main factors determining when the animal should leave. If patches are far apart, the animal should eat almost all the food in a patch, but if patches are close together, they shouldn't let the ingestion rate drop too much before moving to a new patch. Unless the patches are very small, such as one or two plants that a bear may occasionally eat while walking past, grizzly bears feeding in patches of cow parsnip never eat all of it. Although I did not record the proportion of the cow parsnip that remained, it was usually most of it. And, cow parsnip being such a large plant, the bear must have left the patch long before their ingestion rate declined much. There must be other factors affecting their decision of when to move on to another patch.

Back in the WSU captive bear facility, Karyn Rode found that bears could consume 40 g (1.4 oz.) of dry matter per minute when eating cow parsnip because the plants are so large (Rode, Robbins and Shipley 2001). At this rate, a 220-pound (100 kg) female bear in a good cow parsnip patch could consume all that they normally would in an entire day in about two hours and 15 minutes. But Karyn found that captive bears spent the daylight hours in short-term cycles of eating until full and then resting. Do wild bears also follow this pattern? I often found bear beds close to cow parsnip feeding sites, so it seems some bears take this option at times, moving back and forth from feeding to resting. Often, however, they decide to move on, leaving the patch with lots of cow parsnip still standing. The benefits of moving on include finding new patches or checking if other known patches have been depleted by other bears. Another advantage of moving on is the off-chance of finding a deer fawn hiding in the grass, or better yet, a dead moose to eat after chasing off the wolves or mountain lion that killed it. Optimal foraging models (with equations) come in many forms, but a simple model is of two food items, such as cow parsnip and deer fawns, with different costs of searching but with different reward levels. If there are some fawns around, a bear could benefit from not sleeping off a full belly of cow parsnip, but heading off in search of a baby deer or elk or even a dead adult. This is particularly true when the bear knows of other good cow parsnip patches to feed in if, as is often the case, the bear fails to find a little animal to dine on.

The various costs, benefits and handling times of two or more foods can be combined into the disk equation. If the foods are in patches, then I'm sure the marginal value theorem could be added, making a very complex foraging model. It is always interesting to think about all the factors that may affect a bear's foraging decisions, and even put them into a mathematical model of what may be going on, but the ones I've built become so complex and so full of unmeasured parameters that they are basically only computer games. They are a great way to make you think clearly about the numerous factors likely influencing a foraging bear, and are stimulating to build on a cold, snowy winter day. However, the real world of a large, long-lived omnivore in a diverse and dynamic ecosystem is so complex that foraging models likely deviate from reality.

### *8.3.2 Summertime and the Living Is Easy*

In summer, bears most often selected areas that had been burned by wildfire decades before. In these areas, huckleberries were abundant and ants were sometimes present in the dead and fallen trees. Using the same sampling protocols, I recorded plant coverage at 112 feeding sites, 41 bedding sites and 105 random sites within these mostly open, burned-off areas. Unlike when bears fed on cow parsnip, grasses, horsetails or even glacier lilies, I could not estimate how many berries were present before the bear had eaten many if not most of them. Comparing berry abundance between feeding sites and random sites may have found fewer berries in feeding sites because the bear had eaten so many. So I estimated huckleberry shrub coverage rather than berry abundance.

Just like human berry pickers, grizzly bears never eat all the berries on a bush. Bears, and most people picking berries, although they don't know it, are following Charnov's Marginal Value Theorem. A fast picker never picks all the berries on a bush but scans nearby bushes and moves to the next bush, if close by, when it looks better than the one being depleted. The only time someone would likely pick most if not all the berries on a bush is if it was the only bush around. But then, who would pick berries in such a poor berry patch to start with? An optimal berry picker would move to a better patch. A huckleberry bush is really a patch within a larger patch.

Comparing huckleberry plant coverage between grizzly bear feeding sites and random sites also follows the general prediction of the disk equation (Figure 6). Although bears do feed at sites with as little as 5 per cent cover of huckleberry plants, most feeding was at sites with over 25 per cent cover, but bears did not select sites with over 50 per cent cover more than sites with 26 to 50 per cent cover. This result suggests that they can forage as efficiently on huckleberries at all plant coverages above about 25 per cent, about the same as when they feed on cow parsnip in the spring. Also, like feeding sites in riparian habitats in spring, most feeding sites in burns were in areas with less conifer cover than in random sites. However, unlike bedding site selection in riparian habitat during spring, grizzly bear bedding sites were similar to their feeding sites in burns during the summer. Within

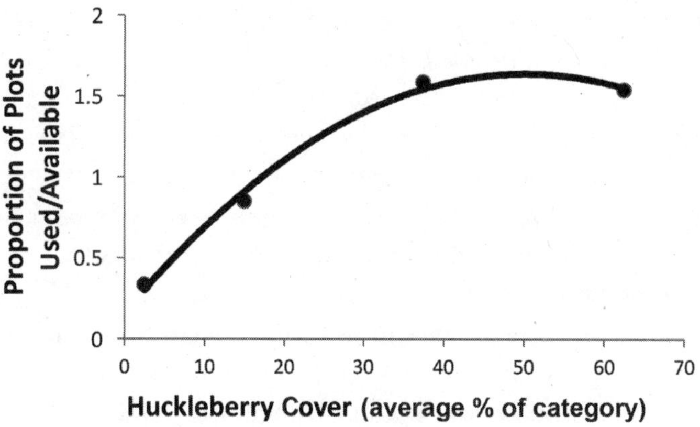


**Figure 6:** Where do grizzly bears stop to feed on huckleberries within areas that had been burned by wildfire decades before? As with the figure on grizzly bear feeding on cow parsnip in riparian areas, grizzlies feeding on huckleberries show a *Type Two functional response* to locations where they fed on these fruits. Bears showed low selection for sites with less than 5 per cent coverage of huckleberry plants, greater selection for sites with 5 to 25 per cent coverage, and even greater for sites with 25 to 50 per cent coverage. Sites with more than 50 per cent coverage were not selected for more than those with 25 to 50 per cent coverage, suggesting berry ingestion rate did not continue to increase with higher densities of berry plants.

the burns, bears often dug a little depression into the hillside where they happened to be, then curled up and went to sleep.

Not only did the foods and habitats selected by grizzly bears differ between spring and late summer, but the pattern of bear food abundance also differed between seasons. Cow parsnip, the number one food in the spring, had greater than 25 per cent coverage in only 11 per cent of the random avalanche chute plots and 5 per cent of the random riparian plots. In the old, wildfire burn habitat used by grizzly bears in the summer, 40 per cent of the random plots had over 25 per cent huckleberry plant coverage. Unlike in riparian habitat used in the spring, bears feeding in the huckleberry fields during summer do not have to be very selective to be in a good feeding site because the entire burn is mostly good. The important selection decision was made at the broader spatial scale.

The investigation of habitat selection, particularly when combined with diet and changes in body composition, suggested that riparian and avalanche chutes were the most important feeding habitats in the spring, while open forest and open burns were most important in the summer berry season. Within these habitats, areas with bear food plants such as cow parsnip or berry-producing shrubs covering about 25 per cent or more of the area were most often selected. With this coverage of large food plants, bears can probably feed at a maximum rate and don't need to walk far between plants. Greater coverage than this is not likely to benefit individual bears while feeding because ingestion rates cannot significantly increase. However, areas with higher coverage of bear foods may benefit the population by accommodating other bears later in the season.

This information on the habitat selection process should help habitat managers decide where to concentrate their efforts to protect habitat, but it does not answer the question of what is more important for grizzly populations, riparian and avalanche chute habitats or huckleberry burns? All are no doubt important, but because at the end of the spring season there is still an enormous amount of plant foods standing or even re-emerging in avalanche chutes and riparian areas, it doesn't seem that these habitats are regulating the Flathead grizzly bear population. Furthermore, while feeding primarily in avalanche chutes and riparian areas in the spring, bears are only ingesting about 3000 to 8000 kcal per day, while later in the year in the buffalo berry and huckleberry fields, they are getting 17,000 to 26,000 kcal per day and packing away the fat needed for hibernation and reproduction. If habitat biologists working across the distribution of grizzly bears can identify the high-energy foods that bears eat in the late summer and fall when they are putting on fat and then protect or enhance these areas, they will make a major contribution to grizzly conservation. Berries of various species are major energy foods in many areas, but spawning salmon fill that role in many, usually coastal areas. I've also caught very fat bears that feed primarily on white bark pine seeds on the dry side of the Coast Mountains in BC, and these seeds are important, high-energy food in Yellowstone National Park as well. Large mammals can be important grizzly bear food where they are abundant, such as elk in Yellowstone or the northern Rocky Mountains of BC, or where the prey migrate in large numbers like caribou in northern Canada and Alaska.

CHAPTER 9

# CRANBROOK TOWNSMAN REPORTS A TOUGH LITTLE TYKE

It was still dark, but somehow I could tell that the sun was starting to strike the upper atmosphere far above the Flathead Valley. I smoothly and quietly snuck out of bed. With my hand over the flashlight to dampen the glow, I checked Michelle sleeping soundly in her little bed. Nothing seems as peaceful as a sleeping 2-year-old. I checked Celine, also sleeping soundly. Nobody seemed more content than Celine did when she was fully pregnant but sound asleep. I went out of the cabin to the overhang to make a coffee and a piece of toast. It was September 27, 1982. This, I had calculated, was the very peak of the elk rut, and being a poorly paid student with a family, I knew that good, healthy super-organic food was critical.

Minutes later I lifted the bow rope on the canoe and slid it silently out into the river. I put my rifle sling over my head and worked it down onto my hunting pack so it wouldn't slip. I stepped in and, standing up, slowly paddled upstream in a back eddy. When the eddy stopped and the water became shallow, I edged the bow into the current. With one stronger paddle stroke, I was cruising quickly, bow just into the current, across the dark river. On the far shore, I shifted my weight to tip the canoe just enough to go over the smooth river rocks. I shifted my weight back and the boat gripped the rocks. I stepped out, pulled the bow out of the river with the rope, and set off for the trail I'd built up the river a few years before. Celine was due to give birth to our second child, and in case action started, I shouldn't be long.

It was dark in the forest, but when the trail went back out along the riverbank, there was enough light to travel quickly over the rounded river rocks. But soon I left the river and went along a game trail through the forest again. There was a meadow in less than a mile where I had seen elk before. I had also seen predators. When doing my daily field work I make noise when moving through thicker brush, particularly in habitats where grizzlies are common. But when hunting, it's all different. When I'm actively hunting, I usually move very slowly and quietly, if indeed I move at all. But when I'm just heading or returning to an area I want to hunt, I travel quickly and quietly.

Going quickly and quietly is when I have bumped into grizzlies at close range. One time I was coming home after a hunt along this same trail. Even though it was dark, I was going fast when I heard the extremely deep guttural growl of a large male grizzly at very close range. So close, I imagined my pant leg shaking in his breath; he must have been less than ten feet (3 m) away, but it was too dark to see him.

"Hey buddy, sorry for intruding, thanks for the warning," I softly and calmly spoke as I gradually moved back the way I had come. When I had backed off about 100 feet (30 m), I began talking a little more loudly as I smashed my way through the totally dark forest to the river and just waded right out in the just above crotch, deep very cold water, and crossed to the other side. It's truly amazing how wonderful I feel when I know I'm safe after a minutes-long, drawn-out flow of adrenaline. Wild grizzlies in wild places have made me feel so amazingly alive.

Once on the same trail, again on an evening hunt, I took out my binoculars three or four trees back from the open meadow to slowly scan for deer and elk. The sun was just about to go behind the western mountains and the light was long and soft. Across the meadow, about 200 feet (60 m) away, was a mother mountain lion with two large kittens, almost as big as she was. She was just lying peacefully in the sun, and looked to be almost asleep. The big kittens were at play, one chasing the other and then rolling together, a few swats, and then running again. I squatted, watching them play until they joined the mother in rest. I remained a little longer and then went elsewhere so as not to disturb them.

Today, I slowed when approaching the first meadow. It was now just light enough to hunt. I stopped, listened and opened my mouth wide and tried to blow some condensing steam from my lungs to see if I could detect any air movement. I imagined molecules being shed from my body and how they would move through the air. Like most mammals, elk have a very keen nose, and I've seen them pick up my scent and bolt when I was hundreds of yards away. Another step and I stopped and listened. Although there were still trees between me and the meadow, I slowly scanned as best I could through my binoculars. I didn't see anything, so I took a couple more steps, stopped, listened and then scanned the meadow and into the forest on the far side. Besides a distant croak of a raven and a chattering squirrel somewhere far away across the meadow, there were no sounds. The best meadow for elk was about a mile further along so I didn't want to spend too much time here. I went to the edge of the opening for one more scan, and then set off across the open, grassy meadow to where the game trail went back into the forest.

There wasn't much point in sneaking slowly through the forest. I'd have to be very close to an elk to get a clean shot, and with the limited light, elk would hear, see or smell me long before I would see them. So once again I moved quickly but silently. Every few hundred yards I would stop, listen and check for any air movement. It's usually so calm in the forest in the morning that it's difficult to know which way the air is moving. But the air always moves a little, even if just back and forth. I approached the meadow and once again stopped, listened, tried to make some fog from my breath to check the wind. There didn't seem to be any, so I took up my binoculars and tried to peer through the remaining forest. I scanned slowly. I could see trees in front, some yellow grass of the meadow, more trees, but something different on the far side. I very slowly bent down to see through a small hole through the layers of branches. Yes, legs; brown, almost black elk legs. It's amazing how my heart raced. I've been that close to elk hundreds of times, but when I'm hunting, the experience is totally different. After a million years or more, there must be something deep in our genes that only awakens at times like this.

Elk are very vocal and communicative. Beginning a little before, and continuing through the rut, the males bugle. Sometimes they start with a deep, chesty roar, but tones rapidly get higher into a haunting whistling. Other times, the bugle starts with a loud whistle and goes up an octave or two, sometimes ending with deep, belly-pulsing grunts. Hunters can mimic the sound and make the males think there's a competitor for his harem of females. Male elk can get very worked up and become almost crazy. But, in 1982, bugles available for hunters were dangerously crappy, curly-Q whistles that sounded silly when close up. I had one in my pack but never liked using it. If I blew it now, I was sure the elk would bolt. I had to stealth hunt instead.

I was too far from the opening to see anything clearly, but any movement would be risky. I continued to look through the tiny holes in the foliage but couldn't see much more than dark legs. Slowly I started my approach. Each step was slow and deliberate through knee-high shrubs and over a few downed logs. I now had a slightly larger hole in the foliage to look through.

Yes, an elk. I could see parts of a darkish body; no doubt a female. I waited, heart racing. She didn't move. But now another walked into view. I could see its head clearly about 75 yards (69 m) away. It stopped, head up, looking, ears shifting their focus. I knew she was also sensing the air for the molecules of danger that were drifting from my body. Sensing such molecules had likely saved her life before. She lived, day in and day out, close to wolves, cougar, bears and people.

A life lower in the food chain is a life of constant vigilance. Those with genes that influence the optimal trade-off between foraging and vigilance live longer and have more babies, and those babies have half the same genes. I scanned behind them, looking for a lighter-coloured and larger body of a male. In 1982, a legal elk to shoot needed at least three points on at least one antler, which generally means that only 2-year-old or older male elk could be shot. The females stood motionless except for their ears that altered directions, trying to detect any sound that was unusual. Elk are so damn patient and I'm so impatient. There must be a male with them; it's the peak of the mating season. Should I just charge out ready to shoot? Stupid idea. Be patient, grasshopper. But I knew my molecules were drifting somewhere, and sooner or later they would be detected. Where is the male?

Should I move more into a better shooting spot? My movement could alert them, but I wasn't in a great spot because I only had a few little clear lines to see through and nowhere to rest my rifle. OK, dude, let's do it when their heads are down, real slowly, please no dry twigs under my step. The female, whose head I could see, finally bent down to feed on some of the dry grass. Now's my chance, and I slowly moved a couple of more steps to where I could see better and there were more clear views through the brush and trees to shoot through. I could see a third female. And behind them, it looked like a lighter-bodied animal. I waited. The lead female took several steps towards me, then stopped and sensed the air. I could see her sniffing the air as well as her ears working. She didn't look alarmed, just vigilant. Sure glad I was born a person and not lower in the food chain. I'm way too impatient to be so vigilant. I looked back towards the lighter-bodied animal, but another female had moved in front. The lead female moved slowly closer to me and then started to feed again. Finally, I thought I saw some antlers move where the light-bodied elk stood but was hidden behind a female. It must be a male. There won't be all these females in late September without one.

I waited, trying to get a sense of any wind, with my heart still racing. I wished I could feel even a tiny breeze coming towards me, but I couldn't.

It seemed totally calm, but I know it wasn't. When would the lead females sense me? No option but to wait and hope the male moves into an open channel in the foliage. Wish I had a better rest to shoot from. Two more steps and I would be next to a lodgepole pine, but would there be a good clear view line from there? I have to try. Wait for the closest female to drop her head, and here I go, one step, now slowly, another step and I'm next to the pine and, yes, there is a good little hole in the foliage to see through. I could see the female in front of the male and, when he raised his head, I could see enough antlers to know it was a mature animal with far more than the three points needed to make him legal. Now I just had to wait until the female moved out of the way or the male moved out from behind her. Elk sure don't move much when you want them to.

The female nearest to me moved even closer and stopped and stretched her neck and sniffed the air. I was expecting her to bolt any second now. But then the male stepped ahead a couple of yards. I could now see his chest broadside through the little clear hole in the vegetation. I raised the rifle and braced it against my hand that was on the tree. I was stable, with the gun not against the tree but against the cushion of my hand, and I had the crosshairs of my scope a foot (30 cm) above his brisket and just behind his shoulder. My gun was very accurate at 75 yards (69 m) and I had full confidence in a clean shot. Don't jerk the trigger, hold your breath and gently squeeze.

Then everything changed. The painfully slow and quiet scene that I had been part of for the past 15 or 20 minutes was totally reversed. It was not only the huge noise of the rifle that echoed across the valley, but the hooves of running elk, as there were more than I'd thought. They seemed to be running from everywhere now. I reloaded as I burst out of the forest and into the meadow. The herd of elk, including the male, were leaving on the distant side. In a few seconds, it was all quiet and there were no elk in the meadow. I first started to run after them but then stopped. No, I can't have missed. Don't chase him. Let him stop, he won't go far if I'm not chasing him. Let him bed down, stiffen up, and die quickly. I went back to where I'd fired the shot, and followed the path the bullet must have taken to make sure there were not small twigs that could have nudged its flight. It was a clean path, I must have hit him where I aimed. My gun is true and I hadn't bumped the scope that I know of. Wait half an hour. I hoped Celine wasn't having a baby.

Waiting is tough. My adrenalin had been pumping for a long time and I was overwhelmed with emotions of excitement, fear and extreme guilt because the elk didn't just drop dead. Nature is cruel, and animals rarely die quickly and painlessly, but I want the ones that I kill to die as instantly as possible. I sat alone on the edge of the meadow. The sun was not yet up over the mountains but it was fully light.

"Sorry, sorry, my friend, I'm so sorry. I wanted you to die instantly, please die quickly, my friend." I waited and waited. I walked in little circles, thinking of life, death, predators and prey, and how species such as our own, as well as the elk, evolved to be good at what we do. We people communicate and can share knowledge and skills among dozens if not thousands of individuals. I couldn't make a gun from scratch. I don't know how to find iron ore, make steel from iron, mould it into a rifle, and the story goes on and on forever. But among thousands of people, we can make guns. Although I know dozens of plants that I can eat and where to find them, and I have sometimes been as close as three feet (1 m) from non-habituated, fully wild elk and deer where I could have killed them with a sharp stick if I had to, living alone in the wilderness like these elk, I know I would have a very miserable time and would likely starve or freeze within a decade. It's our ability to work as a super team that allowed me to shoot and, I desperately hoped, kill the elk.

Okay, I've been walking in circles long enough. It's been a while, I'm ready. "Please buddy, be right there dead in the forest, I'm so sorry." I crossed the meadow and sure enough, there was a small pool of blood. I was half hoping that I wouldn't have found any and the bull would be alive and well. This was the first time in my life that I was in this horrible situation of not making a quick, almost instant kill. I went to the trail that left the meadow; more blood, but not a lot. I quietly walked 20 steps then stopped to listen. Could I hear breathing? Nothing, so another 20 steps but still nothing. I started another 20 when right in front of me, up he stood. He was only 20 yards (18 m) away and he tried to turn and run, but I was fast and shot at point blank range. His front end crumpled. I pounced and was beside him almost instantly. He was a big, majestic animal and had many sharp points on his antlers. Although he was down on his sternum, he could seriously injure me, so I stood back a few yards.

"Die, my friend, please die," I spoke. Our eyes locked and we stared at each other; predator and prey. We stared and stared, and then his eyes started to lose focus, his neck sunk, and he died right in front of me.

"I'm so sorry, my friend, I'm so sorry." My emotions overcame me and tears poured uncontrolled down my face. "I'm so sorry."

Then our relationship, or at least my emotions, began to change from predator and prey to just having enough meat to keep Celine, Michelle, the new baby and I fed for a year. He was a big animal and I was alone, so I had to work efficiently. I quickly took some ropes from my pack, tied one to each front hoof, and pulled him onto his back. His chest was a little higher than his rump so that would make things easier. I suspect everyone has their own method of field dressing an animal, and I have mine. I took my knife and, just under the first layer of skin, cut him from his crotch, up his belly, past his chest to his throat. I skinned back his hide about a foot (30 cm) on both sides, feeling the deep warmth of his body. I then cut through into his chest cavity just under his sternum, so I could put my saw in. I sawed up through his sternum to his throat. I then did the same with the pubis part of his pelvis. I sawed two cuts about two inches (5 cm) apart in his pubic arch and loosened and removed the bone. I then cut around his anus. I then opened him up from the throat down. The chest was full of blood from the shot that went through his lungs just above his heart. I took off my long-sleeved shirt, and cut around his diaphragm. Starting with the esophagus and trachea, I started pulling out his entire entrails. Except for some connective tissues, particularly along the spine, and of course the diaphragm, it's pretty easy to remove everything at once.

My friend was now changing, at least in my mind, from a beautiful, free and wild animal to meat for the family. My emotions were going from a mix of guilt and deep sadness to happiness. The nasty task was behind me and the hard work had begun. I was now thinking of Celine and grizzly bears. I had to get back soon to make sure a baby wasn't on the way, but I also had to move a few hundred pounds of elk meat, in case a grizzly was nearby. I quickly cut off each hind leg where the ball joint of the femur joint the pelvis. I tied one to a short stick, and started to drag it away from the kill and out onto the meadow where I could see it from a distance. I then went back for the second hind, and dragged it back to the meadow. I then peeled back the hide along the spine of the front half. I quickly went through the ribs one by one, just to one side of the spine, with my saw. The larger front quarter, the one with the entire spine, was heavier than the hinds, but with my rope I could drag it away from the gut pile. I put the liver and heart into a big plastic bag and into my pack, and started to drag the smaller front quarter to the meadow. I then took one hind quarter towards the river. When I had both hinds on the riverbank, I thought I should go and make sure Celine was fine and get my canoe to paddle out the elk. I took off my sweaty shirt and put it over the two hind legs. I then peed around the two hinds; maybe that would keep a grizzly away for a little bit. After washing most of the blood from my arms and hands in the river, I grabbed my rifle and pack, and took off at a trot.

I was happy to see Celine and little Michelle on the riverbank below the cabin when I arrived. I grabbed the bow rope of the canoe and slipped it into the river and hopped in. Going back to the cabin was quick, as the current took me right across when the bow was angled upstream just right. I hopped out and Celine could tell by the speed of my movements that something had happened.

"Did you shoot? I didn't hear a shot."

"Got an elk, a nice bull up on the second meadow. Let's get going, I've got to get the canoe up the river."

She wisely said, "It's too slow with me and Michelle to get ready. Why not just take the canoe and just leave the truck up there and get it later?"

"Good idea."

I grabbed the canoe and jerked it up on my shoulders and made for the truck, where I quickly tied it on to one roofrack and tailgate. It had been less than an hour from when I'd left the elk and I was putting the canoe in the river about three miles (4.8 km) upstream of the elk and five miles (8 km) above our camp.

I had canoed this stretch of river many times. It was smooth and slow for the first half mile (0.8 km). I passed the spot where Joe and I had caught poor old Rushes four years before. We then passed where I first saw Blanche with her three cubs early in the spring three years before. The water was very low now and there were places with a lot of shallows and many rocks. Luckily the steepest and rockiest stretch was above the elk, and there the canoe was very light and easy to move around in the water with only myself as cargo. Back and forth across the river I back-ferried and drew the boat through the boulder field in the steep stretch until I hit a series of big waves that ended in a deep pool. I knew the pool well as it was a favourite of mine for fly fishing, but today it was just where the river became easy paddling again. I continued downstream but stopped a few hundred yards above the elk's hind quarters and took out my binoculars. The elk meat was there and no grizzly in sight; perfect. I pulled the canoe to shore at the hind quarters and took my rifle and pack to the meadow. At the edge of the meadow, I spotted the front quarters in the open meadow, and again, there was no bear on them. I hauled one front quarter at a time to the riverside. Perhaps there was a bear on the gut pile. Although I was tempted, there was no point in looking at the gut pile and putting both bear and me in a stressful situation, if indeed a bear was there.

I loaded all four quarters into the boat, and it was now really loaded. With a couple of inches of free board, I started down the river. It wasn't long before I was out of the boat wading. I guided the canoe through the shallows using the stern rope. Back in to paddle in deeper water, but back into the river wading in shallows. Celine and Michelle were both excited when I finally rounded the last corner above the cabin. When I paddled up, both were on shore and even little Michelle tried to help hold the boat as she sensed this was a special time. I dragged the quarters out of the boat and up the bank and over to the meat pole. I used the truck and a pulley to lift the quarters way up, above the reach of most grizzlies. It was now afternoon and it had been a tough physical and extremely emotional day. I ate a fast snack and then headed up the trail to get the truck from where I'd left it when I unloaded the canoe. By dinnertime, all was under control.

**IN THE PAST, WE HAD STORED OUR FROZEN ELK,** moose or deer meat at a Shell gas station in Cranbrook where we had rented a freezer locker. But the gas station had renovated and there was no longer a freezer. We needed to buy one to put in the Fish and Wildlife Branch's warehouse to store the elk meat after butchering. After a couple of days of it hanging behind the cabin, we took the elk to town over the long, bumpy Flathead road. When we got to town, we searched the newspaper for a used freezer for sale. There was only one and they wanted $250. We arranged to check it out at 5 p.m. We then went to the warehouse and started butchering. After an hour, Celine said, "This cutting and wrapping is not good for my back. I don't think I can do it all day." Shortly after, she said, "Uh oh, I feel something is happening."

"What do you mean?" I asked.

"You know, I'm getting cramps."

"You mean the Ruby Creek cramps after butchering so much?"

"No, not those cramps, the real cramps."

"Really? When should we get to the hospital?"

"Not yet. I'm nowhere near ready. I don't want to be in there for days. I'll wait till I'm ready. I'm just going to sit and rest my back for a while."

I was now watching Michelle run around the warehouse, trying to climb on tractors and boats, and generally getting all dirty, while I butchered as fast as I could. Soon, Celine's cramps had turned into contractions, but they were not yet close together and Celine seemed content to just sit, or stand or walk. By late afternoon, they were getting more serious and I could tell they were getting painful.

"Should I call Mr. Freezer and tell him not today but maybe tomorrow or the next day?"

"Oh no, let's go. I'm fine. I know the baby won't come for a few hours yet."

So I got Michelle in her car seat, and Celine and I drove to the house where the guy was selling his used freezer.

We parked in his driveway, and as we left the truck, Celine leaned over, hands on the hood, and stopped talking. She closed her eyes and hummed. This was a bigger contraction. But it ended and we walked up to the house and knocked on the door. A few minutes later, we were in his garage looking at a freezer.

"Two-fifty is a lot, you know they're only four twenty-five new." Celine was dealing.

And just as she was finishing her opening statement of bargaining, a contraction hit.

"*Un moment.*"

Celine put her hands on the freezer, closed her eyes and starting humming again.

"What the hell," Mr. Freezer said, getting noticeably excited. "What's going on here?"

"Well, looks to me that she's going to have a baby pretty soon," I answered.

And then the contraction stopped.

"I think, more like 200is a fair price," Celine said.

Mr. Freezer was in some kind of a shock, as he vibrated his head back and forth.

"Sure, whatever, 200, I don't care, get her to the hospital!"

I was counting out the money when another contraction hit. They were getting closer together. Mr. Freezer didn't look very strong, but he and I seemed to easily almost toss the freezer into the back of the pickup.

As we drove off towards the warehouse, Celine joked, "Too bad we're not buying a house."

I skidded the freezer into a tractor bucket and lowered it, moved it into a good spot and plugged it in. I put the elk meat that we had already cut and wrapped into the freezer, as I thought we might be gone for a while.

"When do you want to go?"

"I'm not yet ready," and then another contraction came.

I cleaned up Michelle, cut a little more elk, and then Celine said, "I think it's time."

I dropped Michelle at a friend's house, and we drove to the hospital. A few hours later a perfect baby boy was born.

Celine was tired and I was looking after Michelle full-time for the first time ever.

"Is pretty good here, they bring me petit bébé when he's clean for me to feed. When he poops, they clean him up. They bring me food, and it's not so bad. Much better than last time with Michelle. I like it here for a day or two."

I was not only looking after Michelle, but I was finishing butchering, wrapping, bagging and freezing the elk. Many years later Celine told me that she didn't mind butchering a deer, but an elk or a moose was too big. She said giving birth was better than butchering.

Again, we needed a name that would work in both English and French. I thought Victor, in honour of my grandfather whom I spent a lot of time with when I was young. In French, Victor is not a good name. Celine thought Boris would be good. Obviously, I wasn't going to burden my son with that handicap (and that was before Boris Johnson!). We settled on Charles. It was fine in French and in English. It honoured Chuck Jonkel, but mostly Mr. Darwin, one of the greatest observers of the natural world of all time.

The four of us returned to the Flathead three days after Charlie was born. It was early October, with beautiful warm, sunny afternoons but freezing nights. Little Charlie slept in a basket that we set on the table. It was sometimes just below freezing in the cabin when I woke early in the morning. Charlie would be sound asleep with a little frost on his blankets near his mouth.

A friend, John Mindek, was helping me trap and collar bears that fall. We set a few snares that October. We were out with the whole family when we caught a large male on the last day of October and Charlie was 4 weeks old. John and I collared him, and I asked Michelle, who was 26 months old, what we should name the new bear. She said, "Pete." I had no idea how she knew of such a name, but Old Pete was now collared. Michelle had been at many grizzly captures by then, but Old Pete was Charlie's first.

The following summer, while I was doing some office work in Cranbrook, Celine took the kids to a nearby lake. Charlie was then 10 months old and sitting on the edge of the water. A newspaper reporter was there and was taking Charlie's picture when a wave lapped up. The photo had Charlie laughing as he was soaked by the wave. The photo made the front page of the paper and was captioned "A tough little tyke." I'm sure the photographer didn't know how tough little Charlie really was after his first fall and early winter in the Flathead.

CHAPTER 10

# HOME ON THEIR RANGE AND MOVING OUT

Bears have amazing spatial knowledge of the area where they live. Not being a bear, I can only imagine how well they remember and find important features in their range, but I know they can find specific points when they need to. For example, I was in the wide, rolling hills of the Flathead Valley bottom, tracking a radio-collared female black bear in the first days of November, just after a snowfall had blanketed the valley. I crossed her cute little tracks in the snow where she had walked through a flat, fairly boring forest of lodgepole pine that just went on and on. I followed her. She was going fairly straight through the forest, sometimes up and down rolling hills. In just over a mile (1.6 km), her tracks ended right at a very large, four foot (1.2 m) diameter larch snag that must have been 50 feet (15 m) tall with a broken top. The radio signal was very strong even without the antenna attached, suggesting that only the shell of the hollow tree was between the two of us. She had climbed up the dead tree, and then down on the inside to the bottom, where she was preparing to sleep for half a year. It was a perfect location; she was totally safe from wolves, cougars and grizzly bears. Unless another black bear came along who also knew of the hollow tree, she was going to sleep safe and sound until spring.

But how did she find such a perfect spot, remember exactly where it was and then walk directly to it through a relatively flat, snow-covered lodgepole pine forest? A big, dead, hollow larch tree with its top broken off is not common; she might have been sleeping in the only one in the entire Flathead Valley. It is almost impossible that the bear just happened to encounter the tree by luck when she wanted to hibernate, and then climbed up and then down inside. I have also found several black bear dens high up in cottonwood trees where a large limb had broken off, letting in water that rotted a big cavity; such features are far too rare to be just found by luck when needed. The bear must have encountered the dead tree sometime earlier in her life, checked it out and remembered its location. That she could walk directly to it, in what to me was a relatively featureless forest, revealed impressive spatial knowledge and ability. Without a GPS, I could probably find the dead tree again, but it would take a lot of searching; there is no way I could walk right to it like the bear had.

Grizzly bears that den in natural caves must also know and remember where these features are. Two of the many caves I've found grizzly bears denning in had small entrances, not much more than a hole about two feet (60 cm) across in the mountainside. When these bears went to den in late November, there was a lot of snow in the mountains. The cave entrances would have been drifted in and completely buried under the snow, like the rest of the mountainside. But the bears went right to the spot, dug the snow away from the entrance and crawled in. Some of these dens were reused by the same bear during different winters. Judging from the various ages of the bedding material and polished rock, where animals rubbed on their way in and out, some caves had likely been used for decades if not centuries by many different bears. It's seems improbable that a bear just happened to find such a spot when it was time for its long winter nap. They must have known and remembered exactly where these cracks in the mountainside were.

AND IT WAS NOT ONLY FOR A WINTER den that at least one grizzly bear was aware of where a cave happened to be. In September 2008, I was darting grizzly bears from a helicopter with Clay Wilson, an exceptionally gifted animal capture pilot I have now worked with for almost three decades. We spotted an adult bear on an open hillside with almost no trees and no cliffs.

"Perfect, this guy will be a piece of cake."

We landed a few miles away and quickly took off the rear passenger door, as we'd done hundreds of times before, and placed it on the ground. I started taping my seat belt shut so it couldn't open by chance.

"Ready, Bruce?" The turbine cranked up and I could feel the machine lift.

One leg was still hanging outside as I folded the end of the tape back and stuck it to itself so I could easily pull it off.

"Ready." But we were already 100 feet (30 m) off the ground.

The Hughes 500D tipped downslope, gained speed quickly and then rose while making a steep bank. I was looking straight down at the ground through the empty door opening.

The bear was almost in the same place.

"Looks perfect, so whenever you're ready," I heard over the intercom.

The bear looked to be a smallish adult male, so while I put a three-vial dart into the gun, I replied, "Ok, I'm ready."

As we gradually approached, the bear slowly jogged uphill about 150 yards (137 m) or so, then stopped just as we rapidly came towards him. Instead of starting to run faster like other bears do when we were coming at them in final pounce mode, this guy just started jogging along again. Then, just as we were upon him, he stopped, looked at us, and then disappeared into a hole in the ground. Clay is an amazing pilot in his agile machine, so before I knew it, he had pivoted us around and, with no door, I was about five feet (1.5 m) from the cave entrance. The cave opening was only a few feet (1 m) across, but it was deep, dark and seemed to go almost straight down. Was it just luck that the bear happened to stumble upon a cave when we approached him and knew enough to crawl in? By his direct and not overly rushed movements, it sure looked like he knew exactly where he was going after we showed up.

Of course ground dwelling rodents instinctively know to run to burrows to take cover; they dig them and are in and out of them every day. But grizzly bears have not evolved to seek cover in holes in the ground. This bear's reaction not only revealed great spatial memory of his home range but indicated some logical response that a hole in the ground is a good place to be when a helicopter is after you. Besides finding the exact location of small features such as caves, it's obvious from bear movements that they know the location of berry fields, productive avalanche chutes, riparian habitats and other important features in their range. But these are not the only features that affect a bear's range.

**GRIZZLY BEAR HOME RANGES,** as well as many other aspects of their behaviour, are also influenced by their mating system, which in turn has been influenced by their reproductive ecology. Most often female grizzly bears have litters every three or four years (more on this in section 14.1), so few are available each spring for mating – in most populations there is a great excess of males. Although both the father and the mother share the genetic benefits of cubs equally, the male only provides a tiny sperm – the mother does 100 per cent of the work raising the cubs for over two years. A mother grizzly will sometimes risk her own life defending not just her, but "their" cubs, as she does need a male.

Out of this unbalanced relationship, a fully polygamous mating system has evolved. In such a system only a few of the males successfully mate, and some dominant males may mate with several females during the mid-May to mid-July breeding season. Males usually spend at least a couple of days with a female but sometimes the pair remains together, and mate often, for over a week. Females may also mate with several males, sometimes in relatively short order. From an evolutionary standpoint, my guess is that she wants males to compete and even fight over her so she is impregnated by the dominant and "best" male and, if she mates with more than one, the one with the "best" sperm becomes the father as there is likely sperm competition going on as well. But females may mate with several males over the two-month breeding season because they also want to confuse paternity. It is likely beneficial that many males at least think they are the father of her litter (more on this in section 16.3). Because of the sometimes fierce and nasty fights males have over females, bears are sexually dimorphic, that is, males and females are physically different. In particular, Flathead adult male grizzly bears are on average 1.7 times as heavy as adult females in the breeding season. Similarly, adult male black bears in the Flathead are 1.6 times as heavy as adult females.

KNOWING THE LOCATION of important habitats and optimal travel routes between them is obviously important, but knowing where the other bears have recently been and are most likely to be found is also advantageous – particularly for breeding adults. We humans generally rely on our eyes and ears to perceive the world, so we often think bears are somewhat asocial because they most often travel alone. But this is because of our eye-ear bias and our inability to understand smell. Bears may rarely feel alone.

Bears have a variety of glands on their feet, particularly between their toes and their foot pads. These glands secrete many chemical compounds, some of which are specific to adult males. Bears also have anal glands that add sex-specific chemical compounds to communicate through their scats – letting others know who has recently been here. Also, both male and female bears of all ages often rub their faces, shoulders and backs on trees and other objects, which, in addition to giving them a good scratch, is another form of chemical signalling. Once in a while, particularly at traditional rubbing sites – but I've also seen it near dead moose and dead elk – bears walk stiff legged while grinding their feet into the ground, making obvious marks in the ground, or what are called "mark trails." Sometimes males even drain their bladders while they strut their stuff – behaviours that are clearly for communication with other bears, and maybe even other species.

I've seen wolves once, very nervously, approach and sniff grizzly bear rub trees for over a minute. Perhaps more interesting, I've often seen trees well rubbed by grizzly bears and even grizzly mark trails right next to hunter, trapper or park warden cabins – communications that the people were usually unaware of until I pointed them out.

From the chemical scents of their feet, droppings, urine and other body parts left on places they rub, bears are likely keeping tabs of the whereabouts of their neighbours, while also letting their neighbours know they are around. Particularly in the mating season, but also other times of the year, it's no doubt beneficial for both males and females to advertise their presence and reproductive status; big, old and dominant animals seem to mark very frequently, likely to let potential mates know that they are still alive and in the game, and worth tracking down to mate with. All of this spatial information helps individuals efficiently forage, avoid conflicts and know where to focus their effort to find the most and best mates during the mating season. Living for years in one area, or home range, where their knowledge accumulates, must be invaluable for bears. Biologists consider a home range to be the area used by an individual for normal activities such as feeding, mating and raising young. A home range is also recognized as an area for which the individual has some form of cognitive map.

**ORIGINALLY, BIOLOGISTS DELINEATED** an animal's home range by drawing lines around the outermost of the radio-collared individual's locations forming what is called a minimum convex polygon, or MCP. This simple method could, however, include large areas such as a big glacier or lake that are not really used by the animal. As computers became more powerful and the number of locations per animal increased because of the development and increased reliability of GPS collars, more complex utilization distributions were developed to estimate home ranges.

Plotting the locations for grizzly bears, particularly of some females that I tracked for decades, suggests that the simple MCP method works well if we are interested in the area for which the animal has a cognitive map. Although the high mountain peaks within their home ranges were rarely if ever used, bears can see them and know they are there, and likely what values they have. I have seen grizzly bears on some of the highest peaks in the Flathead, and in other study areas I've seen grizzly bears travelling miles across large icefields. When a few locations of some bears were outside their more commonly used area, I followed a standard practice and used only the closest 95 per cent of the locations to measure MCPs. This reduction made little difference for most bears but excluded a brief but distant wandering made by some individuals that expanded their MCP to include areas that the bear was unlikely as familiar with.

In the Flathead, I monitored 28 female bears for at least one complete year and all of these were located more than 50 times. Their home ranges varied from 17 square miles (44 $km^2$) for a bear I tracked for five years, to 210 square miles (545 $km^2$) for a bear I followed for six years. Home ranges of females that lived all year in the mountains on either side of the wide Flathead Valley averaged only 33 square miles (85 $km^2$). The average home range size of 20 females that moved to the wide valley in the spring, and sometimes back in the fall after the berries in the mountains were finished for the year, was substantially larger at 82 square miles (212 $km^2$).

The larger range size of females that spent time in the valley likely has little to do with mating but was likely due to the more dispersed nature of the important habitats. The riparian areas mainly used in the spring by these bears are often separated from each other, and from the high-elevation huckleberry fields, by several miles of relatively flat lodgepole pine forests and clearcuts. Bears that live all year in the mountains often have productive avalanche chutes close to huckleberry fields, so their overall ranges are small as they move among these seasonally important habitats. Also, mountains are sloped, so the surface area is much greater per unit of area on a map than are flatter areas. Correcting for surface area that bears actually use would reduce the variation in home range size.

Estimating range size for male grizzly bears, particularly before GPS collars were invented, was more difficult than for females. Males have big, powerful necks (often over 30 inches in diameter) that are almost the same size as their heads, so keeping a collar on them is difficult. Although the bears that I collared have had very few neck problems, and the couple of rubbed necks were initially caused by tooth puncture holes from males fighting each other during the mating season, I take special care when collaring males. I put canvas inserts in all collars for both males and females that will rot and let the collar fall off, but on males, I make cuts in the canvas, so the collars are shed early. I'm happy when males drop their collars in about a year. I also did not collar many males in the later years of my study. For one, they were expensive to keep track of before GPS collars with satellite uplinks were invented because they had to be relocated from an airplane. I collared and tracked only a few males in the later decades of the study because I was more interested in the reproductive rates, cub and yearling survival, and the ecology of females. These are the bears that have the main impact on populations, because they have the babies.

My caution over male collars, and my reduced interest in following them, left me with only nine adult males that I tracked for at least one complete year and for which I had more than 50 locations. Some of these had such large ranges that I know I underestimated their size. Occasionally, even from an airplane, I was unable to find some males. After locating all the other bears, we would climb a few thousand feet (1000 m) above the highest peaks and then fly huge rectangles at over 100 miles (160 km) an hour listening for signals. When we ran too low on fuel, we had to stop with the bear's whereabouts still unknown. But even being biased on several males, their average home range size was 202 square miles (522 $km^2$), or at least three times the size of female ranges. The largest home range of a bear I monitored in the Flathead was 500 square miles (1,300 $km^2$), and this was of a male I tracked for only one year, but he wore a GPS collar that recorded his location four times a day and didn't miss distant locations as I must have when locating other males from an aircraft. It's likely that many other males have ranges that size or even larger.

The smallest range of an adult male I tracked was 69 square miles (179 $km^2$). I monitored this male for three years, and because of his small range size, found him every time I tracked him from an airplane. Like the females with small ranges, he was one of only two males with sufficient data to estimate ranges that were always found in the mountains. The second-smallest range of a male was of the other mountain bear. The mountains surrounding the Flathead are so extensive that all of these male or female mountain bears could have had huge ranges and still not used the wide Flathead Valley.

The much larger home ranges of males is likely related to them wanting to know the whereabouts of many breeding-age females and whether they had cubs or were available to breed. But not only were the annual home ranges and mating season ranges of males about three times larger than those of females, so were the males' berry-season and autumn ranges. Both males and females had the smallest seasonal ranges during the berry season, when they were focused on eating fruit and laying down fat. The seasonal ranges of both males and females were surprisingly a little larger in the autumn than during the spring mating season. This suggests to me that it wasn't only for mating, but that food abundance and distribution also has a strong influence on range size of males. If a home range is a cognitive map, males will learn of dispersed food sources while they are primarily searching for mates. Similarly, they can also learn of the locations of potential mates for the future, while primarily searching for dispersed foods. Searching for potential mates or food sources combine to develop a large cognitive map, and thus can explain the wide-ranging nature of male grizzly bears.

Although I certainly didn't collar all the males that moved in and out of the Flathead Valley, the home ranges of the ones I did collar were so extensive that it is not surprising that they overlapped each other, with individuals often in the same area at the same time. Some adult males that I tracked for several years had home ranges completely engulfed within those of other adult males that had much larger ranges. Although adult males have major battles with each other over females during the mating season, there was no indication of any defence of space outside of a close personal distance. Home ranges and their resources are far too large to be defended by an individual, so there are no territories, just overlapping home ranges of many different individuals. In some coastal areas in North America, the best salmon fishing spots sometimes cover an area smaller than a football field, and there I've seen a couple of dozen adult males resting or fishing almost shoulder to shoulder with big, fat, fish-filled bellies.

Female grizzly bears are also not territorial and have home ranges overlapping those of many others. On several occasions I have seen two or three adult females with cubs or yearlings on one mountainside, and I know some of these mothers were not closely related, or at least they had different mothers and grandmothers. For example, Aggie, who was Blanche's daughter, had almost the exact home range as Elspeth's daughter Mammie, and the ranges of these two adult females were overlapped by half a dozen others.

If spatial knowledge of essential features is important for bears' survival and reproduction, then individuals should benefit from living in one area that meets all their needs, from birth to death. Such bears would accumulate information from the years they spend with their mother that would be useful when, at a tender and vulnerable age, they first separate and live on their own. But what would happen if all young bears remained right in their mother's range? Not only would they end up competing with close relatives over limited resources, but half brothers and sisters would likely end up mating with each other, even if they knew to avoid mating with litter mates or their mother. Therefore, there is a cost to dispersing away from mom's home range, but there is also a cost to staying.

## 10.1 SHOULD I STAY OR SHOULD I GO?

Natal dispersal is the movement from the place of birth to where the young animal establishes its own range and has its own babies. Natal dispersal was poorly understood for grizzly bears yet is an important behaviour for the conservation of these and other animals. Dispersal not only affects population size and trend but, more importantly, is critical for the expansion of growing populations, and for the conservation of small populations. Dispersing individuals preserve genetic connectivity among populations that maintains or enhances genetic diversity. Dispersing bears, particularly females, also maintain demographic connectivity that enables small populations to be rescued from the negative, or even unlucky effects, of just being a small population, or what are called Allee effects (Stephens, Sutherland and Freckleton 1999). These effects were named after Warder Allee, who in the 1930s first described the variety of negative effects on a population when there are only a few individuals.

Dispersal not only reduces competition among close relatives but, perhaps more importantly, reduces the probability of inbreeding. In mammals, males of most species disperse further than females (Greenwood 1980). In birds, the opposite is true and females usually disperse further than males. Furthermore, theory suggests that some individuals of both sexes should disperse, even if dispersers have a lower chance of survival. For bear conservation on an increasingly fragmented continent, understanding grizzly bear dispersal is critically important. We not only have to know how far individuals disperse, but more importantly, how do they go about doing it. Do they one day just pack up and move away never to return, or do they gradually shift their home ranges away from their mother's? Knowing how they disperse is necessary for understanding how we must manage population fractures, or the landscapes that bears must disperse across to move among populations. In the Flathead, I was able to follow many young bears as they grew to adulthood and eventually to old age. One family revealed the variation in how, and how far, female bears dispersed.

**I FIRST COLLARED BLANCHE IN 1979** when she had three cubs. Her home range was in the centre of my study area, and she was one of the bears that I could find every day. In 1982, she had another litter of three cubs. Her old collar had been on for almost three years and I was worried that the batteries might soon run out of juice, so it was time to try to catch her again. I set a few foot snares near a buffalo berry patch that Blanche often fed in, but as luck would have it, I just caught one of her cubs. Catching cubs is never much fun because mother grizzlies are notorious for getting upset when it comes to protecting their babies. Releasing cubs and yearlings without the bears (or me!) getting hurt can be tricky. Fortunately, I've never had to harm either cub or mother in the dozens of times I've faced this situation. Blanche did what I wanted her to do and just ran off when I arrived. Maybe she remembered what snares were all about and that her cub would join her in a day or so. I took out my tracking gear and found Blanche had moved off a few hundred yards. I could have let the cub go, but the little bear was so calm that I thought, maybe I can use it for bait. I went back to camp and got an old hammock and a whole watermelon. I cut the watermelon in half and gave both halves to the cub. She loved it, and in about a minute had scraped both halves clean, leaving only the rind looking like a couple of bowls.

"OK, little bear, I guess I'll call you Melony, if that's OK? Now I'm going to put my hammock way up in the trees above you and wait for your dear old mom to show up to check how you're doing. Then, I'll pop this little dart in her butt. You look happy now with a belly full of melon and you haven't even tightened the snare yet."

So I climbed one tree and then another, and strung the hammock between them about 20 feet (6 m) up and to one side of the cub. There was a third tree that I could climb and from it get in and out of the hammock when way above the ground.

After an early dinner back in camp, I took a sleeping bag, my trusty dart gun, a not-so-trusty flashlight and my tracking equipment, and climbed into the hammock. I got comfortable in my sleeping bag, laid back and waited. For something to do, I listened to the beeps coming from Blanche's collar. She was moving around but not really close. Eventually late afternoon became evening. Then evening gradually shifted to night. It got darker. A couple of stars started to show. It was very quiet. I only heard a few nighthawks squeaking high in the darkening sky. I had expected Blanche to arrive just before dark, but it just got darker and darker. I now could barely see Melony below me. The cub was resting, seemingly peacefully with a belly full of watermelon. Then a great horned owl began hooting far off in the distance. It was now nighttime.

I was going through my plan in my head one more time. When Blanche showed up, would I be able to see enough to put a dart into her butt? I thought so, but if not, I had my not-so-trusty flashlight so, if I coordinated my gun and light by holding both at once, I might get a second or two before she ran off. But then she would know where I was. Would she freak out and climb up and grab me and haul me down? I had seen enough grizzlies 20 feet (6 m) up trees to know some can climb well. But if all went well and I put the dart in her, it would be about ten minutes before she went out. She could go a long way in ten minutes. She was collared and I had my tracking gear so I could track her out. But it would be pretty darn dark wandering around in the bush alone with my not-so-trusty flashlight. Besides, maybe she wouldn't go right out, but just half out. That sometimes happened with the drug I used back then. Dealing with a half drugged, pissed-off and frightened mother grizzly could be exciting in the dark. I finally must have fallen asleep dreaming; what possibly could go wrong with this situation?

It wasn't spring, but enough birds started tuning up their songs at first light to wake me. I thought Blanche would certainly show up now to see what was happening with her baby. It was now light enough to at least see in the forest. I took out my telemetry gear and listened. She was close by, but still not that close. I lay back, watched the last fading star, and waited. Melony was awake, but still seemed relaxed just lying there waiting for something. Would Blanche ever show up? I was feeling guilty enough putting the little bear through all this, even though she didn't seem stressed. But Blanche was not any closer, so I decided to just let the cub go.

I climbed down the tree with my dart gun. I'd leave the hammock until later.

"So Melony, are you going to let me take the snare off your foot?"

She only weighed about 50 pounds (23 kg), but was still a grizzly bear. I crouched down to not look threatening and slowly reached for the snare on her foot.

"Okay, I'll be nice if you'll be nice."

Just as I touched the snare on her foot, she lunged and tried to bite my hand.

"Now Melony, can't you see, I'm trying to let you go so, why are you acting like a damn weed eater? Didn't Blanche read you Androcles and the Lion at bedtime?"

I tried again, but of course, she pounced again.

"Okay, little bear, it must be nap time."

I took a little of the drug out of the dart I had prepared for her mother, and put it into a syringe on the end of a ski pole. I poked her on her left bum cheek. In five minutes she was out and I took the snare off. It wasn't tight at all. She weighed 46 pounds (21 kg) and I put a little tag in her ear so I knew in the future that this was Blanche's cub. She was beyond cute, as all grizzly cubs are.

I caught Blanche three days later in a sneaky snare set along a trail coming towards the same place where I'd caught Melony (49.0993 -114.4744). In September, Blanche and her family had moved from the buffalo berries to where I often watched them feeding on huckleberries on the open mountainside below Commerce Mountain (49.1488 -114.4281), right where Jonkel, Celine and I watched bears several years before.

Almost two years later, on May 10, 1984, Celine and I caught Melony and her sister Ruby, together at the same time and place. The sisters were now 2 years old, so I put collars on both with a well-nicked canvas rot-off. On May 30, I caught another 2-year-old female in one of Blanche's favourite areas. A forester stopped to help me. She acted normal for a grizzly bear, but that was a bit of a shock for the forester. Once we were finished processing her and she had a nice new collar, I asked him, "So, Paul, what should we call her?"

"She sure acts like a girlfriend I once had. So, I think Agatha is fitting."

So Aggie she was.

I located Aggie and Melony together once and I found Aggie in the same spots that Blanche liked, so I presumed she was the third cub of the litter.

**AGGIE WAS NOT ALWAYS COLLARED,** but I was able to follow her most of the time until her death at 32 years of age. She had many favourite spots in her home range, and most were exactly the same locations she had used as a cub with her mother Blanche and litter mates Ruby and Melony. Every year her home range would expand out a little to one side, and the following year expand to another side. Although the boundaries of her annual ranges continued to jiggle back and forth, she, like other adult grizzlies, remained living in the same general area for decades. Most of the annual range expansions and contractions were due to different huckleberry fields being used, or to her shifting from eating huckleberries most years to eating primarily buffalo berries in other years. The last time I saw Aggie eating huckleberries was at the end of August 2013. I could clearly see that her old bones were stiff as she slowly worked her way across the same patch I'd watched her with her mother and litter mates, feeding on Commerce Mountain 31 years before.

Aggie was more philopatric, or a homebody, than was Melony. Melony stayed in her mother's range until she was 4 years old, but that year, I never found her in the southern part of Blanche's range; I located her further north a few times. When she was 5, her range remained similar to the previous year, but she denned even further north, and there she had her first litter of cubs at 6 years of age. Her range stabilized with about half of it north and about half still overlapping her mother's range. When she was 30 years old, Melony got into trouble at a hunting guide's camp seven miles (11.3 km) north of her mother's old range. The conservation officers were called and she was caught in a culvert trap, which, unsurprisingly, is a bear trap made from a section of road culvert. They drugged her, but when they examined her aging body with teeth all but gone, they decided to not let her wake up and she never did again. I think killing an anesthetized bear is a totally humane way to end an old bear's long life – much less traumatic than how most such bears end their lives.

When Ruby, the third daughter of the litter, was 3 years of age, she wandered about 12 miles (19.3 km) westward and far into the mountains. She remained in the western mountains for the entire summer and fall, hibernating there that winter. Over the following two years, she remained in these western mountains but did return once in a while to her mother's range. So of the three female cubs, Aggie lived right in her mother's range for the rest of her life, Melony moved a half a home range away, and Ruby ended up moving completely out of her mother's range.

**IN ADDITION TO THESE THREE BEARS,** I captured, ear tagged and collared 27 other females when 2 years of age or younger (McLellan and Hovey 2001b). Of these, I followed 16 to adulthood. Six of these females I tracked until they were over 20 years old. Of all that I tracked to adulthood, the average centre of their home range was just over six miles (9.7 km) from the centre of their mother's range. Only four had their adult home range centres more than an average female home range diameter of 9.3 miles (15 km) from their mother's range centre, and so would have completely left her range. These dispersal estimates could be biased to bears that remained in the Flathead where I could keep track of them for years. Birth to death sites are less biased because hunters, conservation officers and defence-of-life-and-property kills must be reported no matter where the bear was killed. From where I first caught a 1- or 2-year-old female was an average of 8.2 miles (13.2 km) from where they died when they were adults, so only about two miles further than the bears I had followed for many years. The furthest a female moved from her maternal range was 33 miles (53.1 km) by Tina, one of Mammie's daughters and Elspeth's granddaughters. She was tracked by radio to the edge of the Alberta prairies, where she ended up being shot by a deer hunter (49.4257 -113.9874).

I caught 45 males that were 2 years old or younger. Because males grow faster, I put on collars that would fall off in one year or less, and therefore only followed three to adulthood. All were ear tagged, and 12 of these were killed by people as adults, and their location reported. On average, these 15 males moved 26 miles (42 km) from the centre of their mother's range, and all but three moved at least an average adult male's plus an average adult female's home range radius of 12.7 miles (20.4 km) and would therefore have, on average, completely left the maternal home range. The furthest a male was known to move was 97 miles (156 km) from his mother's range centre southward towards Missoula, Montana, where he was shot when he frightened a deer hunter. In central BC, a 3-year-old male moved at least 211 miles (340 km) from where researchers marked him to where he was shot.

These dispersal results, which showed a few females dispersing but only a short distance, and males moving considerably further from their natal range, qualitatively fits the theory for mammals. But would this amount of dispersal really reduce the chance of inbreeding or competing with close relatives? I built a little computer model to simulate the dispersal behaviour of grizzly bears, based on the actual dispersal distances and home range characteristics. The model suggested that unequal dispersal distance by males and females will greatly decrease the chance of half or full brothers mating with their sisters. Because of the general lack of dispersal by females, there will likely be competition among sisters and with their mother, and there is potential for close inbreeding between fathers and daughters. The chance of inbreeding, however, is greatly reduced by the non-territorial social system of this species. Even if a father was alive and reproductively active when his daughter first bred, usually between 5 and 8 years of age, the home ranges of many other adult males would also overlap her range.

The dispersal behaviour of young male and female grizzly bears and their non-territorial nature should reduce the chance of inbreeding, but because grizzly bears don't reach sexual maturity until 5 or older, there should be no rush for them to disperse. To avoid inbreeding, they could gradually move away. This way they could use important habitats that their mother had shown them, but also start exploring further afield. Both males and females seem to follow this gradual dispersal pattern, which takes several years. For grizzly bear conservation, it is important to know that most males disperse at least out of their mother's home range, but most females hardly disperse at all. It is just as important, or maybe more important, to know that dispersal is a gradual process. There are six grizzly bear populations near the US–BC border with fewer than 100 bears. They are largely isolated from much larger populations to the north by fractures caused by highways, railways, rural settlements, large lakes and, in two cases, the Fraser River. There are many more populations in Europe and Asia that are small and isolated. These small populations, particularly those with fewer than 40 bears, would greatly benefit from bears immigrating, and of course female immigrants are most important. But because grizzly bears disperse gradually, young bears are going to have to live, or at least move safely back and forth, across the fractures. Some males may just cross a fracture in one, final movement, but it is very unlikely any females will. To be functional as demographic connections, fractures have to be managed to not only be a safe place for grizzlies to cross, but a safe place for young female grizzlies to live.

Although we often talk of averages, it's the variability in female dispersal distance, with most staying very close to their mother's home range for their whole life but some dispersing right out of the mother's range, that has likely enabled grizzly bears to persist in the southern portion of their distribution in BC, Alberta and the US. Across this broad area, their distribution is fractured with railways, highways and human settlement. But there are still pockets of wilderness, or at least semi-wilderness, where females and their philopatric daughters can generally live without interference from humans and raise lots of cubs. Most female cubs will stay in the remote mountains, mature there and themselves have cubs. But some will gradually disperse and possibly be attracted to someone's garbage or fruit trees, and then maybe get shot. But, if the habitat is not overly hostile to grizzly bear survival, a few females will successfully disperse and help a small, struggling population. If female grizzly bears dispersed like males do, so many of them would have wandered into lethal situations that people would have likely killed all the grizzly bears over a much larger area than we did in the previous century.

CHAPTER 11

# FAMILY IN THE FLATHEAD

## *Fires and Floods*

For either an afternoon hike or a multi-week adventure, Celine and I used to be quick at packing up and getting out of the house and on the road. I'd like to think it is because we were organized and efficient, but it's more likely that we were well practised. Now, with two kids under the age of 3, we had a couple of anchors that slowed everything down. During the first few days of April 1983, we left UBC in Vancouver in our VW van and drove 12 hours to Cranbrook. There, as usual, we slept in the van parked in the warmth of the Fish and Wildlife Branch warehouse. We had our skis, clothes and bedding already packed, so all we really needed to do was hook up the snowmobile trailer, fill half a dozen plastic five-gallon jerry cans with gasoline, stop by the hardware store for a few items, and get groceries for three or four weeks. It shouldn't have taken much more than an hour, but now it took all morning. We didn't leave Cranbrook until lunchtime, and didn't start unloading the snowmobile and packing the skimmer for the 50-mile (80 km) ride to the Flathead cabin until mid-afternoon. Finally, I got the machine running, Celine got the kids bundled up with their ear protection on, squeezed them between us, and away the four of us went up towards Harvey Pass, all on one old machine. It was a beautiful, sunny and warm afternoon.

There had been other snowmobilers going up towards the pass over the past few days, and the trail was slushy but packed enough that we made good time. Towards the pass, the snow was colder and dry but there had been much less snowmobile traffic. I soon found out why. Just over the pass, a huge avalanche had come down and there was a debris pile of rough, hard-packed snow mixed with smashed bits of trees that crossed the road and must have been 30 feet (10 m) deep. It not only crossed the road but had gone down and even crossed the creek and started up the other side of the valley. I stopped the machine a safe distance away and we all got off.

"Holy smoke, what are we going to do, there's no way we can go over that avalanche, its huge," Celine remarked.

"Well, let's not get near it. There can't be much more snow up there, but maybe there's another big slab just hanging in there further up."

Celine was right; we certainly couldn't drive over the debris pile, but maybe we could go down into the valley, cross the creek and go around the far side of the avalanche, and then, I hoped, we could get back up on the road on the far side of the debris.

"I'll drop the skimmer and we'll try to go around the bottom." I didn't want them to walk across the avalanche path, but I knew it would take much longer to get all four of us down and around the bottom of the avalanche.

It was steep off the road, so I didn't go straight down, as I knew that I might have to make it back up if I couldn't get around the avalanche debris. I drove back maybe a hundred yards where it was a little more gradual off the road. Here, we worked our way down into the valley bottom, making sure my route wasn't so steep that we couldn't return if we had to. The days had been warm, and the creek was no longer completely buried; some was open water flowing below ten-foot (3 m) vertical banks of snow. I had to parallel the creek, just along the edge, for maybe 30 yards (27 m) to get to what looked to be a solid snow bridge to cross. I stopped the machine.

"I'm going to have to side-hill here a bit, so you guys better get off. I'll come back and help you once I cross."

I revved the engine, angled the machine away from the snow-free creek straight below me, leaned my torso out away from the creek, and kept the momentum going. When I stopped at a safe spot, Celine, with Charlie in her arms and Michelle by the hand, were working their way along my trail. Michelle was laughing as she postholed down to her little thighs. Then Celine would count her steps.

"*Un, deux, trois*, posthole," as she sunk into the snow and they all laughed. Celine knew that with little ones, it's always best to make everything a game to keep everyone happy. She also knew to have Michelle's boots done up properly so no snow could get in. Keeping dry is the rule in the wilderness for babies and adults alike.

Once back on the machine, we crossed the creek quickly and skirted the avalanche on the far side of the valley from the road. It was a bit of a side hill, but clear and easy going, and we continued until there was another good solid snow bridge we could use to cross back. Getting back up to the road was not going to be as easy, as it was going down off the road. The last bit was steep.

"You should get off here and I'll giv'er hell," I suggested.

"Yes, let us off, I'd rather walk. I'd always rather walk."

"I'll come back and help you up the steep part."

"No, you get the stuff over the avalanche. We'll go slow and climb up to the road and be fine."

I revved the machine right up and took off to gain as much momentum as I could. The last bit before the road was very steep and the machine, spinning snow out behind it, just barely kept moving up and onto the road bed. Wow, that was lucky. I don't know what we would have done if the machine had spun out. I know we would have made it up somehow. Eventually we always make it, but it would have been a lot more work and a lot more time, and I knew it was getting late.

I started packing all our food, gear, gas and finally the skimmer itself over the debris pile. After a couple of trips across the slide, Celine, Michelle and Charlie had made it up the hill and onto the road. As I came over the debris pile with a jerry can in each hand, Celine was sitting on the snowmobile nursing Charlie, and Michelle was eating an apple. Everyone was still content. This was a very good sign.

Once everything was put back together, we took off from the Harvey Pass and dropped down into the wide Flathead Valley. It always felt so good to enter the big valley where there was no one else but us, especially after being in the city for months. It was now late afternoon and the temperature in the valley was much warmer than in the pass and the snow was very soft and slushy. There had been some snowmobile traffic earlier, but not for many days. The snowmobile trail was narrow with a firmly packed base. Off the track the snow was isothermal, or complete slush right down to the bottom. We still had over 20 miles (32 km) to go, and keeping the machine balanced right on the hardened track while towing a heavy sled with four of us on board was becoming a real challenge. I had to keep my weight just perfect and keep adjusting the steering continuously. I knew it would happen, and finally it did; the skimmer slid to the side, pulling the snowmobile off the track and into the bottomless slush. The machine sunk, then stopped abruptly, and we all tumbled off into the snow.

"What are you doing? It's no time to be stupid."

"What do you think, I did it on purpose?"

A few years before we had kids, I swerved a snow machine on purpose and dumped Celine into deep powder snow because I was becoming bored after hours of motoring into the mountains in mid-winter doing our elk study. Now that youthful stunt was coming back to haunt me.

After helping get the kids settled, I unhooked the skimmer, got out the shovel and dug the snow away to level the machine. I then put on my skis and packed the slush towards the firmer snowmobile trail. Then I drove the machine back on the track. It's always better to spend some time to make a good trail than to keep trying to get going on a bad trail and getting more and more stuck. I then had to get the heavy skimmer back onto the track and hook it up. I could tell that Celine was no longer having fun. Little Michelle could tell this too.

Off we went again. The mileage signs, put on the roadside for logging truck drivers to radio each other their whereabouts, were slipping by; we were doing well. The sun had gone down behind the mountains, and with a cloudless sky, the temperature was dropping fast. We crossed the Flathead Bridge (49.1213 -114.4961) and kept going; 16 miles (26 km) to the cabin. It was now getting cold and the snow was starting to freeze just a little. I was cruising along, keeping my balance just right, when the skimmer slipped to the side once again and there we were, all piled up in the snow.

"What are you doing? We have to get to the cabin, not fooling around out here. It's getting cold now. We are going to freeze to death out here."

That was it. Michelle started crying, as she didn't want to freeze to death. And then baby Charlie started screaming just because everyone else was.

"We have 30 gallons of gas and we're in the middle of a forest of dead trees. We are not going to freeze to death," I forcefully argued.

"Why don't you just leave all the gas and stuff here?"

"Yeh, that's a great idea. Why didn't you say that an hour ago?" Celine so often comes up with the obvious solution that I miss because I'm too focused on how we did it before.

Off went the gas, food, clothes and telemetry gear. I dug out some potatoes, carrots and elk steak for dinner and some cookies just in case we needed to bribe the kids. All I kept was the bedding and our skis. Although with proper tools, some haywire, and enough time I can keep most machines working, I never want to be snowmobiling on such an old machine without skis as a backup. *Un, deux, trois*, posthole is not much fun for ten miles (16 km).

Celine got back on with Charlie still crying, but Michelle didn't want anything to do with the snowmobile and started screaming even more.

"Do you want to stay here alone all night or come with us to our little warm cabin by the river?" I tried to rationalize with a 2-year-old.

She might have calmed down a bit before I just put her on and away we went. It was much easier without the heavy skimmer. Why hadn't I dropped the load way back when we first crashed? Too dumb. The mileage signs went by, the snow was starting to firm up more and more in the cold, and I had the machine under control. It was just after dark when we drove up to the front door and pushed the kill-switch on the machine.

"I know this cabin," Michelle said. She was now happy – so was I.

I took the shovel from where it hung on the outside wall and dug away three feet (1 m) of snow until I could open the door, as, for some unknown reason, it opened outward. The flashlight was still hanging just inside the door with a good battery. The lantern was still hanging over the table and full of gas. Matches were in their metal can on the window sill as always. Dry newspaper, kindling and larger pieces of wood were there just where we had left them four months before. In minutes, the light was on, the fire was on, and the dinner was on. We all felt so good to be back in the cabin by the river.

Before bed, I went outside to make a yellow hole in the snow. There was no moon yet, but it was so clear that the light from stars made the snow shine and even cast shadows on the snow below the trees. I stood and checked out the billions of friends I hadn't seen for months while in the city. There was Cassiopeia just setting, but pointing out Polaris with the big dipper now coming up behind the forest. I searched for my favourite constellation, the banking super-cub coming right at me for a landing, but it wasn't up above the mountains yet. With the bright gas lantern shining light out of the windows, the little log cabin looked so warm and cozy buried in snow. I could see Celine inside dealing with her babies. I was so lucky to have found a country pumpkin, as she sometimes called herself. I mentioned it was supposed to be bumpkin not pumpkin; perhaps she knew.

It froze hard overnight. In the morning, the snow was what some skiers call boilerplate, and the machine easily cruised back to where we had left our stuff. I loaded it back onto the skimmer and returned to the cabin before anyone else was even awake. So simple.

**FOR ME, THE CABIN WAS FINE,** as I was out catching or tracking bears every day. Although Celine and the kids often came along, they spent much more time at camp than I did. On nice days, they went outside most of the time, but when the weather was cold and rainy, the cabin was a bit too small. Michelle, in particular when she got her new tricycle, needed more than a 135 square foot (12.5 $m^2$) cabin.

Ray Demarchi was a big shot in the Fish and Wildlife Branch, but that's not saying much. He often had to scrounge from the Forest Service, because that agency had pretty well all the funding. For a deer study, Ray had scrounged a well-built 1956 Pacific industrial camp trailer that was 33 feet (10 m) long. The deer work had ended so I asked him if I could move the trailer to the Flathead. Within a week, Ray had it brought down to our camp. Now we had 250 square feet (23 $m^2$) of living space with a little bunk bed, a double bed, a propane stove with an oven, and even a tiny bathtub that we converted into a bed for Michelle. But a year later, when Charlie was 1½ and Michelle was almost 4, even 250 square feet (23 $m^2$) was too small on cold, rainy days.

Dave Horning was helping me in the summer of 1984. As in most years, we primarily trapped and collared bears starting in late May and continued to late June. We also used the telemetry gear to track the collared bears and hiked to the locations recorded over the previous few days. One day, after we returned from the field, I paced off an area about 14 by 20 feet (4.3 by 6.1 m) next to the trailer where I thought we should build an addition. I only had a small tape measure for measuring bears so I used a fixed length of rope to measure both diagonals and moved the corner stakes until it was a perfect rectangle.

"What do you think?" I asked Celine, who was the major proponent of this project.

"That will be perfect."

I took my chainsaw into the forest of dead lodgepole pine that surrounded the camp and cut several three inch (7.5 cm) diameter poles. I dragged them to camp and then cut them about four feet (120 cm) long. With these, a few nails and some haywire, I made a couple of three-sided pyramids to hold logs about three feet above the ground for peeling. Every evening, Dave and I would cut some logs, carry them to camp and put the biggest one on the peeling rack. Every day, while Dave and I were out doing bear work, Celine would use the draw knife and peel the logs. When Dave and I returned in the evening, we would scribe the saddle notches where the logs would overlap each other at the corners. We would also scribe long-notches the length of the log, and then follow the scribe lines with a sharp knife to stop any chipping. We would use the chainsaw to remove the saddle and long-notches and then, after rolling the log into place and marking contact points, roll it back out for fine tuning with the knife or a sharp hatchet. We then put fibreglass insulation inside the notches and rolled the log into its final position. Every day we put up one to three logs, and cut another few for Celine to peel. In a few weeks the floor joists, tight-fitting log walls and roof rafters were all done. We then used an Alaska chainsaw mill that I borrowed to cut one-inch (2.5 cm) planks for the floor and the roof. I scrounged three windows and an old door that even had a mail slot. I put 90-pound rolled asphalt roofing on the roof, and a Puffin' Billy, or sometimes called a Hippie Killer, a $35 wood stove, in the corner. In a month, we had added another 280 square feet (26 m$^2$) of living space with a wood stove and three windows for just about $200. Even though we had now lived in the Flathead for six years, I now felt that Celine, with her two babies playing in a warm living room on a rainy day, was even a happier camper than before.

**BUT THERE WERE OTHER CONCERNS** living many miles from pavement. Fire was one. Of course fire has often been a great friend and comforter of mine and perhaps has saved me from hypothermia or even freezing solid a few times. But fire can also be devastating. We were doing the study in the Flathead because the forest had been killed by the mountain pine beetle. Millions of trees were dying and their needles slowly turned red. After the trees had died and life had left the branches, dark hair lichens, commonly called "horse hair" or less commonly called "Neptune's crotch," attached to the dead branches and grew. After a few years the forests became a grey sea of dead wood with hanging lichen. This combination is explosive – a huge fire bomb just ready for ignition. Twice I've had old mountain men comment on the speed with which I could get a campfire going. I'd just break up some dead twigs covered with hair lichen and strike a match and "poof," it was almost like using gasoline.

"What kind of fire starter was that?" each had asked.

And these bushmen had started thousands of campfires but just weren't used to dry lichen mixed with twigs in a dead forest.

I once drove up the North Fork Road on the Montana side of the border with a forester who worked for a logging company. He was looking across the Flathead River at the immense sea of dead lodgepole pine in Glacier National Park.

"What a damn waste," he started. "It's simple stupidity to let all those trees die and just leave them there. Hundreds of people could be employed for a decade logging and processing the timber. If left, it's just going to all fall down and be such a mess that no bears or any other animal can even walk through it."

A second later, after a little thought, he continued. "But it'll eventually burn in one huge firestorm that'll scorch off the topsoil so little will grow for generations. They've been putting out fires for so long, the system's no longer natural at all. I tell you, it's going to be Dante's Damn Inferno when it goes."

And we were living in the middle of Dante's Damn Inferno; all it needed was a spark. What made it more treacherous was that some of the dead trees were starting to fall down. After a windy night, I often had to get out the chainsaw and cut half a dozen trees that crossed the road. After a real windstorm in 1987, it took hours to clear all the dead trees. With forest fires most often being started by lightning storms, there could be ignition in many places in the valley, and trying to escape by driving on a narrow dirt road through miles of forest, with dead trees falling and blocking the way, would probably get us roasted.

We know an old-timer, long gone now, who told us of lying in a creek for two days with a wet blanket over him while a forest fire burned past. Could we just lie in the river for a few days? Maybe, but I had also heard that during a huge firestorm, there is insufficient oxygen to even burn all the gases, particularly near the ground.

"I saw huge explosions with mushroom clouds thousands of feet above the fire," an old forest fire fighter once told me. "There was finally enough oxygen up there for all the hot gases to ignite."

Would we have enough oxygen to breathe lying in the river under wet blankets? Celine usually ended our fire escape discussions with "the Forest Service guys know we are down here with the kids, so someone will send a helicopter. They are good guys and are not going to let us burn to death while they try to save a few trees. If not, we'll take the canoe and be on the river."

So we didn't really stress about Dante's Damn Inferno until big lightning storms blew through. But during the biggest, I was camped in the mountains and Celine was alone with the kids.

**JIM RENNEY,** the butcher who provided meat cutting for bait, and I had been in the mountains watching a female grizzly called Mud as she ate grass in an avalanche chute. Once it became too dark to see her, we hiked back to Jim's truck parked at the end of an old logging skid-trail. Jim slept in the cab of his pickup and I wandered off to find a somewhat level spot and set up my $15 bright orange Taymore tent, with its four corner pegs and one aluminum pole in the middle of the entrance, and another at the foot of the tent. I went to sleep thinking of what Mud was going to do that night. She wasn't very far away, but she was a small female and had little self-confidence. Sure she could kill me easy, but she didn't know it and, more importantly, she didn't want to.

I woke to the noise of the tent flapping. The wind grew stronger. I could now hear it blowing in gusts through the limestone crags towering above. I gripped the front tent pole as it began to shake. Then there was a very bright white flash that lit the tent completely. Maybe half a second later, a loud sizzling sound that seemed to begin high above but almost immediately ended with an explosive boom as loud as a .300 magnum short barrel rifle going off near my ear. Then another lightning bolt hit so close that the light and noise were at the same time. The rain started, but it wasn't really rain, as there were no drops but more like connected sheets of water being pounded by the wind into the cheap tent. In a few seconds all the tent pegs had been torn out. I was out of my sleeping bag, spread-eagled on my stomach in a pool of cold water with my hands and feet holding the tent down and still gripping what now might be an aluminum lighting rod that held the tent up. I had piled my sleeping bag on top of my pack so it wasn't completely in the puddle. Outside, the world was bright with the weird white light of thousands of welding rods, with the odd instant of complete darkness. Lightning was hitting everywhere. I'd been told that the odds are better that a person will be killed by lightning than by a grizzly bear. I wondered what the probability was of both happening simultaneously.

Then the rain and wind slowed enough for me to go out to find rocks to put on the tent corners to hold it down. It was eerie running around in the almost continuous, bright, welding-rod light with only short intervals of total darkness. I found some rocks near the stream I had camped next to. In a few minutes, I was back in my tent pushing the water into a low corner where I hoped it would eventually drain. The storm passed shortly before twilight began.

I got up very early and listened for Mud. I could hear her collar faintly a long way away. I was wet and cold, but the mountains were wetter. There was no threat of a real fire up here, but did it also rain in the valley? We packed up and headed out of the mountains. In a few hours we were back at camp. It was wet everywhere.

"Holy smoke, that was one big storm last night. I never see rain like that before. Was it loud in the mountains?" asked Celine.

"It was by far the loudest noise of any kind that I have ever heard." But, thankfully, there was no fire.

**THE FIRST REAL FOREST FIRE** during the years we lived in the Flathead, called the Red Bench Fire, started in early September 1988, but it was about 20 miles (32 km) south of the border. This fire ended up burning 36,000 acres (146 km$^2$) and about 25 houses plus other buildings near the small community of Polebridge, Montana. The valley was so full of thick smoke that we couldn't really see where the fire was burning from the mountains in Canada, so we monitored its spread by listening, as best we could through the static, to the local radio station. It was a very serious fire for our neighbours in Montana, but by mid-September, it was no longer a threat.

In mid-August 1994 the Starvation Creek fire began about five miles (8 km) to the east of the Flathead cabin. Fortunately, the winds were blowing from the southwest as they usually do, and there were two large creeks with broad riparian areas between us and the fire. It was burning in Starvation Creek valley for a few days, but then one evening, with a strong wind at its back, it exploded up an entire mountainside (49.0 -114.330) in a matter of minutes. There is no doubt that any animal that hadn't moved away and was still on that mountainside was fried. I doubt a mule deer could have outrun the fire going up the hillside, and certainly no human could have. The 7,200-acre fire burned into the upper Starvation Creek drainage, which is totally surrounded by high rock walls with no fuel, so the fire burned itself out.

**IN MID-JULY 2003 THE WEDGE CANYON** fire began about seven miles (11 km) south of our camp. This was a more threatening fire because the winds often blew northward towards the border. It was so threatening that the BC Wildfire Service brought in many bulldozers and excavators. Along about a 100 foot (39 m) wide swath just north of the border, they removed the forest right down to the mineral soil along a ten-mile (16 km) strip to be used for a back burn. If the Wedge Canyon fire had moved northward and appeared that it would cross into Canada, someone would make the decision to start a wall of fire on the south side of this fire break and burn the forest back into the US. I wondered who would make the decision to burn back into another country, particularly the United States.

In 2003, Michelle turned 23 years old and was doing grizzly bear research in Alberta, while Charlie was almost 21 and working for Parks Canada. Celine was now working as a social worker in Revelstoke. The fire break had been finished, and the entire Flathead Valley was closed; I was alone and the only person left in the entire Canadian Flathead. It was hot and very smoky. I waded the Flathead River in front of our cabin and walked in my flip-flops and shorts to the border, just to see the old border crossing that had closed eight years before. I was standing on the BC side against the locked gate between Canada and the US, when a fancy white SUV drove up from the south. It was a US Forest Service vehicle, but it wasn't a pickup with a bunch of smelly firefighters. Two guys got out in clean outfits, almost suits. They were big shots all the way from Denver, Colorado.

"Hey, buddy, you must be a Canadian, eh," one joked as he walked towards the south side of the gate.

"Yahss, Sir, I surely am," I joked back with a southern drawl.

"I hear you guys cut a huge fire break just north of the border?"

"I didn't do it, I promise I didn't," I said as I put up my hands as if I was being arrested.

"Can we come over the line and just take a quick look?" one asked.

"Hey, my friends, this is Canada. Of course you can come over. We are a friendly country. But I'm not sure you can ever go home without Border Security getting you."

The three of us walked 100 feet (30 m) north towards the abandoned Canada Customs Station and talked about what we were doing at this place at this time. We stopped where the fire break crossed the old road. They looked west along the newly cut line to the far mountains. Then they turned and looked east along the new cut as far as one could see.

"If I'd done this on the other side of the border, I wouldn't just be fired, I would be sent to prison," one of them said. They went back to the US, got into their fancy SUV and drove south. I walked north alone – it's a nice feeling to be the only person in the over 600 square miles (1554 $km^2$) of the Canadian Flathead.

**THE NEXT SERIOUS FIRES WERE IN 2017.** The Elder Creek fire started about four miles (6.4 km) to the east of our cabin, but grew slowly northeast with the prevailing winds, and burned only 2,500 acres (10 km$^2$). This fire was overshadowed by the Kenow fire that started about the same time, but high in a basin mostly rimmed by rock. It seemed to burn within the basin for a few days, but then it crept out. Over the next few days it expanded mostly north and eastward, away from our camp. Over the next week or so, it grew to cover about 22,000 acres (89 km$^2$), and then the wind really picked up. It seemed like overnight the fire ripped across the Alberta border into Waterton National Park, and in about a day it had grown to almost 90,000 acres (364 km$^2$). Dante's Damn Inferno had finally arrived, but missed us again. By luck alone, the last fire to burn through our camp was in 1919, about 30 years before the Flathead cabin was built. We are not out of the woods yet, there's still a lot of 40-year-old dead and dry fuel near our cabin.

**THE FLATHEAD CABIN WAS ABOUT 20 FEET** (6 m) from the edge of the river, and the trailer with the new addition we built was maybe 30 feet (10 m) away. We were not as lucky with floods as we had been with fire. In April, when the river is low but ice is usually gone, an average of 920 cubic feet (26 m3) of water flows by the cabin every second. In May, the snow in the mountains is melting rapidly and an average of 3,470 cubic feet (98 m$^3$) go by each second. Every few years, in heavy flood conditions, the flow gets over 10,000 cubic feet (283 m$^3$) per second. At such times the river is fast, churning and the colour of chocolate milk. Full trees with their wide root wads attached come cruising by. Sometimes at a bend they are pushed up over the bank before they pivot back into the river. During floods, our camp was not a restful place to have a couple of toddlers running around chasing butterflies.

We were talking about building a fence, but a conservation officer who was visiting said, "I don't know if a fence is a good idea. It will give you a false sense of security. You might find yourself trusting the fence and not watching the kids, and kids always get around a fence."

"I never, ever let the kids outside without me, never ever and even more so when the river is high. We never go near the river," was Celine's response.

So we never built a fence and the kids never did go near the river when it was in flood, or so we thought.

Several years later, when Charlie and Michelle were about 4 and 6, I was outside in late May replacing broken leaf springs on an old Toyota 4x4 we had. The river was brown and turbulent and full-length trees sometimes floated quickly by. Celine came to me.

"Where are the kids?"

"I don't know, you were watching them."

"No, I was inside, you were watching..."

Before she could finish, "Michelle! Charlie!" I yelled as loud as I could.

No answer. We both yelled and ran around the yard looking. No answers.

I started running down the riverbank looking for something other than brown churning water; a red shirt, blue pants. The river was fast, but I was faster. After a quarter of a mile (400 m) and nothing, I turned and Celine, although she can't really swim so I don't know what she would have done, was not far behind me. I didn't know what to do, so I kept running. They can't have gone this far. After another quarter mile (400 m) downstream, I turned and started jogging back. Maybe I passed them, but nothing. Celine had tears running freely down her cheeks.

"I'm going back, maybe something else happened."

I just couldn't stop running, I certainly couldn't just walk. Celine was right behind me. When we got back to camp, both kids were at the doorstep. It was by far the best feeling I had ever had.

"Where were you guys?"

"Hiding," said little Charlie.

Michelle added, "We just wanted to see what you and Mom would do."

I think we passed the test. After a conversation about inclusive fitness, Hamilton's Rule and the genetics of love and fear, they never tried anything like that again.

**OF COURSE THE "200-YEAR-FLOOD"** doesn't come every year, but over a 42-year study, there is a pretty good chance it will happen – and it did. Fortunately, in 1995 I was doing a second grizzly bear study between Yoho and Glacier national parks, BC, while still keeping the Flathead study going. In early June 1995 I took Charlie, who was 12 years old, out of school a few weeks early and headed for the Flathead. It had been raining on and off for a few days, but on June 7 it was finally a pretty nice day. When we got to the Elk Valley, we realized that the rainfall had been extreme in that corner of the province. Over three inches (7.6 cm) of rain had fallen on June 6 in Fernie, and it likely rained harder in the Flathead. That amount of rain, on top of the winter's remaining snowpack, caused by far the highest water level recorded in the Flathead since 1929 when water measurements began.

The flood wiped out the water measuring station, so the true amount is unknown. A helicopter pilot who surveyed the Flathead said to me, "It's unbelievable. The Flathead River was just standing waves two miles wide. Your camp will be gone. Every bridge is gone. I've never seen anything like it."

We learned that every bridge was not gone, although many were. We also learned that, although the road was very rough, we might be able to get to our camp a few weeks later. On the way in, we knew that the Flathead had changed. The river was still in the valley, of course, but there was so much change that I couldn't remember where it had been before. There were new islands, channels, sandbars and uprooted trees piled up all over, sometimes huge piles of trees hundreds of yards from the current river channel.

When we drove from the higher terrace down towards the cabin, I realized that the old conservation officers had built it on the flood plain. There was a pile of debris piled up on our driveway. We got out and walked to the camp. As we approached from the forest, I could see our trailer and addition were still there – barely. Most of the yard, or cleared meadow, that we had lived in for the past 17 years was gone. The old Fish and Game cabin was gone. Before my brain had processed the new reality, I shut my eyes and tried to visualize what had been there before. The riverbank had moved about 20 yards (18 m) eastward and now was where the very back end of the cabin had been. Just further downstream, perhaps 50 yards (46 m) of the meadow was gone and the river had moved there. The rocky bar on the far side of the river was much wider and piled with uprooted trees. It was painfully raw and dirty. For the first time, the Flathead seemed ugly.

The log addition that we had built had an inch (2.5 cm) of mud on the floor, but luckily the water level had been an inch below the floor of the trailer. We would have to put new plywood on the floor of the addition, but otherwise, our home was fine. With the corner of the addition now being less than ten feet (3 m) from the riverbank, we now really had waterfront property.

CHAPTER 12

# ROADS, MORE ROADS, AND SEISMIC EXPLORATION

When I was an undergraduate student in the early 1970s, I earned money for the following school year by logging. I did a variety of jobs over the four summers that I was a logger, including cutting down huge, old-growth trees in the Coast Mountains of BC. I used a Stihl 070, which I was told was the second-biggest and heaviest chainsaw Stihl made at the time. For one month, I cut right-of-way to build a road network into a pristine valley. I had a deep sense of guilt when the first huge Douglas fir trees, six feet (180 cm) in diameter at the butt, slowly toppled, fell and shook the ground, followed by branches, twigs and dust. I realized that trees would never grow that big again. But even more upsetting was opening roads into valleys that very few people, if anyone, ever went into. Road access, I knew, would change the entire valley forever. But I was 19 years old that summer, needed the money for school and knew that if I didn't cut them down, someone else would. I at least apologized to the first few huge trees I killed.

When I started my grizzly bear study a few years later, it seemed that the expanding road network, with tentacles creeping into almost every side valley, would have permanent effects on grizzly bears and on the rest of the ecosystem. During my earlier elk study, I had read about researchers in Montana and Idaho investigating the implications of roads on elk distribution. But in the 1970s, it seemed to be common knowledge that grizzlies were more sensitive than elk and would respond even more to roads. I thought it was important to investigate how bears would react to industrial roads, as well as to the actual logging and gas exploration. The general hypothesis was that animals were frightened of people but in particular our big, noisy and smelly machines, and so would use areas near roads less than if the roads weren't there. In other words, they would be displaced from roads. If bears were unable to freely use areas near roads, then this habitat would be effectively lost to the animals. If we assume that the more habitat bears had available to them, the more bears there would be, then displacement would ultimately reduce the number of bears that could potentially live in the area. And, of course, the more roads, the more habitat loss, and the fewer bears the area could sustain and, finally, too many roads and there would be no more grizzlies.

By the mid-1980s, I had sufficient radio telemetry locations on enough different bears to investigate the displacement hypothesis (McLellan and Shackleton 1988). First, I thought that if a bear used areas near roads less than areas further away, then *fewer of the bear's locations should be near roads than locations randomly located within the individual bear's seasonal home range.* The Flathead was a good place to test this hypothesis because there were a lot of roads, so if roads had no effect, then I expected a lot of locations near roads. Also, the road network made ground tracking radio-collared bears efficient and relatively accurate.

Locating bears from the road network, however, could bias the data against bears that were far from roads and thus not as likely to be found. Fortunately, I located all the bears from an airplane about once a week, so I could use these locations, unbiased with respect to roads, to correct for biases of ground locations. My analysis was based on individual bears and their own seasonal home ranges. Sure enough, from the airplane I found bears that were more than one kilometre (0.62 miles) from a road about twice as often as I found them that far from a road when I was tracking from the ground. But if the bear was within a kilometre of a road, there was no difference between the ground and aerial locations, so I could use the locations from aircraft to account for this bias. Comparing bear use of various distances to road categories to random locations found that, in the spring and autumn, bears used areas within 250 metres (274 yards) from roads less than they would have if there were no roads. This level of displacement would have caused the equivalent of a 9 per cent loss in bear habitat in my study area.

In this analysis, I did not use summer locations because at that time of year bears were most often eating huckleberries in remote basins where the trees had been burned up in wildfires decades before. Because there were few, if any trees, loggers had no interest in these old burns and so there were no roads. During the summer, most of the bears were eating huckleberries more than a kilometre (0.62 miles) from a road and most of the random points within their summer home ranges were more than a kilometre from a road, so any comparisons would have been meaningless – bears were in remote basins to eat huckleberries, not to avoid roads.

It was obvious that roads were not located randomly with respect to huckleberry fields, but what about during spring and fall when I did my comparisons? Roads often followed valley bottoms but generally kept out of riparian areas. Could the bears' selection of riparian areas confound the effects of roads, or, in other words, could their selection of riparian habitat alone result in an apparent avoidance of roads? Also, many minor roads end up in logging cutblocks, and therefore many roads were surrounded by newly logged areas. Could bears not be avoiding roads but simply not finding much to eat in these recently logged habitats? My first analysis on this topic was done long before modern Geographical Information Systems (GIS) were available, so I had to do this analysis by hand. I had sufficient bear locations in forested habitats and in riparian areas to do habitat-specific comparisons. So, for example, I asked the data, *When a bear was in a riparian area, did it use areas further from roads than random locations within riparian habitat?* Riparian and forested habitat were the habitats with the most cover, so displacement should be less than in the more open habitats, but the results were similar to the general comparison; once again, bears used riparian areas within about 250 metres (273 yards) of a road less than expected.

These results were averages of many bears, but as always, there was considerable variation among individuals. A few bears were found close to roads much more often than others. In general, adult males were found further away from roads than females or younger bears. Bears that separated from their mother when they were yearlings, which is one or two years before most young bears leave mom, were more often found near roads.

**HONEY AND BRANDY WERE 1-YEAR-OLD** female siblings that lived just south of the border in the US and were frequently seen along the main North Fork Road in Montana. These sisters were small bears and travelled together, so Rick Mace and I decided to put a small ear-tag transmitter on one of them. They were easy to find. We drove to where we had been told the young bears were often seen and, sure enough, there they were. They were also the easiest bears to catch. When we were away from the truck setting the snares, we noticed one standing at the back of our pickup sniffing the air. Rick raised his pulaski and ran at them.

"Get out of there!" he yelled, followed by a softer comment.

"I don't want to chase them too far, but they should learn some manners," and then a Rick Mace giggle.

We each finished setting a snare and tossed in a tiny tidbit of bait and just stood back and watched. Both were caught within a couple of minutes.

Laurel and Hardy were Melissa's 1984 batch of cubs, and Knut was the surviving cub of Elspeth's 1983 twins. Like Honey and Brandy, these three males separated from their mothers as yearlings. All five of these yearlings were often seen along roadsides. Sometimes I would pass them when I was driving up a drainage and then pass them again coming back out hours later. We would see them so often it became a joke.

"Knut was hitchhiking on Sage Creek when I went up, and he was still looking for a ride when I came back."

It wasn't only these super-subordinate yearlings, however, that spent time near roads. Unlike these yearlings, adult females were rarely seen from a road, and if they were, they were usually running for cover. But adult females with young cubs used areas close to roads in the spring more often than when they had older cubs or when they were alone. Because adult males kill other bears of all ages, but particularly cubs, perhaps these more vulnerable bears felt more secure with the odd vehicle going by than in areas where they were more likely to encounter a large male bear.

**ALTHOUGH MY ANALYSES SUGGESTED** that most grizzly bears, and particularly adult bears, use roads and areas near roads less than other areas, I often saw tracks of adult grizzlies right on the roads. Their tracks on a dirt road are pretty easy to see from a vehicle if you know how to look. Even if the road is hard and dry, if you look far enough ahead, tracks stand out clearly even when driving at 30 miles (50 km) an hour. After a rain, when roads are a little muddy, tracks are obvious. Most often, I saw fresh grizzly bear tracks on roads early in the morning, and it was not uncommon for them to have walked down the road for several miles. From my unrecorded and unmeasured observations, only wolves seem to travel further on roads than bears. Big cats, such as mountain lions and lynx, along with wolverine, usually just cross roads; I've never seen their tracks follow a road for miles. Since most fresh grizzly tracks on roads were seen in the early morning, I wondered if bears use the roads and areas near roads more when it's dark and people are rarely driving around. If bears did use areas near roads when it was dark, then the effect of displacement would be less than I had estimated.

To test the hypothesis that *bears would use areas on or near roads during hours of darkness more often than during the day*, I could not simply compare nighttime to daytime locations. During the day, I often had to hike miles through the thick forest to get a good location, but miles of bushwhacking through the forest in the dark wasn't wise. So I limited my comparisons to bears spending time in the more heavily roaded portion of the study area. I would locate one or more bears during the day, and then go after the same bears several hours later after dark. Even if they had headed for the distant mountains by nightfall, I could always hear a faint signal and place them in the *greater than a kilometre from road* category. I then compared the matched pairs of daylight vs. dark locations to see if, on average, bears were found closer to roads at night.

Tracking bears at night was uneventful. I only saw one vehicle in all the nights when I recorded 121 bear locations. Although I was rarely out in the middle of the night, when bears were usually sleeping, one night I was parked at 1 a.m. tracking Elspeth when I saw headlights coming towards me. I got into my truck to hopefully avoid a long conversation, but this didn't work. It was the Royal Canadian Mounted Police, and of course they stopped. From a safe distance, one carefully got out and shone a huge flashlight at me.

"What are you up to here?"

"Me? I'm tracking bears like I always am, what are you guys doing way out here in the middle of the night?" The guy laughed.

"Any around here?"

"Yes, I was just honing in on a mother grizzly with three cubs."

They were the only police I ever saw in the Flathead, except for those out for a Sunday drive with the conservation officers. He didn't tell me what they were doing 70 miles (113 km) from pavement on a dead-end road at 1 a.m. This was before onboard GPS, so they were probably half lost, but maybe not. Sometimes there were strange people doing strange things in the Flathead – particularly when close to the border.

Sure enough, I found that bears, on average, were closer to roads at night than they were during the day. What was most striking to me was that during these matched comparisons, I found bears located right on the road 12 times, and ten of these were during the night. Yes, they do use roads at night when there is almost no traffic, likely because it's more secure using darkness as cover.

**MY WORK ON GRIZZLIES AND ROADS** in the Flathead was limited because there were only gravel and dirt roads, with a maximum of about 100 vehicles per day on the busiest roads, and that was only when Shell Oil employees or the loggers were busy in the valley. Most roads had far less traffic. Many roads had no traffic at all except during the autumn when road hunters were slowly prowling around sitting behind the steering wheel. In the Flathead, I couldn't investigate implications of highways or busy road networks. Also, my early analyses were limited because I relied on regular, old-fashioned radio collars that I had to track from the ground or from aircraft myself, and could only use relatively simple analyses because GIS had not been invented.

At the turn of the new millennium, GPS collars that could record an accurate location of an animal many times a day were becoming more reliable. In 2001, I started to use GPS collars in the Flathead. By then, I knew that grizzly bears were not completely a "wilderness-demanding" species, because bears were increasingly being seen in farmers' fields, the Fernie ski hill and even the communities of the lower Elk Valley. This area, where many people lived in several towns and rural enclaves, was immediately north of the Flathead, so I was interested in how bears were coping with so many people doing so many different things. In 2003, Clayton Apps and I raised enough funds to put GPS collars on grizzly bears near the Highway 3 corridor (Apps, McLellan and Servheen 2013) that runs through the lower Elk Valley. This highway can get 7,000 vehicles a day during the summer, but averages about 3,200 from April to November. The Canadian Pacific Railway, which parallels this highway, has between eight and 16 trains each day.

I put 14 GPS collars on bears in the Flathead, and Clayton and I put an additional 32 on bears just north of the Flathead in the vicinity of Highway 3. These collars accurately located the collared bears almost 100,000 times. With this huge number of locations, and the additional complexity in the ecosystem due to all the people living there, Clayton embraced the challenge with his equally complicated multi-spatial scale, multi-causal variable analyses. Understanding what he does on his computer is nearly impossible and describing conclusions is not simple.

First, people who use GIS for analyses of the implications of roads on wildlife no longer use the simple and easily understandable measure of *distance to a road*. Instead, they use *road density*, or the number of kilometres of road in a one square kilometre circle (or square). At each pixel on a computer screen, the total length of all roads in the surrounding circle is measured, and this number is linked to the latitude and longitude of the pixel. The computer goes back and forth, pixel by pixel, across the study area like a moving, circular window, recording the road density around each pixel, and thus forms a road density map, or what is called a road density layer.

Our expanded study area now included all kinds of roads, from a major highway to narrow, mostly brushed-in 4x4 routes. Complicating things more, for example, is that a small dirt road close to the town of Fernie will get far more traffic than a similar dirt track 80 miles (130 km) from pavement in the back corner of the Flathead. Having a road density layer without accounting for huge differences in traffic volume could be misleading. It would have been great if we'd had traffic counters on every road segment in this area, but there are hundreds if not thousands of segments, so this was not realistic. To add traffic volume to the road density layer, Clayton used a network analysis to build a *road-use model*. This model incorporated many factors such as road quality and average vehicle speed, distance over this varied network from a human population centre, size of the population centre, and even the probability that people in various sized towns and cities would go from their homes into remote areas. The result was an estimate of the expected number of vehicles per day on all roads in the extended study area. Now we could weight road density with expected daily traffic, to obtain a more meaningful measure across an area with such varied road use.

As I described earlier, habitat conditions must also be accounted for, because roads are not randomly located with respect to habitat. Clayton doesn't use real, mechanistic habitat units because they are not mapped over large areas. Instead he uses many (33) indirect measures that are correlated, to various degrees, with real ecological habitats. Rick Mace, who was the first to use some of these indirect measures on grizzly bears, called them *pseudo habitats*. Somewhat like road density, pseudo habitat categories are not really recognizable when hiking across a valley, but they can be spotted by a different-coloured hue on a computer screen. Just try explaining these in the field to a forester or road layout engineer; they'll give you a frown and think you've spent too much time alone in the digital wilderness.

Clayton's analyses suggest that some remote-sensed, pseudo habitat variables and terrain features had a larger influence on bear locations than did roads and other forms of human use, although roads did have an effect at all spatial scales. Across the expanded study area that included towns, highways and railways, the influence of roads was most notable at the broadest,

16 square mile (42 $km^2$) spatial scale; bears were found most often in broad landscapes with low road densities and little traffic. Bears showed a slight reduction in their use of these in areas like the Flathead Valley bottom that had fairly high road densities but little traffic because they were so far from town. Bears used areas with similar road densities less often if closer to towns where traffic was higher. But, if bears happened to be in a broad landscape with a high road density, they were only slightly more often found in areas with lower road densities than the average areas. In general, Clayton's complex analyses found that roads had an effect on bear behaviour at all scales, but the effect was greater at broad spatial scales than finer scales. Also, roads had a greater effect when they were closer to towns because there is more traffic on these roads than on similar roads far from towns.

Between the simpler analyses that I had done in the 1980s and Clayton's sophisticated analyses 20 years later, plus a lot of other recent results from research done in Montana and Alberta, a clear picture emerged. Bears use areas near roads that have at least 20 vehicles a day less than they would have if the road were not there. But does this displacement really matter? Or, in other words, does it have implications for population size or trend?

**IN MY FLATHEAD ANALYSES,** I had measured displacement from roads only during the spring and fall because there were no roads going through higher-elevation, burned-off areas where huckleberries were abundant and where bears spent most of the summer. Perhaps bears were more easily displaced during spring and fall because foods at that time of year were relatively abundant but of lower quality, so there was little or no cost to being displaced. Perhaps they could find all the food they needed far from roads, so why feed close to roads? What would the bears have done if roads had gone through the major berry fields where most bears fed intensively to put on the fat needed for hibernation? Displacement in these habitats might have been particularly important for a high-density population like bears in the Flathead where they were near carrying capacity, or in other words, there were enough bears competing for a limited amount of food to affect their reproduction or survival. Bears in the Flathead do noticeably deplete the berry crop in places. We did a small experiment that compared berry abundance every ten days between bushes available to bears and bushes kept away from bears in barbed-wire exclosures. We found bears ate about half the berries in the first three weeks of the berry season in a productive berry field – berries are not an unlimited food source.

I could only guess that displacement from roads would not be as great in berry fields because the cost of avoidance would be high, but I could not test this in the Flathead because there were no roads crossing old burns where huckleberries were common. I could, however, test the effects of another very noisy, mechanized human activity in huckleberry fields: helicopter-supported seismic exploration (McLellan and Shackleton 1989a). Although there had been exploration for oil in the Flathead for decades, Shell Canada got serious in 1980 and began exploring for carbon dioxide. They wanted to use $CO_2$ to force it down into existing wells in Alberta to push the oil from the rock and thus recover much more from adjacent wells.

Seismic exploration involves drilling about 100 foot (30 m) deep holes in the ground every few hundred yards along a straight line that often runs for miles across the valley. At the bottom of each hole, a high-energy charge like dynamite is placed. Then wires with sensors are strung along the line. When the underground charges are detonated, the sensors measure the various shock waves as they penetrate the earth's surface, and from these, the geophysicist estimates what is going on way down deep. In flatter terrain, the seismic lines are made with bulldozers and excavators that simply push in a temporary road for drills and equipment to be moved by truck. In steep terrain, the lines are cut with chainsaws, and the workers with their drills, explosives and sensing wires are moved with light (Bell 206) and medium-sized (Bell 205, 212) helicopters.

In 1981, 1984 and 1985, long before I caught any bears from a helicopter, Shell ran helicopter-assisted programs across a five square mile (13 $km^2$) huckleberry field (49.08 -114.36). Because this area was not roaded, I had previously built a trail network throughout the four drainages that covered the berry field, so I could efficiently hike through the mountains to track bears. For about a week each of these three years, helicopters were busy in the air for an average of 260 minutes per day, as they flew back and forth along the seismic lines moving equipment. At this time, helicopters also made about 35 trips each day back to the staging area, where they would land and wait for drillers to finish each hole. I suspected that this level of very noisy activity should displace bears even from important habitat such as a major huckleberry field.

I divided the five square mile berry field, plus the area beyond, into three zones. Zone One was the seismic line itself and 500 metres (547 yards) on either side. Here, the helicopters were most active. Zone Two was 500 to 2000 metres (547 to 2,187 yards) from the seismic line, provided there was not a mountain ridge that would block the sight and sound of the work. Helicopters crossed this zone every day but not nearly as often as they flew over Zone One. Zone Three was further than 2000 metres (2,187 yards) from the seismic line, or sometimes closer when mountain ridges blocked the direct line of sight or noise. For each year, I compared where the bears were located before, during and after the seismic activity. The hypothesis I was testing was: *bears would use Zones 1 and 2 less during the seismic work than either before or after the work.*

I tracked two adult females, Elspeth and Melissa, during this experiment, as well as subadults Knut and Jennie. When I pooled all locations of these bears, they used the three zones the same before, during and after the seismic work. Of the 11 comparisons of individuals by year, there were only two cases where zones used were different among the three time periods. In 1984, Melissa had two cubs (Laurel and Hardy). I never found this family in Zone One along the seismic line during the activity, but I did find them there before and after the activity. During the activity, I found the family in Zone Two on 11 of the 15 locations.

One day I spotted Melissa and her two cubs on an open hillside about 1,500 yards (1.4 km) from the seismic line. I found a good spot to sit, took out my binoculars, and watched them and the helicopters for an hour and a half until the bears slowly wandered out of view. During this period, there were ten helicopter flights along the line and four underground charges were detonated. When the helicopters flew by 1,500 yards (1.4 km) away, Melissa lifted her head for three to 15 seconds before going back to eating huckleberries. On two of these ten occasions, she didn't lift her head at all. I recorded her head-down and feeding 81 per cent of the time during this period, which is about the same as the 86 per cent of the time when I recorded her activities when there were no helicopters during the same year. The detonations sounded to me like distant rumblings and the bears showed no observable reaction at all. Melissa was not displaced from seismic activity the following year either, when she was without cubs.

During the seismic activity, subadult Jennie used Zone One along the seismic line as often as she had before and then after the seismic work. But she used Zone Two less and Zone Three more than either before or after the activity, which was likely due to displacement. What I observed was that Jennie had been using Zone One a lot and was sleeping there in the forest when the helicopter activity gradually moved towards her. After seven minutes of intensive helicopter activity about 100 yards (91 m) from her, she finally got up and two and half hours later had moved almost two miles (3.2 km) away and out of the drainage. The following morning she was six miles (9.7 km) away and a long way from any huckleberries. These comparisons showed that the hypothesis was not supported because the bears did tolerate a lot of helicopter activity when in the huckleberry fields. It also showed how important it was for me to be there *watching the action live*, and not only interpreting location data.

**SINCE THIS EXPERIMENT WITH SEISMIC EXPLORATION,** I have captured hundreds of grizzlies by darting them from a helicopter. It is very obvious that in the open country where we can spot them, grizzly bears react to helicopters far more vigorously than do black bears. Black bears may look up, but they almost never move unless we are close. In open country, most grizzlies run when we are within about 500 yards (457 m) but stop if we continue past at 120 miles (193 km) an hour and go on our way. Although it was noisy when the helicopters passed half a mile (0.8 km) away, the bears in the berry field did not appear overly threatened by them. If uncomfortable, the bears moved off just far enough to not react further. But when the Bell 212, which is a big machine compared to the one we use for capture, slowed down and hovered to move drills near where Jennie was snoozing in the forest, she had had enough and wandered off.

**AN ANIMAL'S REACTION TO A DISTURBANCE** is not always what we might expect. Like most people, I thought that the louder the activity, the more an animal would be frightened and flee; and helicopters are extremely loud. But this is not always the case. The greatest reactions to people that I have observed occurred when people were not noisy but quiet. I once had a very clear and somewhat intimate evening with a deer that made me realize that our noisy machines are not always what really frightens some animals.

During the winter of 1985/86 I made a little extra money by helping a friend, Keith Simpson, with a moose and deer study. We were catching mule deer in netted box traps on a winter range just above the town of Peachland, in BC's Okanagan Valley, where a major highway was going to be built. These deer were easy to catch, but we didn't want to leave them in the traps for more than a few hours. So before dinner we would set the traps using a snowmobile. After dinner we would get back on the snow machine and check the traps and process any deer we had caught over the previous two hours. Although mule deer are not that large, they can be nasty in a trap. If you're not careful, they can smack you with a strong kick, or they may hurt themselves lunging into the net. Veterinarians like drugs, and one suggested I give them a tiny bit of sedative to make life easier for both deer and biologist. So I poked the captured deer with a jab stick (an injection syringe on the end of an extended ski pole) before we dealt with them.

One evening, I jabbed a deer, but it ended up being smaller than I thought and it almost conked right out. We processed the animal and put on a radio collar. I wasn't a deer biologist, but I had been told that, since deer are ruminants with a big, multi-chambered stomach full of ruminating foods, we should keep them on their chest with their head up while they recovered from drugging. Having their head up would keep the food, liquid and gases that were fermenting away in the rumen, or main part of their stomach, down there where it all belonged; if they were left lying on their side, the food could bubble up and then get sucked into their lungs. So I knelt down with the deer. I had my right arm around its back and down so my hand was under its chest. My left hand was under its jaw, holding its head up. Keith took off on the snowmobile to check the other traps.

It was dark and very quiet. I could see the lights from the town of Peachland far below and more scattered lights down along Okanagan Lake. I could feel every breath and every heartbeat of the deer. After half an hour, I was totally in the groove of the deer's rhythm; breathing and heartbeat. Then I heard the snowmobile coming back. The machine got louder and louder as it approached. Keith stopped about 100 feet (30 m) away and turned off the engine. There had been no change in the deer. But when Keith put his foot down and I could hear the quiet squeak of his boot on the dry snow, the deer's heart immediately raced to an amazing rate and a millisecond later it sprung up, broke my grip and bounded off into the night. The response was overwhelmingly clear. The deer had no reaction to the snowmobile. It was just a loud sound that was new to the species over an evolutionary time scale, and the individual deer I held that evening had no doubt heard snowmobiles often over the winter so had become totally habituated. The sound of a foot on the snow, however, reached back deep into the evolutionary history of not only mule deer but cervids in general. This quiet sound, whether from a person, cougar or wolf, clearly meant death could be close at hand. The deer reacted instantly.

**I HAVE RECORDED REACTIONS OF GRIZZLY BEARS** to me on many occasions (McLellan and Shackleton 1989b). Most often these have been when I'm in a vehicle and they are on or near the road, but also when I'm on foot but near our camp or near a road. But I've also recorded their reactions when I bump into them in the mountains where there are no trails and where people rarely if ever go – I have never seen another person when I have been away from a road in the Flathead. Although almost all adult Flathead grizzly bears run when I drive by in a vehicle, they don't run too far, as they seem to know that vehicles are limited to roads. The strongest responses are always when I'm hiking in remote locations without trails. There, bears almost always run off, and although they may stop running, they usually keep going for a few miles. On several occasions I've watched them climb over 1,000 vertical feet (300 m) to crest a mountain ridge and head off into a distant valley.

An animal's reaction appears to depend on the evolutionary importance of the stimuli and its intensity or distance away. On top of this, an individual's reaction will be modified by what it learned from its mother and what it has learned since being on its own. Most animals, even large carnivores like grizzly bears, seem to have an innate fear of humans that they don't have for other large animals, such as horses for example. People walking in remote areas where human use is rare appears to be frightening to most bears, and they flee. But there are exceptions. Some bears do not seem to be afraid of people even in very remote areas. These bears give me the *willies* and it's me who flees.

Understanding the change in behaviour called *habituation* is important for bear conservation. Habituation happens when an organism learns to reduce or even eliminate its response to a frequent and predictable stimulus that has no negative or positive effect on them. Habituation is highly adaptive because reacting to something that is common but has no effect would be a great waste of time and energy. With bears, habituation can be multi-generational, or a lack of concern can be learned and thus passed from mother to offspring. In addition to habituation, there is *food conditioning.* For bear conservation, this behaviour is also extremely important. Food conditioning occurs when a bear gets a food reward from people, even if the people are no longer there, such as someone leaving some half-burned steak T-bones in the firepit at a campsite. The bear learns to associate food with people or even with the smell of people, and the association of food and people develops. Food conditioning is more problematic for bears than is habituation because a food-conditioned bear seeks people and places where people often leave food, whereas habituated bears simply treat people as if they are not even there. To combat habituation or food conditioning, aversive conditioning or punishment has been often tried, but with varying success. When a bear is habituated, aversive conditioning can work. But when a bear is food conditioned, it's usually too late to change its behaviour, and eventually the bear will likely be shot. People who attract bears, for example by leaving the T-bone in the fire or having a couple of chickens in their yard, may be contributing to the death of bears even if the bears are killed much later and far away in someone else's camp or yard.

## 12.1 HIGHWAYS TO HELL

Not only may roads displace bears from valuable habitat, but major roads such as highways may stop bears from crossing, particularly when associated with towns, rural settlement and railways. Some bears do habituate to the steady, predictable traffic along a highway. But those that spend that much time near a highway are often killed by a car or train, or are attracted to someone's residence and get into a conflict, and are moved or even shot by a conservation officer.

If bears fail to move safely across transportation corridors, then populations can be fragmented, or large populations can be split into smaller ones. Small populations usually have serious conservation problems for a variety of reasons, including inbreeding issues, or unlucky chance events such as the few adult females having male-only litters. But a major problem of small populations arises because of basic geometry that we learned in high school and might even remember; the area of a circle (pi multiplied by half the diameter "squared" or *pi r squared*) increases at the rate of the *square* of the diameter, while the perimeter (pi times the diameter) increases at the *same rate* as the diameter. Or, to put this back into the world of conservation, small populations have a lot of perimeter, where bears must interface with humans, for the area of secure habitat. Larger populations have a lot more area of secure habitat for the amount of perimeter.

In the mid-1990s, a mature, or perhaps I should say an older undergraduate student showed up at the Yoho to Glacier National Park study that I was working on with John Woods of Parks Canada. Michael Proctor was extremely keen on doing field work. He seemed bush-wise and could be trusted to come home safe each evening, so we let him join our team. Within a couple of years, Michael was lining up to do a Ph.D. on the effects of transportation corridors and associated settlement on continental-scale fragmentation of grizzly bears. Using allele frequencies of DNA from over 3,000 grizzlies, he found that rugged mountains with large icefields in coastal BC, Alaska and southwestern Yukon reduced gene flow, but not as much as did the settled transportation corridors near the Canada–US border. Michael's work showed that Highway 3, which wound its way across southeastern BC, had reduced grizzly bear movements more than anywhere else in North America that he could measure, except between Yellowstone and the population in northwestern Montana. Yellowstone has been isolated for many decades.

Do grizzly bears cross highways? That's a simple question that lots of people can answer because they have seen a grizzly bear cross a highway. A better question is not "Why did the grizzly cross the road?" but what proportion of the bears that live near highways cross them, how frequent are these crossings, and what factors influence crossings. Or, how much less do grizzlies cross busy highways than secondary highways? Do they cross more at night when it's dark and there is less traffic? Do they cross more often far from human settlements? Finally, do they cross more often where the broad-scale habitat is good on both sides of the highway? Answering these questions should help mitigate the influence of existing highways, and also into the future when traffic and human uses become busier and busier, as no doubt they will.

Clayton Apps and I used the location data from the 32 grizzly bears that we put GPS collars on near Highway 3 to answer these questions. These collars located the bear every hour, so from two consecutive locations, we measured the distance and direction of 73,000 hourly bear movements, starting and ending at known locations. At each of these *movement vectors*, we had the computer generate a matched possible movement of the same distance as the bear movement vector but in a random direction. Some of the bear movement vectors and some of the random vectors crossed a major highway. If the highway reduced the chance that a bear would cross, then *the number of random vectors crossing the highway should be larger than the actual number of bear movement vectors that crossed the highway.* For each pair of vectors, we also determined the crossing of secondary highways and industrial main roads, as well as the quality of associated habitat, visual cover and human use conditions. We used traffic counters on these highways and roads to determine the hourly traffic volume. We also knew the distances that bears moved each hour of the day when far from people, so we could separate the effect of traffic volume and time of day of crossing from a bear's natural tendency to move different distances at different times of day.

Eight male and eight female grizzly bears with GPS collars were located close enough to the main highway that they could have had at least one random vector cross the road. Of these 16 bears, only four males and three females did cross Highway 3 at least once. For secondary highways and industrial mainlines, 25 of 26 bears located close enough that they could have crossed actually did cross these roads at least once. Only Highway 3 appeared to block some individuals from crossing, at least over the time period that we were monitoring them, but of course they might have crossed either before or after we were monitoring them. For example, we tracked one adult female for three years while she raised two cubs just south of Highway 3. She was often located close to the highway, but she never crossed it, so it seemed like a barrier to her movements. But we know from our earlier DNA sampling project that she previously lived north of the highway. This female dispersed at least 12 miles (19.3 km) and crossed the highway to where she established a new home range. We don't know how many times she crossed the highway before she settled permanently on the south side. But she survived long enough to make this important movement that demographically and genetically linked the two populations on both sides of the highway.

Comparing movement vectors to random vectors and accounting for the other variables, Highway 3 reduced the odds of a bear crossing by 48 per cent. A 10 per cent increase in human settlement density caused a 51 per cent reduction in the odds of them crossing. A 10 per cent increase in broad-scale habitat quality increased the odds by 30 per cent. Secondary highways and major industrial roads reduced the odds of crossing by about 20 per cent, but for these roads, adjacent landscape features had little influence. As might be expected, these results suggest that many, but not all, of the bears cross the highway and most often cross where there is good habitat on either side, and where there is little human settlement.

When in remote areas, the GPS-collared bears moved furthest each hour between 5 a.m. and 9 a.m., and then again between 5 p.m. and 9 p.m. Traffic on the highway is low between 10 p.m. and 5 a.m. but the very lowest between 2 a.m. and 3 a.m. Bears crossed the highway most often between 9 p.m. and 1 a.m. So they didn't cross most often when they normally move furthest, nor did they cross when traffic was at its very lowest, but they

A cubby trap where logs are piled in a "V" shape that directs a bear to step in a spring-loaded foot snare while it is trying to get at the bait that we put in the back of the trap. Bears soon learn to pull the cubby down, so other ways of setting snares are often used. DAVID SHACKLETON

Using a "jab stick," an extended ski pole with a sturdy syringe on the end, to immobilize a bear caught in an aluminum "culvert trap." For grizzly bears, these traps were often built from steel road culverts so they inherited that name. DAVID SHACKLETON

(*top*) Helicopter pilot Clay Wilson and Michelle position a 550-pound male grizzly (post-hibernation, springtime weight) in the south coastal mountains of BC where Michelle did her Ph.D. field work. We called this bear BOB, an acronym for Big Old Bear.
AUTHOR

(*bottom*) Graduate student Fred Hovey and the author carry a young grizzly from a trap site in the Flathead because the mother bear was nearby. After processing at a safe distance, the bear was returned and rejoined the family soon after recovering from immobilization.
DAVID SHACKLETON

(*top*) Michelle and Charlie, at 8 and 6 years of age, keep a close eye on a young bear while the author discusses the procedure with media people who came along for the day.
DAVID SHACKLETON

(*bottom*) Michelle and Charlie, as teenagers, help out on a rainy Flathead day.
CELINE DOYON

(*top*) Michelle uses a "jab stick" to immobilize a large male black bear.
CELINE DOYON

(*bottom*) Michelle and the author weigh an adult male grizzly in the Flathead. Large bears can be lifted by one or two people using leverage. Michelle is keeping the bear's head out of the dirt as I lift.
CELINE DOYON

The author uses a bioimpedance meter with electrodes attached to the bear's lip and anus area to estimate the amount of body fat. CLIFF NEITVELT

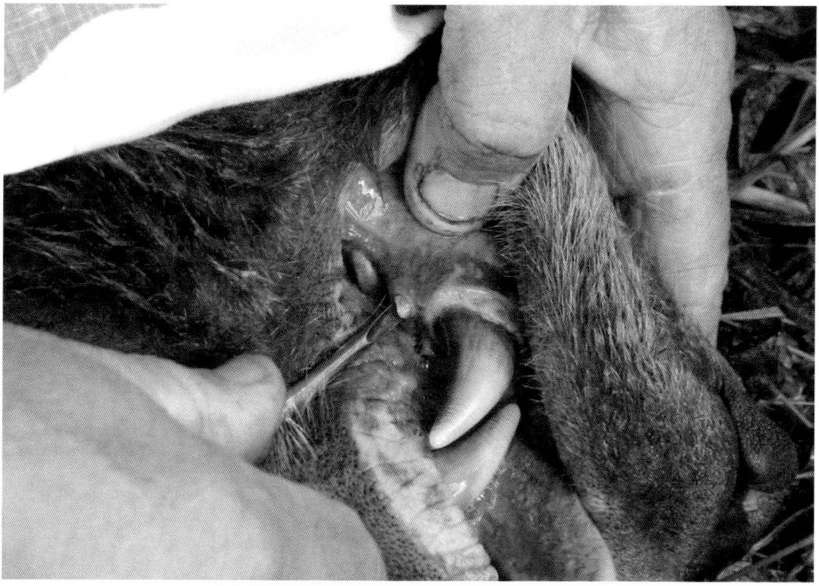

The author uses a dental elevator to remove a premolar that enables an accurate aging of the bear. Being a very small tooth and immediately behind the large canine, these premolars appear to have little use or are "vestigial." Bears evolved from true meat-eating carnivores, but as their diet became more plant-based, their dentition has been gradually changing to resemble many herbivores, with a toothless space between their cutting incisors and grinding molars. CHARLIE McLELLAN

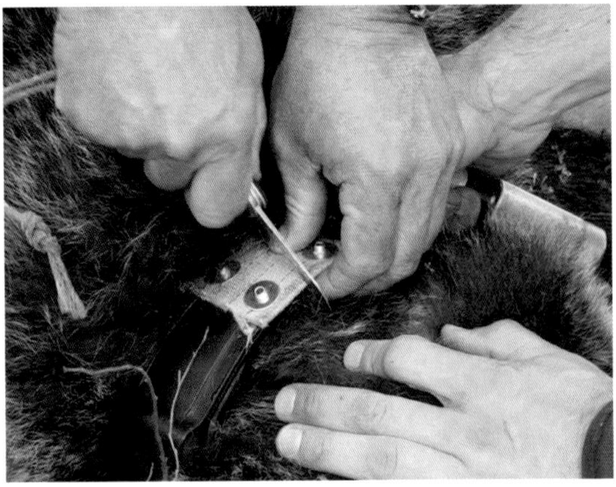

The author cuts the cotton fire hose "rot-off" so it will rot quickly and the collar will drop off this young bear in about one year. Rot-offs of various durability were placed in all collars put on bears. Not only do they greatly reduce the chance of rubbed necks, but they also ensure most monitoring sessions of a bear's survival end with a "known fate" – the collar dropped off and the bear was alive, or the bear died. Without rot-offs there would be far more cases of uncertain fates or not knowing if the collar's batteries wore out or someone shot the bear and destroyed the collar. Many unknown fates make the survival data pretty useless. STEVE ROCHETTA

Like us, bears have five "fingers" and toes. Grizzly bears have much longer and stronger "fingernails" than we do. These claws on the front paws of grizzly bears are used for digging out roots, bulbs and burrowing rodents, as well as digging their dens for winter. Claws on their hind feet are small like those of a black bear. DAVID SHACKLETON

(*top*) Collared bears were located from aircraft about once each week. Once GPS collars were invented and became somewhat reliable (2001), weekly tracking flights were no longer needed.
DAVID SHACKLETON

(*bottom*) Buzz, with his excellent nose and limitless enthusiasm, was used to follow the wanderings of bears in the late 1980s. He was never frightened of the sight or smell of black bears, but at first, even small grizzly bears would make him shake with fear. Finding enough goodies hidden in the fur of immobilized grizzlies soon changed his attitude. He learned to love grizzly bears and was so excited to be able to follow them.
DAVID SHACKLETON

(*top*) Celine, the lifelong unpaid volunteer, records plot data at a grizzly bear bedding site. As is often the case, this bed is in the forest just next to a productive avalanche chute.
AUTHOR

(*bottom*) The author measures Jennie when she was 2 years old while Charlie helps out as best he can. When she was 22 years old, using just a deep, chesty growl, Jennie warned an elk hunter that he was approaching her three cubs too closely and he should back off. The hunter just shot her instead.
CELINE DOYON

(*top*) Michelle keeping a 2-month-old black bear cub warm and happy while the author processes the mother in the winter den. Due to their larger size and unpredictable and sometimes aggressive nature, the author does not go into grizzly bear dens and, perhaps consequently, is still alive to tell you this.
CELINE DOYON

(*bottom*) The log addition that Celine, Dave Horning and the author built in 1984 to provide more space for the two kids. It remains in good shape 39 years later.
CELINE DOYON

(*top*) A bear mark trail, where bears step and often twist their feet in the same footprints, leading to a tree where many bears rub all parts of their body. Clearly, a lot of information about individuals in the neighbourhood is being shared. Bears sometimes mark very near people's camps, as this tree was (note the old plastic). We people just don't have the noses to really understand this form of communication.
AUTHOR

(*bottom*) A highly habituated mother grizzly bear at a popular bear viewing location on the BC coast where Michelle once worked as a viewing guide. An interaction like this would never happen in a wilderness situation where bears do not encounter people in the same places and doing the same actions day after day. Habituation can be intergenerational, as this cub will grow up with little fear of humans, at least when they are at the bear viewing site. The author thinks this person was very lucky a mellow mother bear came along.
MICHELLE McLELLAN

A yearling grizzly bear at McNeil Falls, Alaska, still nursing and spilling a lot of very high-quality milk. The author has seen three 2½-year-olds, that weighed over 200 pounds, still nursing and still making the "chuckling" sound of new cubs. AUTHOR

An avalanche chute that is rich with bear foods, and in particular cow parsnip, a favoured food in the spring. AUTHOR

Grizzly bear feeding sign in a very dense patch of cow parsnip. Bears almost never eat all the plant foods in a patch, but instead eat some and then move off, perhaps seeking a rare but very high-quality food such as a baby elk or deer. AUTHOR

Remains after a grizzly bear digs for glacier lilies and spring beauty. In the churned-up result, new plants will grow and be easy digging in the soft soil. It was hard to find bear scats in these areas, likely because these corms are highly digestible and most scats were buried in the diggings. MICHELLE McLELLAN

Cambium feeding, where a bear first bites across the tree and pulls the bark off, and then scrapes the cambium up and down with its incisors. This feeding often kills the trees and in places is a serious problem for the forest industry. AUTHOR

Black huckleberry is the major high-energy food in the Flathead Valley and many other areas in BC, Alberta, Montana and Idaho. AUTHOR

(*top*) Buffalo berry, or hooshum, is a major high-energy food for grizzly bears across much of their distribution, including the Flathead Valley. Berries are often clumped, so they can be rapidly ingested.
AUTHOR

(*bottom*) Charlie at 5 years old in a clearcut where sweet vetch grew in abundance. Bears dug roots in the soft, machine-scarified soil in this and a few other clearcuts. In this clearcut, a hunter who called himself "Grand Slam" shot a 2-year-old bear, highlighting the sometimes complex interaction between bottom-up and top-down population limiting factors.
AUTHOR

(*top*) Charlie at 40 years old in the same location in the clearcut. The sweet vetch only lasted for about ten years before being out-competed by other plants.
AUTHOR

(*bottom*) Looking out of a typical grizzly bear den that the bear had dug into the mountainside near treeline.
AUTHOR

A grizzly bear is about to leave a tuft of hair on the barbed-wire hair trap. The bear was attracted by rotted cow blood that had been poured on a pile of logs and moss in the middle of a "one-strand corral." Using DNA "fingerprints" and hair traps to estimate bear population size was first developed by the author and co-workers in a study near Revelstoke, BC, in 1995. AUTHOR

One of the several grizzly bear statues in the town of Revelstoke, BC, where the author and his family lived between 1992 and 2003. Between 1986 and 1995 at least 120 grizzly bears and 311 black bears had been removed (killed or relocated) from Revelstoke as conflict animals. The author and many others started the Bear Aware Society in 1995, and this led to reduced attractants and almost the end of grizzly bear conflicts (some issues with black bears remain). Other communities followed Revelstoke, which led to the formation of WildsafeBC. AUTHOR crossed when traffic was fairly low and at the time of night when, even in wilderness, they made some long movements.

As always, there are exceptions to how, where, when, and probably for what reason, bears cross a highway. An old female named Power was an exception in more ways than just crossing a highway. Her known movements were, as far as I know, unique for an old female grizzly bear that had never been captured and moved by conservation officers for getting into trouble.

**IN 2010, MY TRUSTY PILOT, CLAY WILSON,** and I were putting GPS collars on grizzly bears with Steve Rochetta, a district biologist in Squamish, BC, in the southern Coast Mountains just north of Vancouver. By 2010, Clay and I had caught several hundred grizzlies together from CYIP, his Hughes 500D helicopter. Although we kept improving our technique, we were pretty comfortable with how we went about our job. Steve and Clay were, in some ways, pretty similar fellows. Both were very competent in the bush. Both were strong and physical, and both had redder necks than me. For example, when Steve was a teenager, he played hockey and baseball in Ontario. Clay was a boxer and bull rider in Saskatchewan. Meanwhile, for west coast Bruce, it was skiing and track and field – what a comparable wimp. Steve hadn't worked with Clay before and I wondered how they would get along.

We spotted a grizzly in Rutherford Creek (50.276 -122.990), just northwest of Whistler, BC, a resort town settled by ski bums with highly variable net worth. The bear was on a very steep mountainside just above the water intake for a mid-sized hydro power project. We dropped down and landed the machine at the intake. Steve got out to lighten the load so the machine would be more agile, and off came the back door where I sat. A few seconds later Clay and I were searching for the bear again in a huge avalanche chute full of slide alder. Now slide alder is either a huge shrub or a small tree between ten and 30 feet (3 and 10 m) tall, but to protect itself from avalanches, it grows out of the mountain horizontally for most of its length before turning up towards the sun. It grows very thickly and can become almost impenetrable for a person because we walk upright on two feet. A bear, running on all fours, can put its nose down and run through it if they need to. While searching for the bear after dropping Steve off, Clay and I never saw it, but the moving alders gave it away. We backed the machine off, not wanting to make it run fast, but just keep it slowly jogging along.

"I'll take her to that small opening, you'll have a half second if we're lucky."

"Sounds good," and I flipped the speaker of my headset up and out of the way so I could aim the dart gun. With no door, my left foot hung out in space, I turned to prepare myself, and the wind blasted in when Clay banked the machine.

As the shaking alders got close to the opening, Clay pounced the machine. The bear came into the opening for just a second, but we were there and I shot.

"Got her, 8:15," and we pivoted, and swung back to not press her anymore.

We could see the alders moving from a distance. A few times we had to swoop in down low to turn her away from the forest where she would be very hard to follow. We could tell her movements were slowing down, even though we were far away.

"Should we check her out?" Clay asked.

"I think so, there's going to be a creek or two down there and I bet she's close to one."

Water and cliffs are my biggest worries. Although I've never lost a bear to either, Clay, the bears and I have had some adventures with both.

"Where did you last see the alders move?" I asked.

In the back seat, I often lost sight of the bear when Clay shifted the machine to catch favourable wind.

"I think right about here somewhere."

We hovered over the alders, but we couldn't see anything under the madly thrashing sea of moving branches and leaves.

"Let's back off, watch for a minute or so," I suggested, but Clay replied, as he usually does, "I'm sure she's down there, she must be out."

Here we go again, easy for him to say.

"Okay, let me out just above and I'll try to find her."

I grabbed my .30-06 pump action with a short barrel and iron sights and snapped in the clip with 220 grain bullets. I undid my seat belt and stepped out and down onto the skid. The wind blasted. I slung the rifle strap over my shoulder.

"I'm out of here in one second."

I removed my headset and tossed it back into the machine. I stretched one leg out along the skid, and in one semi-smooth motion, hung and then dropped into the alders thrashing in the wind-blast of the helicopter, hoping I wasn't landing on top of a half-drugged and very pissed-off grizzly. Clay spun the machine and dropped downhill about 50 feet (15 m), hovered as he always did to let me know where he thought the bear might be, and then he was gone.

"Easy for you to say," I thought as I was left alone.

I jacked a shell in the chamber of the rifle and put the safety on. It was very thick, and I was not yet standing on the ground but lying sort of sideways, tangled in alders. I liked it when he was gone because after all the helicopter noise, it was just so refreshingly quiet. I knew that I'd hear a bear long before I saw it, so when he and his deafening machine were gone, I could listen. Yes, we were over a small creek. Big enough to be a little noisy and, I suspected, to drown a drugged bear if all went wrong. I blocked out the sound of the creek as best I could and listened for panting; nothing.

I straightened myself. I got my feet down and my head up, and started to half walk, half swim, downhill on the alders. After moving maybe 15 feet (5 m), I stopped and listened. How many times have I done the old "listen for a pissed-off grizzly at 15 feet" routine? I always think of Clay's "she must be out" as he flies down, lands, gets out to put his door back on, before picking up Steve, while I try to find the bear, which may not be immobilized yet.

I wallowed in the alders another 15 feet (5 m) and listened. The sound of a creek yes, but no bubbling bear with its nose in the water. That's good. I wallowed on downhill, stopping every 10 or 20 feet (3 to 6 m) to listen. Finally, yes, there was panting, I was near now. I set myself as best I could in the alders and shouted, "Hey, buddy!"

Nothing but panting. Another bit of wallowing around bouncing on and under the alders and there she was, all tangled, head down but not in the creek. I had to get her ready for Clay to pull her out of this vegetative tangle and take her to a good spot to work on her.

My ski-touring coat was once bright red and easy for Clay to spot from a distance. It was now very worn, with duct tape over the tears and much less bright. But it has four good-sized pockets and in these I had what I needed to get the bear ready to get lifted out. Top right pocket was the eyeball lubricant, blindfold and electrician's tape. Even putting a dab of lubricant in each eye was difficult in our respective positions. Putting on the blindfold was worse, but after fighting with branches and her heavy head, I got it on. I then taped around the blindfold to make sure it stayed on and wouldn't let wind blow in. Out of my lower left pocket I took out the hobbles to put her feet through. This was also difficult in the alders, as both bear and I were mostly suspended. So far, I could see only one of her four feet.

I could hear the helicopter in the distance coming back, so I took my radio out of the top left pocket.

"Things are good," I said into the radio.

"Great, where are you?"

"I'm jumping on an alder, so look for movement."

He must have seen the movement, as the machine pulled right up over and hovered for a few seconds just uphill from where I was. I put my hands over the bear's ears and tried to shield her from the wind that was blowing the alders all over. I knew this was the test. I had seen it before – almost everyone failed. After hovering just uphill for a few seconds, Clay then moved the helicopter across the slope and briefly hovered about 100 feet (30 m) away. I knew this was to tell me of a spot where he could hover low enough to pick us up. He then took off to hook up his long line. A minute later, Steve was stumbling and rolling through the alders. It looked like Steve had passed the test.

Now with two of us, we could move the bear enough to get the hobbles on and then could work on getting her free from the alders. I took my collapsible saw from my bottom right pocket and started to cut a few alders so we could pull her straight up. I knew Clay wouldn't wait for a radio call but would guess at how long it should take for us to get her ready, then just show up with his long line. He always shows up when I'm not quite done. It's always rushed. And, now I could hear him coming up from the valley.

Clay uses a light rope made of Kevlar that he says is much stronger than a steel cable of comparable size. He had put a radio collar on the end of the line as a weight to keep the rope hanging downward. It was still waving around but I knew, even though mountain winds were blowing, that he would put the rope right in my hand from 100 feet (30 m) above. It waved around, but slowly dropped to where I grabbed it. We hooked the hobbles into the carabineer, and gave Clay the wave. The bear started to go upward and out of the mess of alders we were still in. I grabbed my rifle, unloaded it and put the clip back in my lower right pocket where it belongs next to my saw. After catching hundreds of grizzlies, I've still never had to shoot a bear with anything but a dart gun. Steve and I started stumbling and swimming through the alders towards the spot where Clay had hovered. I knew he would be back there in a couple of minutes, so we wallowed through the slide path as fast as we could.

Sure enough, we were not yet out of the alders when Clay was heading back for us. Just ahead, he hovered the machine a couple of feet above the ground on very steep terrain. I stumbled my way around the front of the machine to get to my side. I had been working hard in many awkward positions for over half an hour, and the white sticky stuff was now sticking to my lips. I was getting tired. Clay gave Steve the nod. Steve stretched up to the door handle, put his foot on the skid and hoisted himself up. Then, standing on the skid, he opened the front door and got in. My turn, but I had a rifle and had to get into the back seat, which, due to the steepness of the mountainside, was much higher up. I grabbed the handle and the rifle at the same time, and kicked my foot up and onto the skid and hoisted myself up. I then had to walk back along the skid but was pleased to see Clay had not put my door on yet, as that would mean a longer walk to the end of the skid and fooling around with the door. I got in, put on my seat belt just as we peeled off down the mountain. I never did get my headset on. The bear was lying on the green lawn at the hydro power intake. We processed the female we called Power and headed back home to where Celine and I now live, snuck in under one of our huge cottonwood trees, and landed in our backyard just before it was really dark.

I have a lot of respect for both Clay and Steve, they are both very competent, but I was interested, so later asked Steve about the test. "We just roared right up and started to hover, and all Clay said was 'Bruce needs help,' that's it. No suggestions or directions on what to do. So, I opened the door and jumped out."

**POWER WAS AN OLD FEMALE.** She'd had cubs in the past and we knew from their genetics that several of these were still alive and having cubs of their own. Many bears in the expanding population in the mountains west and northwest of Whistler were now her descendants. But in 2010 and 2011 she travelled alone. In the two years that her GPS collar located her every hour, she lived in the mountains and never came down into the main valley where the highway, railway and busy town of Whistler were located. Then, at 4 p.m. on September 28, 2011, she started moving downhill and directly towards the Whistler townsite. By 7 p.m. she was under a transmission line, and 60 yards (55 m) from an expensive home (50.116 -122.987). She spent an entire day along the transmission line and close to houses by a lake, but she wasn't located in anyone's yard. By midnight, she moved into the Nicklaus North golf course, where she spent time on the fairways, but during the day she slept in a small patch of trees in the middle of the course (50.137 -122.963). By 8 p.m. on September 30, she moved to some trees right behind

Nesters' mini-mall. Most of October 1 she spent just behind the shopping area, often 20 yards (18 m) from buildings (50.1285 -122.9555), and at least once crossed the highway back and forth. After hanging out for a while near a main junction in Whistler where Lorimer Road crosses Highway 99 (50.123 -122.960), she crossed the highway again just before 11 p.m. She didn't hang around much longer, and by 2 a.m. on October 2, she was heading up Fitzsimmons Creek and into the big mountains on the east side of the valley. She could have crossed the highway and valley quickly in many places where there was no human settlement, but she didn't. She could have quickly moved through Whistler, but she didn't. Instead, she spent three days in a populated town. Perhaps it was human foods that attracted her, but she was found more in small pockets of natural habitat, not at dumpsters. Whatever the reason for spending three days in town before crossing the valley, her adventure had just begun.

Power was heading directly away from her home range on the far side of the valley and the town of Whistler. She kept mostly to the high country while she wandered southeast, usually on rock and ice, far above treeline. She crossed several large glaciers, full of crevasses. After three weeks, she came out of the high mountains and crossed the Pitt River near to where it flows into Pitt Lake (49.550 -122.609). Salmon were spawning in this river, but she only stayed for a couple of hours. By Halloween, a month after she crossed through Whistler, she was 45 miles (72.4 km) south and only 14 miles (22.5 km) from the edge of the metropolis of Vancouver. Maybe she was the first grizzly bear to ever, in the history of the earth, cast her eyes on or sniff the air from almost three million people. For whatever reason, she then turned back northward. Her route north was far to the west of her southern jaunt. She skirted the east side of Whistler on November 13 and crossed the highway just north of town on November 14. She had now returned to her home range, and there she denned for the winter. She stayed in her old home range at least until her collar stopped working in 2012. What that month and half walkabout was all about is anyone's guess. I have followed dozens of adult females for many years, and Power is the only one that went for such a vacation. Conflict animals that have been captured and then moved by conservation officers sometimes wander over huge areas as if they are lost and looking for home, but Power had never been moved. She went on her walkabout all on her own.

## 12.2 THE END OF THE ROAD

Roads displace some bears from nearby areas, resulting in a loss of usable habitat. Highways can stop some bears from crossing and therefore moving into new areas. But the main effect of roads is simply allowing lots of people to effortlessly access grizzly country. All of these people, usually unknowingly, may contribute to habituating bears to human presence. Some of these people may be sloppy with their coolers or garbage, and thereby food condition some bears. A few will have guns and some of these will kill bears (McLellan et al. 1999; McLellan 2015).

Honey and Brandy, the 1-year-old sisters who were frequently seen along the main North Fork Road in Montana, were highly habituated to vehicles and people. Although it wasn't a highway, there was enough traffic that the young bears got used to vehicles and learned to ignore them passing by. Using my tracking equipment, I located Honey on September 26, 1979, in the creek bottom just beside the road. I went back to Montana to find her on October 1, but found only the ear-tag transmitter that we'd put in her ear. It had been cut off and tossed into a huge pile of brush that a crew clearing the roadside had stacked up to burn. Neither of the two young bears was ever seen again. Rumours circulated that the sisters, who only weighed about 110 pounds (50 kg), had been shot by a movie "extra" who was there for the great Hollywood flop *Heaven's Gate*, which was partly filmed in the Flathead in 1979. Losing two young female grizzly bears was a nasty blow to the recovering population, but their death was just the start of my education on the real effect of roads on bears.

A year and a half later, Rushes was shot by a hunter from the road. The next spring, Josey, one of Blanche's 1979 daughters, was shot by a hunter while she was feeding on the side of a road. She was only 3 years old. The next spring, little Knut was once again hitchhiking on the side of the road when a hunter stopped and shot him. He too was 3 years old at the time and, like Josey, a pretty small bear. I asked the proud but very fat grizzly hunter if he planned on making a toilet seat cover out of the cute, tiny hide.

That same spring, one of the local outfitters had a client from Cincinnati. When I met them along the road, the short and dumpy client introduced himself. "They call me Grand Slam."

Grand Slam is a term some hunters call themselves when they have killed all four varieties of North American wild sheep. That spring, a 2-year-old collared bear we called Sue and her two brothers had just separated from their mother. They had remained together and had been digging sweet vetch roots in clearcuts along a major side road. Well, Slam no doubt had a reputation in Cincinnati that he had to maintain, so he really had to get his grizzly. The young bears were pretty habituated to vehicles, so his .375 Weatherby Magnum downed one of the 2-year-old brothers pretty easily from 100 yards (91 m).

"I know he's not a huge bear, but I liked his colour," Slam told me.

I'd guessed he weighed 130 pounds (59 kg) before his blood had drained over the ground – maybe 120 (54 kg) after.

All the collared bears that had died by 1986 had been shot from a road. But none affected me like the one gunned down on my birthday that year. I was loading my mountain bike in the back of my pickup when an elk hunter stopped and asked, "Did you see the dead grizzly on the Border Road?"

I asked him a few specifics, thanked him and jumped in my truck and took off for the Border Road. I had located Blanche and her latest batch of three yearlings near there that morning and had set up an activity monitor to record her resting patterns. There was no grizzly bear hunting season in the fall, but there were lots of guys driving around with high-powered rifles looking for moose, elk or deer. Some would be itching to shoot something.

I drove fast, as I had a bad feeling about what I would find. Sure enough, there was the body of the old mother bear that had had nine cubs over the seven years that I had followed her pretty well every day. She lay about 15 feet (5 m) from the ditch. A pool of blood was seeping into the hard-packed surface in the middle of the road. A small tree on the side of the road had a fresh scar where a bullet had grazed it, and showed that the shot came right down the road. There were empty shells on the roadside about 75 yards (69 m) away. I looked for dead yearlings, as they would have been right by her side when it happened, but I didn't find any. Her carcass had not been touched. She had simply been shot from the road and left near the ditch. There was no apparent reason for killing her. That some person had killed a mother bear when she had three yearlings with her for no reason made me realize, once again, that there are people with totally different ethical standards driving the backroads of the Flathead and elsewhere. Can we really hope to conserve grizzlies and the ecosystems they are part of with these kinds of people in our society? Let's hope their numbers are in rapid decline.

Many other bears that I was tracking were killed from roads in similar ways. Jennie had three cubs when a deer hunter needlessly gunned her down on the side of a road. The hunter told me that he was walking by and Jennie gave him a warning growl from 30 yards (27 m) away as bears usually do. The hunter could have simply turned and walked back from the direction he had come, but he didn't. He just shot her. Sally was shot next to a road by a moose hunter when she had two cubs, Elizabeth was shot when she came into an elk hunter's camp, and Genevieve was with a cub when a hunter shot her while she ate grass on a roadside.

**THE DEATH OF ANOTHER MOTHER GRIZZLY** and the fate of her two yearling sons provides a good example of the relationship between roads, people and dead bears. A graduate student, Fred Hovey, and I were driving along a straight stretch on the main Flathead road late one afternoon during the fall hunting season (49.1063 -114.4952). About a mile ahead I could see an animal on the road, moving slowly but very erratically, often back and forth across the road. I thought it must be a bear so we stopped the truck and I took out my binoculars. It was a person. As we drove up, the guy got right down on his knees on the road. Both of his hands were full of bullets, so he held his rifle by pressing it to his chest with his forearms. He was scratched, a little bloodied on the face, and his camo jacket was torn. Tears ran freely down his face. He was shaking. He had both of his bullet-full hands up towards his chin as he prayed for us to stop, and we did.

"They, they, are huge, they, there are lots of them, please, please help, they are coming after me, I know it, they are after me." He sobbed out the words.

"What's after you?" I asked.

"Huge bears, they're after me, I know they are," he said, shaking.

"Get in, buddy, they won't get you in here." He got into the truck but kept breathing hard, crying and shaking.

"Where's your camp, buddy?"

He could no longer talk, but just pointed a shaking finger. I drove on.

He soon pointed to a side road and I drove in to where a wall tent was standing; smoke was still coming out of the chimney. I stopped and got out, and we helped him out of the truck. We went into the tent and sat him in a lawn chair next to the wood stove. His body was still trembling uncontrollably.

"You going to be okay?" I asked.

"Yes, yes, yes," he panted the word with each breath. "I think, think so."

"Okay, we'll come back in a few hours and see how you're making out," and we left.

When we did return it was after dark. A gas lantern was hissing away, casting shadows through the big tent. He was still sitting in the same chair blubbering away and shaking. His two hunting partners were there, but they had no sympathy for him. They were calling him a fat, yellowbellied chickenshit, and were laughing at him. But we learned three things from them. First, they told us where they had dropped him off for his hunt. Second, that he might have shot at one of the bears he was babbling about. Third, he was a detonation expert in the Canadian Armed Forces.

The next morning, I went with Fred and his helper, Randy, to investigate. Sure enough, as we drove up to where Yellowbelly had been dropped off (49.1069 -114.4881), we spotted two young grizzlies, one light blond and one darker. We found two .30-06 casings on the side of the road, and a pool of blood on a seismic line that crossed the road about 50 yards (46 m) away. We followed the blood trail and found the dead mother bear about 100 yards (91 m) further in the forest.

I had no doubt that Yellowbelly thought he was a goner and shot the bear in perceived self-defence. His nervous system had melted down and he was left a sobbing, shaking blob of soft tissue. But, at 50 yards (46 m), I doubt he was yet in real danger. Likely, he could have simply backed off and the bear would have not found him a threat to her yearlings, who were old enough to look after themselves.

Fred, Randy and I set a couple of snares near her carcass to catch the yearlings so we could learn how they would make out without their mother. We caught the dark one that night, but we missed catching the lighter one, which we thought was more likely to be a female. This was disappointing because I liked to monitor females more than males. Females had smaller necks compared to their heads, so we could have them carry a collar for a longer period of time, and they did not go on huge wanderings like young males do, and so would be less expensive to track. And of course, female vital rates are what are needed to understand what the population is doing. So I wanted to catch the light-coloured bear if we could.

"Let's put him in the culvert trap. A nice safe place for him to recover and we can use him for bait."

So, while I processed the male bear, Fred and Randy drove off to get the aluminum culvert trap. It was a little eerie processing the young grizzly alone and so close to his mother's corpse while knowing that the blond sibling was nearby. A couple of times I leapt to attention because of a noise in the forest, but I don't think anything was really there. When the boys returned, we put the culvert as close as we could, but it was almost 200 yards (183 m) away.

To move a bear that is small enough to lift, I wrap my arms around its chest and lock my hands together, and then stand up. A second person grabs the bear's hind feet to keep them from dragging. I hoisted the bear, Randy grabbed his feet, and off we went towards the culvert. As Randy and I packed the bear, Fred packed a light PVC plastic tube that contained a ski-pole jab stick we used to inject drugs instead of a dart gun. The bear was not really small and the terrain was covered with shrubs and, here and there, a few dead trees lay in our path. I was breathing heavily and certainly feeling the exercise when Fred called out, "Here comes Blondie!" I couldn't see or turn with the bear in my arms.

"How close?"

"Twenty feet!"

Two seconds later, "Ten feet!"

"Freddy, smack her with the tube."

"Two feet!"

"Smack her, Freddy!" I was preparing my bum for a bite. Fred had the PVC raised and gave her the "Yahh!" roar, and it must have worked. He didn't give her a whack and I didn't get my butt bit. The bear in my arms was really feeling heavy. We got to the culvert and let him down – he ended up weighing 165 pounds (75 kg). We called him after Yellowbelly's real name, but here I'll call him Frank to protect the guilty.

We set and baited two snares. We filled the water basin that was welded inside the culvert trap so Frank could have a drink when he woke up, and then went back to camp for the night. The next morning Frank was wide awake in the culvert. Blondie was there beside the trap, but not caught in a snare. Blondie didn't run, but just wandered away. Fred put a bucket of lightly rancid fat on the ground near the culvert. I loaded a small dart, opened the truck window, and we sat quietly. Within half an hour, Blondie was back, sniffing the air. It approached cautiously but within a few minutes, pop – I put a dart right in its rump – and the bear ran off into the forest. Now with the drug we used in the 1980s, the bear might still be mobile for ten minutes. We quietly waited. We were in a flat lodgepole pine forest with no creeks around, so the bear was safe to get sleepy and settle down wherever it ended up.

After ten minutes, I set off tracking the bear. I didn't take a rifle, as it was only a yearling, and like the brother, would be under 200 pounds

(91 kg). It was difficult tracking because, between the bear and ourselves, the grass had been trampled in many places. Luckily, it didn't go far. Unluckily, it wasn't out, but got up and staggered off.

I went back and loaded an even smaller dart, and resumed the hunt. I walked slowly, knowing the bear wasn't far. Sure enough, I hadn't gone 100 feet (30 m) when Blondie got up from behind some trees and again staggered off. I couldn't shoot a dart through the trees. How long to wait? Too soon and the bear wouldn't settle back down. Too long and the drugs might wear off and it would never settle down.

In five minutes, I very slowly and quietly went after Blondie. I was close when the bear got up, but before it could get away, pop – another little dart in the rump. Fortunately, the bear only went a few dozen yards before lying down again. Unfortunately, it was a brother, not a sister. All that and we decided there was no point in putting a collar on the second bear, when they would likely travel the rest of the autumn and spend the winter denned up together.

With their mother dead, Frank and Frank's brother did travel together. Like all other independent yearlings I've tracked, they were often seen on or next to a road and became habituated to people and vehicles. The following spring, they separated and travelled alone.

Celine and I were away from camp tracking bears and a friend's 17-year-old sister, Anne-Marie, was staying with us and keeping an eye on Michelle and Charlie, although they were now 11 and 9 years old, almost old enough to look after themselves. Charlie was playing around with his homemade bow and arrows and Anne-Marie was washing her hair in the river when Frank arrived. At 250 pounds (113 kg), Frank was much more than Charlie was hunting for with the little sticks he had whittled for arrows; Charlie bolted for the cabin, but the door, with an old, finicky knob, was locked. Charlie's screaming at his sister to open the door finally startled Frank enough that he jumped into the river and started swimming. Anne-Marie's head was down in the water rinsing when Frank paddled by about three feet (1 m) away; she didn't even notice him. He was a bold bear, and bold bears don't live long in a place like the Flathead.

Sure enough, three months later he came into a popular Forest Service Recreation site that was full of elk and deer hunters. They were much less tolerant than we were, and someone shot him. The following month Frank's brother was stirring up trouble by just being in the very small community of Polebridge, about 25 miles (40 km) south of the border. He was caught by the authorities and sent to the bear lab at the Washington State University.

In the end, the mother and both of her sons were removed from the ecosystem. The family was wiped out. The people were there because roads gave them easy access.

FINALLY, MAGGIE WAS JENNIE'S DAUGHTER and Melissa's granddaughter. I tracked Maggie from her birth in 1989 to her death when she was 21 years old. She had three yearlings with her when she died in mid-October 2010, when a lot of hunters were in the Flathead after a deer or elk. Her body was not right next to a road but about 100 yards (91 m) away. She was too decomposed for us to tell for sure if she had been shot, but we were very suspicious – she was close to a road, and bears very rarely die for other reasons without obvious trauma such as being killed by another bear or a major rock slide. We were so suspicious that my new partner in the study, Garth Mowat, took a metal detector to where Maggie had been killed as soon as he could get into the valley the following spring.

"I checked out Maggie a few days ago. I couldn't find any metal, but I'm not sure the machine was working right. But it was really weird. The site had been visited and moved around. It was really pretty strange. There was still a foot of snow or so, but what was eerie was that something had dug up her bones, like lots of bones, and placed them on top of the snow all around. The tracks were too melted out to really tell what they were from, but it wasn't like there was any meat to be scavenged, and they were placed on top of the snow, not just messed up like a scavenger would do. It was sort of like what we hear elephants sometimes do with the bones of dead ancestors. Wonder if it was her yearlings coming back to pay their respects. Wish we would have put a camera on her."

OVER THE YEARS, 18 FEMALE AND 12 MALE radio-collared bears died while their collars were still working and I was following them. I also had good evidence that four other radio-collared males had been killed, but I didn't have real proof such as a dead bear. Of the 34 bears that died or I suspected had died, 28 (82 per cent) were killed by people, and only six (18 per cent) died of natural causes. I knew exactly where people killed 25 of the collared bears, and 17 (68 per cent) were on a road and five others (20 per cent) were within 170 yards (155 m) of a road.

Until 2018, grizzly bear hunting was legal in BC, but only where it was thought there were sufficient numbers of bears for a sustained kill, which was across most of the province. Hunters living in the province could put their name in a computerized hat to be drawn for a limited number of grizzly permits. Hunters from outside the province were required to hunt with a registered outfitter that had a territory with exclusive guiding rights. The five outfitters in the Flathead each had a small quota, usually less than one bear per year. Between 1980 and 2015, there were more grizzly bears shot by hunters for the area (i.e., per square mile) in the population unit that included the Flathead and adjacent Wigwam drainage than were killed anywhere else in BC. Yet of the 23 collared bears that were killed by people on the BC side of the study area where there is legal grizzly bear hunting, only 11, or less than half, were killed by legal bear hunters. As with Frank and Elizabeth, several were killed at hunter camps, while others like Jennie, Sally and Frank's mother were shot because they scared a hunter. Others, like Blanche and Sven, were shot for no apparent reason; certainly they weren't threatening anyone. Of the 11 collared females that were killed by people in BC, only four were legally shot by grizzly hunters.

All collared bears that were killed by people for reasons other than legal bear hunting were within 120 yards (110 m) of a road when shot, yet most of these deaths would not have been recorded in the government's dead bear database if I hadn't been doing the research. Comparing the ratio of bears legally killed by hunters to bears killed by people but for other reasons, between my research sample of animals and the uncollared bears in the government database for the BC Flathead, suggested that only 12 per cent of the non-hunter kills would have been reported. Since 1995, the reporting rate may have improved to 21 per cent. Although I'm sure most managers have a hard time believing it, I had been telling them for years about the large number of bears that people kill that they don't know of, so they did include an estimate of unreported kill when calculating the number of hunting permits allowed.

When their collars were on and working, 28 bears were killed by people, while only six died of natural causes. I don't know the details of how an old female we called Alexis died. In the late autumn when the snow was a couple of feet deep in the mountains, I located her from an airplane in a steep but lightly forested basin, high up in the mountains. Her collar was on mortality mode, suggesting it hadn't moved in six hours. I assumed she was hibernating because it was late in the year, she was in typical denning habitat and sometimes bears are so still in their dens that the bubble switches in their collars don't move for many hours. I was wrong. The next spring, all I found were Alexis's scattered bones. There is a chance that she too was shot by a hunter, but she died in a remote area when only deer were open for hunting. It is unlikely that anyone was deer hunting where she died.

Melissa was the largest female I caught in the Flathead and had ten cubs in four litters over the 12 years that I followed her. She died when her den collapsed. For years Melissa had dug her dens in one of the southern basins on Miskwasini (49.061 -114.337) and Kenow mountains, but for the winter of 1991, she dug her den (49.0639 -114.3546) in a mostly open scree slope, on the north side of the mountain. Without plant roots to hold the soil and rocks together, it eventually collapsed on the sleeping bear.

Two collared adult females, Janice and Sylvia, as well as young Mitch, were killed by other bears. Mammie, whom I tracked from birth, died at 28 years of age. She seemed to have been walking across a meadow when she just lay down and died. She, and perhaps Alexis, were the only ones that died peacefully without major trauma.

In summary, almost all bears that were old enough to carry a radio collar ended up killed by people and almost all of these were on or very near a road when they died. Most were not killed by legal bear hunters but for other reasons. Very few of these non-hunting deaths would have been recorded in the government bear mortality database. So it is easy to conclude that roads that access wild country represent a major issue for grizzly bear conservation, not only because most bears end up being killed on or near a road, but also because many of these deaths are unrecorded. From government databases, Clayton Lamb has estimated that there are over 900,000 km of roads in British Columbia – enough to go around the earth more than 20 times.

CHAPTER 13

# FAMILY IN THE FLATHEAD

## *Predators and Weirdos*

Since we began our work, the Flathead has increasingly become well known for its very healthy populations of all BC's native large carnivores. These include not only grizzly and black bears but also wolves and mountain lions. There are also meso- or mid-sized carnivores such as wolverine, coyotes and lynx roaming the valley, as well as many smaller carnivore species. Although it might have been safer and less stressful to raise a family in the wilderness than in a big city, our neighbours with big teeth certainly kept us vigilant.

Compared to bears, wolves are very cautious animals. Sightings from our camp were infrequent. Once every couple of years we would see a lone wolf trotting in and out of the forest on the far side of the river, and a few times I've seen packs of seven and eight in open grassy meadows maybe 200 yards (183 m) from camp, but not often. Similarly, we have heard packs howling in the distance, but never close by. They no doubt know of our camp, and perhaps see it as our territory and avoid us. I've seen them more often when out tracking bears, but even then they are cautious. Over the years I've been within spitting distance of all the large animals in the Flathead, but I've only been within five yards (4.6 m) of a wolf once. I was alone and sitting quietly when a lone black wolf trotted by. I don't think it saw, smelled or heard me.

Although wolves are cautious, they are seen much more often than mountain lions. I think I've been lucky to have seen a couple of dozen of these large cats over the years, and none were close to our camp. Celine, however, almost bumped into one, or at least that's how she tells the story.

"I was slowly riding the old bike down the road, just enjoying myself, and I started picking up speed going down a hill. My body is shaking on the bumps and rocks, so I'm just focusing a few feet in front of me and then, there he is, a huge mountain lion on the side of the road. I put on the brakes as hard as I can and they do nothing except make a big squeaking noise. This scares the lion and he jumps across the road. He was so big with such a huge tail that he covered the entire road. Holy smoke did I get my exercise I tell you pedalling hard all the way home."

The only time we knew of a mountain lion being very close to our cabin was when a hunting guide's 14-year-old daughter, Tracy, had been visiting. She had ridden her horse down to our camp and tied it to some trees on the edge of a meadow near the cabin. After spending a few hours with Celine and the kids on the beach near our cabin, she and her dog wandered back to the horse. Just past the cabin, she bent down to pick a pretty wildflower. When she stood up, there was a mid-sized, maybe 100-pound (45 kg) cat, three feet (1 m) away staring into her eyes. Tracy's dog took off running and the cat instantly ran it down and smacked it over with its paw. Tracy bolted back to our cabin, screaming to alert Celine. The dog was unhurt. After, when Tracy had calmed down, she said she thought the young cougar wanted to play more than eat. Lucky, or one of them would have been lunch. She felt safer once in the saddle, high up on a horse, and she rode back to her camp.

Although it was certainly not a daily event, bears, and particularly grizzly bears, came through our camp much more often than did the other large carnivores. Our cabin was right along the river, and there were good feeding areas for both sweet vetch and buffalo berries just upstream and downstream. Over the 40 years we worked out of the camp, we never had a bear conflict or a bear get into garbage, because we really don't have any garbage. Almost all foods that were not eaten can be composted a long way from camp, burned or washed clean. When I butcher a deer, elk or moose, I usually don't leave bones in the meat, but if we do have any, we freeze them in our propane fridge/freezer and take them elsewhere. But bears did come a few times each year, and only once was the situation really concerning.

It was autumn and the river's water level was very low and moved smooth and slow. Big yellow cottonwood leaves were falling, and those in the river drifted slowly downstream. Michelle was 3 years old and playing along the river catching leaves with a stick. Celine was cleaning the old VW van while 1-year-old Charlie was playing in the dirt just outside the vehicle. Celine stepped out of the van and spotted Eddy, a 220-pound (100 kg), 4-year-old male grizzly on the far bank of the river about 25 yards (23 m) from Michelle and staring at her; he could have crossed the shallow river in two seconds.

"Michelle, come here right now," Celine stated firmly but not loud enough to agitate the bear.

"Not now, I'm busy," little Michelle replied.

"Michelle, get here now, there's a big bear right across the river." Michelle kept playing in the water.

As protective as a mother grizzly, Celine grabbed the kindling axe from the splitting stump and ran down the bank. She is less than 110 pounds (50 kg), but probably would have split Eddy's skull in two if he came for Michelle. Michelle was dragged up the bank and into the van, then Charlie was tossed in, and they all drove off.

Eddy was a bold and likely food-conditioned bear. I caught and collared him that night. He then worked his way south of the border where there are many rural homes. Being food conditioned, he associated good grub with people. Eddy just walked into people's yards during the day and ate whatever he could find. I always located him among homes for two weeks, and then his radio signal disappeared forever.

"Yes, didn't we hear some gunshots in the middle of the night a while ago, dear?"

"Yes, but it's hard to say what direction they came from." Rumours were out that Eddy was gone.

**OF ALL MY CLOSE ENCOUNTERS WITH FREE-RANGING** (i.e., not captured) large predators, including being within 15 feet (5 m) and sometimes much less, of wolves, mountain lions, grizzlies and black bears, one of my most memorable was a golden eagle. I was sitting on a rugged limestone ridge, far above treeline, with my legs dangling over a small, southward-facing cliff and watching Mud and her cub through my binoculars. After an hour or so I stopped watching to rest my eyes and arms. I spotted a golden eagle, wings set, a little lower than I was, but floating up towards me riding the updrafts caused by the sun warming the mountain face. Then, of all places, it pulled up on the ridge about three feet (1 m) to my left. It slowly tucked away its wings. We sat together, side by side, for maybe five seconds. I was totally motionless, hardly even breathing. I tried to focus on the bird by just rolling my eyeballs. He wasn't really clear in my peripheral vision, so I very slowly moved my head just an inch. Then the eagle's eye facing me opened really wide and the big bird exploded from the ridge, dropped a bit and then soared away.

**MORE THAN LARGE CARNIVORES,** people are of greater concern for parents raising kids, whether you live in a huge city or 50 miles (80 km) from your nearest neighbour. Distant places seem to attract odd people. Maybe Celine and I are a little odd, but nothing like a man we called the Nut. As one good old Fernie redneck told me one day, "That fella really needs fixing." I never met the Nut, and I'm half glad I didn't. But I still wonder what he was all about.

I first noticed that someone odd was spending time in the valley when the kids were about 3 and 5 years of age. I was tracking a bear past the old 1940s oil derrick near to where Joe Perry and I had first caught Rushes seven years before. There were two leaky old shacks near the derrick, but they were full of pack rat filth and grime. But evidently, someone had moved in. There were two old, broken-down kid's swing sets in front. Only one had a swing that might have worked if the second chain was hooked to the seat. There were a few small wrecked bikes, toy-sized baby buggies and a variety of other toys that obviously had been scrounged at a garbage dump. But what was really striking were all the dolls. There must have been a dozen or more rubbery pink dolls. Few were intact. Most had a leg or an arm missing. None had any clothes, and they were nailed to trees all around the camp. There were also half a dozen doll's heads on sticks in the ground or on branch stubs on the trees. It was extremely weird.

The door of the old shack skidded on the floor when I lifted it and pushed it open. I stepped in. There was now plastic on the windows that let in enough light that I could at least see. The shack had been cleaned up a bit, but it was far from clean. A bunk had been made in one corner, and on it was a filthy old stained mattress and an equally disgusting sleeping bag that also must have come from a dump. But what was really strange is that there was a pit toilet, or what would have been called an outhouse, except this one was *inside* the shack – why go outside into the cold just to take a crap? This was all too weird. I left to track a grizzly. At least bears are clean animals just trying to make a living in the wilderness, not mentally messed up like this person was.

I mentioned my discovery to Celine that evening. She was horrified. "Holy smoke, that's way too weird. You're not making this up, are you?"

"Of course not, how could I dream up such a weird story?"

"I don't mind grizzly bears and wolves, but I don't like crazy people, they creep me out. Did you see this nut case?"

"No, he doesn't live there. He must just come down once in a while with a pickup full of junk that he scrounges at some garbage dump and then hangs it in the trees."

The next day I took Celine to the Nut's camp. We drove up slowly and made sure he wasn't there. We certainly didn't want to let him know we had children.

"Why don't you stay in the truck with the kids? I don't want them near this weirdo's place."

The way she said this suggested that this level of sickness could be a communicable disease that could spread and infect innocent people. Celine got out and headed straight towards the shack. It didn't take her a second to realize that I hadn't exaggerated. There was no need to exaggerate, with all the dolls and doll heads staring down at her. She went inside.

I could only stay in that dirty little shack with the inside outhouse for a few seconds before I got so uncomfortable I had to get out. Celine had been in for a while and I was starting to wonder what was going on.

"You guys stay in the truck. No fighting. I'll be back in a minute," I told Michelle and Charlie.

I put on the parking brake, took the key and shut them in. I walked to the shack.

"You cleaning this place up a little more or what?"

"Did you see dees books? He is one messed up pervert. Let's get out of 'ear."

"What about the books?"

"Dey are about sex tings avec kids and pervert shit comme dat."

Celine was upset, her accent was fully back and she was mixing French with English. Yes, she was upset.

THE NUT WASN'T THE ONLY HUMAN WEIRDO haunting our world in the wilderness. The following week, we heard that some crazy mountain men near Yellowstone National Park had kidnapped a young woman and taken her into the mountains to make a bride out of her – reminiscent of the classic cartoon of the caveman with the club over his shoulder, pulling a woman by the hair. These crazies then shot and killed someone who tried to rescue her. They then left the woman and took off into the mountains and now were on the run. We heard that they hadn't been caught for weeks so we assumed that they were still on the move. It didn't seem possible that the police hadn't hired someone who could track out these guys by now if they were still in the Yellowstone area.

Celine, who should have been a detective, and I, just for fun, would make up theories of what crazy, murdering mountain men would do. I thought they would head to Alaska, because all fully crazed mountain men must think Alaska is the place to go. It's only a little over 300 miles (483 km) from Yellowstone to our camp, and that couldn't be very far for a real mountain man. Even I could likely wander that far in a couple of weeks, and I'm not a mountain man. I don't wear buckskin; I'll even wear Gore-Tex if I get it at a good price at the Salvation Army. And if they did head up through the Rockies towards Alaska, they would probably go up the west side of Glacier National Park and right up our driveway to our cabin. I had fun making up such stories, but I think Celine took them too seriously.

"You must give me a new lesson with the rifle. I don't like these weird perverts near us."

"Sure, we'll go over it again. We'll have to anyway for hunting season. But you've really got to practise, which means shooting at some targets to get used to the feel of having a rifle in your hands."

I had gone over firearms with Celine before because she wanted to hunt too. She would buy her licence and a deer tag every year, and occasionally take my rifle and hunting pack, and head off from camp for a few hours. Sometimes I would drop her off in a spot where I had seen some deer. I would take the kids and track bears before picking her up.

"I don't see any blood on your hands."

"No, I didn't see any deer, but there were some fresh rubs that looked more like deer rubs than elk rubs. I sat and waited in a good spot with a good view for maybe an hour, but nothing showed up."

Many years later she confessed that she never would have shot a deer, even if she saw a buck standing broadside. Then again, she never would have seen one because she told me that she would sing loudly when hunting to scare bears away. She really used hunting as an excuse to go walking for a few hours alone in the forest while I looked after the kids.

One day an RCMP officer stopped by for coffee with the conservation officer. We talked of the Yellowstone mountain men, as well as the Nut who pooped in the corner of the shack that was just up the road.

"What should I do if one of those crazy men comes into my home and try to get my kids?" Celine asked. I thought that was an interesting question, so added, "Should she shoot them in the leg just to stop them?"

"Well, tell him you have a gun, and if that doesn't make him go, put the slug right between his eyes," was the answer. "Just make sure there is a knife in his hand when we show up. There isn't a jury in the country that would convict a mom protecting her two little kids way out here when they see photos of that guy's camp."

This was way too graphic for both of us. I never did go over the operation of the shotgun with Celine, and I often took my rifle with me.

**I HAVE NO IDEA HOW THE NUT FOUND OUT** we had children, but it was likely important to him, because he did find out. I was out following bears and Celine was at camp alone with the kids. Luckily, they were inside when she heard a vehicle approaching. Up came an old pickup that she didn't recognize.

"Charlie, Michelle, you get back in the bedroom," as she grabbed them and led them into the back room.

"Be quiet like a mouse." The door of the addition was closed but not locked. She slid the bolt to lock the door between the trailer and addition and went to the back room near to where the kids were. The truck stopped and a man got out. She had never seen him before. He walked around a little, checking things out. He then came to the addition door and knocked. Celine and the kids stayed quiet. He knocked again.

Then he went back to his truck and took out an old, small purple bicycle and put it in the yard. Then he grabbed a green Tonka truck and left it too. He got in his pickup, turned it around and drove back down the driveway.

After he left, Celine waited a while, and then went out. Charlie and Michelle were so excited to see the new toys. The Tonka truck was fine, but the bike was junk and I didn't want to spend the effort and money to get it working. Clearly the Nut knew where we lived, that we had kids, and no doubt that I was gone every day. Luckily we can hear vehicles approaching, and the trailer door opens outwards, so once the bolt slid shut, it would be difficult to get in. But Celine also spent a lot of time on the beach where I had built a big shade structure, and where the breeze along the river kept the mosquitoes down.

Two years later, I noticed the Nut had moved to another place in the valley and much further away. He moved most of his stuff, plus a lot of more recent junk, to a plywood shed that once housed a big diesel generator at one of Shell Oil's recent drilling camps. The shed stank of diesel fuel and grease, but that was likely better than the indoor outhouse in the last shack he was in. Then, a few years later, the Nut moved again. He was back in a different 1940s oil drilling camp. He had all the toys and dolls hanging on his walls and in the trees, but this time he had painted the entire inside of one shack a very light blue and painted the other shack a light pink. Then, after about five years in the valley, he vanished.

CELINE AND THE KIDS OFTEN CAME ALONG with me when I trapped and tracked bears, and not because she was afraid of the Nut or other weirdos. They came because they enjoyed getting out and being involved with the bear work. Besides, they were very helpful, even essential at times, because someone had to keep an eye on drugged animals while they recovered. After all, where is the last place you would want to be lying while recovering from a general anesthetic? Likely not next to a pile of rotting flesh in the wilderness full of grizzly bears, black bears, wolves, cougar and wolverine. If we could, we usually moved the drugged bear away from the trap site and put it in a place such as a small stand of trees in the middle of a clearcut, where an encounter with another carnivore would be very unlikely. Usually, however, this was not possible because the bears were too heavy to move and we couldn't drive close enough to get them into the truck. With many traps out, Celine and the kids were often left, at a safe distance, to babysit drugged grizzly bears until they woke up. And this usually was uneventful and went well.

Rick Mace and I caught Jennie in one of the first traps we checked, but we had several others set far back in the mountains. Celine had planned on driving the old Toyota to an area more central to where we were working. There was a little beach along Sage Creek where she and the kids, who were 4 and 2 years old at the time, could play and wait in case we needed help. Once Rick and I were finished with the bear, I went to get Celine so she could watch Jennie recover while Rick and I went on to check the rest of the traps.

Jennie was lying in the shade of some trees on the far side of a very rough log-landing. Celine parked about 50 yards (46 m) from the bear. As is often the case, it was not possible to get the vehicle parked for a rapid escape as well as to have a clear view of the bear. Celine would have to make a sharp turn to get out fast, and even then had to bend her neck or use the mirrors to see a bit of the bear lying behind the uneven ground.

After finishing checking the traps and Rick tracking one bear and I another in the mountains, we got back to camp near dinnertime. The Toyota was there, so all must have gone well. Celine and the kids were on our beach as usual on a fine day.

"How was Jennie?"

"Jennie was first very boring, but then way too exciting," Celine answered. "We sat for an hour, maybe more, and nothing happened. I got out once in a while and shouted, but Jennie just sleeps and sleeps. Then, the kids are both on the floor of the jeep having a great game. I'm reading my book, sort of looking at Jennie a bit, but she was just sleeping. Then Michelle takes Charlie's toy and he screams a big mad scream. I go to grab Michelle and then I just catch a little motion in the jeep's mirror. I look, and here comes Jennie full blast at us. Lucky I left the key in the jeep, and when I turn it, rur rur rur, before the engine start, I see Jennie try to turn away and she flips over, and there's dust all over just behind me. Lucky again that the crappy old jeep starts the first time for a change, and lucky again I don't stall it when I take off out of there as fast as the jeep can go. Kids were bouncing up and down and all over."

It wasn't Celine's first surprise with a fast-waking bear, nor her last. But for the past 20 years, we have been using a different drug and the bears don't wake up fast, so monitoring their recovery has few exciting moments.

**I CAUGHT AGGIE IN MID-OCTOBER** when she had two cubs. I processed her and changed her collar. It was a cold day, so I left her in the open under a weak sun behind thin clouds. I found a comfortable spot, leaning back against a tree to watch her from about 75 yards (69 m) away. Her cubs were there, just lying next to her sleeping body. It was very quiet and peaceful in the forest. After maybe half an hour, both cubs jumped up, ran, leapt and stuck like Velcro to a tree and then scrambled up. I too jumped up, just as a large adult male grizzly came towards Aggie. I raised my rifle and let go a shot aimed far above the bears and it echoed across the Flathead Valley. The big male bolted instantly. Luckily, I didn't have to decide who should live and who should die. I'm sure that my monitoring of Aggie's recovery saved her life and her cubs.

Two decades later, again in late October, Celine, Michelle and I were checking traps. I drove and Celine sat in the middle. We stopped at a landing where there was a trap just over a big pile of earth on the far side. I grabbed my rifle and Michelle and I went to check the scene. As we approached, a big male grizzly came right at us.

We calmly backed off.

"You want to dart him or be backup?" I asked. Michelle replied, "It's your rifle, you're backup."

I mixed the drug, as Michelle prepared the dart. She loaded the dart gun and we went back towards the bear. I jacked a shell in and put on the safety.

"He'll charge again, get ready."

"I know, I'm ready."

Out he came. Pop – she shot him perfectly in the thigh. We went back to the truck. He was a big bear; we estimated him at 500 pounds (227 kg). While we waited in the truck, I told her of when Joe Perry, the cowboy, and I caught Rushes for the first time. He too was a big male in the fall. But Michelle had caught a lot of grizzly bears with me and by now I'd caught many hundreds. Both Michelle and I were alert, but we were no longer winging it like I had been with Joe decades before. We weighed big Grant using a small digital scale and he was 535 pounds (243 kg). His tooth age came back and he was 20 years old, and one of his alleles at all 15 loci matched one of Aggie's, suggesting that this big male was one of those little cubs I had saved by waiting for Aggie to wake.

CHAPTER 14

# THE FLATHEAD GRIZZLY POPULATION

## *How Many Bears Are There?*

"So how many bears are there in the Flathead?" is the most common question I'm asked from the few people I meet when I'm out doing field work. This question is simple to ask but difficult to answer. But to test my hypothesis that the salvage logging, gas exploration and hunting would be harmful to the bear population, I needed to measure how many bears lived in my core study area. And to compare this number with other places, I needed to estimate bear density, which for bears is standardized by the number of individuals in a 1000 $km^2$ area.

Knowing bear density is important for both wildlife managers and research biologists, so people have been trying to measure it for decades. When I started my bear work in the 1970s, biologists would spend the summer hiking around with binoculars trying to identify bears that they thought were different individuals in an area such as a national park or portion of a park (Mundy and Flook 1973; Martinka 1974). They realized it was difficult, particularly in forested areas where bears were rarely seen, to reliably identify individuals by just looking at them. Grizzlies are not a walking bar code like a tiger, nor do they have distinct colour patterns like a whale's tail or a wolverine's belly. Although females with one, two or three cubs certainly helped, and many males have obvious battle scars that can be seen, particularly in a sharp, close-up photograph, many females without cubs often look very similar. I thought Elspeth had a uniquely yellowish face until her daughter Mammie grew up and looked the same, and then so did Tina, her granddaughter. Melissa looked a lot like her daughter Jennie, granddaughters Maggie and Irene, and great-granddaughters Liz, Genevieve and Becky. I could go on, but a lot of females look alike, and many young males are hard to tell apart as they wander over huge areas. Without a fairly clear mug shot of their face for an analytical comparison (Clapham et al. 2020), it's really difficult to reliably identify individuals, particularly in a densely forested area, by observation alone.

Even in the 1970s biologists knew it was very unlikely that all bears that lived in a forested area would be seen, and several bears that looked alike could have been counted as one, so the result of their counts was called a minimum estimate. In reality, though, the number of bears counted may not have resulted in a minimum density estimate but rather an overestimate. Because of their large home ranges, some bears with home ranges that overlap the census area boundary may have been counted even if they spent only a small amount of time in that area. If the census happened to have been done in the adjacent area, then the same bear could have been counted there as well. The larger the bears' home ranges and the smaller the census area, the greater geographic closure was a problem, and minimum estimates may have been even higher than the real number.

So there were, and still are, two main problems when estimating bear density. The first problem is knowing what proportion of the whole population was counted. If the final count was, for example, 20 different bears, then was this half of the true population, or maybe three-quarters? The second problem is knowing what proportion of the time these bears spend in the census area. In a small area, it could be a small proportion of their time. In a very large area, this proportion of time would be higher, but not all of the time for all bears, unless the area is on an island, or has an isolated population. There is a trade-off between these two problems. A small census area has a big problem with *geographic closure*, while it is more difficult and costly to estimate the proportion of the bears that were counted in a very large census area.

In the Flathead, I was primarily interested in testing the effects of intensive salvage logging and gas exploration on population density as well as on the mortality rates and causes, and on reproductive rates. The industrial activity was mostly in the southern portion of the valley and focused in the wide valley bottom dominated by beetle-killed lodgepole pine. This 85 square mile (220 km$^2$) area was my core study area, and where I really wanted to know the number of bears that would be there, on average, every day of their active year. Although I trapped bears outside of this area to learn many aspects of their ecology, I put more effort into the core area.

In the first four years (1979 to 1982), I caught and radio-collared ten females in the core. When first caught, they averaged 7.5 years of age and ranged from a cub to 18-year-old Blanche. Over the next 34 years (1983 to 2017), I caught another 29 females in the core area a total of 110 times. When first captured, they averaged only 2.8 years of age and ranged from cubs to 7 years old; 22 of the 29 were 3 years old or younger. I also caught and collared another 44 females a total of 72 times outside of the core area. I am confident that after the first four years of work, I had caught all the adult females that lived in the core study area at that time, and from then on, I only caught their offspring or immigrating younger female bears.

Unlike with females, which have relatively small home ranges, I don't think I caught all the adult males that came into my core area. In the first four years (1979 to 1982), I caught 14 males in the core area and, when first caught, they averaged 4.9 years of age, with the oldest 15 years. Although I stopped collaring all males in 1990 and actively avoided catching them, the average age of the 46 males when they were first caught in the core area between 1983 and 2017 was 4.1 years, not much different from the first four years. I caught the odd old male in the 1990s and even 2000s, but these lived most of the time in Alberta or Montana. Although I caught 61 males in the core area and another 39 just outside the core, I did not catch all of the males that had home ranges overlapping my study area; their home ranges were just too large.

For females, I had solved the first problem, or what proportion of the population I had counted. I was counting pretty well all of them. This was not true for males, so I was underestimating their numbers. The second problem of determining the proportion of time each bear spent in the core study area was significant because the area was small. But, because I had put radio collars on all males before 1991 and all females for over 40 years, I estimated the contribution for each individual by the proportion of their locations that I recorded from the airplane or GPS collar that were in the core area. Only bears that were never found outside the core area counted as a whole bear. The rest were fractions of bears (McLellan 1989). For example, if half of a bear's locations were in the core study area, then this individual would add half a bear to the total tally. Because adult bears have fairly stable home ranges from year to year, I could use all locations I collected on them over all years that I tracked them to estimate their individual contribution. If their collars fell off or batteries wore out, but they were later recaptured, then I included them each year, even when they weren't collared. If they were never caught again or if I knew they had died, then they were no longer used in the population estimate.

I estimated the annual density from 1980 to 2011 in the core area for adult females and their dependent offspring. The density of adult females increased from 13 in 1980 to 26 per 1000 km² in 2003. When the cubs, yearlings and 2-year-old cubs who were with their mothers were included, then the density in the core area increased from 31 in 1980 to 56 per 1000 km² in 1990, and fluctuated around the latter estimate until 2004.

When the known males were added to the total density estimates, the highest density was 79 per 1000 km² in 1991, but after that, data on males were incomplete. I also found that the number of females and their dependent offspring began to decline in 2003. This decline was during a decade-long (1998 to 2009) severe reduction in huckleberry production. One major berry field on the edge of my core area has yet to recover to anywhere near the production levels in the 1980s.

**WHEN I FIRST ESTIMATED THE DENSITY** of bears in the Flathead there were few estimates from elsewhere in the world for comparison, and the other estimates at the time usually didn't deal with the two problems of measuring density outlined above. But my estimates were higher, and usually much higher, than those from other areas, except for coastal Alaska, where bears had access to huge numbers of spawning salmon. I knew my density estimates were correct because they were based on real bears that I had personally caught, handled and tracked day after day – the bears were there. But my estimates were only for the small area of intense logging and gas exploration, so maybe the size and location of the area was a problem. My observations over the years suggested that there were fewer bears in the northern half of the valley than in the south where I was mostly working. I would have liked to have estimated the density over a larger area, at least the whole Flathead Valley in BC, which covered 612 square miles (1585 km²). But I couldn't use my method of *catch and collar every bear* because I would have had to catch dozens more bears every year.

In the 1980s and 1990s, Sterling Miller and other Alaskan biologists were using a method called mark-resight to estimate grizzly bear density over larger areas, comparable in size to the entire BC Flathead (Miller et al. 1997). This method involved catching and radio collaring a sample of grizzly bears. After the radio-collared bears had time to move around and mix, the *resight team* would fly around in an airplane looking for bears. When they saw one, they would record whether or not it was radio-collared. At the same time as they were resighting the bears, a *tracker*, in a different airplane, would locate all the collared bears so they would know how many of these bears were actually in the census area that day. The proportion of the collared bears in the census area that were seen by the resight team was called the *capture probability*. Because they knew the number of marked and unmarked bears that had been seen by the resight team as well as the capture probability, they could calculate the total number of bears in the census area that day and thus measure density. For example, let's say they first caught, radio-collared and released 30 bears. A month later they did their resighting but then the tracker found that only 20 collared bears were in the census area that day; ten had moved outside that area. The resight team did their flight and saw ten collared bears and 50 uncollared bears. Since ten collared bears were seen out of the 20 collared bears that were in the census area, the capture probability would be 0.5. Assuming that uncollared bears had the same capture probability as collared bears, this would mean that the 50 uncollared bears seen were 0.5 (half) of all the uncollared bears, so there was a total of 100 uncollared bears. Adding the 20 collared bears in the census area gives a total of 120 bears. Using this method, the Alaskans found very high densities of up to 551 bears per 1000 $km^2$ in some coastal areas that had huge amounts of spawning salmon, but densities of between 10 and 30 bears per 1000 $km^2$ where there were few or no salmon. The densities I estimated in my core area were much higher than areas in Alaska, other than those with lots of salmon.

The Alaskans' method of estimating density using collared bears to deal with the problem of geographic closure, and knowing the proportion of the bears counted, could only be done in open habitats where bears could be easily seen. In forested areas, like the Flathead, too few bears are seen from an aircraft to use the mark-resight method. In Montana during the late 1980s, Rick Mace and Tim Manley linked a motion-sensitive switch to film cameras (digital cameras had yet to be invented) and put them into strong military ammunition containers (Mace et al. 1994; Mace, Manley and Aune 1994). They bolted a few dozen of these cameras to trees just in front of where they hung smelly bait just above the reach of a bear. Rick and Tim had previously caught and radio-collared about 15 grizzly bears so, following the same arithmetic as the Alaskans, they could estimate the capture probability from the collared sample and then the total population size from the number of collared and uncollared bears in the pictures. Because their resight sessions with the cameras took about ten days each, geographic closure was a problem, even though they had collared animals. The bigger problem was estimating the proportion of bears they were counting because there was great variability in the capture probability among different individuals, or what is called capture heterogeneity, and they often could not tell which marked bear was in a photo.

Capture-recapture methods have been used extensively for hundreds of species, and capture heterogeneity is common. It can be accounted for with large sample sizes, provided individuals can be identified and there are several recapture sessions.

**WHEN I STARTED WORKING WITH JOHN WOODS** in Glacier National Park, BC, in 1994, we copied Rick Mace and Tim Manley and used film cameras in military ammunition containers to resight bears in our census area where we had radio-collared 15 grizzly bears. Our area was 2,120 square miles (5490 km$^2$), or almost ten times larger than the area Rick and Tim had worked in. We had problems because film cameras were limited to 36 pictures, we couldn't always tell if animals were collared or not, nor could we always tell collared individuals apart, and we had tiny sample sizes for such a big, expensive effort. Although wildlife managers in BC were very excited about the cameras, I wondered if the method would work over an area much larger than what I was already doing in the Flathead.

John Woods and I had started a research group we called the Columbia Mountains Institute in the early 1990s, and in 1995 we held a workshop on our bear project. Because of recent developments in the amplification of DNA microsatellites, which are repetitive bits of DNA that can be used to generate a *genetic fingerprint*, John had received special funding from Parks Canada to use DNA in wildlife research. With this funding we started working with Dr. Curtis Strobeck, an animal genetics professor at the University of Alberta, and his star Ph.D. student, Dave Paetkau.

Unlike the agency I worked for, Parks Canada always had lots of goodies at their workshops, so I was helping myself to a second muffin and cup of coffee when I starting talking to Dave Paetkau.

"We've been trying to get blood from tiny black bear cubs that we get out of the dens. They are so small, wiggly and darn cute and of course they cry like babies. I hate poking holes in the little guys trying to find a tiny vein. Any better ways to get a DNA sample than taking blood out of babies?"

"Well, for about a year now, we can get enough DNA out of the roots of a few hairs to run microsats," Dave answered.

The old light bulb went on. I took my muffin and coffee and wandered across the room to where Woods was talking to someone. I butted in: "Johnny, let's get rid of those damn cameras. I've been talking to Paetkau. He says we can get enough DNA from the roots of a few hairs to do microsats. A tuft of hair is the perfect mark."

John puckered his lips and looked deep into his coffee mug for about three seconds.

"We won't even have to catch bears to count them," he finally said.

"No, well, except dealing with closure."

"So, how will we get hair?" he thought out loud.

"About ten years ago, Rich Harris came to the Flathead to test ways of getting a simple index of bear abundance by hair trapping. He used wire brushes and horse curry combs nailed onto cubby logs – like a trap site with no trap."

The following week, Woods and I were talking to Dave Lewis, who was one of the toughest moose wrestlers in the moose wrestling business and a very practical cowboy. He told us about all the bear hair that was on the barbed-wire enclosures that we had put around berry plants in the Flathead to keep bears out, so we could estimate how quickly they depleted the fruit. Of course, Dave had it. Barbed wire was the way to get hair.

The following month was when Michael Proctor showed up in Woods's office looking for work and maybe for a graduate school program. Right away, John and I knew he was keen, smart and, above all, competent in the wilderness. We gave him the task of testing various ways of getting bear hair. Barbed wire, pulled tight about a foot and a half (46 cm) above the ground and around four or five trees making a little corral with bait in the middle, worked best (Woods et al. 1999). From the hair, Dave Paetkau could tell us the species, the individual over its entire life, its sex and the likelihood that it was related to all other individuals – way more information than we needed for the capture/recapture method.

**THE ANALYSIS OF CAPTURE/RECAPTURE DATA** has had a century-long history, and because it is highly mathematical, many of the more analytical ecologists have been lured there by their love of math. In the 1990s, many complex models and the software to run them had been developed, and home computers had become powerful enough to rapidly deal with many thousands of computations. These models could incorporate different capture probabilities for individuals, as well as how capture probability might change with time, and whether or not an animal became trap happy or trap shy after the first capture. These analytical methods were aimed at the problem of estimating the proportion of the population that was counted, but they had not yet solved the problem of geographic closure. Locating a census area that was somewhat closed to bear movement was helpful, as was having animals radio-collared to know how often they left the census area.

The DNA hair trapping in a capture/recapture design for estimating grizzly bear numbers that we developed soon became very popular. Finally, bear numbers could be estimated across large areas without physically catching animals, and as a result, people began calling it *non-invasive*. But also important, the field work did not require special skills or knowledge about bears. Since we developed the method, about 25 inventories have been done in BC alone (Garth, Heard and Schwarz 2013; McLellan et al. 2017) – more than any other jurisdiction on Earth – and others were completed on bears and other species all over the world. In 2004, Kate Kendall led a team that did a DNA hair trapping grid across 12,100 square miles (33,480 km$^2$) that covered the entire range of grizzly bears in northwest Montana (Kendall et al. 2009). To me this was exciting because there were now grizzly bear detection data for Glacier National Park, Montana. Kate's project sampled bears across the lodgepole pine flats in the Flathead Valley just south of the border that had not been logged or explored for gas, and where the bears were not hunted. Only the border line, a fully human concept, separated the national park from where I worked in BC, where the valley was far from pristine.

Working with Alberta, we received funding in 2007 to do the same seven by seven kilometre grid north of the US border, just as Kate had done to the south three years before, and used the same lure – rotten cow blood. To avoid any bias, I had no input on where to put the hair traps, so my years of experience in the area had no effect. But the bears in my core study area had been captured using bait for over two decades, so they would be much less apt to carelessly barge into a hair trap and leave lots of hair than would naïve individuals who had never been trapped. There was potential, therefore, for a significant negative bias north of the border when detection rates were compared.

The 2007 DNA hair trapping grid covered an area of 2,365 square miles (6125 km$^2$) in BC and Alberta (MacHutchon et al. 2008). The Flathead Valley covered 612 square miles (1585 km$^2$) and extended, like a big wedge, from the US border up into the middle of the DNA grid. The Flathead Valley and the mountains that bounded it (a five-mile buffer) covered about half the census area but had 84 per cent of the grizzly bear detections. Areas sampled further to the west on the BC side, and to the east in Alberta, had few detections, indicating low densities of bears.

Around the same time, Murray Efford in New Zealand (Efford 2004), and then Andy Royle in the US, were developing what they called *spatially explicit* capture/recapture methods (Efford 2004; Royle et al. 2013). For these methods, information on the location of the traps and the locations of where each individual bear was detected were used, along with individual capture histories, to estimate capture probabilities. Using the spatial information that was ignored in earlier methods improved the estimates of bear density and avoided the ongoing issue of geographic closure.

Murray Efford's spatially explicit capture recapture program (SECR) resulted in a density estimate of 42 females and 23 males, or a total of 65 bears per 1000 $km^2$ for the entire Flathead Valley in BC. These results suggested, once again, that there were a lot of grizzlies in the Flathead. These DNA-based capture/recapture results over the entire drainage supported my earlier estimates in the core area and even my observations of bears during helicopter capture. Except for some coastal areas in Alaska where there were lots of spawning salmon, the Flathead had the highest density of bears so far recorded on the continent. Grizzly bear densities in the Flathead were as high, or higher, than any of the six estimates from the BC coast where bears ate salmon, and much higher than most areas in the interior of BC or Alberta where there were no salmon. For example, the density in the Flathead Valley was four to five times higher than a similar-sized area in Canada's flagship national park, Banff.

The density estimates also found almost twice as many females as males in the Flathead. This is not surprising because the population had been hunted for at least a century, and between 1980 and 2014 twice as many males were killed by hunters as were females. Although most of the males shot by hunters in the Flathead, as elsewhere in the province, were only between two and six years old, the unequal kill would have depleted the number of males. In all population inventories of hunted populations in BC, there were far more females than males. Although not as extreme, an unequal sex ratio was also found in Montana and Banff, where grizzly bears were not hunted; for many reasons besides hunting, people kill more males than females.

**THE EVIDENCE CONTINUED TO FALSIFY** one of the main hypotheses that I set out to test when I began the Flathead study. In other words, my original prediction about the impact of the human activities in the Flathead was wrong. There was not a low density of bears in my core study area where there had been a lot of logging and gas exploration as well as hunting; there was a high density of bears there. Similarly, the SECR analysis of the 2007 hair trapping grid found a high density of bears over the entire Flathead Valley of BC. And now, I could compare an index of abundance between my core study area, with its logging, gas exploration and hunting north of the border, to the relatively pristine conditions in the same valley immediately south of the border in Glacier National Park.

In my core study area, an average of 0.63 female grizzly bears and 0.21 males were detected at each hair trap. In the matching area just south of the border, Kate Kendall's crew detected only 0.16 females and 0.07 males per hair trap. In the mountains on either side of my core study area, the difference was not as striking, but still, about twice as many females, though about the same number of males, were detected per site in the BC Flathead as south of the border in Glacier National Park.

Many of the bears that I had radio-collared and tracked over the years spent time, some most of their time, south of the border in Glacier National Park. None of these bears led me to any large berry fields in the park. Kate Kendall and Rick Mace had both worked on grizzly bears in Glacier for years, so I asked them if they knew of any major huckleberry fields on the west side of the park and within 30 kilometres of the border. Both said "Nope." Clay Wilson and I looked for huckleberry fields on the west side of the park in his Hughes 500D during mid-September when huckleberry leaves are a deep purple colour and easy to see. Again, nope. No major berry fields, no major grizzly density. More ecological interactions were becoming clear.

Finding such a high density of bears in the BC Flathead when there was so much logging, gas exploration and hunting made my life more difficult. It would have been easier had the evidence supported what the environmentalists and the media had been preaching for decades – industry and hunting, more or less, means the end of grizzly bears. Unfortunately, reality was much more complicated.

By the mid-1980s I knew there were a lot of bears in the Flathead, and when I was asked, as I often was, about the effects of industry and hunting on grizzly bears I usually responded with something like, "If I were to manage the logging and hunting with the goal of getting rid of grizzly bears, I likely could do it. But if my goal was to make the same amount of money, or even more over the long run, while logging and hunting grizzlies, and yet have no effect on the size of the grizzly population, I could do that too. It's about how you log and hunt, and that's where knowledge becomes important."

## 14.1 VITAL RATES AND TREND

"Tell me, Bruce, how are the bears doing?"

Next to "How many bears are there?" this was the most common question I was asked. As an ecologist, I interpreted this question as, "Is the population increasing or declining?" Answering this question is perhaps even more challenging than estimating density.

There are several ways to estimate population trend. Indexes of abundance based on systematic track, scat and observation surveys have been used, particularly in small populations in Europe where there is abundant and easy access for human observers. Similarly, the number of bears showing up at some salmon spawning streams has been monitored for years. These counts may reflect the number of bears over a greater area, but they usually fluctuate, sometimes greatly, due to changes in salmon abundance and water conditions, not only at the census streams but at all the other streams that the same bears may also fish. Fluctuating numbers of bears seen at salmon streams will also be due to changes in the productivity of other foods, such as berries, that can draw bears away.

The systematic and long-term use of game cameras shows promise, and younger biologists began to investigate their use in the Flathead. After only a couple of years, however, there are signs of waning interest because of cost and the amount of work required, in checking cameras and dealing with a million photos. Currently, indices of abundance based on bear sign or camera trapping have many inherent problems that must be well thought out and tested before they should be assumed to be reliable.

For grizzlies that live over rugged and mostly forested areas, there are really three ways to measure trend in their populations. One obvious way is to carry out two DNA-based capture/recapture population estimates several years apart, and we have done this in three areas of BC, and so have biologists in Alberta. Fortunately in all of these areas, populations were increasing rapidly and there was little doubt that the trend was upward. But often grizzly bear populations don't change quickly so there may be considerable uncertainty in estimated trends. When asked, "How's the population doing?" the answer from two estimates several years apart may be something like, "Well, it looks like they increased, but there's also a 20 per cent chance they declined." This is a nice answer and people are usually happy with it. But populations can't always be going up, so if the answer was, "It looks like they declined, but there's a 20 per cent chance they increased," then there will be more questions.

"So why are they declining?"

"I don't know; we just counted them a decade apart and there were likely fewer." So even if something changed like logging the valley or doubling the hunting quota, the mechanisms of change might not be clear without replications in an *experimental design*, to confidently estimate the amount of population change that was due to the particular known factor, and how much change was due to other uncontrollable, and likely unknown, confounding factors.

Since the mid-1990s when our team developed the hair traps to sample DNA from bears, a second way to estimate trend without catching and radio-collaring bears was developed. This method estimates the number of new recruits, or individuals entering the population either by birth or immigration, as well as those leaving a population by death or emigration. This is often done by carrying out lower-intensity DNA sampling in the same area year after year, or maybe every second year, for many years. For example, after the intensive hair sampling in the Flathead in 2007 most of the bears had been genetically identified. In 2010, Garth Mowat started collecting grizzly hair at rub trees and a few baited hair traps to detect new bears recruited into the population, as well as to measure when it was probable that individuals were permanently missing. Each year he sampled sites several times.

Over time, Garth developed a long detection history for each individual grizzly bear. From these histories, probabilities of survival, and if they survived, the probability of detection, were estimated for each session and all sessions combined. These probabilities were estimated going forward in time to estimate survival, and backward in time to estimate recruitment. Although this method does not have to estimate the actual number of bears in the sampling area, it could measure trend from the number of bears entering and the number leaving. Now if someone asked, "So why do the bears seem to be declining?" The answer could be, "Too many are dying compared to the number being born." Then someone will no doubt ask, "Well, what's killing them?" And the best answer is likely "I don't know."

**THE THIRD WAY TO ESTIMATE POPULATION TREND** requires more intrusive actions and much more skill than taking hair off a wire and putting it in an envelope. This other method measures the actual birth and survival rates of female bears, or, more precisely, the *age-specific survival and age-specific reproductive rates.* To do this, a sample of female bears is radio-collared and monitored over time and the number of cubs they produce at each age is recorded. How many of these cubs survive to their first, and then second birthday is also documented. It also requires knowing what proportion of the female bears of each age survived from one birthday to the next. Once all these vital rates are known, then an estimate of the population's trend can be calculated. This measure of trend is unlikely to be exactly the same as that calculated by the other two methods, because it does not account for immigration and emigration, and it assumes the population has a stable age distribution, which happens when birth and death rates remain similar for a few years.

Of the three methods that estimate population trend, the one that relies on knowing age-specific survival and reproduction provides the best measure of how the population is coping with its current situation; it has been called a measure of *demographic vigour* (Caughley 1977). Therefore, this measure of trend was the best test for my hypothesis that the salvage logging and gas exploration had negative effects on the grizzly population. Also, because I estimated huckleberry production in the major Flathead berry fields each year, I could test if cub production and survival were related to the previous year's berry crop. This hypothesis was often suggested but had not been tested with data. This method of estimating population trend was also being used in Yellowstone, northern Montana, Banff, Alaska and northern Canada, so population trends as well as each vital rate could be compared, providing greater insight into what causes grizzly bear populations to increase or decrease.

In the Flathead, we put radio collars on and then tracked 80 different female grizzly bears that were over 2 years old. Most had their old collars replaced with new ones a few times. All collars had canvas spacers that gradually rotted, so that the collars dropped off the bear leaving a *known fate* for the tracking session. Mortality rates of these females were estimated from monitoring them for a total of 300 *bear-years.* While they were being tracked, 18 died. Five died of natural causes, four were legally killed by grizzly bear hunters, and nine were shot and killed by people but for reasons other than legal hunting. The total annual mortality rate of these female bears was about 6 per cent. As I have mentioned, but think it's worth repeating, more grizzly bears were legally killed by grizzly bear hunters per square mile in the Flathead than in any other area in British Columbia, yet more than twice as many collared females in the Flathead were shot by people in other circumstances than by legal hunters.

Mortality causes were similar for males, but rates were much higher. Although for many years I avoided catching males, I ended up collaring and following 67 of them in the Flathead. The canvas spacer used in collars put on males was thin and rotted more quickly than the spacers I put on females. This safety measure reduced the amount of time each male was monitored after they were captured. Consequently, I only tallied 79 bear-years monitoring the survival of males, but during this time, 16 died or I strongly suspected that they had been killed, which gave an annual mortality rate of 19 per cent – about three times the rate of the collared females. All deaths of males except one were human caused. With three times the mortality rate, no wonder there were so many more females than males in the Flathead.

Legal grizzly bear hunters killed the collared male bears at an annual rate of 9 per cent. This was much higher than the female hunter-kill rate of just under 2 per cent. The difference is not surprising because it was illegal to shoot a female with cubs or yearlings, and hunters were told not to shoot any bear in a family group. Because 2- or 3-year-old grizzlies usually split up from their mother during the breeding season in mid-May, and the grizzly hunting season ended on June 5, productive mothers might only be alone and thus vulnerable to be legally shot by a hunter for two or three weeks every three or four years. The human-caused annual mortality rate, excluding legal hunting, was also 9 per cent for the collared males. Some were shot for being near people's homes in the US, where there was permanent settlement. Others were shot in deer and elk hunting camps where they had been attracted by garbage, hanging game meat or pelleted horse food. The natural mortality rate of both males and females was between 1 and 2 per cent.

Ideally, to measure the population trend from vital rates, I would have to know the mortality rate of female bears of each age or, for example, what proportion of bears that turn 5 years old die before their 6th birthday. Clearly I haven't followed enough bears to do that for all ages, but I do have enough to split them into a few categories or age groups. Subadult females, which are 2-, 3- and 4-year-olds, or old enough to have left their mother's care but not old enough to have cubs of their own, had a mortality rate of

3.4 per cent. Young adult females from 5 to 10 years of age had a mortality rate of 5.2 per cent, while 3.8 per cent of the 11- to 16-year-olds died, and 12.1 per cent of the over-17-year-old grannies died each year.

Cubs and yearlings are rarely collared, so estimating their survival rates is challenging. Ironically, black bears are likely the best large mammal for estimating mortality rates of juvenile animals, while grizzlies are among the worst. Like many biologists, I have gone into the winter dens and immobilized dozens of mother black bears when their cubs are newly born and tiny. Sure, a few times I've noticed, in the view cast from a dim, pre-LED headlamp, that the mother bear had partially woken up. Then, I was most often upside down in a dirty, tight hole with tree roots jabbing me in the ribs, and my face about two feet (60 cm) from hers. Some have blown snot in my face. Once, during a warm, early spring, a feisty one even swatted at me. But recording the number and sex of black bear cubs that were born, or at least were there before they left their den, is pretty straightforward. Carefully sneaking up on a radio-collared black bear mother to count her cubs a few times over the summer is possible, and then going back in her den the following winter to see how many cubs lived to their first birthday can confirm cub survival. Den work, as we called it, was logistically difficult in the rugged terrain and deep snow of the Rocky or Selkirk mountains, but I always enjoyed it for a couple of weeks in March. It provided clear, unquestionable data of how many cubs were born and survived to one year of age.

Unlike with black bear dens, I haven't gone into a mother grizzly bear's den to count her new cubs. I'm pretty sure I could have done this a few times, particularly with the moms that were gentler, as Elspeth may have been. But I'm also sure that if I had made a habit of counting newborn grizzly cubs that way, I wouldn't be here writing about it. At least one would have woken up fast and blown snot in my face before shredding me. Melissa, I'm pretty sure would have. Just thinking of being a couple of feet from Melissa's big face makes me nervous. Yes, Darwin is one of my heroes, but I don't seek his award.

After they leave their winter den, usually in early May, some moms with new cubs are not easy to see in a heavily forested valley like the Flathead. Once in a while they are in open enough terrain to be spotted from an aircraft. But if the mother is seen and she has no cubs, does this mean there aren't any, or has she run off and left the little guys behind? I've been fooled from aircraft a couple of times. On the ground I've often tracked families when hiking through the forest, but because many moms get excited when someone sneaks up on them, counting new cubs when on foot is challenging. Often, after I've bushwhacked for miles trying to get close to a collared mother grizzly, she ends up being in thick vegetation where it's not possible and certainly not safe to get close enough to count her cubs. Although most of the cubs that I used to estimate their mortality rates were first seen in May or June, the estimate would be likely too low because some cubs may have died before the family was seen. Fortunately, the reproductive rate, or the number of female cubs born per female per year, will be equally biased low if some cubs died before they were counted, so the effect on the estimate of population trend should equal out.

In addition to not being able to reliably count grizzly bear cubs when they are first born, there are other problems when estimating cub mortality rate. Most young grizzly bears separate from their mothers during the spring breeding season when they are 2 years old, but some stay with their mother for three or four years. Sometimes, however, they separate from their mother when they are only 1 year old. On a few occasions I saw a mother grizzly with her family of 8-month-old cubs in the autumn just before they hibernated for the winter, but when I saw her the following year, the cubs were gone. Did they die or just separate from the mother as yearlings? Some, I know, just left their mothers as yearlings because I caught and collared them early in the year just before they separated or just after they separated during the breeding season. On these few occasions, I had to calculate both maximum and minimum survival rates for cubs by first assuming that all the cubs lived and just separated from their mother when they were yearlings and then assuming they all had died.

I followed 109 cubs of radio-collared mothers for the entire first year of life and the mortality rate was 25 per cent. There were four other cubs that I saw late in the autumn, just before they would have hibernated, but then the mother's collar fell off so I didn't get to see them the following spring. They probably survived to their first birthday in late January when they were hibernating, and if they had, then cub mortality would have been 24 per cent. There were 13 more cubs that I saw in the autumn but whose mothers I didn't see again until after the breeding season the following year, and by then they were alone. The cubs, which would then be yearlings, could have died, or they could have left their mother as 1-year-olds. Does excluding these cases bias my estimate of cub mortality rate? If the yearling cubs had still been with their mother, then I would have included them as survivors. So excluding them might be a bias. So if all of these cubs lived, then the mortality rate would be 21 per cent, but if all died it would have been 35 per cent. In the cases of six of the cubs that died, or at least I assumed died, it was because their mother was shot. The natural mortality rate would be about 4 per cent less than these estimates.

**I ONLY PUT COLLARS ON A COUPLE OF CUBS** and therefore I didn't know the details of the causes of death. I didn't really know for certain that they had died when they separated from their mother during their first year of life, but I think it's safe to assume that they had. But an unfortunate incident in Jasper National Park in the 1970s shows that cubs orphaned as early in the year as July, or about 5 months old, can survive. The incident also shows that mother grizzlies, once in a while, can get ridiculously aggressive. Perhaps some of these extreme acts towards people were intensified by an encounter with another bear or a pack of wolves an hour or two before that had wound up the mother grizzly. I've seen mother grizzlies get very aggressive with other bears, and I sure wouldn't like to be strolling happily along a trail and encounter one of them shortly after. Both my son Charlie and I, in separate incidents, have found first-hand that moose can be a little nasty just after they fight off a pack of wolves.

On July 21, 1975, before Chuck Jonkel and his students invented bear spray, a Jasper National Park warden encountered a mother grizzly with three cubs near the treeless Cairn pass in the Rocky Mountains. The warden saw the family of grizzlies about 400 yards (366 m) away feeding on vegetation, and then the mother bear noticed the intruder. She immediately came running towards the warden at a moderate speed. He took out his rifle and fired a warning shot when she was about 100 yards (91 m) away. The bear slowed a bit but continued through a ravine where she was out of sight. She reappeared when 25 yards (23 m) away when the warden fired a second shot into marmot diggings, spraying her with dirt. She stopped, stood for a second, then came at the warden, ears flat back, at a full charge. He shot and killed the bear when she was ten feet (3 m) away. A sad, but not totally uncommon event, that left three orphaned cubs in July of their first year of life.

The three orphans were spotted in September by some hikers, but then they were not seen until the following May. They were seen together several times over their second summer. They were once seen separated, with one yearling about half a mile behind the other two, before it caught up. When they were next seen a month later, there were only two and they seemed very nervous and restless; the wardens speculated that the third yearling might have been killed by another bear. The remaining two were seen the following year as 2-year-olds, and then Canadian Wildlife Service biologists captured them and put a radio collar on one. Both bears were small for their age but healthy. They survived that year and, once again, dug their own den and hibernated together. They survived at least until they were 4 years old when the biologists took off their radio collars and the study ended. This event shows that some cubs, particularly in wilderness areas where they will not be attracted to human food sources, can survive on their own when they are only 5 months old – a consideration for people deciding what to do with orphaned cubs.

Estimating mortality rates of yearlings is also a challenge because, like cubs, they too are rarely collared themselves but are monitored by being with their radio-collared mothers. So, as with cubs, their fates were sometimes unknown and I had to estimate maximum and minimum mortality rates for them. From the 96 yearlings that I monitored, their mortality rate was between 15 and 18 per cent.

**GRIZZLY BEAR REPRODUCTIVE RATES** vary due to different ages at which females have their first litter of cubs (age of primiparity), variation in the time period between litters (interbirth interval), and in the different numbers of cubs in a litter (litter size). These three factors are certainly worth documenting, but to estimate the age-specific reproductive rates, I simply measured the average number of female cubs born per female in each age or groups of ages. For example, I monitored the status of 30 four-year-old females and none had cubs. Sometimes, 4-year-old females have had cubs in Yellowstone, the eastern side of the Rockies in Montana, and in Alaska, but so far, no Flathead 4-year-olds have had cubs. Of the 30 5-year-olds I monitored, five had cubs, including three single-cub litters and two litters of two cubs. If we assume an equal sex ratio at birth, then the reproductive rate of 5-year-old females was thus seven cubs out of 30 females, or a rate of 0.233. When divided by two, this gives 0.117 female cubs per 5-year-old female. Reproductive rates increased with age until females were 8 years old and then remained just under 0.30 female cubs per mother per year until they were 22 years old. Once reaching 23 years old, Flathead bears stopped having cubs. In other parts of the world however, a few 28-year-old females have given birth, but this is the oldest age that has been reported.

I can estimate reproductive rates without knowing the average age of primiparity, interbirth intervals and litter sizes, but it's important to document these parameters because they are all along the mechanistic chain of why populations are trending the way they are. Flathead females had their first litters between 5 and 12 years of age. The average of the 18 females that I was monitoring when they had their first litter was 7.0 years. But this estimate would be biased because some females I monitored past that age had yet to have their first litter, but then dropped their collars or were killed. So, by using proportions that had or did not have first litters at each age, I found the average age of first litter was really 8.25 years.

From the 42 interbirth intervals, I estimated an average of 3.18 years between litters. But this average would also be biased because some females were monitored for more than this time and then their collars fell off, or they died before *closing the interval* with another litter. Accounting for *open-ended intervals*, the average was 3.6 years between litters.

Just over half of the 72 litters of collared bears had two cubs. There were a few more single-cub litters than there were litters of three, so the average litter size ended up being 1.9 cubs per litter. I didn't see any litters with four in the Flathead, although I have seen one in the BC Coast Mountains and they have been recorded elsewhere.

Three- or four-year interbirth intervals and litters of three cubs can make an intimidating pack of grizzly bears and a good reason to make some noise while strolling through the forest. But I think the overgrown cubs are still babies in many ways. After all, I've watched three 2.6-year-old grizzly bears, that weighed about 200 pounds (91 kg) each, still noisily chuckling away like babies as they nursed on their 280-pound (127 kg) mother.

THE COMBINATION OF AGE-SPECIFIC MORTALITY and reproduction suggests that, without immigration or emigration, the Flathead population would have been increasing at about 4 per cent per year. At that rate, there should be about five times as many bears in 2020 as there were when I began working there in 1979. There were a lot more bears in 2020, but the increase had not been steady. In the first 20 years, including the decade of salvage logging and gas exploration and the decade that followed, the number of adult female bears in the core of my study area increased about 2½-fold. But in 1998, things began to change.

Between 1979 and 1997, the huckleberry crop varied in production, as fruit usually does, but there were more good and great years than there were bust years. But in 1998, after four good or great berry years, we had a total bust. No big deal, I thought, we'd had them before. The following year was not a bust but was a poor year, and it was followed by two more years with almost no fruit. And this pattern was repeated for 11 years until production picked up a little. In the last decade, we have seen some good years again, although none has been a great year.

During the first two decades (1979 to 1997), when huckleberry production was good most years, and there were relatively few bears in the Flathead, cub mortality was 20 to 22 per cent. During the decade of poor huckleberries (1998 to 2008), cub mortality was 28 to 40 per cent. In the last decade, when berry production had improved, cub mortality was down to 16 per cent. During the entire study, three mothers with cubs were killed so I assumed their six cubs died. All three were killed during the decade with poor huckleberries, and these six dead cubs were the reason for cub survival being low during that decade. A statistical analysis to test the importance of factors influencing whether or not a cub would die or survive suggested that if the cub was in a female's first litter, it had a higher chance of dying, and suggested a female's level of experience affected her cub's survival. The density of female bears, the huckleberry crop, or if adult males were killed in their range had little notable effect.

The change in huckleberry abundance seemed to have a greater impact on cub production than it did on cub survival. In particular, the age at which females had their first litter increased from about 7 years of age in the first two decades to over 10 years in the decade with poor huckleberries. It returned to an average of 7 when huckleberry production improved. Similarly, the average interval between litters increased from just over three years both before and after the decade of poor huckleberries, to over four years when the huckleberries were doing poorly. A statistical analysis of factors influencing cub production suggested that the previous year's huckleberry crop and bear density both played a role, but they only explained about 40 per cent of the variation in cub production. Unmeasured factors explained the rest. Some good old moms like Elspeth, Aggie, Maggie and Trixie still had triplets following a bust huckleberry year, but in general, small or no litters were more common following very low berry years.

Knowing the vital rates and how they changed as the population grew and huckleberry production changed gave me the information to answer most questions about the Flathead grizzly population. The salvage logging and gas exploration alone didn't make a notable difference, because the bears were recovering from many decades of overkill before I began my work. Berry production turned out to be more important to the recovery of the population, although the roads left by industry enabled people to efficiently move throughout the valley and continue to kill grizzly bears. So now when people ask, "Tell me, Bruce, how are the bears doing?" I sometimes give them such a long-winded and complex answer that they may wish they'd never asked.

CHAPTER 15

# KEEPING THE STUDY ALIVE

Many people see going to university, particularly when they are old enough to be a graduate student, as the pathway to a career – a hoop to hop through. But for me and Celine, living in the Flathead and having our family while following the lives of many grizzly bears was nearly perfect, provided we had enough income to keep food on the table and avoided any student debt. However, at UBC there were time limits for students to finish or they got the boot, and I had maxed out my five-year M.Sc. and now my seven-year Ph.D. I needed to defend by the summer of 1990.

By the end of the 1980s, there were other pressures suggesting that we would not be able to remain forever living in the Flathead following bears every day. Michelle was in school and even little Charlie started Grade 1 in 1988. Being pre-adolescents, they were still having fun living along the Flathead River. Michelle had been to several different schools for a few months here and there when we wintered at UBC, but mostly she had been home schooled. Now, Celine and I thought it was fine to take kids out of school for a one- or two-year adventure, but to remove them from society for their entire youth was unfair. It would be too selfish on our part to keep them from having at least a somewhat normal upbringing as they approached adolescence.

There was also the continued issue of having sufficient funding to buy radio collars, rent aircraft for the weekly tracking flights, pay someone to help me trap and collar bears, and keep gas in a vehicle. The project was mostly on the Canadian side of the border, but the BC government rarely had funding for our bear project. Although I was following the lives of over a dozen collared bears in 1983, the BC Fish and Wildlife Branch decided to put all the grizzly bear research money into a new coastal bear study and zero into mine. The coastal study had enough funding to even hire a camp cook; that cost alone would have covered my entire aircraft budget. Ray Demarchi argued to have some of this money go to my project, but the bureaucrats in Victoria turned him down, and being a regional biologist, he had no funding in his own budget for research. He helped the best he could, but this was really limited to letting us use the warehouse to park our van in so we could sleep where it was warm in the late autumn. We could also use the Flathead trailer that I had built the addition to, and an old snowmobile, but mostly Ray gave me a key to the gasoline bulk station, where I would fill up a couple of 55-gallon gas drums every time we came to town. He might have been fired if anyone had found out, but he saved the project many times with his unique form of financial risk management.

I had tried a lot of ways to get funding, and had to be a salesman as much as a biologist. With the goal of continuing to get some funding, particularly from south of the border, I used to tell the audience at the numerous presentations I made that the most important grizzly bear habitat in the US was actually in Canada. I often stressed that it was through a relatively narrow band of occupied grizzly bear habitat, just north of the US border in the Flathead and Elk valleys, that the US grizzlies as well as other large carnivores such as wolves and wolverine, were connected to the rest of the continent's bears, wolves and wolverine. This strategy worked in two ways. First, Harvey Locke, a lawyer who worked for the Canadian Parks and Wilderness Society (CPAWS), saw a slide show I gave in Alberta. He later told me that while listening to my talk about the importance of the Flathead and southern Elk Valley to the connectivity of large carnivores through the Rocky Mountains, his light bulb went on and the Yellowstone to Yukon, or Y2Y, initiative was spawned.

More importantly to my project, Chris Servheen, the Grizzly Bear Recovery Coordinator for the US Fish and Wildlife Service (USFWS), also knew that the fate of grizzly bears north of the border was important for the conservation of US bears. The USFWS, through Chris, helped with funding even though most of the bears I was tracking lived north of the border. Beginning in the late 1980s, Chris provided a truck or two and a field assistant, and even paid for some radio collars and tracking flights. The logging industry would always come up with a little funding when the project was completely broke and I needed a few more tracking flights. But when I defended my Ph.D. in the fall of 1989, my ability to apply for scholarships ended, so I was no longer paid even the very modest stipend of a student. Chris continued to help out with contracts to analyze data and write reports, but even between both countries, the project was struggling to stay alive.

A few months after I defended my Ph.D. and my scholarships ended, we were in Fernie doing a supply run. I was in the hardware store with the kids when Celine snuck off to her favourite shop, the Christian Women's Charity, which was the almost-free second-hand store in town. The kids and I got back to the truck first and were inside waiting when Celine crossed the road with a huge smile suggesting she'd found the deal of the day.

"You won't believe how I got these muffins; it's just too funny," she started.

"I was in the second-hand store just checking things out when the nice old lady comes up to me and very discreetly whispers, 'You know, for people like you, we have day-old muffins from Tim Hortons for free.' She is such a funny old lady."

Well, the kids were at the age where they found this hilarious, and between mouthfuls of muffins, "Mom, you're just a bum," Charlie starts off.

"No she isn't, but she will take food from the bums," Michelle continues.

"I'd say that people who take food from a bum is a double bum," Charlie laughs.

"No, the muffins are a gift for my good karma for not being a crazy consumer. The world is just full of crappy stuff and most people are addicted to shopping and buying more and more junk. Because I don't need much and I don't need new stuff to make me completely happy, it's my duty to not buy new stuff to clutter the poor world with more and more junk. I buy good-quality things that others don't need anymore and I feel very good about it."

"But if everyone was like you, the world economy would collapse," I said, just so the kids would know that solutions are not always simple.

"No, everyone would need a little less so everyone would have to work a little less. Everyone would have more quality time with family and friends." Celine had it all figured out in the 1980s.

While driving back into the Flathead, I was wondering if learning so much about foraging theory would help an unemployed, homeless family forage more efficiently in a landscape of rare but big garbage dumpsters, and common but smaller garbage cans. How long to stay in a patch given their distribution and average reward? That would be a simple study, but there could be more complex and interesting behaviours for an unemployed Dr. McLellan to investigate while scrounging food in various sizes and distributions of garbage containers. Somehow, I had to get a real job with a real salary that would allow us to continue to be good parents and also enable me to continue my bear work.

For a while, Ray had been telling me that I should apply for some wildlife biology jobs just to experience the government interview process.

"It's government, so it puts the illusion of fairness even above getting the best person. So in this game, the more you play, the better your chance of winning if you ever do really want a job." And Ray always added a little more to his suggestion. "Besides, they will buy you a dinner and even put you up in a hotel where you can have a real shower instead of lukewarm water dribbling out of a bag hanging in a tree."

In the autumn of 1989, a job as a provincial wildlife research ecologist with the Forest Service Research Branch was posted. This was a rare job as there were only two in the entire province. I applied to see what would happen. I got the interview, a flight to Victoria, the dinner and the hotel with a shower. Air Canada lost my luggage and I waited and waited for it that evening and the next morning, but it never arrived. At the last minute I ran half a mile to the interview through the pouring coastal rain and showed up in a ratty old rain-soaked T-shirt. I was invited into a small room, wiped the water from my face, and sat down across the table from the suits and ties.

The position being a Forest Service wildlife research ecologist job, the interviewers had questions on animal ecology and how it related to forestry and old-growth forests, but they also touched on forest management, including various harvesting systems. Likely all biologists interviewed could answer the biology questions fairly well, but because I had been a logger in my teens and early 20s, I could talk about main lines, haul-back lines, tight lines and straw lines. I got the job likely because of my knowledge of forestry and the forest industry, more than my knowledge of bats, birds and bears.

My new job was to do research on wildlife and forestry issues that were of provincial significance. This was good because grizzly bears were an issue wherever they were found, and they were found across most of the province. Only mountain caribou, or the caribou that feed all winter on hair lichens that grow best on very old trees, were a greater issue. After all, these lichens grow on many of the same old trees that the loggers wanted to cut down. But caribou and forestry was a winter issue. In the summer, the caribou were most often high in the mountains, at or above treeline. So I worked on mountain caribou in the winter, but switched back to grizzly bears from May until November.

I did it. I got a job with a real salary and could keep working in the Flathead, at least part-time. This was fine, but we could no longer live in the Flathead as we had for over a decade. With a real job, particularly one that involved both caribou and grizzly bears, there were many other tasks. We managed to spend a few months each year in the Flathead; it was enough time to keep a sample of females collared, monitor their cubs and estimate the berry crops. For our understanding of Flathead grizzly bears, it would have been better to have kept living in the Flathead and following the bears every day as we had for the past dozen years, but I already knew a lot about the Flathead bears; the law of diminishing returns was at play. It would be better to work on grizzlies in other places as well.

MY CARIBOU PROJECT WAS IN THE COLUMBIA MOUNTAINS north of Revelstoke, BC, where I worked with John Flaa, a Parks Canada warden. John was an extremely reliable mountain man in the modern sense. In 1994, John Woods became the research biologist for Parks Canada and he wanted to do a grizzly bear study between Glacier and Yoho national parks, but neither Flaa nor Woods had worked on bears. Because I was already doing caribou work with Parks Canada, I soon found myself catching, collaring and monitoring bears also with Parks Canada. As this work was during the spring and summer, it really reduced the amount of time I could spend in the Flathead. But Parks had something that I had never experienced in the 15 years I had worked on bears – real funding.

For a month we tried catching and radio-collaring bears in the national parks, just as I had in the Flathead; we set traps along the road network. We did catch a lot of black bears but only a couple of grizzlies. Woods suggested we set traps from a helicopter. Unlike the Flathead, this study area was dominated by remote mountains, many miles from any roads. Using a helicopter had never crossed my mind when working in the Flathead because the cost was way beyond my limited funds, but it was essential in the Columbia Mountains.

By using a helicopter to access remote locations, we did catch grizzly bears, but once in a while we saw other grizzlies while flying past. I knew that Alaskan biologists didn't trap bears like we did but simply darted them out of a helicopter. But the Alaskans worked in areas with far fewer trees. The Columbia Mountains were mostly in the interior wet belt with old-growth forests of often immense cedar, hemlock, spruce and fir trees, so were far too dense to see into. If an uncollared bear was darted and got into the trees, it would be very difficult to find. After all, it takes five to ten minutes for the drug to take effect and a bear can run a long way in that time.

In September, we began to see grizzly bears in more open areas where, just as in the Flathead, forest fires had killed the trees and huckleberries were common. Don McTigue was the pilot we had been working with. Don had never flown for animal capture before, but he was an excellent pilot so we thought we would get ready and try.

Bluewater Ridge (51.625 -117.305) was a perfect place to practise. Not only had the area been burned by wildfire, but forestry people had cut down every snag, I presume so it could be safely replanted. The open area was over half a mile (800 m) across, so we should be able to keep a bear in view with a little herding, until the drug took effect. So, in late September 1995, I darted three young male grizzly bears from Don's helicopter. The school of hard knocks taught us that it took almost twice as much drug to immobilize a bear from a helicopter as one in a foot snare. The next fall, while running a helicopter-assisted trap line, we caught six grizzlies in snares, but darted another six from the machine. Although helicopters are expensive, they are efficient, and when time is limited, efficiency is important.

In 1996, Chris Servheen's US crew and I trapped in the Flathead and caught nine grizzlies. Except for two adult males that lived mostly in Alberta, all were young bears that were unfamiliar with our trapping tricks. After I'd been working in the same area for 18 years, the older bears were wise to our culverts and foot snares and were difficult to catch. They were pretty adept at setting off very sneaky sets without getting caught. Most bears would not enter culverts no matter how much syrup we poured on a choice chunk of fat. I had only seven adult females collared in the spring of 1996. In late August, I thought I would try darting some from a helicopter when they were in mostly treeless huckleberry fields. Clay Wilson of Bighorn Helicopters was developing his business as an animal capture specialist. In the winter, he worked across western Canada catching all types of large mammals, from wolves to bison. I was lucky because Clay lived in Cranbrook, very close to the Flathead. Dave Lewis, who, as I have mentioned before, was one of the toughest moose wrestlers I have worked with, came along with Clay and me. In one weekend, even though we were just learning, we caught and collared eight adult females. These including Elspeth, Jennie, Aggie and Cindy – all smart bears and very tricky to catch in traps.

During this weekend of helicopter capture, we searched all open huckleberry fields across an area of 380 square miles (985 $km^2$) and saw at least 14 adult females, 12 of which had a total of 19 cubs and yearlings. We also saw ten other bears, of which we thought six were males. At that time six of our previously collared bears were in the area we searched, but we only saw one of these. All tallied, there were at least 48 grizzly bears in the area we searched, and no doubt many more. But how many more, and whether they really lived there or just happened to be on the edge of their home range in the good habitat we searched – all that was unknown. So helicopter capture worked well even in southern, mostly forested grizzly bear range, and we could use it to complement more traditional trapping methods, particularly where bears were wise to culverts and snares.

Helicopter capture in forested, mountainous terrain, however, presented many factors beyond our control. After our weekend of capture, and after Clay flew away and the silence of wilderness returned to the Flathead, Dave summed it all up with "Man, I need to sit by the river and just listen to it flow by for a few days." Then he giggled as only Dave giggles. "Helicopter capture is damn stressful," and he giggled some more. "I mean, how many times were we chased up trees? Twice in three days. Man, we're lucky we survived," and more giggling. We were at the beginning of the learning curve, and it was a long, steep one.

**SOMETIMES HELICOPTER CAPTURE** goes amazingly smoothly. One late afternoon Clay surprised us by showing up a day early to catch bears. Graduate student Fred Hovey, Celine and I were doing some major carpentry work on the log addition to the trailer when we heard the high-pitched whine of a 500D in the distance.

"That sounds like Clay," I said.

"He's not supposed to be here until tomorrow," Fred replied.

The 500 came in just above the trees at 120 miles (200 km) an hour, made a very steep, almost vertical bank and came back down the river. It flared and set right down on the rocky beach without any hesitation. I could tell by how he was flying that Clay was alone and in a good mood. He let the turbines cool and then shut down.

"You guys ready to catch some bears?" he said as the blades slowed down above his head.

"Not really, since you're a day early."

"Better early than late, and besides it's just a beautiful evening to catch a few bears. Best day we've had since yesterday. I'd say it's perfect. What do you think?"

We put away our hammers and I started to mentally psych up for a capture session. I calmed myself right down and began the process of mental transition from carpentry to capture. I put some sterile water in the vials of drugs and gave them to Clay to shake to dissolve the powdered drug, and started putting on my capture clothes.

"What are you doing here a day early?"

"Some crazy climber went for a tumble in Waterton. It was so damn windy and the guy was all smacked up so close to the cliffs that the wardens thought they better bring me in to do the long lining. There I was in the old Waterton wind, hovering with my blades a foot from the rock wall, thinking, the guy's good and dead. What's the rush?"

In ten minutes we were airborne, but the sun had gone down over the western mountains. It was going to be dark soon. Through the intercom Clay asked, "So, where's the nearest bear?"

"The lookout's closest, but we'll have a better chance of finding one in Elder," I answered.

"Sounds good. There is a slight chance we may be rushed." And Clay laughed.

"Yeh, I sort of figured that seeing how the sun has already gone down."

We entered the area where the 1936 fire had burned off most of the forest across a half-dozen mountain basins. We hadn't searched for more than half a minute when I spotted a grizzly eating huckleberries.

"There's a bear," I quickly said before anyone else saw it, so I could claim the sighting (49.07153 -114.36189). Who first spots the bear becomes a good-humoured competition often leading to insults.

"Okay, Freddy, I'll set you off right up, let's see, yep, up here on this ridge."

Without fussing around looking for a landing spot, Clay set it right down and we all jumped out. I put on my red capture coat because it might be cold in the wind. Clay had my door off, Fred was out, and I was back in and taping my seat belt closed. All that took a minute, and Clay and I took off.

"Okay, where is that little feller, oh, right in the same spot. Perfect, are you ready?"

"Small dart, do you think?"

"Yep, it's not a big bear. Okay, I'll take her just up the hill away from those trees."

In far less than a minute, we pounced and I shot.

"Got her, 7:14."

She was on an open hillside so we backed way off and let her jog along. Clay can always keep an eye on the bear, whereas in the back seat I lose sight of bears when he moves the helicopter around. A couple of minutes after darting her, I asked, "Did you see a stumble?" because I always want to see if the drug is taking effect quickly.

"Yep, I think she's feeling it, oh yeah, time for the old Macarena."

Her rear end started running a little to the side, she slowed, and then she sat down. Her head began waving back and forth, and in half a minute she put it down.

"I'll drop you off and get Freddy."

"Okay, sounds good."

In a few seconds, Clay toed the front end of both skids of the helicopter into the mountainside. I hung up my headset, transferred my weight gradually as I stepped out and crouched down, plugging my ears. The wind blasted hard and then he was gone.

I could see the bear from where I was let off and she was just lying there on level ground. We wouldn't even have to move her. I walked up and clapped my hands. After all the helicopter noise, I'm sure she wasn't really interested in a little hand clapping, but it was a habit from trapping so many bears. I put lubricant into each eye, put the blindfold on, and then rolled her onto her chest. Clay came roaring back and landed 100 feet (30 m) away.

We measured different parts of her body, weighed her and were adjusting her radio collar; I could tell it was getting a little dark because it getting difficult to see all that I was doing.

"When should we be out of here?" I asked.

"Oh, about 20 minutes ago," Clay answered.

Being a young bear, she was starting to recover and was lifting her head a little. With all our roaring around, there was likely no other bear in this little basin. Clay wanted to get going.

"She'll be up before you know it. I packed some elk steaks all the way to Waterton and back. I should have been preparing them an hour ago. Let's get in my little buggy and wander our way back to camp."

And with that, we loaded up, and in five minutes were landing on the beach. Clay got to work cooking dinner as he always does. In about 45 minutes from beach takeoff to beach landing, we had collared Debbie.

IN DARTING GRIZZLY BEARS from a helicopter, uncontrollable factors make every capture unique, and we had to adapt to new circumstances continually. For an example at the other extreme from Debbie's capture, which went about as smoothly as possible, catching Lucky gave us a lot more exercise. Clay and I were putting GPS collars on grizzly bears in the Elk Valley, just north of the Flathead, with Clayton Apps. It was the 1st of June 2008, on an evening capture session, and we'd already caught one adult female, and with only a little time left before dark, thought we should go straight after a bear that was already collared but with batteries about to die. Using the telemetry gear on the helicopter, we located her, but it being the mating season, she was with a large adult male.

"Might as well collar him first. We can always track her and get her tomorrow," Clayton suggested. The two bears were in a high, southwest-facing basin that was partly covered with snow.

We followed the usual procedure. Land, drop off Clayton and my door, put on my capture coat, and tape the seat belt closed. I was glad I had my darting clothes on because it was darned cold high in the mountains travelling at 100 miles (160 km) an hour with no door. The male was big and running steadily across a large, smooth snow patch, so he was very easy to hit with a dart. Then we backed off, far away, to watch. He kept up with the female for maybe a minute before starting to fall behind. We were high up and over a mile (1.6 km) away but could see his big body clearly against the snow as he slowly climbed towards the ridge.

"Let's check the basin on the other side of the ridge," I suggested.

"He's starting the Macarena, he'll never make the ridge," Clay responded.

"Let's check it anyway."

It took just a few seconds to fly a mile or so to see what was on the other side of the ridge. It was another smooth, mostly snow-filled basin with no cliffs.

"Looks good, no problems there."

The big bear was on a little flat bench that was half-free of snow and a hundred yards below the ridge.

"Perfect place to go down, I can set my buggy down right beside him."

But, very slowly, the bear staggered his way up.

"Hope he doesn't make the ridge," I mumbled over the intercom.

"He won't make it. The big fella's about done."

But up he slowly staggered on.

"Let's get over there and keep him out of the far basin," I suggested.

"Hate to turn him downhill now."

"Let's get over there and stay high and see if we just stop him where he is," I suggested again.

"Okay, but he won't make the ridge, he's done."

Clay flew back over to the distant valley. We were high above the bear, not wanting to turn him and make him lope downhill. But he kept slowly staggering up and soon was approaching the ridge top. Clay zoomed in.

"Come on, big fella, turn around."

We were right in front of him, just a few feet above the snow. But the big bear was too far drugged to care. He just slowly came right towards us. The wind from the blades blew his fur flat. He would pull us out of the sky unless we moved, so Clay just backed off as the bear crested the ridge and started down the distant valley.

"Sorry, Bruce, my fault, I should have turned him earlier."

"No, it's not your fault. Turning him early would have sent him down the other valley. He's got to go out soon, he can hardly walk."

But, almost fully drugged going downhill on snow, he got into a steady, repetitive lope and just kept going and going towards the bottom of the basin.

"We better get in his face or he might make the trees."

At this, Clay zipped down and hovered right in front of him. It seemed like the bear didn't even notice. He just kept up the staggering lope right at us. Clay had to lift the machine a little and the bear went underneath and into the tall spruce forest in the bottom of the basin.

We tried to keep an eye on him, but he was out of sight in the darkening forest.

"Ok, I got his tracks, he's still going downstream." Clay pivoted the helicopter and I could no longer see for a few seconds. In this basin, the sun had set a while ago and the cold wind blew hard through the open side of the helicopter, making my eyes water. I could see his tracks in the snow where he had crossed a small opening in the forest. They went into a creek. When almost fully drugged, bears almost always go downhill, and at the bottom of downhill, there are creeks. We flew a few circles looking for more tracks or the bear, but the canopy was too thick. We then flew downstream, right over the creek, but much of it wasn't visible under the tall spruce trees. Maybe we could find him if we kept looking, but his tracks went into the creek. We might not have much time. He was likely still in the creek.

"Better let me out, I'll track him. Why don't you go get Clayton and I'll call you on the radio." There was no need to tell Clay that I was worried about the creek. We have never lost a bear to drowning but, over the years and hundreds of bears, I have pulled a few of their heads out of the water just as they were losing all control. I know Clay wanted to stay in the air and follow me as I followed the big male, but I needed all my senses working, in particular my hearing.

A minute later I was running on the snow following the big guy's tracks. Clay was gone. It was now so nice and quiet. I followed the bear's tracks down through the forest, and yes, he'd gone right into the water. The creek had snow on both sides and was only about three feet (1 m) wide but looked deep for a little creek. There were no tracks anymore. The bear had to have staggered right down the stream, and with the snow on both sides, I knew he wouldn't get out; this was not good. I ran quickly on the snow – it was firm and I didn't sink more than a few inches. The bear had looked pretty drugged so I wasn't too worried that he could catch me if I caught up to him. But then, maybe he'd hit the bottom of his immobilization and was waking up and gaining control? I had my rifle so kept running quickly.

It wasn't more than 200 yards (183 m) and there he was, right in the creek, but luckily his big head was lying on a little snow bridge. He was licking rapidly as he panted. His eyes followed me but he could only move his head a little. I took out the radio. "Clay, you there?"

"Find him?"

"Yeh, he's in the creek, but his head's out. I'll need help getting him ready to lift out, if your line can reach him. I'll direct you to me. He's a big dude."

"We're off."

I got out the hobbles. I was sure glad that I had caught a big salmon-eating male on the coast the previous fall with feet so big that I had to really work hard to get my old hobbles on him. So I had invested five dollars in webbing and made myself a set for really big feet. They were much easier to get on a bear like this guy. I was in the creek now, bent over, down to my chin in about two feet (60 cm) of muddy, ice-cold water trying to hobble his front feet by feel. Water was slowly seeping in through my Gore-Tex.

"What are you doing going out in a place like this?" I asked the bear. "Sure, your relatives are polar bears that swim in the arctic waters all winter. My relatives are chimps sweating their ass off in the jungle. I didn't evolve for this."

I could hear Clay coming in the distance. "You there?" I dug my radio out of my pocket.

"I'm in the creek with my red coat. I'll direct you in."

Then the snow bridge with the bear's head on began to fail. I grabbed his stubby ears that had been torn in old fights and jammed my knee under his chin so my vertical lower leg bones took the weight; otherwise, his head would be too heavy to hold for long.

Clay was coming, but I had tossed the radio onto the snow when I had to grab the bear's ears. I reached but couldn't quite grab it. I lifted his head and switched knees, and then reached and just got the radio. By now I was fully soaked to the waist as well as my arms.

"Okay, downstream maybe 200 yards, you're close, okay, over top."

Clay turned and then I could hear him set down. Clayton should be here soon. There wasn't much more I could do on my own, so I just waited in the creek.

"Wow, he's a big guy," Clayton said as soon as he got there.

"And heavy. Why don't you grab his head and I'll see if I can get the hobble on his hinds."

I had the hobbles on his front feet, but his hinds were deeper in the water. I was floundering around when I heard Clay winding up the machine. There was no way I'd get the hobbles on in time.

"Maybe we can get Clay to just pull him out of the creek by his fronts, and we can hobble his rears out of the creek. We should help push his ass up to take weight off his arms."

Clay was now hovering above the spruce trees and dropping the long line slowly down through the tall canopy.

"You get the line, Clayton, I'll hold his head." Clayton wasn't really that wet yet, so there was no point in both of us being soaked in the ice water.

Clay slowly dropped the line down between the tall trees, but it stopped about 15 feet (5 m) above us. Over the radio he said, "That's as low as I can get, my skids are in the trees."

"Do we have any more ropes?" I asked.

"I've already put two together, that's all I have," Clay said over the radio.

"I've only got my six footer," I replied.

"No worries. I'll park and then we'll drag him out of there."

"Okay, Clayton, we're going to have to make a ramp to roll him out on. Use your boots and kick that snowbank down."

I could now hear Clay shutting down. He must have found a new little hole to land in. Clayton was kicking away at the snowbank on the edge of the creek. I was just standing in the creek with the bear's head on my knee again. I was getting very cold. Clay showed up and saw me in the ice water.

"Ohh, looks like you'll need a couple of hot rums tonight."

"Doubles, man, doubles. I'm thinking we can make sort of a ramp out of the snow and then roll him out."

"Wish I had my shovel. I pack a good one most of the winter to dig dead people out of avalanches. I just took it out last week," Clay said, and started kicking the snow down.

"Okay, someone else want to join me in the creek? The other can grab his ears and keep his head turning with his body?"

Clay jumped in the creek and reached into the water and grabbed the bear's hind leg.

"I sort of feel like a few hot rums myself, and they're always so much better when you're just about half froze solid," Clay laughed.

Clay lifted the bear's hind leg while I lifted his front leg, and with our knees under his body lifting as well, like tossing a huge hay bale, we rolled him, spread-eagled, just onto the snow ramp.

"Looks like he's been scrapping," I said.

Once we rolled him, I was looking right into an open wound that went from his chest about a foot (30 cm) long and into his armpit. It was beyond deep, it was peeled back right to his ribs like someone had been butchering him. His face was also torn open across his nose, but cut-up faces are so common with adult males in the spring that we didn't pay much attention.

The bear was now just out of the water a few inches. We had to roll him at least once more, but his back was now towards the creek and his legs pointing up and away from the creek. We pulled his rear legs straight back and dug one front leg into the snow right against his body. All three of us got into the creek below and, with a "one, two, three," rolled him over one more time. Now his legs were pointing back towards the creek. We could now lift his hind and front leg, and lever him over as we had before when we first got him out of the water. We were just getting him spread-eagled again when Clay said, "Wow, he's really been tussling, look at that hole."

There was a nice circular hole, the size of a grizzly bear canine tooth, or about three-quarters of an inch (1.9 cm) in diameter, right through his scrotum. It was fresh and clean with no infection at all. I looked in and could clearly see a testicle rolling around.

"Well, now, that's what I call ultimate fighting, not the wimpy stuff with no biting or even hitting below the belt," I commented.

"Yes sir, a little biting below the belt would sure keep a guy on his toes. Amazing he didn't get the old jewels ripped right off with that big tooth sunk right in there," Clay joked.

"Maybe the other guy lost his jewels first. After all, this guy was with the girl," I replied.

We finally had him out of the creek and Clay started getting the collar on. After taking his temperature, which was fine because he was so big and still pretty fat from the previous year, I went to find something that might act as a barrier to stop him from rolling back into the creek. Clayton started moving snow in for a barrier and I found a rotten old piece of log to add to the snow barrier. It was getting pretty dark under the forest canopy when we finished adjusting the collar. We didn't have time to measure him and certainly no chance of weighing him, but he was big. No doubt at least 500, but more likely 600 to 700 pounds (272 to 318 kg). In the last few days he could have lost his testicles in a fight. Just now he could have drowned. However, except for a few battle scars, he was fine. We named him Lucky.

The sun had gone down, but flying back to camp through the high mountains towards the remaining sunset glow was an almost magical experience, even when wet, cold and exhausted. Over the intercom, we chatted about the tooth hole in the scrotum. I told them about a bear Dan Carney and I had caught decades before that we called Singleton.

"I once caught an old Flathead male that had one of his nuts ripped right off, but the other one must have been working overtime because it was about the size of a grapefruit. He also had half of his face, including one eye, removed. His body seemed to be about half scar tissue. But that wasn't slowing him down. He was with a bear we called Mud, because we first caught her on a very rainy day and she was just covered, head to toe, with mud. When she was with him that spring, she was a cute little 5-year-old, but maybe his one nut wasn't working for him because she didn't have cubs the next year. She was pretty scrawny for a 5-year-old, though, I think she only weighed 135 pounds."

We were flying at the elevation of the mountain passes. The peaks, all a faint orange in the last alpenglow at the highest points, towered above us. We blasted through a pass at 120 miles (200 km) an hour and the earth fell away to almost darkness in a basin below. There was a small lake and some bare ground likely greening up beside it and a few stands of spruce trees. It was a long way from any road and I wondered when someone would have been there last. It would sure be a nice place to camp, just like the previous basin, the one before it and the next one would be.

"But old Singleton only had one eye. I think it was his left eye. He must have been digging roots most of the spring because the claws on his left paw were worn right down, but on his right paw they were the longest claws I've ever seen. It was pretty obvious that he only used his one eye and left paw when digging and eating roots."

"But I recall you telling me that their whole world comes through their nose," Clay said.

"Well, at a broader scale of space and time. From old Singleton, it seems that at the fine scales of feeding, or about a metre in distance and a second in time, they use their eyes; then they need instant and fine details. That's why they're active picking berries during the day but not at night. But to know what's going on over a few square miles and a few days, then they use their nose. But we don't really use ours. We can't really understand smell because our noses are so poor. We can see a bear walk by, but a minute later we wouldn't know it had been there. A bear can smell that another bear, that they of course know, went up the trail two days ago and another, perhaps one they mated with months before, crossed right here yesterday. And once in a while, they will know there is a dead elk two miles away. We sense mostly in three dimensions while they can sense in four. Their mental model of reality may be way more complex than ours. Imagine if light travelled at varying speeds and, in addition to what we can see right now, we could see fading images from the past few days. Nobody knows what a bear's nose knows."

"Dude, your brain's froze. We've got to pour a couple of rums into you pretty quick." Clay's remedy for most capture events.

**HELICOPTER CAPTURE WAS MORE EXPENSIVE** than having a graduate student, earning less than minimum wage, spending weeks trapping in an area like the Flathead where bears could be effectively snared from roads. But helicopter capture was cost effective in most situations, and now that I was collaring bears in many places in the province, I was most often doing it from a helicopter. It's a fast way to catch a lot of bears, and we could catch bears that had learned how to avoid traps. So by catching them every three years, we could keep monitoring some females year after year.

Based on measurements of stress hormones in the blood and movement rates shortly after capture, Marc Cattet, a vet who helped catch bears in Alberta, thinks helicopter capture is less stressful on the bear than is snaring (Cattet et al. 2008). Although snaring and using culverts may be necessary in many areas to get an unbiased sample of animals, perhaps the best feature of helicopter capture is that you don't need to deal with bait. Bait, which is generally rotting animal flesh, can get disgusting. Using putrid animal tissue week after week can, if you're not careful, get everything you own or wear a little bit gross.

Not that there aren't some good things about bait. In the early years of our study we used to get most of the bait from the B & B grocery store in Columbia Falls, Montana. This store had a policy that all meat had an expiry date, and then they'd toss it out. When we showed up to ask for meat scraps, the butcher would say, "You can take all of this, but you know, an hour ago it was on the shelf for sale."

Being students without much money, we interpreted that statement as "Fill your freezer, folks," and once we got so much good meat, we did try to find a freezer locker in Columbia Falls. We often had a few dozen big sausages hanging from the upper ceiling rafters of the cabin to dry. Once we had 17 picnic hams hanging from the rafters to dry like Jamon Iberico in a Spanish bar. Joe Perry, the Montanan cowboy, and Celine and I had a great dinner after being given all the seafood that was on display, after we showed up late on a Saturday afternoon. But that ended, and all the meat that was good enough for us to eat had to be sent to the dog food factory. After that, and for many years, we got all our grocery store cuttings from Jim Renney, who was the meat manager at Safeway in Cranbrook. Jim had a great interest in wildlife and our work, so always kept a few big buckets of the best pork and beef fat trimmings for us, a dream meal for a bear but nothing edible for us.

We also used a lot of road-killed animals for bait and, not surprisingly, dead elk and moose seemed to work best. I would usually carry a very sharp machete and a file in my truck. I could slice off the four legs of a dead elk in a couple of minutes and toss them in my pickup. That would leave the head attached to the oval-shaped, legless torso. Passing vehicles would slow down, and probably wonder what was happening when they saw me struggling to get the head and torso of an elk into my truck.

Death is the only guarantee in life (yes, taxes too), but death of animals, as well as death of people, is well hidden in our society. People kill a couple of billion large domestic animals every year, but how many people in North America have ever seen a dead cow or pig? For most people, meat comes on a Styrofoam tray, wrapped in cellophane. Dealing with death and dead animals greatly disturbs most people in our culture, but some bear trappers, who get used to dead animals and rotting flesh, develop a somewhat odd sense of humour over it all.

It was a very hot day near the end of July 1995, and I was working in my office in Revelstoke, BC. The phone rang. It was Parks Canada at the operations compound at Rogers Pass.

"There has been an unbelievably horrible smell in the warden's office for the past few days and it was getting worse and worse so we went on a full check of the place. The walk-in freezer downstairs has broken down and John Woods has it full of dead things. We can't find John and we don't know what to do. Can you come up and help us do something?"

For starters, I knew we had put hundreds of dead beavers that had been trapped and skinned in northern Alberta into that freezer. The greasy, fat rodents, with their stinky castor glands, are darn good bear bait, so we brought a pickup load of frozen beavers down in the late winter when it was still cold. What do you do with almost a ton of rotting beavers? I phoned Bob Forbes, the biologist in Cranbrook (after Ray Demarchi retired), where they also had a big walk-in freezer.

"Sure, bring them down. No problem. Phone me when you're ready to leave and I'll meet you at the compound."

I drove to Rogers Pass, and Kelly Stalker, who was working for Woods, was there to help me. Like all mammals that live in cold water, the beavers had about an inch (2.5 cm) of fat over their entire bodies. The fat was now a green, rancid slime with an extra touch of rotting castor gland. They were a total mess, but looked to me like perfect bait. Kelly and I grabbed them by the flat tail, one in each hand, and carried them out of the freezer and over to my pickup truck, where we tossed them onto a tarp I had spread out in the box. We did this for half an hour until the truck was obviously way overloaded. I certainly had some slime on my pants, but after so many beavers, Kelly wasn't strong enough to keep them held away from her. Her pants were saturated with slime. I phoned Forbes, and then we drove for five hours on the hot July afternoon to Cranbrook. There, once again, we had to carry the beavers into the Cranbrook freezer. By then we were used to the smell and didn't really notice it too much and didn't really think about it.

When we finished, it was 7 p.m. and I was very hungry.

"Kelly, how about we grab a quick burger for the road, I'm starving."

"Good idea, all that rotten beaver sure makes a gal hungry."

We pulled into McDonald's (before there was drive-through). It was crowded with locals and tourists on such a wonderful July evening. Kelly and I walked in. There were lineups to order food. In five seconds, at least

100 eyes were looking at us. In ten seconds, the place was clearing. In 20 seconds, we had a lot of space; the lineups had all but disappeared. It looked like the manager had stepped in to serve us. We ordered, had our burgers and fries in about five seconds and we left and started the long drive home.

"Didn't you order a Quarter Pounder?" Kelly asked me.

"No, I asked for a Big Mac."

"I guess they just gave us what they had ready. We got four fish burgers. I know we didn't order that."

"Good deal. They must have enjoyed our 'perfume de castor' so much they gave us a couple of extras."

We drove northward. An hour later, "You know, Kelly, this wasn't the first time I've grossed out that same McDonald's. There was this really funny Italian backyard butcher in Cranbrook I sometimes got bait from. It certainly wasn't legal, but he had just shot a cow right in his shop that was right downtown. We put all the very fresh guts into a 45-gallon (55 US gallon) drum in the back of my pickup. The barrel was full almost to the top. We had three hours to drive to the Flathead and I was hungry, so I suggested we stop for a quick burger. Of course the kids thought that was a great idea and Celine couldn't veto all of us. I drove in and, without thinking, I backed in right in front, with the tailgate of my truck facing the biggest window in the place. We were just sitting there having our burgers and then the guts started to bloat in the warm sun. The intestines almost crawled out of the barrel. After a while they were hanging all over. Some customers were wondering what was going on. I asked the kids if I should sneak out to the truck, slam the door and come back in and yell, 'Hey, your beef's here, where do you want me to put it?' but Celine vetoed the idea."

We continued northward. An hour later, "And that wasn't the first time I've horrified people when using beavers as bait. In the early 1980s a buddy of mine, Keith Simpson, started a bear project just north of Revelstoke and asked me to show him how to trap bears. He also had scrounged up some skinned beavers from the trappers. We were using one for a drag, you know, pulling it along a logging road for a mile or so to make a good scent trail right up to a trap for bears to follow. Well, Keith had some banking to do one afternoon so we drove to town and he parked in front of the bank. I went for a walk around the block to check things out, and when I returned, there was a small crowd at the back of Keith's truck. Lo and behold, we forgot to untie the beaver carcass from the truck and we had hauled it 50 miles

(80 km) down the highway. The bottom half had been ground away right to the ribs. They were all there but polished white. One poor, horrified guy asked me if I had forgotten to untie my dog."

I dropped off Kelly where she lived and I got home at 2 a.m. I stripped naked in the yard. Put all my clothes in a five-gallon pail and filled it with water from the hose. I had a long, hot, soapy shower. My work truck stunk for weeks. It probably still does.

CHAPTER 16

# WHY AREN'T THERE MORE GRIZZLIES?

From a conservation point of view, and in understanding the population ecology of grizzly bears, "Why aren't there more bears?" is the question that it's all about. As Charlie Krebs's textbook would say, "Grizzly bear ecology is the scientific study of the interactions that determine their distribution and abundance."

Recently it's been trendy to divide forces that limit abundance into top-down and bottom-up factors. Top-down factors are those driven from a higher trophic level. Most often, top-down refers to being eaten by a predator, or eaten by a herbivore for plants. Top-down also includes being killed by people and sometimes even parasitism or disease. Bottom-up factors are those from a lower trophic level, and in particular the quality, quantity and distribution of food. This simplification, of course, masks some interactions. Risk-sensitive foraging theory, as well as what has been often seen in the real world, suggests that a hungry bear, due to limited food, will take greater risks to obtain food, such as apples owned by a grumpy old codger who hates bears breaking branches off his trees yet is too cheap to buy an electric fence. Such a bear may then get top-down limited by being shot by the codger, when it's really a bottom-up factor that led to its demise. Interactions between top-down and bottom-up can get even more intertwined and complicated.

## 16.1 TOP-DOWN FACTORS

It's pretty obvious that top-down limitation, or people killing way too many grizzlies, was the major factor limiting, and often eliminating, these animals over most of the continent for almost two centuries. The eradication of grizzlies and other large carnivores from the Canadian prairies and from almost the entire lower 48 states of the US in the late 19th and early 20th centuries has been well documented (Brown 1985; Storer and Tevis Jr. 1955). There is no reason to believe that people in British Columbia were any different – many were the same gold-seeking 49ers who moved north from California when gold found in BC became known to the outside world in 1858 (Marshal 2018). Excessive human-caused mortality of grizzly bears continued into recent times.

When I began working on grizzly bears in the late 1970s, two old-timers in their 80s told me that the logging and mineral exploration crews they worked on in the 1930s and 1940s killed every bear they saw. Both said, "I really thought we were going to kill them all." Even in the Flathead, a logger who died years ago had told me that they had a garbage dump 100 yards (91 m) from camp in Ruby Creek, and there they shot six grizzlies in the summer of 1968, only ten years before I started my project. Until 1964, grizzly hunters didn't even need to buy a specific grizzly bear tag before they set out hunting, so they could legally kill a grizzly even if they just happened to come across one when hunting deer, moose or elk. It was also legal to kill a bear that wandered near their camp. If they wanted to actually go out and hunt for a grizzly, they often used a dead horse or the gut-pile of a deer or moose they had killed as bait. They could legally kill bears all year round, except during July and August when the bears were moulting and the hides were of no value. And North America was not the only continent where *Ursus arctos* was being persecuted. They were extirpated from North Africa, decimated in most of Europe and annihilated in much of Asia.

Although a light breeze of change in human values towards nature had been in the air since the writings of Henry David Thoreau, John Muir and Aldo Leopold, the wind seemed to pick up with Rachel Carson's *Silent Spring*. For grizzly bears in BC, the change happened in the early 1960s, and gained momentum in 1964 when Ray Demarchi became regional wildlife biologist in Cranbrook. The same year Ray began working as a biologist, it became mandatory that grizzly bear hunters buy a species tag before they went hunting; no longer could an elk or deer hunter legally shoot a grizzly whenever they happened to see one. Then in 1968, Ray had a major role in banning the use of bait to hunt bears, and in 1971 he closed the autumn hunting season in his region. Ray's encouragement led, in 1976, to the provincial policy having every grizzly bear killed by hunters, or anyone else, inspected and recorded by a government agent. He then limited the number of permits available for hunters and put these in a lottery system.

Legal hunting, once a major top-down factor, was under greater control in BC, but legal hunting is relatively easy to manage. Grizzly bears were, and still are, being killed for other reasons, and these deaths are rarely known and recorded by managers and therefore are far more difficult to control. Flathead data suggests that being killed for "other reasons" was much more common for females than the legal hunt was. Importantly, these forms of mortality do not have a feedback mechanism that reduces the rate at which people kill bears, even when the number of bears decline.

Historically, the lack of an ecological feedback mechanism enabled people to kill all the grizzlies across much of North America. Unlike in most predator/prey relationships, the number of predators (in this case, people) didn't depend on the abundance of prey (in this case, grizzly bears), so people remained abundant and even increased in numbers while continuing to kill bears until the bears were exterminated from large areas.

Today, there still isn't an ecological feedback mechanism for bears killed by trains and vehicles, or by deer and elk hunters defending themselves or their camp, or for conflict animals around settlements. The mortality rate of bears need not depend on the density of bears. The human-caused mortality rate is what ecologists call *density independent*. Density-independent factors sometimes cause local extirpation because the death rate is not reduced even at low population numbers.

Although closed in 2017, the legal hunter kill of grizzly bears depended on many factors, and the rate may or may not have been density independent. If the hunt had been an open season for a limited time period, as is common for species like deer, then the kill rate would likely have depended, at least to some degree, on the density of animals, and so would have been *density dependent*. In that case, as the number of the hunted species declined, then hunter success rate would likely decline at about the same rate. Additionally, however, the number of hunters would also decline because they would go elsewhere to hunt where there were more animals, or they might not hunt at all. If, on the other hand, animal numbers increased, then hunter success would increase, but also more hunters would go to where there were more animals, so the number of hunters would increase. These hunting regulations likely result in a somewhat density-dependent kill rate, with the rate increasing at high densities of animals and decreasing at low densities of animals. Density-dependent factors keep animal numbers from going very high or very low. Ecologists sometimes call density-dependent factors *regulating factors* because they stimulate a population to grow when there are few animals but reduce and even stop population growth when populations get high or close to carrying capacity. Regulating factors are most commonly related to competition over food sources, but I used hunting as an example to explain the concepts of *density dependence* and *population regulation.*

Hunting regulations for grizzly bears in BC were unlike rules for most other hunted species, in that there was no open season but only a limited number of permits for restricted areas. These much more restrictive regulations enabled great control over the number of male and female bears killed by hunters. The success rate of the hunters would likely change as bear populations gradually fluctuated in size, but because the number of hunters would usually remain the same (i.e., same number of permits), the hunter kill rate would likely be density independent, much like other forms of human-caused mortality. Legal hunting would become somewhat density dependent if the number of bears got so high, or so low, that the number of permits changed, or individual bear hunters put in more or less effort. In many areas of the US, Alberta and southern BC, the number of permits was reduced, often to zero, when populations were thought to be too small, making the hunter kill a density-dependent factor.

**ACROSS MOST OF THEIR DISTRIBUTION,** people remain the major top-down limiting factor of grizzly bear populations, and the rate is usually density independent. The importance of human-caused mortality ranges from minor in remote protected areas to very high where grizzly bear habitat overlaps with highways, railways, farms and other types of human settlement. In these human-dominated areas, almost all grizzly bear deaths are due to people, and most are ultimately due to bear attractants such as garbage, fruit trees and other crops, compost and barbeques, as well as to living and dead livestock and chickens, and livestock feed – the list goes on and on. Attractants lead to bears being near people and therefore becoming habituated or, in other words, becoming accustomed to being near people. Many bears in these areas also become food conditioned or learn to associate good food with people. Food-conditioned bears expect to find good food where people are, and some bears seeking food may get a little too bold and even intrusive for most people's comfort.

Black and grizzly bears that become habituated, or food conditioned, sometimes swat or bite people, and although extremely rarely, sometimes people are more seriously injured. Not surprisingly, the news media, which is in the entertainment business, highlights these sensational events and consequently most people are frightened of bears near their homes or camps. Then some people will shoot the bears, or they call the conservation officers, who have to deal with the situation as best they can. Once a bear is food conditioned, it almost always ends up being shot by someone. As is often stated, *a fed bear is a dead bear.*

There have been efforts all over the globe to reduce or manage attractants to decrease human-bear conflicts, along with conflicts with many other species. Reducing and managing attractants is complex and can be a huge task, but it is necessary if we want to stop killing bears that we unwittingly encourage to be near us. Situations vary enormously, but one example in a human-dominated area that ended up having major ramifications across BC occurred in the town of Revelstoke, BC. Celine, the kids and I moved to Revelstoke in 1992 to work with John Flaa of Parks Canada on caribou in the winter when bears were hibernating, while keeping the Flathead grizzly study going the rest of the year.

**IN THE EARLY 1990S, REVELSTOKE** had a serious problem with both black and grizzly bears, or, more accurately, both black and grizzly bears had a serious problem with Revelstoke. As in most communities, there were fruit trees growing in people's yards. But there were also well-pruned and maintained apple trees in playgrounds right next to swing sets and slides for kids to play on. There were also hundreds of feral (wild) fruit trees, germinated from discarded cores, scattered throughout the town and in nearby rural areas. Open public garbage disposal bins were placed about town, and people put out their garbage cans on the roadside the night before pickup, giving bears all night to dine out. There were also the usual rural attractants of chickens, ducks and sheep. Revelstoke also had an open garbage dump about half a mile (800 m) from a subdivision. There were no conservation officers stationed in town at the time, and they couldn't get there until about 7 a.m. because they had to cross a ferry that stopped operating at night.

Charlie and Michelle were teenagers when we lived in Revelstoke. When they were not home when they were supposed to be on a Friday night, we were much more concerned that they had bumped into a mother grizzly with cubs than that they had drank too much booze or got into drugs. At night, there were a lot of black and grizzly bears wandering around the neighbourhood, although some were also around during the day.

The management strategy in Revelstoke had been simply to trap and shoot most black bears and either move or shoot the grizzlies. In the eight years between 1986 and 1993, at least 69 grizzlies and 256 black bears had been either shot or moved a great distance away. In September 1994, an electric fence was built around the garbage dump. In 1994 and 1995 alone, 51 grizzlies and 55 black bears were removed. Clearly, with 120 grizzly bears, including at least 50 females, being removed in a decade, Revelstoke was a major *population sink*, sucking in and eliminating bears from the mountains all around the town, including from Mount Revelstoke and Glacier national parks.

Because there were no conservation officers in town, John Flaa and I were sometimes phoned when a trap set for a black bear ended up catching a grizzly cub instead. Having a very pissed-off mother grizzly in town was not a healthy situation. This happened three times in Revelstoke when I lived there. In one case, the trap with the cub inside was between a trailer park and an elementary school. John and I were phoned at around 4 a.m. with the request to trap or dart the mother grizzly, and if we couldn't, we were to let the cub go if the mother would let us get close enough. If not, well, we were to do what we thought was best. Celine asked, "Who phones in the middle of the night?"

"There is a bit of a bear issue. I have to go meet Flaa. I'll be back soon."

As is apparently common in horror movies, it was a dark and very rainy night. Flaa and I, towing a culvert trap on wheels behind a Parks Canada pickup, pulled up to the address we'd been given. We stopped next to the mobile home. The dim, yellowish porch light provided some visibility, but also cast long, dark shadows. No mother grizzly to be seen. We got out into the steady, cold rain. John loaded his shotgun with the standard four three-inch magnum slugs. We quickly walked to the door next to the yellow light. Before we had a chance to knock, the door opened maybe a quarter of the way. The mom, dad and son, who was about 8 years old, were huddled together inside. There was fear in their eyes, and in everything else about them. We came in. John cracked a joke about Revelstoke weather to lighten the mood. We then told them about the extra trap we'd brought and, if that didn't work, how we could likely shoot the mom with a dart gun from a window. They seemed very happy to have us there to help. Nothing like diluting risk among more people – the selfish herd. They had been in a state of fear since they watched the cub enter the trap from their window and the immensely large and powerful, human food-fed mother bear proceed to bang the heavy trap around. We took our dart guns and drug kits into the home.

We had already baited our culvert trap with some wonderful bait. John skilfully backed the trap next to the trap the cub was in. I rode shotgun, literally. We were prepared for a good strong thump somewhere, but luckily, mom didn't show up. Most often a truck is too much for a mother grizzly, but certainly not always. I also think town bears are more understanding, at least when in town, than are wilderness bears. When in town they know they are in a risky place and are somewhat cautious there. We left the trap hitched to the truck and turned off the engine and headlights. Damn, it was dark. The rain seemed to increase when the wipers stopped. We couldn't see anything from inside the pickup and all we heard was rain. Where was mom? We felt a little safe inside the truck but knew we had to step out into the dark and walk around to the front of the mobile home.

"Do you get overtime for this?" John asked, likely to postpone us leaving the dry warmth and comparable safety of the truck.

"At 4 a.m. I'm a volunteer," I answered.

"I've always thought so of you, but maybe both of us are the real definition of dumb," John joked, or maybe he was serious.

"We'd better do it. Wish they had a back door. I'll go out first. We'll walk together. If I hear her coming, well, I guess I empty the gun at her."

We walked side by side with our headlamps on. There seemed to be a lot of shrubs and bushes for a bear to hide in, but we made it back to the door under the dim yellow light and went inside. We mixed drugs, loaded two dart guns. I found a little window in the bathroom that overlooked the traps. I removed the screen and stood on the edge of the tub and waited. John found another window facing the backyard. It was now 5:30 a.m. We had maybe two hours before school opened, and then things could get really complicated.

In about an hour I saw some shrubs moving. Out of the bush came the mother and her second cub. My dart gun was ready, but she moved towards our trap. I waited to see if she would go in. She sniffed the air. She sniffed the trap with the cub inside. She sniffed the new trap with the wonderful bait. She ate the nice fat morsel of porch bait we had placed just at the entrance. That's all it took. She hopped inside – beautiful. Her cub followed – even better. A second later – bang, the door slammed shut.

"Fucken A!" the father yelled.

"Don't swear, you asshole!" the mother yelled.

John and I had a round of high fives with the family and told them we had heard swearing maybe once or twice before.

The conservation officers arrived a few hours later and three more grizzlies were removed from the local ecosystem. They were moved far away. But who knows what happened to them and, perhaps more importantly, who knows what effect the newcomers had on the society of local resident bears? After all, these were big, fat bears that had been living well on a diet fortified with human foods. How would smaller, wilderness bears deal with the newcomers? We don't know. Out of sight and out of mind, and all the people are happy and feeling good.

The entire bear situation in and around Revelstoke was chaos and almost everyone in town knew it, but nothing was changing. Bears were simply being attracted to town, caught in traps and then shot or moved to unknown terrain a long way away. After watching a mother grizzly with two cubs eating apples in a playground next to a swing set, I went to city hall and told the mayor, whom I knew from caribou issues, to have the trees removed. He balked, as politicians usually do, so I said, "If a kid gets beat up or killed, I'll make sure the parents and their lawyer know that I came here and warned you. I suspect the town will be liable for a huge pile of money, and it should be. We know better."

Nothing happened, at least not right away. More bears were shot. Finally, an outspoken and well-known woman in town had seen enough bloodshed. She was so upset that she punched a conservation officer who was about to shoot a black bear out of a fruit tree. The time had finally come to do something.

We formed a local bear management committee that included elected officials from the City and Regional District, Parks Canada staff, the Royal Canadian Mounted Police, Friends of Mount Revelstoke and Glacier national parks, the Revelstoke Rod and Gun Club, and myself. Most importantly, we got the head conservation officer in the region, Richard Deloise, to be the chair. Finally, things were starting to change. But change takes effort and effort needs money. The "Friends" offered up some funding, but they didn't have much.

The Columbia Basin Trust allocates money to communities affected by the numerous hydroelectric projects on the Columbia River. There was such a huge variety of interest groups wanting funding that to have written proposals reviewed by a few people would no doubt have led to accusations of bias and favouritism, so they had a different process. They held an open forum where individuals representing many groups had five minutes to get up in front of everyone and state their case. Then a fairly large committee ranked them. I was asked to present the case for the bear management committee. I didn't use up my five minutes but maybe five seconds.

"To continue, year after year, to attract dozens of bears into town by our sloppiness, and then to kill them, is simply wrong and ethically bankrupt. We now have a bear management committee, but we need funding to begin to fix this obviously ridiculous situation." I sat down. We got our funding.

With it, we hired a bear awareness coordinator and provided her with enough funding to do a host of tasks, from talking at schools, being on the local radio station and reporting in the newspaper, to organizing fruit tree removal teams. We removed hundreds of trees – most were scrawny feral trees. The city started to replace open garbage bins with bear-proof containers and developed new bylaws about garbage and fruit. Sure, there were old grumpy guys who thought we should just continue to kill bears, but that generation was passing on quickly. The town showed its spirit and only four grizzlies and 60 black bears were euthanized or moved away over the next decade; not perfect, but from 31 to six black bears a year, and 12 grizzlies per year to less than one every two years, was a huge change. Maybe the Revelstoke sink had drained almost all of the grizzly bears over a huge area by the time we started the bear awareness program, but there are bears in the forests and mountains now. Revelstoke is so proud of their grizzly bears that there are large statues of bears in several places in town.

Three years later, other communities became interested in what we had done in Revelstoke and the program expanded across the region. The BC Conservation Foundation began to administer the regional program and then it spread across the province, becoming Bear Aware and then WildsafeBC. Although there are a few population sinks for grizzly bears in BC, such as the Elk Valley just north of the Flathead and Bella Coola on the coast, they are considerably less common and less of a drain on their local bear populations than they had been. Furthermore, moving conflict bears great distances away is less common now. More often these bears are moved only a short distance and effort goes into reducing or eliminating the attractant.

THE FLATHEAD IS SIMILAR to most of the current grizzly bear range in North America in that it has no permanent human settlement or highways, but it is certainly not a remote, protected wilderness. In the Flathead, people remain by far the dominant top-down limiting factor, at least for bears old enough to be independent of their mother. Once they reached two years of age, over 80 per cent of the bears that died ended up being killed by people.

Although Flathead bears were legally hunted up to 2017, the high proportion of them that ended up killed by people was about the same as in areas without hunting, but where there is considerable human interface. Between 1981 and 2001, in and around Yellowstone National Park, where there wasn't a grizzly bear hunt, 19 (83 per cent) of the 23 radio-collared grizzlies that died from known causes were killed by people (Schwartz et al. 2006). In northern Montana, where there is also no legal hunting of grizzly bears, two studies by Rick Mace found 15 of 20 (75 per cent) deaths of radio-collared bears were caused by people (Mace and Waller 1998; Mace et al. 2012). In and around Banff National Park, where bears were not hunted, 15 of 18 (83 per cent) collared bears that died were killed by people (Garshelis, Gibeau, and Herrero 2005). In central BC, where, like the Flathead, there was legal grizzly bear hunting, 11 of 13 (85 per cent) of the collared bears that died were killed by people (Ciarniello et al. 2009).

This level of human-caused mortality, however, does not mean the death rate is causing these populations to decline. Populations in the Flathead (McLellan 2015), Yellowstone (Schwartz et al. 2006), northern Montana (Mace et al. 2012), the south Chilcotin Mountains (McLellan et al. 2019), and maybe even Banff (Garshelis, Gibeau and Herrero 2005) have generally been expanding over the past several decades. The human-caused mortality, however, does affect the population structure even of expanding populations. In all of these areas, female survival rates were consistently 94 or 95 per cent, sufficient to have population growth. Male bears, however, died at much higher rates than did females, with annual survival rates of only 84 to 86 per cent in Yellowstone, northern Montana and Banff and, at 81 per cent, a little lower in the hunted Flathead Valley. The higher rate of human-caused mortality of males is why there was a much higher density of females than males in the 2007 Flathead DNA-based inventory.

**IT IS CERTAINLY NOT SURPRISING** that human-caused mortality continues to be the major top-down limiting factor in areas with towns, subdivisions and farmland in settled valleys. It is a little more surprising that human-caused mortality remains so dominant in areas such as Yellowstone, Montana, Banff and the Flathead, where bears and people overlap less often. But what happens in very remote wilderness areas where bears are not hunted? Are there any top-down factors limiting grizzly bear numbers in such areas?

These populations should be at or near ecological carrying capacity, or the maximum population size a species can sustain in a given environment. Unfortunately, due to human intrusion, such areas are rare in BC, as well as almost everywhere else in North America. But research has been done in both Denali (Keay, Robbins and Farley 2018) and Katmai national parks in Alaska (Sellers et al. 1999) and in Kluane National Park, Yukon (McCann 1998), as well in northern Yukon (Maraj 2016) and the barren grounds of the Northwest Territories (McLoughlin et al. 2003), and in remote mountains in eastern BC (Ciarniello et al. 2009). In these studies, 47 independent bears (not with their mother) died when wearing a radio collar. Of these, 85 per cent died of natural causes; only 15 per cent were killed by people. The proportions of the bears that were killed by people in these remote areas were nearly the exact opposite to those of bears living in the Flathead, Yellowstone, Montana and Banff.

In these remote areas, what kills a grizzly bear? The actual cause of death in these wilderness areas was only known for 24 of the natural deaths, and 18 of these (75 per cent) were killed by other grizzly bears. In the southern study areas, where the majority of radio-collared bears were killed by people, 60 per cent of the 38 natural mortalities with a known cause were also due to grizzly bears killing each other. When the killer was known, it was always an adult male grizzly. Murder and cannibalism is not rare with grizzlies, as is also the case in many other species. In all of these areas, both northern wilderness and southern areas with more human contact, the cause of death was known for 62 natural (not caused by people) mortalities of bears over two years of age, and only three bears were thought to have starved, while six seemed to have died of old age. The data suggest that once old enough to be independent of their mother, grizzly bears can keep their body charged up enough with energy and protein to almost always avoid starvation.

The grizzly bears in the northern wilderness areas with no hunting were probably near to carrying capacity, where bottom-up factors, or competition over a limited amount of food, are expected to be severe. Maybe some of these bears were killed by other bears while fighting over limited food, or perhaps they were almost starving so they were easy for other bears to kill – we know a few were. But if near starvation predisposing bears to being killed by others was common, then the natural mortality rate in these unhunted wilderness populations should be higher than in populations that are kept below carrying capacity by human-caused mortality. But the natural mortality rate of independent bears in Denali, Kluane, northern Yukon and the barren grounds of the Northwest Territories averaged about 3 per cent a year, about the same as in the southern populations where grizzly bear deaths were dominated by human causes.

In Katmai, however, things were different. There, bear densities were at least ten times higher than in the other populations (Miller et al. 1997) where survival has been measured, and the natural mortality rate was 9 per cent, or about three times higher than other populations. In seven of the nine cases where the cause of death was known in Katmai, the bear was killed by another grizzly, and an eighth starved because her jaw and tongue had been damaged in a fight with another bear. Grizzlies killing other grizzlies, and in particular males killing females, is a top-down limiting factor, and appears most common in unhunted wilderness populations that attain very high bear densities.

In these unhunted wilderness populations, 100 per cent of the 34 deaths of females were due to natural causes. But even in these very remote areas, seven of the 13 deaths of males were due to people. If males captured and collared in these remote and often protected areas still die most often at the hands of people, then it is likely that almost every male grizzly bear on the continent is vulnerable to being killed by a person. There is just not enough room left anywhere, including remote portions of Alaska and northern Canada, for these wide-ranging male bears to spend a lifetime safely away from people.

## 16.2 BOTTOM-UP FACTORS AND POPULATION REGULATION

It may seem to be the science of proving the obvious, but without excessive human-caused mortality, it seems food supply, interspecific conflict or both will ultimately limit the population size of apex carnivores such as grizzly bears. After all, not much else will kill a grizzly bear but a person or another grizzly bear, although packs of wolves have killed some on occasion.

A simple comparison of bear densities across the continent clearly shows the importance of food. On the Alaskan Peninsula and on some Alaskan Islands where huge numbers of salmon spawn in many small streams so the best fishing sites are not all dominated by big fat males, population densities are 10 to 50 times higher than for any interior population or even coastal systems with fewer small spawning streams (Miller et al. 1997; McLellan

1994). This is not surprising because these fish have grown from nutrients they have consumed across the enormous North Pacific Ocean, only to return by the millions to spawn and die in very restricted areas. Lots and lots of salmon available to females results in lots and lots of bears.

In the Flathead, black and grizzly bears put on the fat needed for hibernation and reproduction primarily when feeding on huckleberries and buffalo berries. When these fruits were scarce, female grizzlies failed to reproduce as often as when fruits were abundant (McLellan 2015). Large huckleberry fields growing after wildfires burned in the 1920s and 1930s is the only obvious reason why so many more bears were detected in DNA hair traps north of the border than just south of the border in the northwest corner of Glacier National Park, where there were no major berry fields. Recently, both Michael Proctor working in the Selkirk and Purcell mountains (Proctor, Lamb and MacHutchon 2017) and my daughter, Michelle, working in the southern Coast Mountains (McLellan 2020), have found the extent of huckleberry producing habitat to be the best predictor of grizzly bear densities. No doubt other foods are also important to bears, but some, such as roots and green vegetation eaten in the spring and early summer, are abundant both north and south of the border in the Flathead and don't fluctuate in abundance from year to year like fruit does. Also, bears do not seem to have put much of a dent in the supply of these other foods by the time berries become ripe, so these food are unlikely to be limited in the Flathead.

In areas without salmon or fruit, other high-energy foods eaten by bears in the late summer or fall must be available; otherwise there will be few grizzly bears. In the Yellowstone ecosystem, an abundance of elk and bison, army cutworm moths and, in particular, whitebark pine seeds are the foods that enable that population to thrive (Schwartz et al. 2014). Similarly, whitebark pine seeds are the primary food for grizzly bears along the dry side of the Coast Mountains in BC; there I have caught and put radio collars on some very fat grizzlies. These bears had been climbing high in whitebark pine trees and eating seeds while sitting way up in the tree canopy. They also broke off large branches and then came down out of the tree and cleaned up the cones scattered all over the ground. In the Rocky Mountains, my son Charlie and I once watched an entire grizzly bear family, way up in the canopy, picking apart cones and eating seeds. The mother and both cubs were literally head and shoulder above any tree branches. Sometimes grizzlies let squirrels do all the hard work and just raid the rodents' caches

(Kendall 1983). In other ecosystems, large mammals, including migratory barren-ground caribou, are the dominant high-energy food that supports the local grizzly bear population (Maraj 2016).

The abundance of some of the most important foods, such as berries, salmon, whitebark pine seeds and migrating caribou, often fluctuates enormously from year to year. But it wasn't the number of bears that caused the amount of these foods to change. A very hot and dry July can wither berries whether there are 100 bears in a valley or only 50. But there will always be some berries and many other less preferred foods, so if there are only 50 bears, there will be less competition for these foods than if there are 100 bears. If bears do compete over a fluctuating food source, then it's a complex interaction of density-independent change in annual food abundance, and density-dependent competition over the foods available, particularly during poor food years.

Although grizzly bear populations, like the one in the Flathead, will gradually fluctuate in size over the years due to inconsistent food abundance, food is usually a regulating factor. When the population becomes small, there is more food per bear, so their reproduction and cub survival will be high, as it was in the Flathead when I began my study. When the population is very high and there is a lot of competition among bears for food, reproduction and usually cub survival will decline. Regulating factors, such as competition over food, cause what some people call the *balance of nature*.

The effect of food as a density-dependent regulating factor is best seen in the unhunted wilderness areas such as Denali, Katmai, Kluane and northern Yukon, where populations are at carrying capacity. What mechanisms regulate these populations? First, as I found in the Flathead during the decade of poor huckleberry crops, reproductive rates were low mostly because females had their first litter when they were a year or two older than females in nearby populations that were below carrying capacity. During the prolonged period of poor berries, the females also had a year or so longer interval between litters (Miller, Sellers and Keay 2003). What is most striking, however, is that cub mortality in these unhunted wilderness populations was much higher than elsewhere. In Kluane, 51 per cent of the cubs seen in the spring perished in their first year (McCann 1998), while 60 per cent died in northern Yukon (Maraj 2016) and 66 per cent died in both Denali (Keay, Robbins and Farley 2018) and Katmai (Sellers et al. 1999). Causes of death are rarely known; cubs are seen one day and then next time the radio-collared mother is seen, she has fewer or no cubs.

**SOME CUBS,** however, have been known to be in poor condition. In mid-June following a very poor huckleberry year in the Flathead, I saw Monique with one tiny cub we called Festus. It was about the size of a small house cat. The little fellow could only keep up when she was walking slowly, but struggled to crawl over a downed log. It was so scrawny that I didn't think Festus had much of a chance, and sure enough, Monique was alone a month later. I don't know what actually killed the little cub, but I'm pretty confident it was at least related to its very poor condition.

I tracked Sally from when she was a cub in 1986 to her death at 19 years of age. Sally had two cubs when she was shot by an elk hunter in perceived self-defence two days before Halloween in 2005. It had been a total bust of a huckleberry year and Sally's family had been digging sweet vetch roots near the edge of a clearcut. The conservation officer was called and he did what he hated to do and euthanized both cubs. He told me that the cubs were so scrawny that he didn't think it was humane to let them slowly starve. The conservation officer skinned out all three bears. He told me that none of them had any fat and he was sure the cubs would not have survived the winter, and doubted Sally would have either. There is little information from the remote northern studies on the condition of cubs when they died, although three yearlings starved in their winter den in Denali. There is little doubt that cub survival is affected by food abundance in some cases.

## 16.3 INFANTICIDE

Cubs in the unhunted wilderness areas, as well as cubs in many other areas including the Flathead, were killed by other bears and, once again, adult males are the ones usually holding the smoking gun – but not always. I was once watching bears feeding on salmon at McNeil Falls in Alaska with other biologists Stephen Herrero, Larry Aumiller and Derek Stonorov, when we saw a female grizzly kill a cub. On the far side of the river from where we were, almost two dozen big fat males were either sleeping on the riverbank or in the water fishing. There were no females over there. Then, just downstream from where the males were, a mother with two cubs approached along a trail through dense shrubs. Then another female with cubs came along a different trail. Both mothers looked to be on high alert with so many males around. Then one mom became separated from her cubs along the narrow and braiding trails. She seemed to panic and rushed through the bush. She veered to the right as if she heard a cub bawl. But it wasn't her cub that she found standing alone. The excited mother grabbed it and crushed it in her jaws. She dropped it and then found her own cubs. It was over in a second or two.

By far, however, it has been adult males that have been seen killing cubs, and most, though certainly not all, were killed in the spring during the grizzly bear mating season. Males killing cubs during the mating season has led biologists, particularly those working in Scandinavia, to discuss the possibility of sexually selected infanticide in bears (Swenson et al. 1997; Swenson 2003; Gosselin et al. 2015; Gosselin et al. 2017; Leclerc et al. 2017), shortly after this behaviour became known and documented in other species (Hrdy 1974; Hrdy 1979; Bertram 1975).

Sexually selected infanticide happens when a male kills infants that are not his own and are not yet weaned so that the mother will more rapidly become receptive to mating and there is a high chance it will be with the male that did the killing. But the grizzly bear mating season is at the same time of year when some grizzlies prey, with great focus and zeal, on newborn animals of other species, such as moose, elk and caribou, so the ultimate reason for males killing cubs has been debated.

Sexually selected infanticide has been shown for many species but perhaps is most clearly documented in African lions, and that species provides a good example to explain a behaviour that some people consider to be maladaptive or even pathological. Lions often live in prides of usually closely related adult females, their young, and a "coalition" of one or more adult males. The pride is territorial and defends their area from other lions. Within the pride, the males have exclusive breeding rights with the females; outsiders are not welcome. Young males are evicted from the pride when they approach maturity and, often with their brothers, become nomadic, or wander widely without a pride or territory. When they encounter another pride they may, if they think they will win, fight with the pride's coalition of males. If the new immigrant males drive out or kill the males in the pride, then they kill the young cubs so the mothers return to breeding condition quickly. Male tenure in a pride of lions is not long, so infanticide enables males to father many more cubs than if they waited for the cubs that had been fathered by a member of the previous coalition of males to grow up. If the behaviour of infanticide in these cases has a genetic component, then it won't be long before all males are infanticidal in these conditions. Trophy hunting may cause unnaturally rapid turnover of adult males in prides, and result in an increase of infanticide and cause cub survival to become low in some areas (Loveridge et al. 2016; Mweetwa et al. 2018).

This form of infanticide, where a male immigrates after an adult resident male dies, and then the immigrant kills cubs that would not be his, has been shown for several other territorial species, and has been suggested for both grizzly and black bears. It has been argued that with this mechanism of "immigrant male" infanticide, killing adult males by hunting would cause cub survival to become low just as it does with lions. Bears, however, are not territorial and both sexes have large, overlapping home ranges. In a place like the Flathead, every female will be within the home range of about a dozen adult males. Many if not most adult males I've caught in the breeding season were wounded from fights they had over females; competition for mates is often fierce. If a male dies, there isn't a vacuum of empty habitat to be filled by an immigrant male, as there would be in a territorial animal like a lion. If a male does kill an entire litter of cubs, then there is a good chance he will not get to mate with the female without fighting off other males; limited data suggests it takes between two and seven days for a female to go from being a lactating mother to estrus once her entire litter is killed (McLellan 2005; Steyaert et al. 2012). This major difference in social structure between bears and lions does not mean that sexually selected infanticide does not exist in bears, but if it does, it is likely a slightly different mechanism.

In bears, why wouldn't any male who did not mate with the female the previous year, so is not the father, kill her cubs and wait for her to become receptive? Why would it be limited to an immigrant male, who would likely be younger and smaller than the adult males he would have to fight with, once the mother became receptive again? Most young dispersing males are not much larger than the mothers they would have to overcome. It has often been suggested that female promiscuity in species with sexually selected infanticide is to confuse paternity, and therefore is a female's counter-strategy to infanticide (McLellan 2005; Steyaert et al. 2012; Ebensperger 1998). Confusing paternity only works if males recognize who they mated with. With a "mate recognition" form of sexually selected infanticide, any male who did not mate with the mother the previous year could kill cubs, provided he would not do better by just continuing to search for a female without cubs that is already in breeding condition (McLellan 2005). So which form, if any, of sexually selected infanticide operates in bears? You may ask, "Who really cares?" The difference, however, is important because killing male bears will have opposite effects for each form on cub survival and therefore on population trend and status.

Can we follow the scientific method and test these two competing hypotheses? First, based on the different mechanisms, we will deduce testable predictions. The mechanism behind the immigrant male hypothesis suggests that populations with high levels of adult male mortality would have rapid male turnover. Immigrant males would be frequently filling the void left by the dead adult males, resulting in frequent infanticide and therefore high cub mortality. The prediction of the immigrant male mechanism is therefore a positive relationship between male mortality rates and cub mortality rates; populations with high male mortality should have high cub mortality.

The mate recognition mechanism makes the opposite prediction. High male mortality would result in populations with fewer adult males to kill cubs and a greater chance that each male would be the father of a female's cubs. Also, there would be more females per male so the males would be spending more time mating, not killing cubs and waiting for the mother's body chemistry to change from being a lactating mother to one in estrus. The mate recognition hypothesis predicts low cub mortality in populations with high male mortality. A high ratio of male mortality to female mortality, such that the living sex ratio becomes dominated by females, should be the best predictor of the mate recognition mechanism.

From academic journal papers and from detailed reports and raw data, I summarized cub, female and male survival rates from 12 grizzly bear populations in North America. The studies ranged from Yellowstone in the south to Denali, northern Yukon and the barren grounds of the Northwest Territories in the north. They included the fates of 954 cubs, 2,038 bear-years of tracking females and 872 bear-years of tracking males. The main test statistic is whether cub mortality rates are positively correlated with male mortality rates as predicted by the immigrant male hypothesis, or are negatively correlated as predicted by the mate recognition hypothesis – or, perhaps, infanticide is not totally sexually selected but occurs because some bears are focused on preying on neonates (i.e., babies) of large mammals at that time of year (Griffin et al. 2011; Brockman 2017).

Let's use a simple regression analysis, weighted by the sample size of each study (although this weighting does not affect the conclusions in this case) to test the predictions of the two hypotheses. We find a negative correlation between male and cub mortality rates; when male mortality is high, cub mortality is low (Figure 7). The probability that the relationship was due

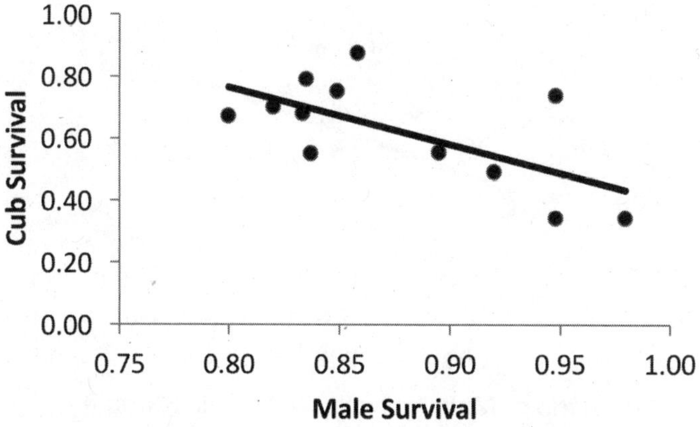


**Figure 7:** Two hypotheses of how sexually selected infanticide (SSI) may operate in bears have been proposed. First is the immigrant male hypothesis, where high male mortality results in rapid turnover of males. The new immigrant males, that cannot be the father of cubs in the area, kill cubs so the mother will soon become receptive for mating. This hypothesis predicts a positive relationship between male survival and cub survival. The second hypothesis has been called the mate recognition hypothesis, and here any male who knows that he did not mate with the mother the previous year, so knows he is not the father, may kill cubs so the mother will soon become receptive for mating. The results from 12 studies in North America show that when male survival is high, cub survival is low ($r^2 = 0.48$, $p = 0.012$), suggesting that if SSI operates in grizzly bears, it is more likely the mate recognition hypothesis.

to chance alone is about one in 85. If the infanticide that has been observed in grizzly bears during the mating season is sexually selected, then it likely follows the mate recognition mechanism and thus populations with high male mortality rates will have low cub mortality.

What about the prediction that the ratio of male to female mortality should be the best predictor of the mate recognition hypothesis? Is cub survival higher in populations where males have a high mortality rate, but females have a low rate? These populations would have the most unbalanced adult sex ratio; the relatively few adult males would have a higher chance of being fathers of the litters and these males would be busy mating because there are many more adult females than adult males. The regression of cub mortality rates to the ratio of male to female mortality rates is strongly positive with virtually zero chance (< 0.001) of being due to chance (Figure 8). The results suggest that 72 per cent of the variation in cub mortality can be explained by the ratio of male to female mortality rates. The evidence suggests that populations where females have much higher survival rates than

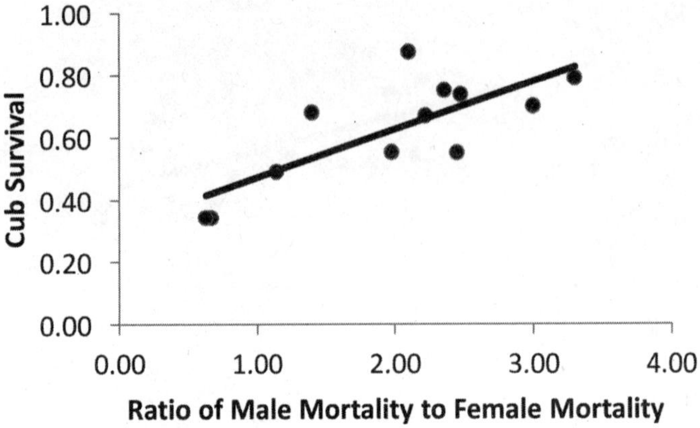


**Figure 8:** The mechanism underlying the mate recognition hypothesis of sexually selected infanticide suggests that the ratio of male to female mortality rates should be the best predictor of cub survival. When male survival is low but female survival is high, there would be far more females than males living in the population. There are two reasons why males would kill cubs less frequently in a population with fewer males than populations with a more equal sex ratio. First, with fewer males, each male would have a higher chance of being the father of litters, and if they can recognize a female they mated with the previous year, they should not kill her cubs as they may be his own too. Female promiscuity to confuse paternity is thought to be a female's counter-strategy to this form of SSI. Second, the relatively few males would be more occupied mating so would be less likely to kill cubs and have to wait for the female to become receptive. This hypothesis is supported by the data ($r^2 = 0.72$, $p< 0.001$).

males will have high cub survival. This result is also supported by a population of brown bears in northern Sweden. There, illegal killing of male bears was so high that very few (22 per cent) survived to become adults, so there were many more adult females than adult males (Swenson 2003). In that study area, cub mortality was only 4 per cent, the lowest ever recorded (Swenson et al. 1997; Swenson 2003).

The relationships between male, female and cub survival rates are really just correlations and do not necessarily explain the underlying mechanisms. Perhaps cub survival is low in populations with high male survival because these populations, such as Denali, Katmai and Kluane, are remote, unhunted and likely near carrying capacity. Low cub survival may be caused by bottom-up factors as much as, or even more than, sexually selected infanticide. Similarly, populations with low male survival, such as the Flathead or Susitna drainage in Alaska, are heavily hunted, so the number of bears is more likely to be kept below carrying capacity; high cub survival may be due to less competition over food in these populations. Can we continue to use the data to tease apart the alternative hypotheses explaining why there was low cub survival in populations with high male survival?

Hypothesis 1: populations with high male survival are closer to carrying capacity and therefore there would be more competition among bears over food, leading to low cub survival.

Hypothesis 2: populations with high male survival would not only have more adult males but less of a chance that each male is the father of a litter, and thus, following the "mate recognition" mechanism of sexually selected infanticide, low cub survival.

If Hypothesis 1 was correct, and how close the population was to carrying capacity was the major factor causing low cub survival, then female survival, even more than male survival, should be the better predictor of low cub survival. After all, it's females that raise the cubs, and if their survival is high then the population should be nearer carrying capacity than if their survival is lower. A regression analysis across the 12 populations suggests no relationship between female survival and cub survival. This result suggests that the mate recognition form of sexually selected infanticide is likely to be at least a contributing factor leading to cub deaths.

Understanding the interactions that affect cub survival remains a challenge, but I believe there is enough evidence to support sexually selected motivation by males who know that they did not mate with the mother the previous year – 10-pound to 15-pound cubs just can't be tasty enough for even a large male to risk injury from the mother.

**SO, AFTER ALL OF THIS, WHY AREN'T THERE MORE GRIZZLY BEARS?** Let me summarize. Where grizzly bear range overlaps with highways and railways, plus rural and urban human settlement and lots of open roads nearby, density-independent human-caused mortality will keep populations low and be a drain on the surrounding area. Where human-caused mortality is low, however, bear numbers will increase to where food limits their numbers. Most importantly, bear foods fluctuate in abundance, both annually and over decadal time periods, so there will be good years when females do well and many have cubs that survive, and there will be poor years. During poor years the females themselves will almost always survive, but fewer will have cubs, and if they do, the cubs will more likely perish. The interaction between density-independent food production and density-dependent competition for foods during periods of food scarcity will regulate the population. In areas like the Flathead where there are few adult males, cub survival will generally be higher, but reproduction will still suffer following years of poor food production. Evidence suggests that shifting the adult sex ratio to favour females will increase cub survival.

CHAPTER 17

# THE FUTURE

The power of the scientific method is most clearly seen in the ability of scientists to accurately predict the future. This capacity is perhaps most obvious in astronomy, where celestial events such as eclipses and the passing of comets are predicted with great accuracy decades in advance. But all around us are skyscrapers, huge bridges and jet aircraft, all of which have been predicted to work the way they do because many detailed measurements were made, hypotheses were deduced and tested, and mathematic formulas linking variables and constants were developed. Many equations I learned in high school physics and mathematics classes are still embedded in my memory half a century later.

When personal computers became common in the early 1980s, I programmed equations into my father (the engineer)'s brand new Commodore 64. He used these equations when designing tramways, chairlifts and suspension bridges, so he could quickly know, for example, the height above ground a cable, with a certain tension, would hang between two towers at different elevations on a mountainside. I assume the equations gave correct answers because he made dozens of cableways and they all worked fine. If the equations hadn't worked, then the hypotheses would have been rejected and others developed that did work.

Ecology, unfortunately, is not so simple. As many others have pointed out, ecology is not rocket science; it's far more complex than that. We may know to the minute that there will be an eclipse a century from now, or that a cable will hang 50 feet (15 m) above the ground, but no equation, and I'm pretty sure there will never be one, will predict the size of a specific grizzly bear population in 2100. There are simply far too many interacting factors, all with great uncertainty, that will affect the outcome. By far the dominant factor is what we humans decide to do in the future, and we all know how unpredictable that is. The global human population, which is ultimately the root of almost all conservation issues, almost doubled, from 4.3 to 8 billion people, over the years that Celine and I followed Flathead bears. The population of British Columbia did double, going from 2.6 to 5.2 million people. How long will the human population continue to grow? Will we continue extracting and burning more and more fossil fuels with little carbon sequestered? Will a conservation ethic leading to reduced consumption and more ecological care spread beyond a few localized areas? Although, out of the millions of species that have evolved on Earth over the past couple of billion years, we are the first with the cognitive ability to plan for a more sustainable and utopic society, does that mean will we gradually reduce our numbers to a couple of billion caring souls? Due to the complexities of human nature, I doubt we will ever work collectively towards this obvious goal, but it is certainly possible. The endless list of what people may or may not do in the future sure fogs my crystal ball. Ecologists might, in some cases, be able to determine that "if people do this, then populations of this species will do that." For grizzly bears, we can project bear densities based on areas and production levels of berry fields, as long as we consider some other foods too, and as long as people keep behaving the same as they do today. But without knowing what people will actually do over the next century, any long-term predictions are highly speculative.

In the past, projections have been made for grizzly bear populations and time has proven most of them wrong. When I began my research in the 1970s, I never heard anyone suggest that the grizzly population in northern Montana would grow to over 1,000 bears and continue to increase and spread into the Great Plains. I don't recall anyone suggesting that the population in the Yellowstone ecosystem would grow to over 700 bears as it has. Most predictions in the 1970s were for shrinking populations and continued extirpation. Famously, John and Frank Craighead, who studied grizzlies in Yellowstone between 1959 and 1971, predicted extirpation, or at least a dangerously small population, after the garbage dumps were closed in the national park (Craighead, Varney and Craighead Jr. 1974). The National Park Service, however, guessed there were more bears in the ecosystem than the Craigheads estimated, and that grizzlies would not disappear. Neither side of this well-publicized debate suggested there would be over 700 bears half a century later. If they had made such a suggestion, I think they would have been laughed out of the room. This sensationalized argument over the fate of the Yellowstone grizzlies helped spawn considerable theoretical work on how small populations can become and yet remain viable (Shaffer 1981).

Since the 1970s, population viability analysis, often based on Yellowstone grizzlies, has become one cornerstone of conservation biology.

**MUCH HAS BEEN LEARNED** about grizzly bear ecology and human-bear conflicts since the Craigheads worked in Yellowstone. We also know more about people – our tolerance and limits to our tolerance. We know that in all grizzly bear ecosystems with a conservation concern, by far the dominant top-down factor remains human-caused mortality. We know that where people have settled, habituation of grizzly bears combined with attractants leading to food conditioning results in high human-caused mortality at levels that are sometimes unsustainable and result in a localized population sink. Unsettled but well-accessed areas, particularly when close to towns, may have enough people fishing, hunting, hiking, biking and camping to have a similar effect as a settled area, and thus be a population sink. In areas further from towns and with fewer roads, like the Flathead was over the decades we worked there, bears will suffer less human-caused mortality, and if the habitat is good, the area can sustain a source population. We can reduce the level of human-caused mortality in all of these areas by managing all attractants and having a greater tolerance of bears. This will take some effort, but is not difficult; after all, Celine and I raised our family in a valley with a very high density of grizzly bears without a single incident, and many other people do as well. But, unlike other people, we also spent most of our days working in avalanche chutes, riparian habitat and huckleberry fields where grizzlies concentrated. We still had no serious issues. Bears will almost always take care of the situation, as long as you let them know you are there so they are not surprised.

**HUMAN-CAUSED MORTALITY** of grizzly bears (and other large carnivores) was historically such a dominant and obvious factor affecting grizzly populations that, until recently, it overshadowed the importance of bottom-up factors. We now know that food is the driver of most grizzly bear populations. Areas with an abundance of high-energy foods such as salmon, berries or whitebark pine seeds not only attain higher densities of bears but can withstand higher mortality rates. The Canadian Flathead has an abundance of both huckleberries and buffalo berries, which sustained a high density of bears that was a source population of male and female bears that gradually dispersed into adjacent parts of Alberta, Montana and the Elk Valley in BC. In these more settled areas, many bears went down the drain in localized population sink. As human populations in these sink areas increase, as they no doubt will, their rate of drain will likely increase. Keeping the Canadian Flathead, and the many areas like it, functioning as population sources will become increasingly important. Fortunately, some female bears gradually disperse but most remain in or near their mother's home range. Even with population drains all around, the Flathead is large enough for a high density of female bears to thrive and produce cubs, if the area continues to be managed wisely.

The future of the Canadian Flathead grizzly population is bright if conditions remain similar to those of the past half century, and in particular if road access continues to be limited, and most importantly, if there are no permanent human residences. Currently there is no threat of settlement, but a change in policy is always possible. Enabling even one settlement, such as an established campground, a gas station or a small store, would likely be the thin edge of the wedge leading to more settlement and a dismal future for Flathead bears, as well as the wild nature of the valley on the Canadian side of the border. Individual developments are like a ratchet; they click and advance only one way. Once developed, very rarely are areas undeveloped. When they are, it's usually left to private, non-government organizations to raise enormous amounts of money to buy back land to correct the short-sighted blunders made by governments. If the Flathead ever becomes settled to the point where it is no longer a source population supplying bears to adjacent areas, then a much larger area will become a population sink and the bears in northern Montana will become much more isolated from the bears to the north. Keeping the Flathead unsettled by people and a source for neighbouring areas is critical for more than just Flathead bears. Let's hope that government blunders of privatizing land in remote areas are forever finished. A simple solution, of course, is, after a century of delay, to finally put the finishing touches on the International Peace Park. In 2011, the province banned all mining and oil and gas developments in the Flathead, so it's partway towards becoming some form of protected area – why not finish the job and make it a fully protected area? At least protect the east side of the valley to match the Castle Wildland Provincial Park in Alberta.

Keeping the Flathead free of human settlement is only part, and a relatively simple part, of the solution to having grizzly bears in the Rocky Mountains of southern BC and Alberta plus northern Montana a few hundred of years from now. The greatest challenge will likely continue to be the lower Elk Valley from the small settlements of Jaffray and Elko, through to the larger towns of Fernie and Sparwood and over the Crowsnest Pass to Pincher Creek in Alberta. Over the decades of carnivore cleansing (1880–1975 in this area), the lower Elk Valley was an almost impenetrable barrier to bear dispersal that resonated in the differences in bears' genetics on either side of the valley (Proctor et al. 2005). However, since the 1980s, when Chris Servheen, the US Fish and Wildlife Grizzly Bear Recovery Coordinator, and I began highlighting the significance of the Lower Elk Valley for the grizzlies in the lower 48 states, some very positive changes have been taken place.

Importantly, an effective environmental group, now called Wildsight, relentlessly lobbied for change and, combined with the Yellowstone to Yukon Conservation Initiative, the Nature Conservancy of Canada, and the Ktunaxa Nation, have secured at least some form of management control of 50,142 acres (20,292 ha) primarily from recent owners Teck Resources (mining company) and Tembec Industries (forestry company). WildsafeBC, which evolved from our community work in Revelstoke in the 1990s, is now actively trying to limit bear mortality in the Elk Valley. An up-and-coming bear researcher, Clayton Lamb, is monitoring bears in the lower Elk Valley and also trying to reduce bear mortality. Clayton was instrumental in having over 200 road-killed elk and deer moved, each year, to a bear-proof bunker instead of having them just dumped in gravel pits where they attracted dozens of bears from the mountains towards the highway, railway and settlements in the valley. The Lower Elk Valley still has more conflicts with grizzly bears than anywhere else in BC and remains a population sink (Lamb et al. 2020), but an amazing number of grizzlies still live at least part of the year in the valley, and many do cross from wild country on one side of the valley to wild country on the other side.

**FUTURE CHANGES** in bottom-up factors are more difficult to assess than top-down factors mostly because we know a lot about where and why people kill bears. Understanding human-caused mortality is relatively simple, and the future of this factor depends on changes in human numbers and distribution, as well as on human attitudes and behaviour. Although future technological advances (i.e., all-terrain vehicle improvements, personal mini-aircraft, e-machines) and, perhaps most importantly, the number of climate refugees from areas with weather that has become too hot, dry or otherwise just unlivable, make accurate estimates difficult, we do know the number and mobility of people will probably increase. But over the past

40 years, the Canadian Flathead bear population trend has been driven more by the abundance of berries than by human-caused mortality, and this trend will hopefully continue into the future. During the periodically warm and generally dry climatic conditions in the late 1920s and 1930s (Pederson et al. 2006), when high-temperature records for Idaho, Montana and every prairie province of Canada still stand and contributed to the "Dust Bowl," great wildfires swept the Flathead as well as other areas. These fires eventually resulted in the large berry fields that were productive over most of the decades that I monitored both berries and bears. In these berry fields, bears put on the fat needed for hibernation and reproduction. After the Dust Bowl years, there were over 40 years of generally cooler weather (Pederson et al. 2006; Pederson et al. 2010), and with active fire suppression contributing, there were relatively few wildfires (Barrett, Arno and Key 1991). A strong warming trend began in the late 1980s (Pederson et al. 2010) and is continuing. In 2021, the 80-year-old high-temperature record was broken in British Columbia. Once again, there have been large, hot wildfires much like those almost a century ago. In portions of these more recently burned-off areas, huckleberry and buffalo berry plants will likely thrive. Berry production should be good in the decades to come if climatic conditions remain within the bounds of the past 40 years.

**AS WE HAVE KNOWN FOR SEVERAL DECADES NOW,** climatic conditions are very unlikely to remain within the bounds of what we now consider to be normal. With increasing carbon dioxide, methane and other greenhouse gases, some climate models suggest a much warmer and perhaps slightly wetter future for the Flathead and much of the Rocky Mountains (Pacific Climate Impacts Consortium). Models predict that by 2070, the climate in the Flathead may be more like it is now at low elevations on the west side of the southern Selkirk Mountains, where cedar and Douglas fir forests are more prevalent. Some climate scientists think we will likely see a combination of seasonal precipitation and temperatures that do not currently exist anywhere, making conditions, and particularly ecological transition through a period of rapidly changing climate, very difficult to predict – trees and other plants can quickly die, but species new to an area can't rapidly become established and grow.

Even during a 40-year period of so-called normal climate conditions, I have seen dry years when the few berries shrivelled into tiny raisins and fell to the ground. I've also seen so much snow in the berry fields in June that bumblebees couldn't pollinate the flowers. If, as predicted, extreme variation in weather increases, then I suspect we will have more extremely hot and dry years and more large wildfires, and perhaps more berry fields. However, we may also see more years with berry failures, creating a greater boom-and-bust huckleberry and buffalo berry economy for the bears. Other fruiting species, and in particular Saskatoon berries, which do well in open areas in warmer climates, may increase in the Flathead and elsewhere and become an increasingly important food in places.

Across the distribution of grizzly bears in North America, berries may be the only major high-energy grizzly bear food that has a reasonably bright future – the future of most others is bleak. Whitebark pine seeds, a major food in the Yellowstone ecosystem, portions of the Canadian Rockies, and the dry side of the Coast Mountains in BC, are doing poorly and their future generally looks grim. Many stands of these trees have been hit by the one-two punch of the exotic white pine blister rust and mountain pine beetles. In many areas, about half the trees are dead, and in some areas almost all are. But, thanks to genetic diversity, some trees seem resistant to rust, some to the beetles, and a few to both rust and beetles. Foresters are working hard to obtain seed from resistant trees and, while still trying to maintain the genetic diversity, plant more resistant individuals. This may work a bit in the US but will likely not be very successful in Canada, where the area currently covered by whitebark pine is large and the resources to help it are far more limited than they are south of the border. Grizzly bears on the "dry side of the mountains," whether the coastal or interior ranges, will suffer from declining whitebark pine. In these dry habitats, it is unlikely that a great increase in berries after more wildfires will be enough to maintain current numbers of bears.

Cervids, including mule deer, whitetail deer, moose, elk and caribou, are significant food sources for grizzly bears in many areas from Yellowstone, through the Canadian Rockies to the Northwest Territories, Yukon and to central and northern Alaska. Due to their large body size and numbers, these species have important ecological roles. Because they are also important sources of food for people, they receive a disproportionate amount of attention from managers. Unfortunately, this effort does not mean they will be maintained at numbers where they remain an important food for bears. Changing climates will likely be hard on the more northern species, such as moose and caribou, while the distribution of elk and whitetail deer will likely continue to expand. Increasing numbers of wolves and cougar, and the public's general distaste for control of these predators, a common management action in the past, will also affect densities of these species, except for perhaps migratory caribou that move beyond, or *out-distance*, territorial predators like wolves.

I think, however, that large herbivores cannot be the dominant energy food for even a moderate-density bear population. After all, animals that eat plants generally attain much higher densities than animals that eat other animals – the energy pyramid is a fundamental concept in ecology. More specifically, when wolves reach a density of between about two and ten individuals per 1000 $km^2$, depending on the vegetative productivity of the system, they start to have significant impact on prey populations. Wolves are the world's largest canid and, compared to bears, very efficient predators. But wolves are usually less than a third the size of a grizzly bear, and so each grizzly bear will need to eat a lot more than each wolf. If prey populations become depressed when two to ten wolves per 1000 $km^2$ are eating them, then grizzlies could not even reach these low densities if they relied primarily on these prey animals for food. This hypothesis certainly needs further testing, but grizzly populations are usually between 15 and 50 bears per 1000 $km^2$ – much higher than wolves.

Finally, we have salmon – obviously an enormously important group of fish that spawn and die by the millions in rivers and streams along the entire Pacific coast from central California through BC to Alaska, as well as northeastern Asia. Where they have access to an abundance of spawning salmon, grizzly bear densities get much higher than where the bears only have plants or large mammals to eat. But beyond bears, the influx of tons and tons of nutrients within their dying bodies that were amassed from across the vast North Pacific Ocean, has a huge and complex impact on coastal ecosystems. Unfortunately, salmon face a very uncertain future, with negative forces coming at them from many directions. First, they are killed by the millions by commercial (including bycatch), recreational and Indigenous fishers from all north Pacific Rim countries, including the US, Canada, Russia, Korea, Japan and China. But this is far from their only problem. Many of the spawning rivers have been dammed. Others have been compromised by logging and clearing for agriculture. To compensate for reduced spawning capability, fish hatcheries have been built. Hatchery fish may be fine for human consumption, but these fish compete with, and thus may reduce, numbers of fully wild salmon that are more apt to spawn naturally where bears can catch some. Fish farms, especially those using

Atlantic salmon, are the source of a variety of threats to wild salmon ranging from disease and sea lice to possible competition and genetic issues from escaped fish. Wild salmon need cold, clean water, and a warming world will be hard on them. With depleting and disappearing snowfields and glaciers and people using more and more fresh water, spawning streams will shrink in size, becoming more ephemeral and warmer. Salmon do not do well in such conditions because warm water streams hold less oxygen. Similarly, warming oceans will not provide the nutrients that salmon need for optimal growth or survival. On top of all these issues, it now seems that even chemicals added to tires to make them last longer degrade into a deadly poison for at least Coho salmon (Tian et al. 2021).

Along the BC and southeast Alaskan coasts, a warming climate, combined with more weather extremes, will likely result in large wildfires that previously were relatively rare in the wet coastal rainforests. We have had some foreshadowing of this possibility during recent relatively hot and dry summers. In 2015, there was a wildfire in the coastal Squamish Valley of BC that burned over 30,000 acres (12,140 ha) and in doing so turned 1,000-year-old Douglas fir trees, with their extremely thick, fire-resistant bark, into ash. Perhaps future generations of coastal bears in British Columbia and southeast Alaska will rely more and more on berries growing after wildfires than on the likely reduced salmon populations.

Across their entire distribution, grizzly bears eat a variety of grasses, horsetails and dozens of species of green forbs, particularly in the spring. Although these plants are not high in energy and are abundant in most areas, and thus likely not regulating many grizzly populations, they are important, and an abundance of these plants leads to higher ingestion rates. Many of these plants flourish in riparian habitats and avalanche chutes. Both of these habitats may become increasingly rare in the future in many areas. For example, avalanche chutes in the Flathead and many other parts of the Rocky Mountains are relatively unproductive compared to the rich, massive chutes in the much wetter Columbia Mountains to the west. A reduced snowpack due to a warming or drying winter climate will further reduce the size and productivity of avalanche chutes, and likely their value to bears.

**I THINK I'VE BEEN LUCKY** to have spent most of my life doing research on grizzly bears during a time when populations across their southern distribution have generally been recovering after a century or more of excessive killing.

I've also been lucky to have done this research in the Rockies, Selkirks, Purcells and Coast Mountain ranges of southern British Columbia. Although I've worked in totally pristine wilderness areas both inside and out of national parks, most of my studies have been in areas with some logging, mining and settlements, yet populations in these areas have been doing well and expanding in most but not all cases. Some populations in south coastal British Columbia are struggling to hang on. But that is a story for my daughter to write.

It is clear to me that grizzly bears are very intelligent and adaptable and do well in a huge variety of habitats as long as people do not kill too many of them. My experience in the town of Revelstoke in the 1990s, where we went from killing or moving a dozen grizzlies each year (and killing four dozen black bears) to having almost no conflict issues with grizzlies (still a few with black bears), showed me that people can deal with these conflicts if they really want to. Now, in our retirement, Celine and I have spent $500 on electric fences that are simple and effective at keeping bears out of our vineyard, orchard and garden. With a little money and effort, it's not difficult to avoid all conflicts with bears. These experiences have made me a grizzly bear optimist. I know it's much easier to sell a story of doom and gloom and insist that disaster is rapidly approaching, but that conclusion is not supported by the data in most areas. Yes, we have some small isolated populations in the southern Coast Mountains of BC that are all but extirpated. We know the challenges well and are gradually working on these despite higher-level bureaucratic complexities. The days of grizzlies living in vast expanses of pristine wilderness with little or no human intrusion, if such conditions ever really existed, are long gone. Almost all bears will have to live with hikers, hunters, bear viewers, loggers or miners. But with continued effort to limit human access and expand our tolerance, I'm sure grizzlies in North America will continue to do well for another 40 years and likely many more.

Brown bears, as grizzlies are called in other parts of the world, are unlikely to fare as well elsewhere, particularly in Asia. Although there are vast expanses of high, arid plateaus and mountains with very few people in this huge continent, there are still a lot of people, and many are struggling to provide for themselves and their families. With improving economies, a conservation ethic is developing in some areas, but it is nowhere near the level it is in North America or Europe, where millions of dollars or Euros are spent each year on brown bear research and management. Very little work has been done in Asia. I sometimes feel guilty of spending almost all of my life working on bears in British Columbia that are relatively secure – but this wasn't known in the 1970s when we began. Much more must be done in Asia for brown bears as well as the other species. Unfortunately, most large mammal research and conservation funding in Asia only goes to four species: giant pandas, tigers and snow leopards and orangutans. I hope this situation changes for the next generation.

CHAPTER 18

# SUCCESSION

For most of my life, I thought succession was the process that an ecosystem gradually goes through following a disturbance such as a forest fire, logging or even the retreat of glaciers in a warming climate. But spending over 40 years in one study area meant that succession became a clear, personal reality for me, not just a theory or a series of photographs taken over time from the same location. I was able to observe forest being removed by fire, flood and loggers, and then some plants initially flourish, which then gave way to others, until forests had either returned or were clearly on the way to returning. But, as I approached 60 years of age, people started asking me about my succession plan. I had never thought about myself as part of a system changing over time, or my eventual replacement. But even old growth doesn't last forever.

Fortunately, younger, smarter and stronger people were there, perhaps like saplings, just waiting for an old tree to topple. And, as they say, sometimes apples don't fall far from the tree. My succession strategy just happened without planning. Charlie did his master's thesis on fire ecology and grizzly bears in the Rocky Mountains. But now he is more interested in wild and prescribed fires than bears, so is now a fire ecologist. Michelle did her Ph.D. on factors limiting two threatened grizzly bear populations in the southern coastal mountains, and still works on these and other populations. Unfortunately, neither of our kids ended up working in the Flathead where they grew up.

In 2010, Garth Mowat began working with me in the Flathead, and when I retired, he applied for and got the job I'd had. Although Garth is no sapling, his role in the Flathead study is increasing as mine declines. Celine and I are now senior citizens, retired and even receiving pensions. But I still go out in Clay's helicopter and catch bears, although in the Flathead, Garth sometimes does the darting, as he will have to take over one day. Often I'm the one waiting on the ground. That job is usually much less stressful, but not always.

**WHILE DOING THE CAPTURE PROGRAM** the year after I retired, we spotted a mid-sized grizzly bear in a small, mostly treeless huckleberry field in the back corner of an otherwise mostly sparsely forested subalpine basin (49.18174 -114.5551). Clay immediately turned his helicopter away and we all looked for a landing site.

"We could probably land there just below her, but it's pretty close," I said over the intercom.

"Yes, I could set down there, but it is close, let's quickly check out…over here,… no, nothing here. Damn…nowhere here," Clay was scooting here and there further away from the bear, but there wasn't a spot open enough to set down for half a minute to get the door off.

"Let's do it in that spot right below her…we'll have to be fast or she'll bugger off," Clay finally decided. He banked sharply and dove down into a slightly wider spot in the sparse forest. We were only a couple of hundred yards below the bear (49.1790 -114.5550).

The skids were not fully settled when both Garth and I were in action.

I hopped out just before Clay. He took off the rear door and I could see Garth through the back window taping his seat belt closed while organizing the capture pack, dart gun and .30-06 rifle so nothing would fall out if the machine did a steep bank with the doorless side facing down. That was the job I had done hundreds of times, but now, on the ground, I really had nothing to do except take the door to a safe spot away from the helicopter's wind blast. The jet engine revved up and the blades whined. The machine zipped straight up out of the hole we were in. Garth is light so it was like Clay flying alone.

I could easily see the bear just above me. She was now moving away, but so far mostly walking. She was still close and I thought, no matter how well she's herded by the helicopter, she'll very likely run right down this little gully that I'm standing in. Over the five to ten minutes that it takes for the drug to take effect, bears usually end up going downhill in a gully. I could climb a tree, but the trees were small, with weak, drooping branches almost to the ground, sort of like Christmas trees about 25 feet (8 m) tall. So I thought, if I just hunker down under the low branches, she'll run right past without ever knowing I'm there. Garth had the rifle, as he would be the one to get out of the helicopter to check the bear.

I watched as they swooped in, darted the bear and then backed away to monitor her while the drug took effect. I enjoyed watching the machine manoeuvre. At higher speeds, helicopters bank sidewise to turn, but when mostly hovering, it banked more front to back; sometimes the tail was almost straight down for backward acceleration. The bear ran towards the ridge top. I knew there was some cliffy terrain over the ridge and, just as I thought, they flew over to the ridge to herd her back into the basin. She turned and ran quickly downhill. She was coming right down the gully, and if they couldn't turn her she would, as I expected, run right past me in a few seconds. I squatted down in a low crouch on the downhill side of the largest, bushiest tree and waited.

I could hear the helicopter right above me. It dropped low, just above the tree I was hunkered next to. Then it pivoted and hovered just below me. This was bad; I thought the bear must be coming right at me and they couldn't turn her back up the basin. Then they flew back uphill, over my tree, and continued up. This was really bad; I thought they couldn't turn her so were trying to keep her moving downhill past me. We never push bears down into the trees. This was a desperate action. She must be very close to me. Where was she?

Then, over the noise of the 500D, I heard something to my right. There she was, just standing there, I'd guess eight feet (2.4 m) away. There was only one branch between the two of us. She had a collar on and a little one-inch-long red ear tag. She didn't look panicky. She was just standing there. I didn't look panicky either; I didn't even twitch. If I had sneezed, I'm sure I would have had a fight on my hands. It was less than two minutes since she'd been darted, so who knows, maybe she was a little groggy, but maybe she was just pissed off. She didn't look upset, but she must have been wound up. I thought to myself, if she sees me, she will attack – no bluff charges today. I'm going to have to punch her as hard as I can right on her tender nose and then get into the opening where I hoped Garth could shoot her from the helicopter. I wonder if he even has the .30-06 loaded and ready. Probably not. More likely they were cracking jokes: "The idiot picked the wrong tree."

Once in the trees, sometimes half-drugged grizzlies just stand there and don't move even when the helicopter is right above them. As the seconds went by I watched her chest moving as she slowly panted. She was not looking right up at the helicopter but more into the forest. Luckily for both of us, her focus seemed to be distant. If she moved downhill, she would most likely pass about three feet (1 m) from me, and if she kept going down, there would be no branches between us for a few steps. But then, unless she turned her head, she would not likely see me as she went past. Finally, she took a step down towards me. Then she stopped, turned right and moved away. This was good. Very good. She then walked out of sight behind some small shrubs just uphill from the tree I was under. Should I stay put, or should I try to get to the top of the tree? I waited. I couldn't see where she had gone, but the helicopter was still right above me so I knew she hadn't run off. I thought she must still be close by.

My knees had become stiff in that awkward squat under the tree. I thought, I'm 66 years old now, not 24 like I was when I first caught bears in the Flathead. It might not be wise to remain in the squat, but I don't think it would be a good idea to be sitting on my bum on the ground. It would be best to very smoothly climb the tree. I slowly stood up. My knees had had enough. I couldn't see her anywhere, so I grabbed a drooping branch and, as smoothly and slowly as an orangutan, just went up the tree. I hadn't felt a huge, instant rush of adrenaline over the past minute or so, but I must have had a steady increase in some hormone because I seemed to have an exceedingly strong grip and could simply pull myself up, branch after branch. In a few seconds I was at the top of the tree. I grabbed the narrow trunk of the tree and leaned way out and waved to the boys in the helicopter. Clay tipped it back and forth in reply.

From the treetop, I could see the bear going uphill maybe 20 yards (18 m) from me. In another minute she began the Macarena and soon after that she lay down. I climbed out of the tree and walked towards the bear. I waited about 30 yards (27 m) away for Garth with the rifle. We processed the bear. It was one we had called Hasting. Clay and Garth hadn't seen that she still wore a collar. We put on a new one, did our measurements and left.

"We were sure happy to see you in that tree," Garth said.

"I felt pretty darn happy in the tree too," I replied, and then I told them of what happened from my point of view.

"I think it's time to put our feet up and have a nice relaxing glass of red. That was two close calls in a day," Garth said.

Earlier in the day Garth and I had done what we used to call the "old Harry Jerome," but the name has evolved through Ben Johnson, Donovan Bailey, and now it's the old Usain Bolt – although I doubt we are getting faster. That happens maybe once every hundred bears when they seem to be conked out until you get right up to them. We had been topping one up with a little more drug in a hand syringe when she jumped right up and, we presume, came after us. BOOM, we were both fast out of the blocks. I knew to run uphill, as three-quarter-drugged bears can't go uphill fast. Garth went across the slope. I had the rifle so I was trying to keep an eye on Garth while still running uphill from the bear. Luckily the bear went elsewhere.

"Whatever, we earned our rums today," says Clay, as he always does, every day that we get at least one bear.

"I earned my old age pension," I replied.

We flew into camp, landed and went about our end of the day routines. I was in the log addition that we'd built 35 years before, cleaning the capture kit, when Clay came in and went into the trailer.

"Did you earn your rum and Pepsi today, Clay?" Celine asked.

"Hey, I'm on a health kick these days, it's rum and cranberry juice now. The way I see it, that gets me one fruit group serving each drink," Clay joked, and then continued, "I'm cooking, Celine, you don't do a thing. I've got ribs, potatoes, the works." Clay always does the cooking on the first and sometimes the second night.

"Sounds good, I'll make the salad." Celine always needs a salad.

"Salad, yes, that's that green stuff you tried to feed me last year, isn't it?" Clay joked.

"It's not just green stuff, it's actually good for you. It's LT," Celine joked back.

She continued: "You know, last winter I was telling an American friend, I guess still with a tiny French accent, that I made a very healthy salad. He turned to me and said, 'I'm not up on all these damn acronyms, what the hell is an LT salad?' You know, even after 45 years, it's really hard for me to make that silly H sound, and TH is even worse."

**GIVEN THE TITLE OF THIS BOOK,** I hope you were not expecting a detailed guide to living in the wilderness that ranged from how to properly sharpen a chainsaw to ways of pickling elk tongue. There are hundreds of skills that one should have in order to live comfortably in the wilderness. Some are essential, some just make life more pleasant and interesting. There are many books and YouTube videos that cover these skills (don't believe them all). But having a variety of skills is not really the art that makes wilderness life a wonderful experience. A few tips. First, know your own skill level and that of anyone else you happen to be with. The wilderness is no place to push skills to the limit. Second, know your optimal pace for doing things. Go fast enough to make satisfactory progress at whatever you're doing but not so fast that you fail to absorb the sights, sounds and smells of the environment around you – I hope these are the main reasons you are there. Besides, whether the task is cutting firewood or bushwhacking for miles, if you go too fast, one year you will make a mistake and hurt yourself in a location where you really don't want to be hurt. Finally, we humans are highly social animals. The real art of wilderness life is probably the same as in all types of life: pick the right partner to share it all with. I sure did.

## APPENDIX

### *Family Trees of Major Bear Characters*

Blanche, Elspeth and Melissa were three adult female grizzly bears that were, among several others, living in the Flathead Valley near the US border when we began our study in 1978. They are some of the major bear characters mentioned in this book. This is a summary of their families.

#### Blanche (1964 to 1986)

1979: Josey (1979 to 1981) and two others
1982: Aggie (1982 to 2014), Melonie (1982 to 2012), Ruby
1985: Ernie (1985 to 1994), Birt and one other.

AGGIE (BLANCHE'S DAUGHTER)
1990: Jack (1990 to 1992), Grant
1993: three cubs
1996: two cubs
2001: Pamela (not certain)
2007: Dude (2007 to 2013), maybe others

#### Melissa (1970 to 1991)

1981: Jennie (1981 to 2003), Butch (1981 to 1991), Byron
1984: Laurel, Hardy
1986: Sally (1986 to 2005), Cindy, Bill
1989: Paul and one other

JENNIE (MELISSA'S 1981 DAUGHTER)
1986: Lorna, Donald (1986 to 1990)
1989: Maggie (1989 to 2010), Sammy
1992: Irene
1995: one cub
1998: two cubs
2001: Joel (2001 to 2005)
2003: three cubs

MAGGIE (JENNIE'S 1989 DAUGHTER)
1997: two cubs (lost both between autumn and spring)
2001: Liz (2001 to 2003), Genevieve (2001 to 2006), one other
2004: three cubs (lost all between autumn and spring)
2008: Becky
2009: GM174 and two others

## Elspeth (1973 to after 1999)

1979: Trouble (1979 to 1984), More Trouble
1982: two cubs (one died in den and one shortly after emergence)
1983: Newt (1983 to 1986) and one other
1985: Mitch (1985 to 1989), June
1988: Mammy (1988 to 2016), Luke (1988 to 1992), Tyson (1988 to 1998)
1991: three cubs
1994: three cubs

MAMMY (ELSPETH'S 1988 DAUGHTER)
1995: one cub
2001: Tina (2001 to 2014), one other
2006: one cub

# BIBLIOGRAPHY


Andrews, Gerald S. 1930. *Survey and preliminary plan of management of the Flathead forest*. BC Forest Service Survey Division. Forest Survey R.36. 82 pp.

Apps, Clayton D., Bruce N. McLellan, Trevor A. Kinley and John P. Flaa. 2001. "Scale-dependent habitat selection by mountain caribou, Columbia Mountains, British Columbia." *Journal of Wildlife Management* 65:65–77.doi.org/10.2307/3803278.

Apps, Clayton, Bruce McLellan and Christopher Servheen. 2013. "Multi-scale population and behavioural responses by grizzly bears to habitat and human influence across the southern Canadian Rocky Mountains." Version 2.0. Aspen Wildlife Research in collaboration with Ministry of Forests, Lands and Natural Resource Operations, and the US Fish and Wildlife Service. Unpublished.

Barrett, Stephen W., Stephen F. Arno and Carl H. Key. 1991. "Fire regimes of western larch–lodgepole pine forests in Glacier National Park, Montana." *Canadian Journal of Forest Research* 21:1711–20. doi.org/10.1139/x91-237.

Bentley, David M.R. 1990. "Set forth as plainly may appear: The verse journal of Henry Kelsey." *ARIEL* 21:9–30.

Bertram, B.C.R. 1975. "Social factors influencing reproduction in wild lions." *Journal of Zoology, London* 177:463–82. doi.org/10.1111/j.1469-7998.1975.tb02246.x.

Boutin, Stan. 1990. "Food supplementation experiments with terrestrial vertebrates: Patterns, problems, and the future." *Canadian Journal of Zoology* 68:203–20. doi.org/10.1139/z90-031.

Brockman, Christopher J., William B. Collins, Jeffery M. Welker, Donald E. Spalinger and Bruce W. Dale. 2017. "Determining kill rates of ungulate calves by brown bears using neck-mounted cameras." *Wildlife Society Bulletin* 41:88–97. doi.org/10.1002/wsb.733.

Brown, David E. 1985. *The grizzly in the southwest: Documentary of an extinction*. Norman: University of Oklahoma Press. 304 pp.

Burroughs, Raymond D. 1961. *The natural history of the Lewis and Clark Expedition*. East Lansing: Michigan State University Press. 340 pp. And see October 7, 1804 episode at lewis-clark.org/day-by-day/ypr/#.

Cattet, Marc, John Boulanger, Gordon Stenhouse, Roger A. Powell and Melissa J. Reynolds-Hogland. 2008. "An evaluation of long-term capture effects in Ursids: implications for wildlife welfare and research." *Journal of Mammalogy* 89:973–90. doi.org/10.7589/0090-3558-39.3.649.

Caughley, Graeme. 1977. *Analysis of vertebrate populations*. New York: John Wiley and Sons. 234 pp.

Charnov, Eric L. 1976. "Optimal foraging: The marginal value theorem." *Theoretical Population Biology* 9:129–36. doi.org/10.1016/0040-5809(76)90040-X.

Ciarniello, Lana M., Mark S. Boyce, Dale R. Seip and Douglas C. Heard. 2009. "Comparison of grizzly bear *Ursus arctos* demographics in wilderness mountains versus a plateau with resource development." *Wildlife Biology* 15:247–65. doi.org/10.2981/08-080.

Clapham, Melanie, Ed Miller, Mary Nguyen and Chris T. Darimont. 2020. "Automated facial recognition for wildlife that lack unique markings: A deep learning approach for brown bears." *Ecology and Evolution* 10:12883–92. doi.org/10.1002/ece3.6840.

Cole, Glen F. 1972. "Preservation and management of grizzly bears in Yellowstone National Park." *International Conference on Bear Research and Management* 2:274–88. doi.org/10.2307/3872590.

Cowan, Ian M., Douglas G. Chapman, Robert S. Hoffmann, Dale R. McCullough, Gustav A. Swanson and Robert B. Weeden. 1974. *Report of Committee on the Yellowstone grizzlies*. National Academy of Sciences. 61 pp.

Craighead, Frank. 1979. *Track of the grizzly*. San Fancisco: Sierra Club Books. 261 pp.

Craighead, John J. 1976. "Studying grizzly bear habitat by satellite." *National Geographic* 150:148–58.

Craighead, John J., Jay S. Sumner and John A. Mitchell. 1995. *The grizzly bears of Yellowstone: Their ecology in the Yellowstone ecosystem*. Washington, DC: Island Press. 535 pp.

Craighead, John J., Joel R. Varney and Frank C. Craighead Jr. 1974. "A population analysis of the Yellowstone grizzly bears." Bulletin 40. Montana Forest and Conservation Experiment Station. University of Montana. 20 pp.

Dormaar, Johan F., and Rob A. Watt. 2007. *Oil city: Black gold*. Lethbridge, AB: Lethbridge Historical Society. 97 pp.

Ebensperger Luis A. 1998. "Strategies and counterstrategies to infanticide in mammals." *Biological Reviews* 73:321–46. doi.org/10.1017/S0006323198005209.

Efford, Murray. 2004. "Density estimation in live-trapping studies." *Oikos* 106:598–610. doi.org/10.1111/j.0030-1299.2004.13043.x.

Erlenbach, Joy A., Karyn D. Rode, David Raubenheimer and Charles T. Robbins. 2014. "Macronutrient optimization and energy maximization determine diets of brown bears." *Journal of Mammalogy* 95:160–68. doi.org/10.1644/13-MAMM-A-161.

Evans, Alina L., Navinder J. Singh, Andrea Friebe, Jon M. Arnemo, Timothy G. Laske, Ole Fröbert, Jon E. Swenson and Stéphane Blanc. 2016. "Drivers of hibernation in the brown bear." *Frontiers in Zoology* 13:7:1–13. doi 10.1186/s12983-016-0140-6.

Farley, Sean D., and Charles T. Robbins. 1994. "Development of two methods to estimate body composition of bears." *Canadian Journal of Zoology* 72:220–26. doi.org/10.1139/z94-029.

Farley, Sean D., and Charles T. Robbins. 1995. "Lactation, hibernation, and mass dynamics of American black bears and grizzly bears." *Canadian Journal of Zoology* 73:2216–22. doi:10.1139/z95-262.

Felicetti, Laura A., Charles T. Robbins and Lisa A. Shipley. 2003. "Dietary protein content alters energy expenditure and composition of the mass gain in grizzly bears (*Ursus arctos horribilis*)." *Physiological and Biochemical Zoology* 76:256–61. doi:10.1086/374279.

Garshelis, David L., Michael L. Gibeau and Stephen Herrero. 2005. "Grizzly bear demographics in and around Banff National Park and Kananaskis Country, Alberta." *Journal of Wildlife Management* 69:277–97. doi.org/10.2193/0022-541X(2005)069 <0277:GBDIAA>2.0.CO;2.

Gendle, Scott M., Thomas P. Quinn and Mary F. Willson. 2001. "Consumption choice by bears feeding on salmon." *Oecologia* 127:372–82. doi.org/10.1007/s004420000590.

Gosselin, Jacinthe, Martin Leclerc, Andreas Zedrosser, Sam M.J.G. Steyaert, Jon E. Swenson and Fanie Pelletier. 2017. "Hunting promotes sexual conflict in brown bears." *Journal of Animal Ecology* 86:35–42. doi.org/10.1111/1365-2656.12576.

Gosselin, Jacinthe, Andreas Zedrosser, Jon E. Swenson and Fanie Pelletier. 2015. "The relative importance of direct and indirect effects of hunting mortality on the population dynamics of brown bears." *Proceedings of the Royal Society B: Biological Sciences* 282:20141840. doi.org/10.1098/rspb.2014.1840.

Greenwood, Paul J. 1980. "Mating systems, philopatry and dispersal in birds and mammals." *Animal Behaviour* 28:1140–62. doi.org/10.1016/S0003-3472(80)80103-5.

Griffin, Kathleen A., Mark Hebblewhite, Hugh S. Robinson, Peter Zager, Shannon M. Barber-Meyer, David Christianson, Scott Creel, Nyeema C. Harris, Mark A. Hurley, DeWaine H. Jackson, Bruce K. Johnson, Woodrow L. Myers, Jarod D. Raithel, Mike Schlegel, Bruce L. Smith, Craig White and P.J. White. 2011. "Neonatal mortality of elk driven by climate, predator phenology and predator community composition." *Journal of Animal Ecology* 80:1246–57. doi.org/10.1111/j.1365-2656.2011.01856.x.

Hamer, David. 1974. "Distribution, abundance and management implications of the grizzly bear and mountain caribou in the Mountain Creek watershed of Glacier National park, British Columbia." M.Sc. thesis, University of Calgary. 164 pp.

Hamer, David, and Stephen Herrero. 1983. *Ecological studies of the grizzly bear in Banff National Park – Final Report.* University of Calgary. 303 pp.

Hearne, Samuel. 1911. *A journey from Prince of Wales's Fort in Hudson's Bay to the Northern Ocean in the years 1769, 1770, 1771, and 1772.* New Edition with Introduction, Notes, and Illustrations by Joseph B. Tyrerell. Toronto: The Champlain Society. 438 pp.

Herrero, Stephen. 1970. "Human injury inflicted by grizzly bears." *Science* 170:593–98. doi.org/10.1126/science.170.3958.593.

Herrero, Stephen. 1976. "Conflicts between man and grizzly bears in the national parks of North America." *International Conference on Bear Research and Management* 3:121–45. doi.org/10.2307/3872761.

Hewitt, David, and Charles T. Robbins. 1996. "Estimating grizzly bear food habits from fecal analysis." *Wildlife Society Bulletin* 24:547–50. www.jstor.org/stable/3783342.

Hilderbrand, Grant V., Stacy G. Jenkins, Charles C. Schwartz, Tomas A. Hanley and Charles T. Robbins. 1999. "Effect of seasonal differences in dietary meat intake on changes in body mass and composition in wild and captive brown bears." *Canadian Journal of Zoology* 77:1623–30. doi.org/10.1139 /z99-133.

Hilderbrand, Grant V., Charles C. Schwartz, Charles T. Robbins and Tomas A. Hanley. 2000. "Effect of hibernation and reproductive status on body mass and condition of coastal brown bears." *Journal of Wildlife Management* 64:178–83. doi.org/10.2307/3802988.

Holling, Crawford S. 1959. "Some characteristics of simple types of predation and parasitism." *Canadian Entomologist* 91:385–98. doi.org/10.4039/Ent91385-7.

Hrdy, Sarah B. 1974. "Male–male competition and infanticide among the langurs (*Presbytis entellus*) of Abu, Rajasthan." *Folia Primatologica* 22:19–58. doi.org/10.1159/000155616.

Hrdy, Sarah B. 1979. "Infanticide among animals: A review, classification, and examination of the implications for the reproductive strategies of females." *Ethology and Sociobiology* 1:13–40. doi.org/10.1016/0162-3095(79)90004-9.

Jansen, Heiko T., Shawn Trojahn, Michael W. Saxton, Corey R. Quackenbush, Brandon D. Evans Hutzenbiler, O. Lynne Nelson, Omar E. Cornejo, Charles T. Robbins and J.L. Kelley. 2019. "Hibernation induces widespread transcriptional remodeling in metabolic tissues of the grizzly bear." *Communications Biology* 2, 336. doi.org/10.1038/s42003-019-0574-4.

Jones, Elena S., Douglas C. Heard and Michael P. Guillingham. 2006, December. "Temporal variation in stable carbon and nitrogen isotopes of grizzly bear guardhair and underfur." *Wildlife Society Bulletin* 34:1320–25. doi.org/10.2193/0091-7648(2006)34[1320:TVISCA]2.0.CO;2.

Kaczensky, Petra, Djuro Huber, Felix Knauer, Hans Roth, Aaron Wagner and Josip Kusak. 2006. "Activity patterns of brown bears (*Ursus arctos*) in Slovenia and Croatia." *Journal of Zoology* 269:474–85. doi:10.1111/j.1469-7998.2006.00114.x.

Keating, Kim A. 1986. "Historical grizzly bear trends in Glacier National Park, Montana." *Wildlife Society Bulletin* 14:83–87. www.jstor.org/stable/3782474.

Keay, Jeffrey. A., Charles. T. Robbins and Sean. D. Farley. 2018. "Characteristics of a naturally regulated grizzly bear population." *Journal of Wildlife Management* 82:789–801. doi.org/10.1002/jwmg.21425.

Kendall, Katherine C. 1983. "Use of pine nuts by grizzly and black bears in the Yellowstone Area." *Bears: Their Biology and Management* 5:166–73. doi.org/10.2307/3872534.

Kendall, Katherine C., Jeffrey B. Stetz, John Boulanger, Amy C. MacLeod, David Paetkau and Gary C. White. 2009. "Demography and genetic structure of a recovering grizzly bear population." *Journal of Wildlife Management* 73:3–17. doi.org/10.2193/2008-330.

Krebs, Charles J. 1978. *Ecology: The Experimental Analysis of Distribution and Abundance.* Harper & Row Publishers. 678 pp.

Lamb, Clayton T., Adam F. Ford, Bruce N. McLellan, Michael F. Proctor, Garth Mowat, Lana Ciarniello, Scott E. Nielsen and Stan Boutin. 2020. "The ecology of human-carnivore coexistence." *Proceedings of the National Academy of Sciences* 117:17876–83. doi.org/10.1073/pnas.1922097117.

Leclerc, Martin, Shane C. Frank, Andreas Zedrosser, Jon E. Swenson and Fanie Pelletier. 2017. "Hunting promotes spatial reorganization and sexually selected infanticide." *Scientific Reports* 7:45222. doi.org/10.1038/srep45222.

Lewis, Meriwether, and William Clark. 2004. *The Lewis and Clark journals: An American epic of discovery.* Edited and Introduction by Gary E. Moulton. Lincoln: University of Nebraska Press. 413 pp.

Loring, Stephen, and Arthur Spiess. 2007. "Further documentation supporting the former existence of grizzly bears (*Ursus arctos*) in northern Quebec–Labrador." *Arctic* 60:7–16. www.jstor.org/stable/40513153.

Loveridge, Andrew J., Marion Valeix, Guillaume Chapron, Zeke Davidson, Godfrey Mtare and David W. Macdonald. 2016. "Conservation of large predator populations: Demographic and spatial responses of African lions to the intensity of trophy hunting." *Biological Conservation* 204:247–54. doi.org/10.1016/j.biocon.2016.10.024.

MacDonald, Graham A. 1992. *Where the mountains meet the prairies: A History of Waterton Lakes National Park.* Parks Canada. Microfiche Report Series 524. 165 pp.

Mace, Richard D., Daniel W. Carney, Tonya Chilton-Radant, Stacy A. Courville, Mark A. Haroldson, Richard B. Harris, James Jonkel, Bruce N. McLellan, Michael Madel, Timothy L. Manley, Charles C. Schwartz, Christopher Servheen, Gordon Stenhouse, John S. Waller and Erik Wenum. 2012. "Grizzly bear population vital rates and trend in the Northern Continental Divide Ecosystem, Montana." *Journal of Wildlife Management* 76:119–28. doi.org/10.1002/jwmg.250.

Mace, Richard D., Timothy L. Manley and Keith E. Aune. 1994. "Factors affecting the photographic detection rate of grizzly bears in the Swan Mountains, Montana." *Ursus* 9:245–51. doi.org/10.2307/3872708.

Mace, Richard D., Steven C. Minta, Timothy L. Manley and Keith E. Aune. 1994. "Estimating grizzly bear population size using camera sightings." *Wildlife Society Bulletin* 22:74–83.

Mace, Richard D., and John. S. Waller. 1998. "Demography and population trend of grizzly bears in the Swan Mountains, Montana." *Conservation Biology* 12:1005–16. doi.org/10.1002/jwmg.250.

MacHutchon, Grant, John Boulanger, Gordon Stenhouse, Bruce McLellan, Garth Mowat, Michael Proctor, Jerome Cranston and David Paetkau. 2008, August 31. *Grizzly bear population and density estimates for Alberta Bear Management Unit 6 and British Columbia Management Units 4-1, 4-2, and 4-23* (2007). Report Prepared for the Alberta Sustainable Resource Development, Fish and Wildlife Division, British Columbia Ministry of Forests and Range, British Columbia Ministry of Environment, and Parks Canada. https://open.alberta.ca/dataset/2f768c90-4bad-457a-9d0f-6523813194f1/resource/d9bc44da-cf4f-4543-bed3-6b31aa085e9f/download/2007-grizzly-bear-2007-dnapopulationest-2008.pdf.

Maraj, Ramona. 2016. "Yukon north slope grizzly bear population estimation and demographic analysis." Yukon Fish and Wildlife Branch, TR-15-01. Draft 75 pp., and unpublished data.

Marshal, Daniel P. 2018. *Claiming the land: British Columbia and the making of a new El Dorado.* Vancouver: Ronsdale Press. 424 pp.

Martinka. Clifford J. 1974. "Population characteristics of grizzly bears in Glacier National Park, Montana." *Journal of Mammalogy* 55:21–29. doi.org/10.2307/1379254.

Mattson, David J., Stephen Herrero and Troy Merrill. 2005. "Are black bears a factor in the restoration of North American grizzly bear populations?" *Ursus* 16:11–30. doi.org/10.2192/1537-6176(2005)016[0011:ABBAFI]2.0.CO;2.

Mattson, David J., and Troy Merrill. 2002. "Extirpations of grizzly bears in the contiguous United States, 1850–2000." *Conservation Biology* 16:1123–36. doi.org/10.1046/j.1523-1739.2002.00414.x.

McCann, Robert K. 1998, October 21 & 22. *Kluane National Park grizzly bear research project: Interim report to accompany the project review.* Kluane National Park, Yukon. 144 pp.

McLellan, Bruce N. 1986. "Use-availability analysis and timber selection by grizzly bears." In *Proceedings: Grizzly Bear Habitat Symposium*, edited by G.P. Contreras and K.E. Evans, 163–66. General Technical Report INT-207. USDA Forest Service Intermountain Research Station, Ogden, Utah. https://books.google.ca/books?hl=en&lr=&id=b549ALryPQQC&oi=fnd&pg=PA1&dq=Contreras,+G.P.

+and+Evans,+K.E.+(eds).+Proceedings:+grizzly+bear+habitat+symposium.&ots=t2iTAx-t56&sig=EtHdtDw1DKDL2T_fpyIcQl9CKiY#v=onepage&q&f=false.

McLellan, Bruce N. 1989. "Dynamics of a grizzly bear population during a period of industrial resource extraction. I. Density and age–sex composition." *Canadian Journal of Zoology* 67:1856–60. doi.org/10.1139/z89-264.

McLellan, Bruce N. 1994. "Density dependent population regulation of brown bears." In *Density dependent population regulation in black, brown, and polar bears*, edited by Mitchell Taylor, 15–24. Ninth International Conference on Bear Research and Management. Monograph Series No. 3.

McLellan, Bruce N. 2005. "Sexually selected infanticide in grizzly bears: The effects of hunting on cub survival." *Ursus* 16:141–56. doi.org/10.2192/1537-6176(2005)016[0141:SSIIGB]2.0.CO;2.

McLellan, Bruce N. 2011. "Implications of a high-energy and low-protein diet on the body composition, fitness, and competitive abilities of black (*Ursus americanus*) and grizzly (*Ursus arctos*) bears." *Canadian Journal of Zoology* 89:546–58. doi.org/10.1139/z11-026.

McLellan, Bruce N. 2015. "Some mechanisms underlying variation in vital rates of grizzly bears on a multiple use landscape." *Journal of Wildlife Management* 79:749–65. doi.org/10.1002/jwmg.896.

McLellan, Bruce N., and Fredrick W. Hovey. 1995. "The diet of grizzly bears in the Flathead drainage of Southeastern British Columbia." *Canadian Journal of Zoology* 73:704–12. doi.org/10.1139/z95-082.

McLellan, Bruce N., and Fredrick W. Hovey. 2001a. "Habitats selected by grizzly bears in a multiple use landscape." *Journal of Wildlife Management* 65:92–99. doi.org/10.2307/3803280.

McLellan, Bruce N., and Frederick W. Hovey. 2001b. "Natal dispersal of grizzly bears." *Canadian Journal of Zoology* 79:838–44. doi.org/10.1139/z01-051.

McLellan, Bruce N., Fredrick Hovey, John Woods, Michael Gibeau, Dan Carney, Richard Mace, Wayne Wakkinen, and Wayne Kasworm. 1999. "Rates and causes of grizzly bear mortality in the interior mountains of British Columbia, Alberta, Montana, and Idaho." *Journal of Wildlife Management* 63:911–20. doi.org/10.2307/3802805.

McLellan, Bruce N., Garth Mowat, Tony Hamilton and Ian Hatter. 2017. "Sustainability of the grizzly bear hunt in British Columbia, Canada." *Journal of Wildlife Management* 81:218–29. doi.org/10.2193/2008-330.

McLellan, Bruce N., Michael F. Proctor, Djuro Huber and Stefan Michel. 2017. *Ursus arctos (amended version of 2017 assessment). The IUCN Red List of Threatened Species*, e.T41688A121229971. doi.org/10.2305/IUCN.UK.2017-3.RLTS.T41688A121229971.en.

McLellan, Bruce N., and David M. Shackleton. 1988. "Grizzly bears and resource extraction industries: Effects of roads on behaviour, habitat use and demography." *Journal of Applied Ecology* 25:451–60. doi.org/10.2307/2403836.

McLellan, Bruce N., and David M. Shackleton. 1989a. "Grizzly bears and resource extraction industries: Habitat displacement in response to seismic exploration, timber harvesting and road maintenance." *Journal of Applied Ecology* 26:371–80. doi.org/10.2307/2404067.

McLellan, Bruce N., and David M. Shackleton. 1989b. "Immediate reactions of grizzly bears to human activities." *Wildlife Society Bulletin* 17:269–74. www.jstor.org/stable/3782383.

McLellan, Michelle L. 2020. "Identifying mechanisms of population change in two threatened grizzly bear populations." Ph.D. thesis, Victoria University of Wellington, Wellington, NZ. 170 pp.

McLellan, Michelle L., and Bruce N. McLellan. 2015. "Effect of season and high ambient temperature on activity levels and patterns of grizzly bears (*Ursus arctos*)." *PLoS ONE* 10:e0117734. doi.org/10.1371/journal.pone.0117734.

McLellan, Michelle L., Bruce N. McLellan, Rahel Sollmann, Clayton T. Lamb, Clayton D. Apps and Heiko Wittmer. 2019. "Divergent population trends following the cessation of legal grizzly bear hunting in southwestern British Columbia, Canada." *Biological Conservation* 233:247–54. doi.org/10.1016/j.biocon.2019.02.021.

McLoughlin, Philip D., Mitchell K. Taylor, H. Dean Cluff, Robert J. Gau, Robert Mulders, Ray L. Case, Stan Boutin and François Messier. 2003. "Demography of barren-ground grizzly bears." *Canadian Journal of Zoology* 81:294–301. doi.org/10.1139/z02-245.

Miller, Sterling D., Richard A. Sellers and Jeffrey A. Keay. 2003. "Effects of hunting on brown bear cub survival and litter size in Alaska." *Ursus* 14:130–52. www.jstor.org/stable/3873014.

Miller, Sterling D., Gary C. White, Richard A. Sellers, Harry V. Reynolds, John W. Schoen, Kim Titus, Victor G. Barnes, Jr., Roger B. Smith, Robert R. Nelson, Warren B. Ballard and Charles C. Schwartz. 1997. "Brown and black bear density estimation in Alaska using radio telemetry and replicated mark–resight techniques." *Wildlife Monographs* 133.

Monahan, Pat A. 2000. "The geology and oil and gas potential of the Flathead Area, Southeastern British Columbia." *Petroleum Geology Special Paper 2000-2*. Monahan Petroleum Consulting.

Mowat, Garth, Douglas C. Heard and Carl J. Schwarz. 2013. "Predicting grizzly bear density in western North America." *PLoS ONE* 8(12): e82757. doi.org/10.1371/ journal.pone.0082757.

Mundy, Keith R.D., and Donald R. Flook. 1973. *Background for managing grizzly bears in the National Parks of Canada*. Canadian Wildlife Service Report Series No. 22. 35 pp.

Mweetwa, Thandiwe, David Christianson, Matt Becker, Scott Creel, Elias Rosenblatt, Johnathan Merkle, Egil Droge, Henry Mwape, Jones Masonde and Twakundine Simpamba. 2018. "Quantifying lion (*Panthera leo*) demographic response following a three-year moratorium on trophy hunting." *PLoS ONE* 13(5): e0197030. doi.org/10.1371/journal.pone.0197030.

Nagy, John A., Richard H. Russell, Arthur M. Pearson, Michael C.S. Kingsley and B.C. Goski. 1983. *Ecological studies of the grizzly bear in Arctic Mountains, Northern Yukon Territory, 1972 to 1975*. Canadian Wildlife Service. 104 pp.

Nagy, John A., Richard H. Russell, Arthur M. Pearson, Michael C.S. Kingsley and C.B. Larsen. 1983. *A study of grizzly bears on the barren grounds of Tuktoyaktuk peninsula and Richards Island, Northwest Territories, 1974 to 1978*. Canadian Wildlife Service. 136 pp.

Nelson, Ralph A., G. Edgar Folk, Egbert W. Pfeiffer, John J. Craighead, Charles J. Jonkel and Dianne L. Steiger. 1983. "Behavior, biochemistry, and hibernation in black, grizzly, and polar bears." *International Conference on Bear Biology and Management* 5:284–90. www.bearbiology.org/publications/ursus-archive/behavior-biochemistry-and-hibernation-in-black-grizzly-and-polarbears/.

Oftedal, Olav T., Gary L. Alt, Elsie M. Widdowson and Michael R. Jakubasz. 1993. "Nutrition and growth of suckling black bears (*Ursus americanus*) during their mothers' winter fast." *British Journal of Nutrition* 70:59–79. doi.org/10.1079/BJN19930105.

Olsen, Jack. 1969. *Night of the grizzlies.* New York: G.P. Putnam's Sons. 221 pp.

Ordiz, Andrés, Jonas Kindberg, Solve Sæbø, Jon E. Swenson and Ole-Gunnar Støen. 2014. "Brown bear circadian behavior reveals human environmental encroachment." *Biological Conservation* 173:1–9. doi.org/10.1016/j.biocon.2014.03.006.

Pacific Climate Impacts Consortium. Plan2Adapt. pacificclimate.org/analysis-tools/plan2adapt.

Pearson, Arthur M. 1975. *The northern interior grizzly bear Ursus arctos L.* Canadian Wildlife Service Report Series No. 34. Ottawa. 86 pp.

Pederson, Gregory T., Lisa J. Graumlich, Daniel B. Fagre, Todd Kipfer and Clint C. Muhlfeld. 2010. "A century of climate and ecosystem change in Western Montana: What do temperature trends portend?" *Climatic Change* 98:133–54. doi.org/10.1007/s10584-009-9642-y.

Pederson, Gregory T., Stephen T. Gray, Daniel B. Fagre and Lisa J. Graumlich. 2006. "Long-duration drought variability and impacts on ecosystem services: A case study from Glacier National Park, Montana." *Earth Interactions* 10(4): 1–22. doi.org/10.1175/EI153.1.

Pigeon, Karine E., Etienne Cardinal, Gordon B. Stenhouse and Steeve D. Côté. 2016. "Staying cool in a changing landscape: The influence of maximum daily ambient temperature on grizzly bear habitat selection." *Oecologia* 181:1101–16. doi.org/10.1007/s00442-016-3630-5.

Pritchard, Geoffrey T., and Charles T. Robbins. 1990. "Digestive and metabolic efficiencies of grizzly and black bears." *Canadian Journal of Zoology* 68:1645–51. doi:10.1139/z90-244.

Proctor, Michael, Bruce N. McLellan, Curtus Strobeck and Robert Barclay. 2005. "Genetic analysis reveals demographic fragmentation of grizzly bears yielding vulnerably small populations." *Proceedings of the Royal Society, London* 272:2409–16. doi.org/10.1098/rspb.2005.3246.

Proctor, Michael F., Clayton T. Lamb and A. Grant MacHutchon. 2017. *The grizzly dance of berries and bullets: The relationship between bottom up food resources, huckleberries, and top down mortality risk on grizzly bear population processes in southeast British Columbia.* Trans-border Grizzly Bear Project. Kaslo, BC. 73 pp.

Ramsay, Malcom A., and Robert L. Dunbrack. 1986. "Physiological constraints on life-history phenomena: The example of small bear cubs at birth." *American Naturalist* 127:735–43. doi.org/10.1086/284522.

Robbins, Charles T., Merav Ben-David, Jennifer K. Fortin and O. Lynne Nelson. 2012. "Maternal condition determines birth date and growth of newborn bear cubs." *Journal of Mammalogy* 93:540–46. doi.org/10.1644/11-MAMM-A-155.1.

Robbins, Charles T., Jennifer K. Fortin, Karyn D. Rode, Sean D. Farley, Lisa A. Shipley and Laura A. Felicetti. 2007. "Optimizing protein intake as a foraging strategy to maximize mass gain in an omnivore." *Oikos* 116:1675–82. doi.org/10.1111/j.0030-1299.2007.16140.x.

Rode, Karyn D., and Charles T. Robbins. 2000. "Why bears consume mixed diets during fruit abundance." *Canadian Journal of Zoology* 78:1640–45. doi.org/10.1139/z00-082.

Rode, Karyn D., Charles T. Robbins and Lisa A. Shipley. 2001. "Constraints on herbivory by grizzly bears." *Oecologia* (Berl.) 128:62–71. doi.org/10.1007/s004420100637.

Rogers, Matthew C., Grant V. Hilderbrand, David D. Gustine, Kyle Joly, William B. Leacock, Buck A. Mangipane and Jeffrey M. Welker. 2020. "Splitting hairs: Dietary niche breadth modelling using stable isotope analysis of a sequentially grown tissue." *Isotopes in Environmental and Health Studies* 56:358–69. doi.org/10.1080/10256016.2020.1787404.

Royle, J. Andrew, Richard B. Chandler, Rahel Sollmann and Beth Gardner. 2013. *Spatial capture-recapture*. Oxford, UK: Academic Press. 612 pp.

Russell, Richard H., James W. Nolan, Norman G. Woody and Gordon H. Anderson. 1979. *A study of the grizzly bear in Jasper National Park, 1976 to 1978*. Prepared for Parks Canada. Canadian Wildlife Service, Edmonton. 136 pp.

Saris, Wim H.M., Marie-Agnes J. van Erp-Baart, Fred Brounds, Klaas R. Westerterp and Foppe Ten Hoor. 1989. "Study on food intake and energy expenditure during extreme sustained exercise: The Tour de France." *International Journal of Sports Medicine* 10-suppliment 1:26–31. doi.org/10.1055/s-2007-1024951.

Schwartz, Charles C., Jennifer K. Fortin, Justin E. Teisberg, Mark A. Haroldson, Christopher Servheen, Charles T. Robbins and Frank T. Van Manen. 2014. "Body and diet composition of sympatric black and grizzly bears in the Greater Yellowstone Ecosystem." *Journal of Wildlife Management* 78:68–78. doi.org/10.1002/jwmg.633.

Schwartz, Charles C., Mark A. Haroldson, Gary C. White, Richard B. Harris, Steve Cherry, Kim A. Keating, Dave Moody and Christopher Servheen. 2006. "Temporal, spatial, and environmental influences on the demographics of grizzly bears in the greater Yellowstone Ecosystem." *Wildlife Monographs* 161.

Sellers, Richard A., Sterling Miller, Tom Smith and Rick Potts. 1999. "Population dynamics of a naturally regulated brown bear population on the coast of Katmai National Park and Preserve. Final Report." Resource Report NPS/AR/NRTR – 99/36. National Park Service, Alaska Region, and Alaska Department of Fish and Game.

Shaffer, Mark L. 1981. "Minimum population sizes for species conservation." *BioScience* 31:131–34. doi.org/10.2307/1308256.

Shoalts, Adam. 2017. *A history of Canada in ten maps: Epic stories of charting a mysterious land*. Toronto: Penguin Random House. 352 pp.

Sinclair, Anthony R.E. 1989. "Population regulation in animals." In *Ecological Concepts*, edited by J. Malcolm Cherrett, 197–241. Oxford, UK: Blackwell Scientific Publications.

Stenvinkel, Peter, Alkesh H. Jani and Richard J. Johnson. 2013. "Hibernating bears (Ursidae): Metabolic magicians of definite interest for the nephrologist." *Kidney International* 83:207–12. doi.org/10.1038/ki.2012.396;2.

Stephens, Philip A., William. J. Sutherland and Robert P. Freckleton. 1999. "What is the allee effect?" *Oikos* 87:185–90. doi.org/10.2307/3547011.

Steyaert, Sam M.J.G., Anders Endrestøl, Klaus Hackländer, Jon E. Swenson and Andreas Zedrosser. 2012. "The mating system of the brown bear *Ursus arctos*." *Mammal Review* 42:12–34. doi.org/10.1111/j.1365-2907.2011.00184.x.

Storer, Tracy I., and Lloyd P. Tevis Jr. 1955. *California grizzly*. Berkeley: University of California Press. 382 pp.

Swenson, Jon E. 2003. "Implications of sexually selected infanticide for hunting of large carnivores." In *Animal behavior and wildlife management*, edited by Marco Festa-Bianchet and Marco Apollonio, 171–207. Covelo, CA: Island Press.

Swenson, Jon E., Finn Sandegren, Arne Söderberg, Anders Bjärvall, Robert Franzén and Petter Wabakken. 1997. "Infanticide caused by hunting of male bears." *Nature* 386:450–51. doi.org/10.1038/386450a0.

Tardiff, Sandra E., and Jack A. Stanford. 1998. "Grizzly bear digging: Effects on subalpine meadow plants in relation to mineral nitrogen availability." *Ecology* 79:2219–28. doi.org/10.1890/0012-9658(1998)079[2219:GBDEOS]2.0.CO;2.

Tian, Zhenyu, Haoqi Zhao, Katherine T. Peter, Melissa Gonzalez, Jill Wetzel, Christopher Wu, Ximin Hu, Jasmine Prat, Emma Mudrock, Rachel Hettinger, Allan E. Cortina, Rajshree G. Biswas, Flávio V.C. Kock, Ronald Soong, Amy Jenne, Bowen Du, Fan Hou, Huan He, Rachel Lundeen, Alicia Gilbreath, Rebecca Sutton, Nathaniel L. Scholz, Jay W. Davis, Michael C. Dodd, Andre Simpson, Jenifer K. McIntyre and Edward P. Kolodziej. 2021. "A ubiquitous tire rubber-derived chemical induces acute mortality in Coho salmon." *Science* 371(6525):185–89. doi.org/10.1126/science.abd6951.

Tøien, Øivind, John Blake and Brian M. Barnes. 2015. "Thermoregulation and energetics in hibernating black bears: Metabolic rate and the mystery of multi-day body temperature cycles." *Journal of Comparative Physiology B* 185:447–61. doi.org/10.1007/s00360-015-0891-y.

Tøien, Øivind, John Blake, Dale M. Edgar, Dennis A. Grahn, H. Craig Heller and Brian M. Barnes. 2011. "Hibernation in black bears: Independence of metabolic suppression from body temperature." *Science* 331 (6019):906–9. doi.org/10.1126/science.1199435.

Tumanov, Igor L. 1998. "Reproductive characteristics of captive European brown bears and growth rates of their cubs in Russia." *Ursus* 10:63–65. www.jstor.org/stable/3873111.

Welch, Christy A., Jeffrey Keay, Katherine C. Kendall and Charles T. Robbins. 1997. "Constraints on frugivory by bears." *Ecology* 78:1105–19. doi.org/10.1890/0012-9658(1997)078[1105:COFBB]2.0.CO;2.

Wood, Barry P. 2000. "A multi-regional analysis of heritage management: An approach to building new partnerships." Master's thesis of Environmental Design. University of Calgary. 339 pp. doi.org/10.11575/PRISM/21323.

Woods, John G., Bruce N. McLellan, David Paetkau, Michael Proctor, David Lewis and Curtis Strobeck. 1999. "Genetic tagging free-ranging black and brown bears." *Wildlife Society Bulletin* 27:616–27. www.jstor.org/stable/3784082.

Young, Cameron. 1988. *Coming of age in the Flathead: How the British Columbia Forest Service contended with the mountain pine beetle infestation of southeastern B.C. 1976 to 1986*. B.C. Ministry of Forests, Pest Management Report Number 10. BC Ministry of Forests and Range, Victoria. 31 pp.

Zhang, Tong, David G. Watson, Rong Zhang, Rong Hou, I. Kati Loeffler and Malcolm W. Kennedy. 2016. "Change over from signalling to energy-provisioning lipids during transition from colostrum to mature milk in the giant panda (*Ailuropoda melanoleuca*)." *Scientific Reports* 6:1–10. doi.org/10.1038/srep36141.

# INDEX

*Note*: Locators in *italic* indicate figures.